SHINOBU OHTAKA

Enjoy Magi volume 26!

MAGI

Volume 26
Shonen Sunday Edition

Story and Art by
SHINOBU OHTAKA

MAGI Vol.26
by Shinobu OHTAKA
© 2009 Shinobu OHTAKA
All rights reserved.
Original Japanese edition published by SHOGAKUKAN.
English translation rights in the United States of America, Canada, the United Kingdom,
Ireland, Australia and New Zealand arranged with SHOGAKUKAN.

ORIGINAL COVER DESIGN / Yasuo SHIMURA+Bay Bridge Studio

Translation & English Adaptation ◇ John Werry

Touch-up Art & Lettering ◇ Stephen Dutro

Editor ◇ Mike Montesa

Printed in Canada

Published by VIZ Media, LLC
P.O. Box 77010
San Francisco, CA 94107

10 9 8 7 6 5 4 3 2 1
First printing, October 2017

WWW.SHONENSUNDAY.COM

PARENTAL ADVISORY
MAGI is rated T for Teen.
This volume contains
suggestive themes.
ratings.viz.com

www.viz.com

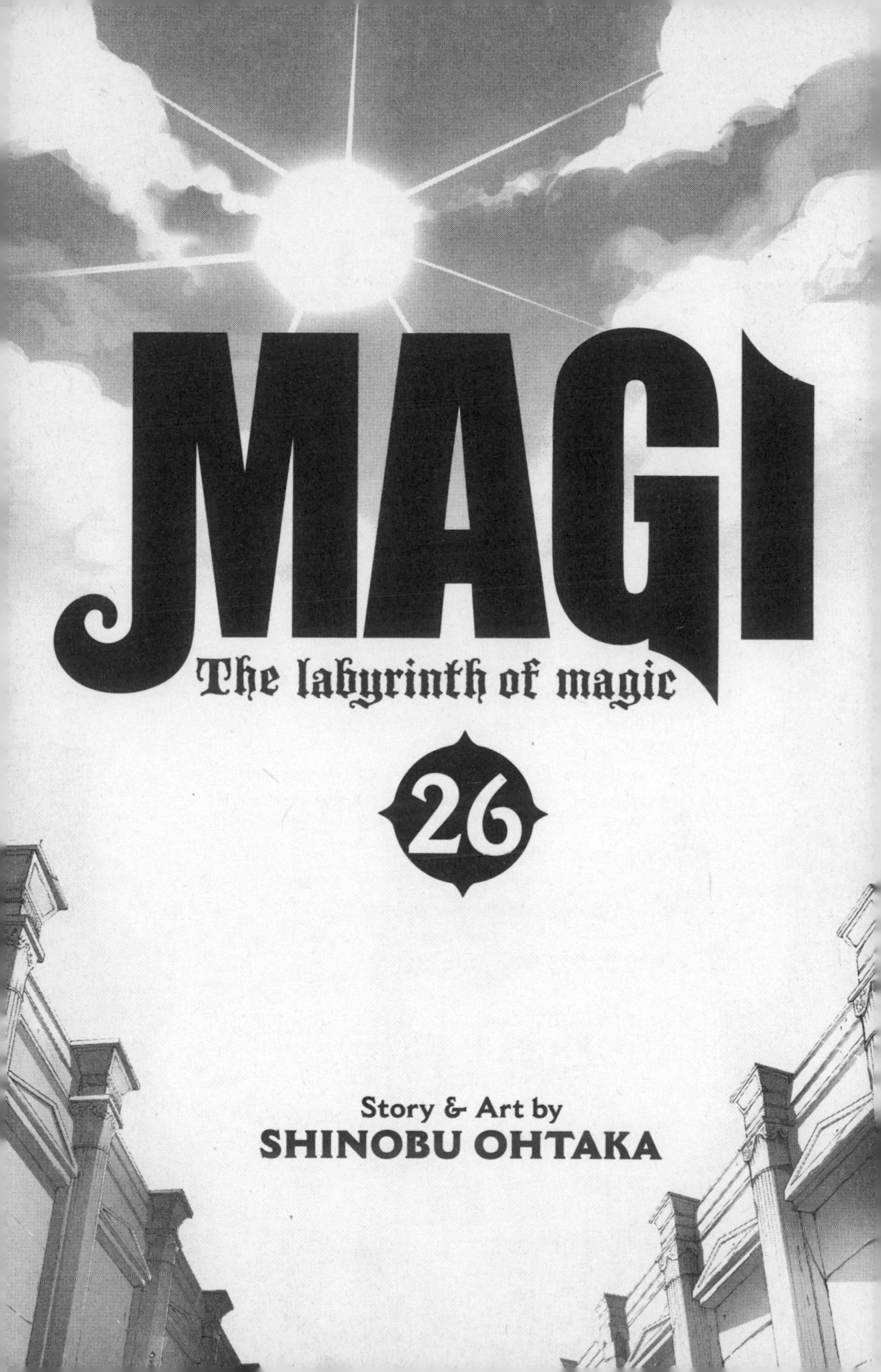

MAGI

The labyrinth of magic

26

Story & Art by
SHINOBU OHTAKA

MAGI
The labyrinth of magic

26

CONTENTS

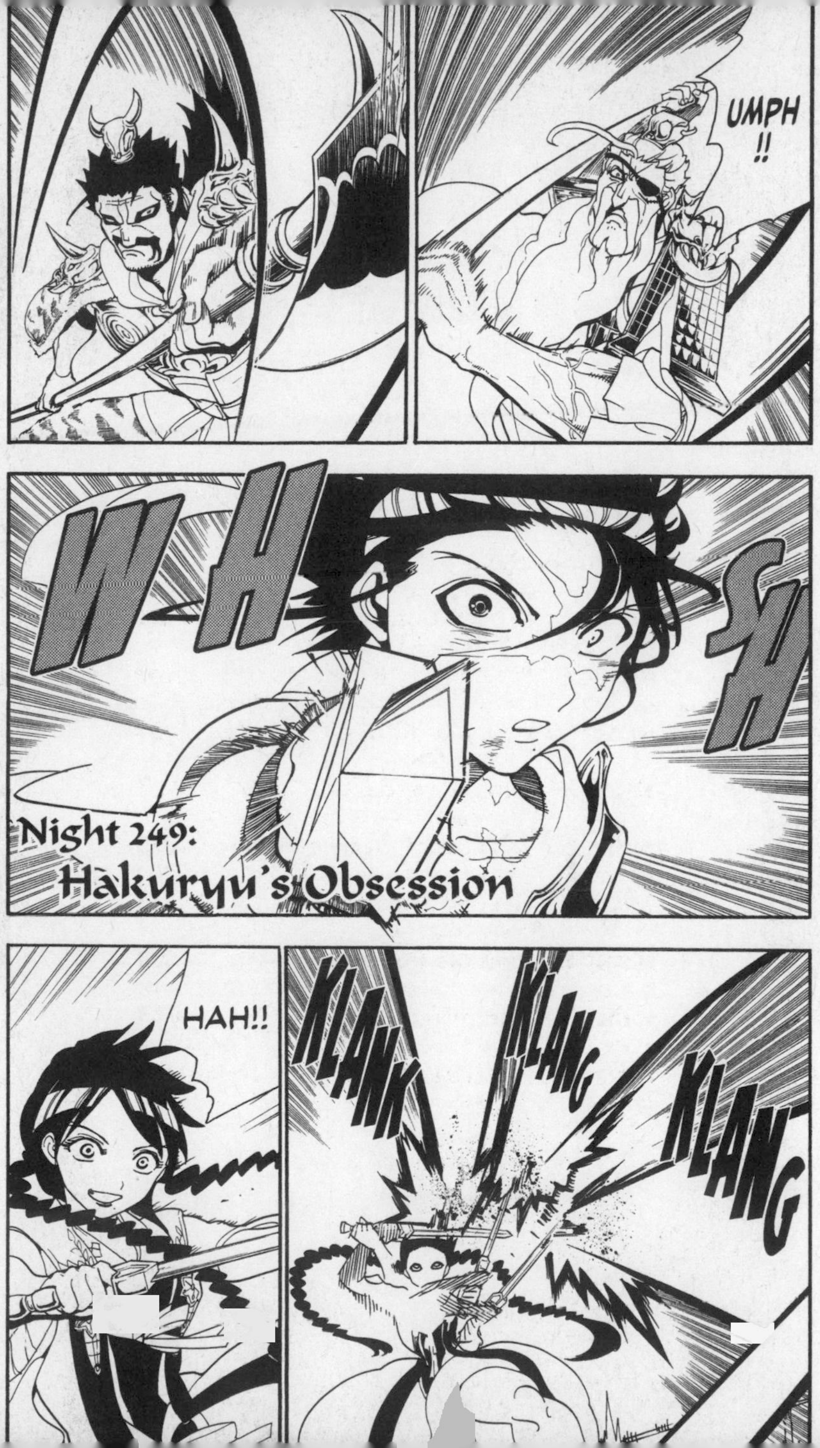
UMPH !!
Night 249: Hakuryu's Obsession
KLANK
KLANG
KLANG
HAH!!

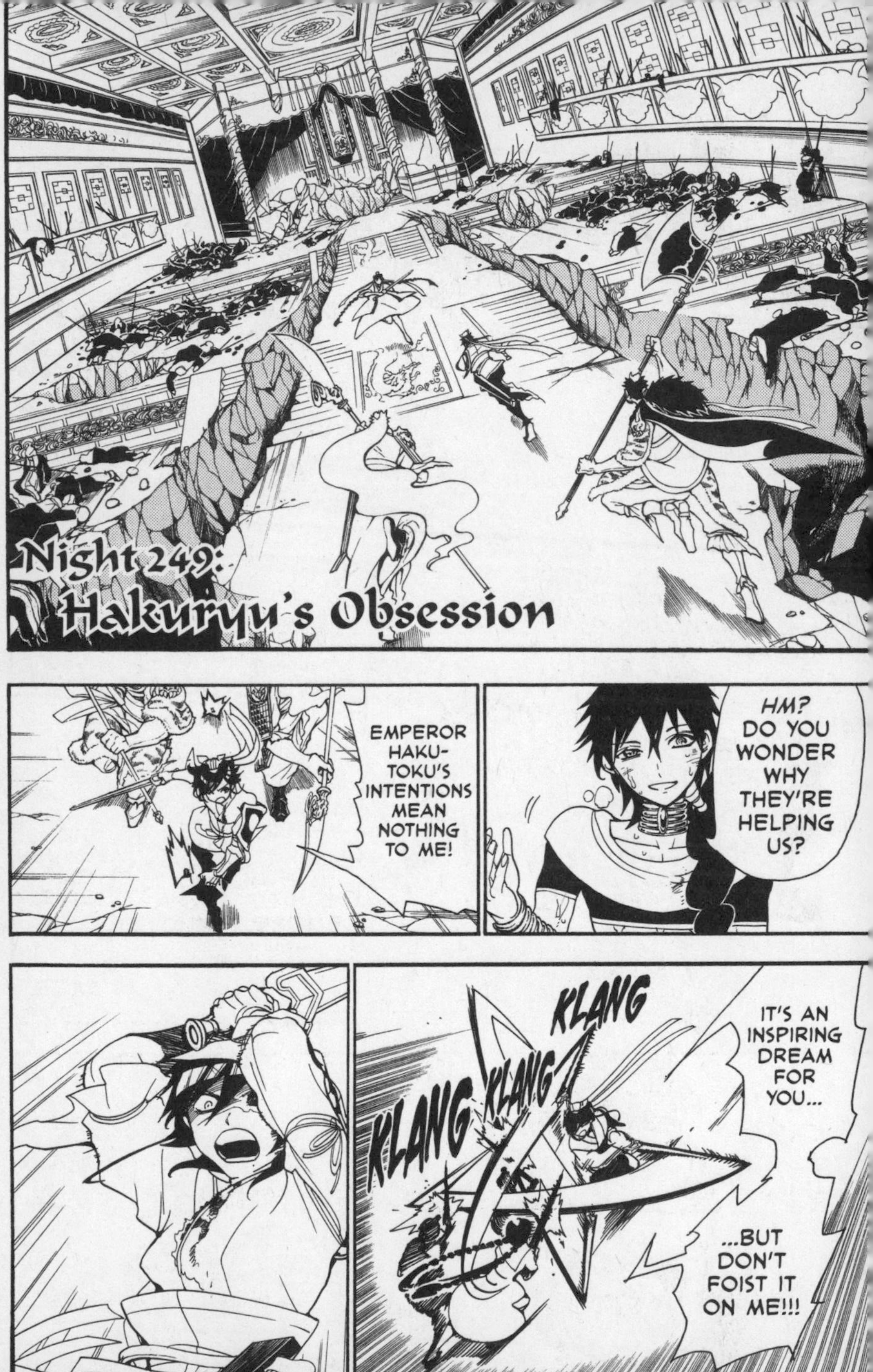
Night 249: Hakuryu's Obsession
HM? DO YOU WONDER WHY THEY'RE HELPING US?
EMPEROR HAKU-TOKU'S INTENTIONS MEAN NOTHING TO ME!
KLANG
KLANG
KLANG
KLANG
IT'S AN INSPIRING DREAM FOR YOU...
...BUT DON'T FOIST IT ON ME!!!

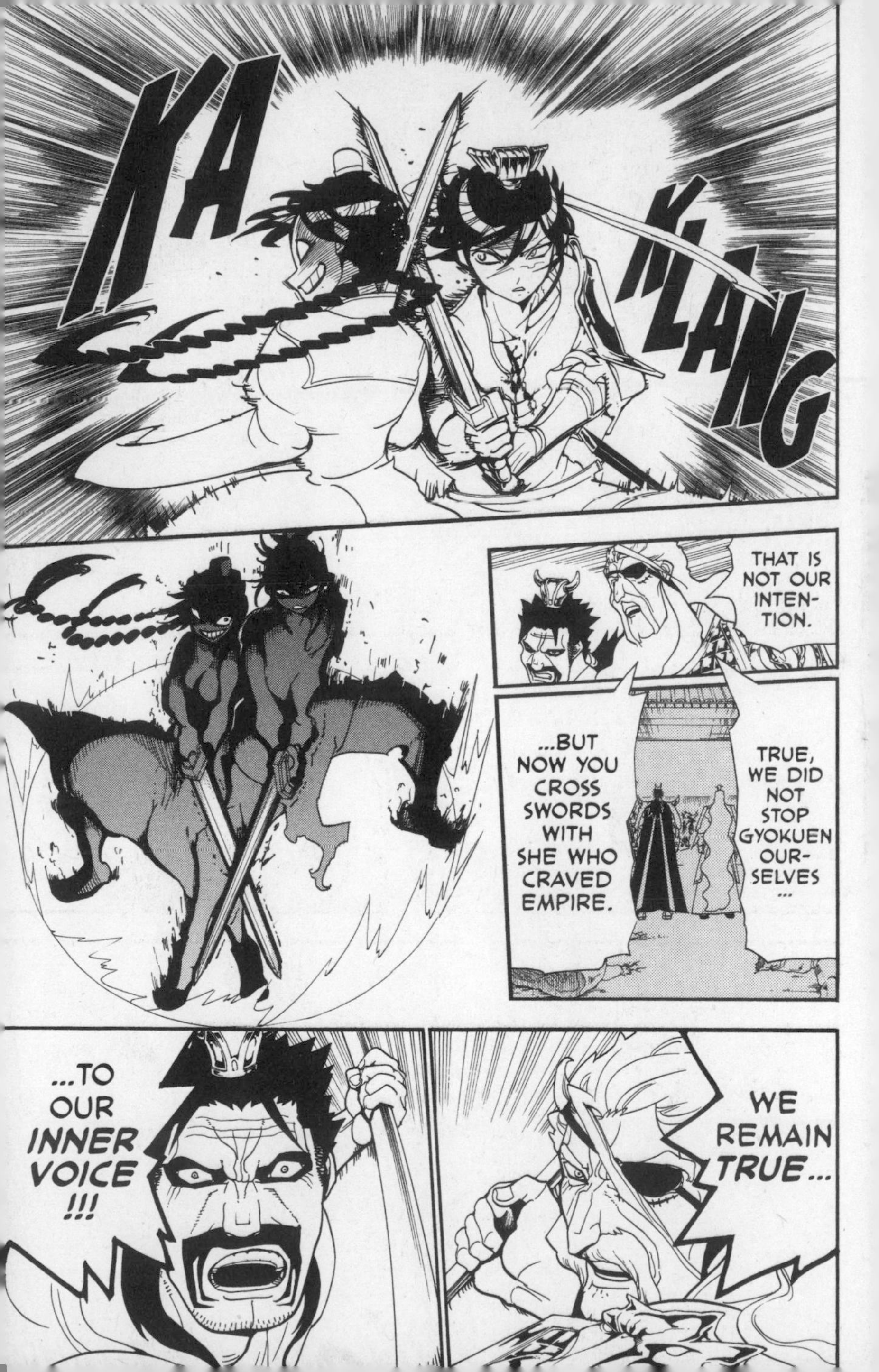
KA KLANG
THAT IS NOT OUR INTENTION.
TRUE, WE DID NOT STOP GYOKUEN OURSELVES ...
...BUT NOW YOU CROSS SWORDS WITH SHE WHO CRAVED EMPIRE.
WE REMAIN TRUE...
...TO OUR INNER VOICE !!!

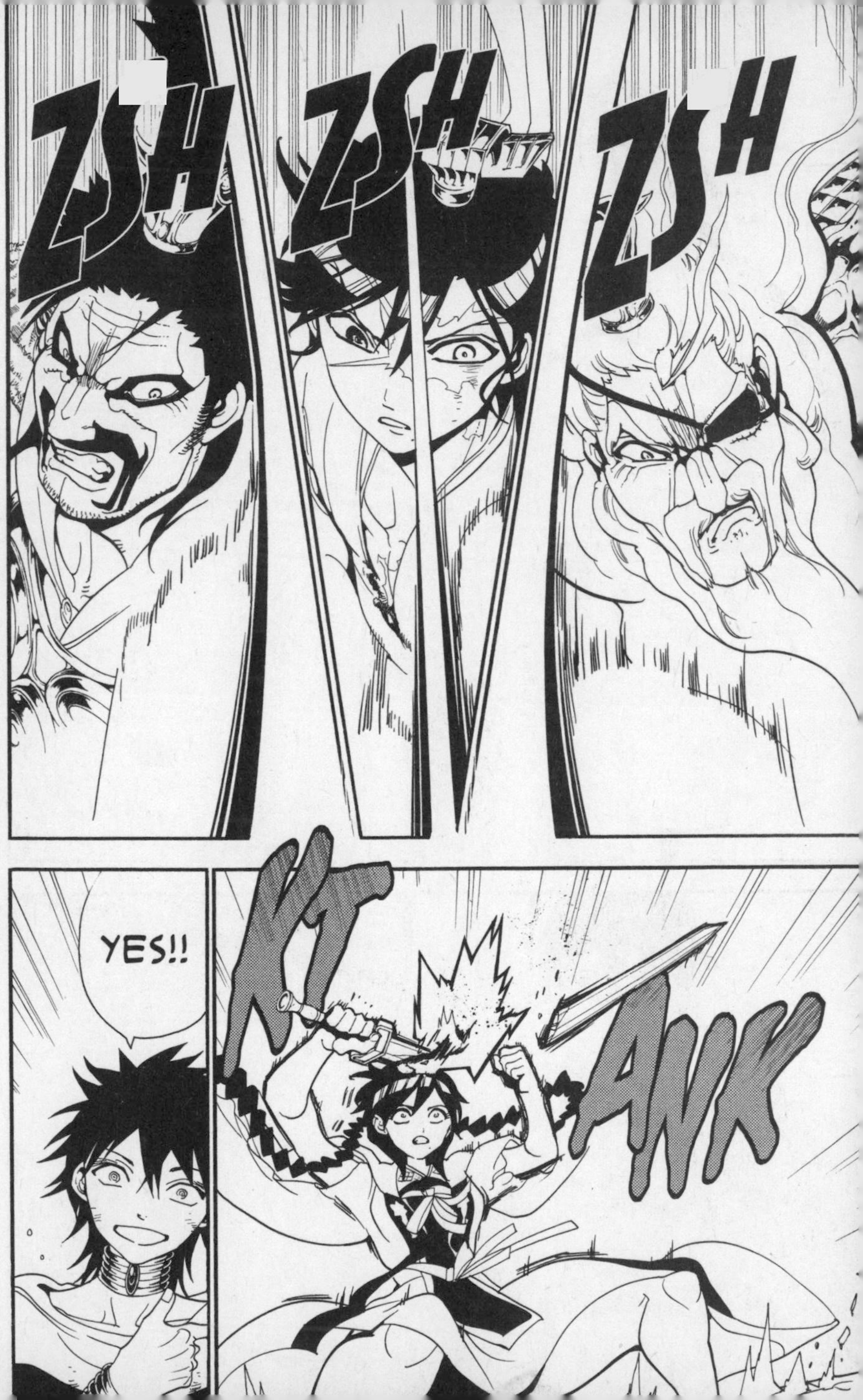
ZSH
ZSH
ZSH
KTANK
YES!!

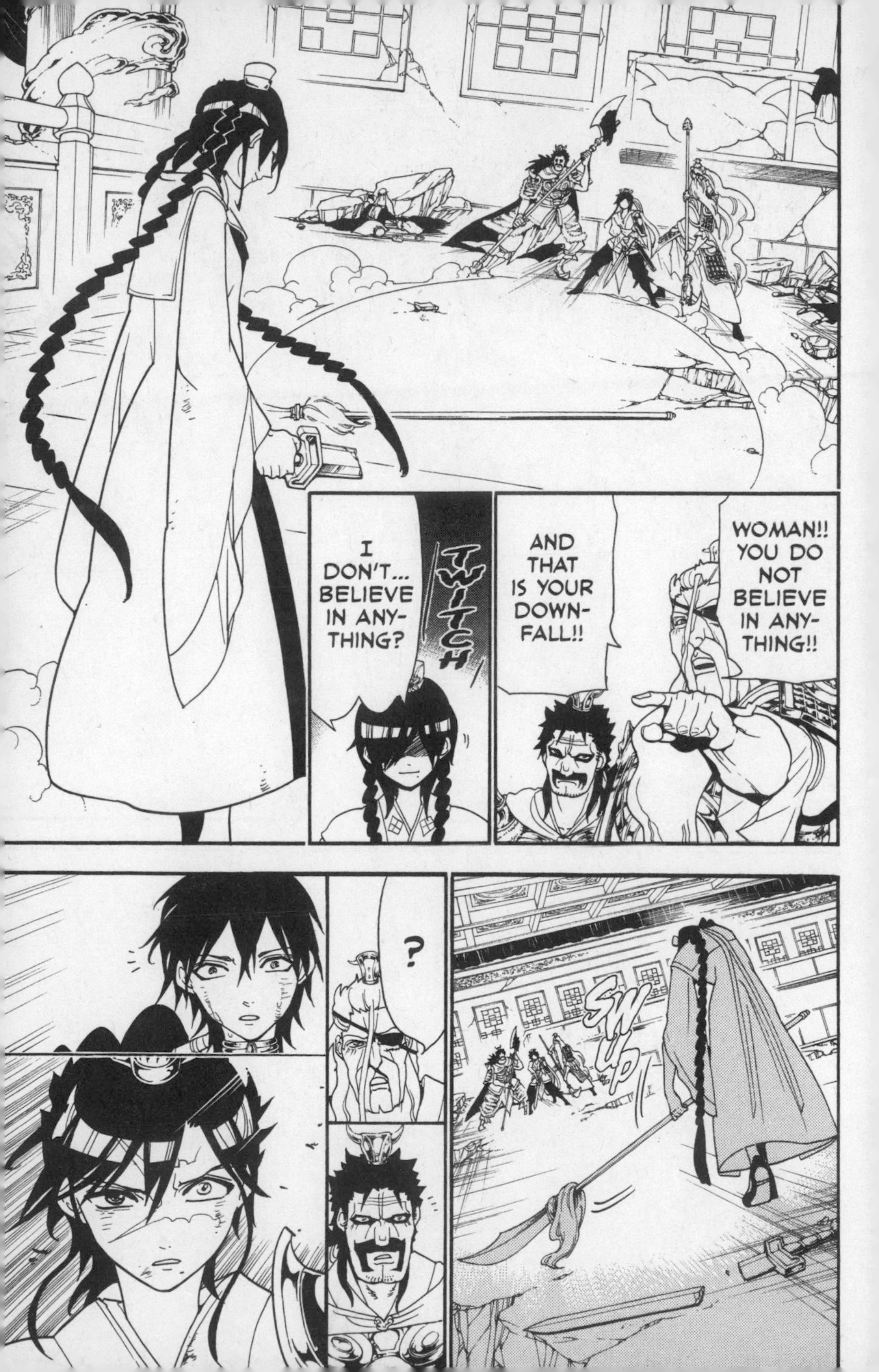
WOMAN!! YOU DO NOT BELIEVE IN ANY-THING!!
AND THAT IS YOUR DOWN-FALL!!
I DON'T... BELIEVE IN ANY-THING?
TWITCH
SWUP
?

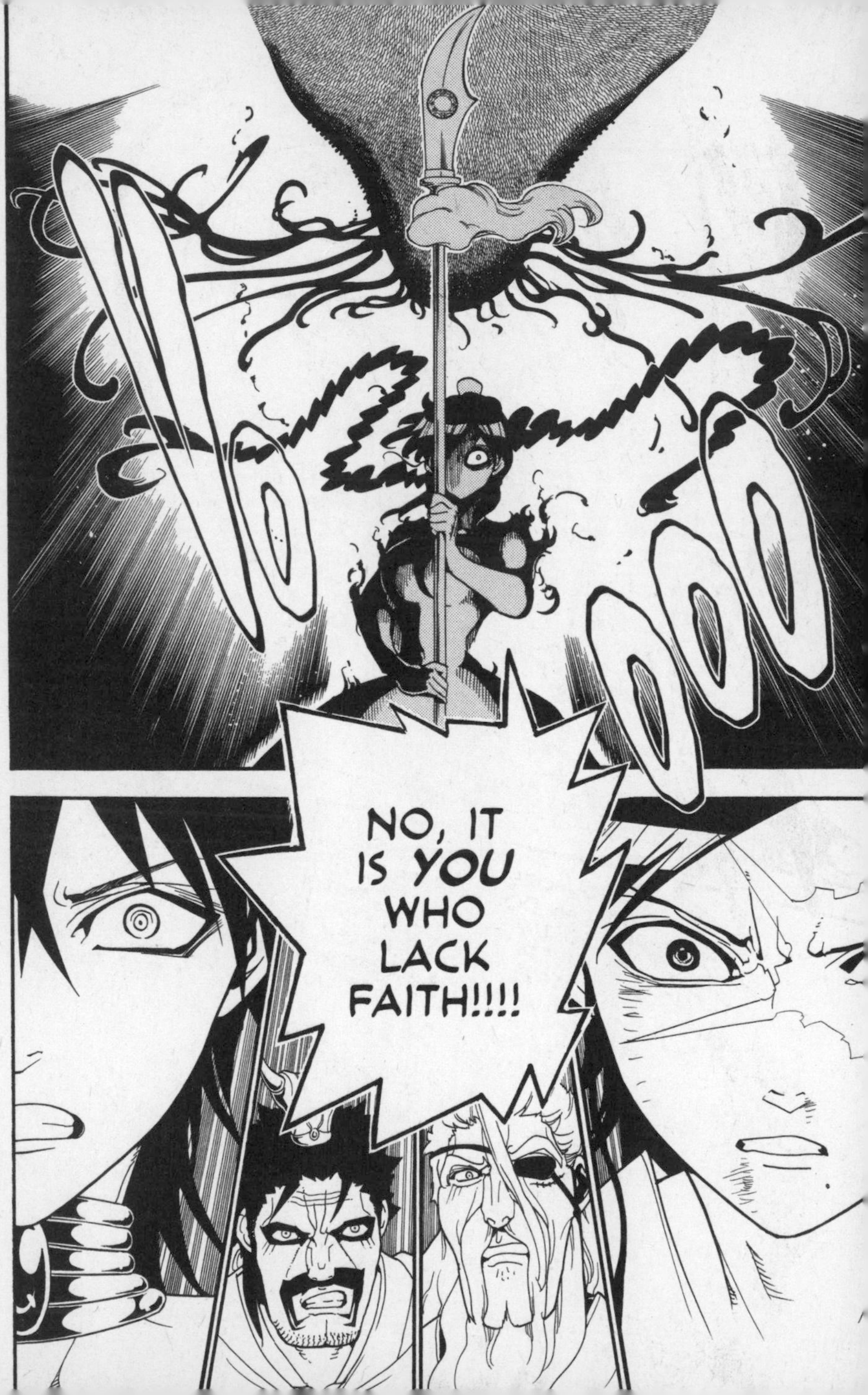
NO, IT IS YOU WHO LACK FAITH!!!!

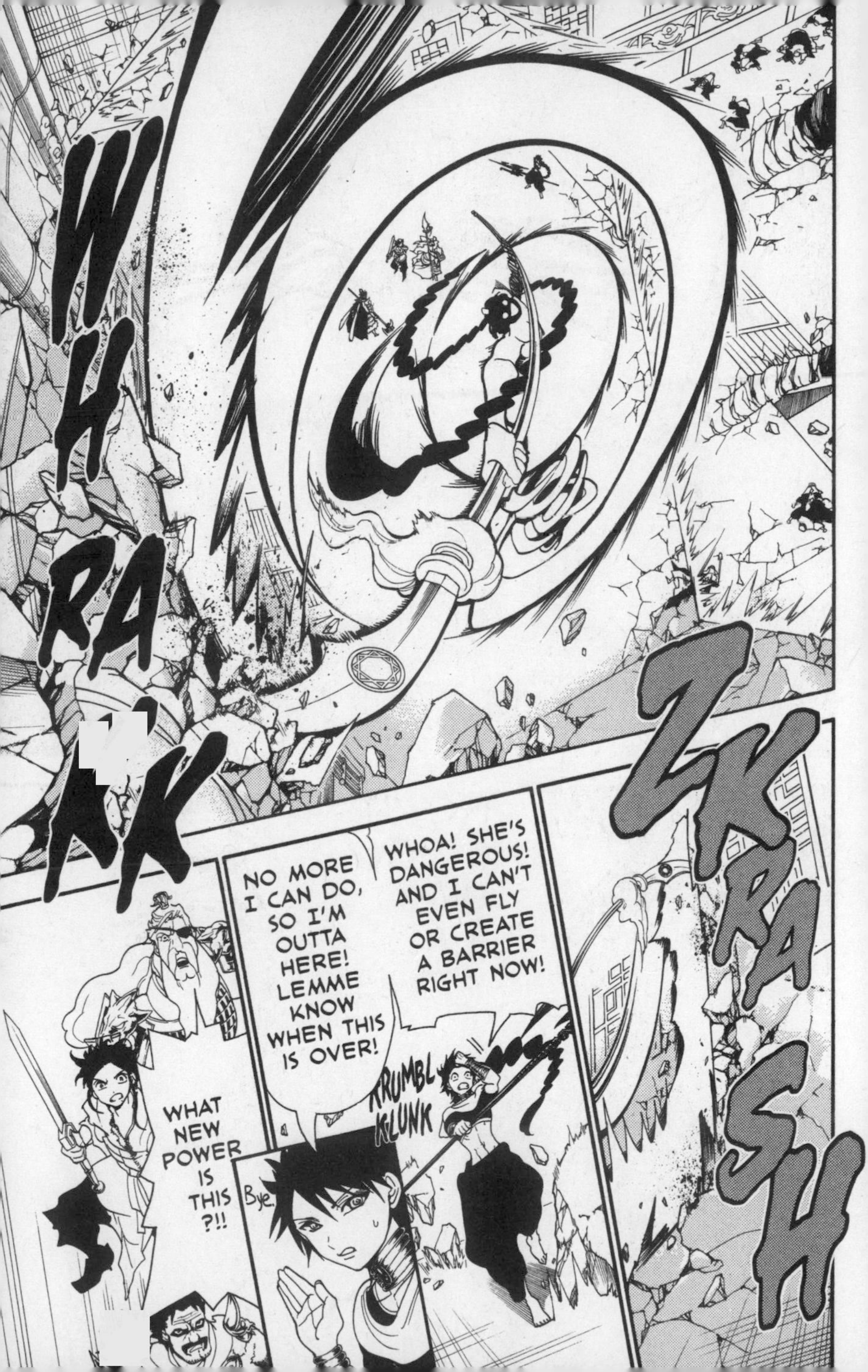
WHRAKK
ZKRASH
WHOA! SHE'S DANGEROUS! AND I CAN'T EVEN FLY OR CREATE A BARRIER RIGHT NOW!
NO MORE I CAN DO, SO I'M OUTTA HERE! LEMME KNOW WHEN THIS IS OVER!
KRUMBL KLUNK
Bye.
WHAT NEW POWER IS THIS?!!

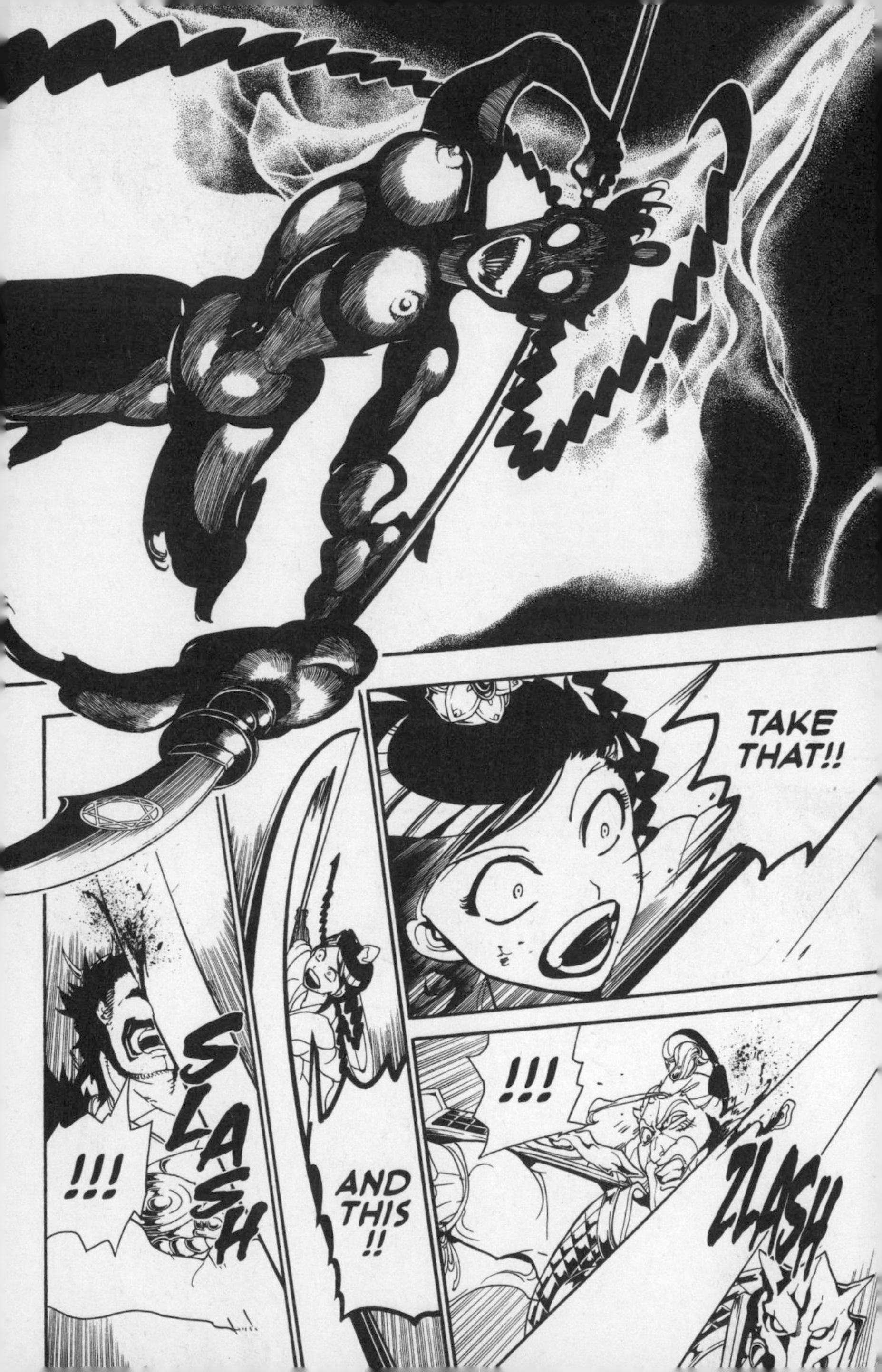
TAKE THAT!!
!!!
ZLASH
AND THIS !!
SLASH
!!!

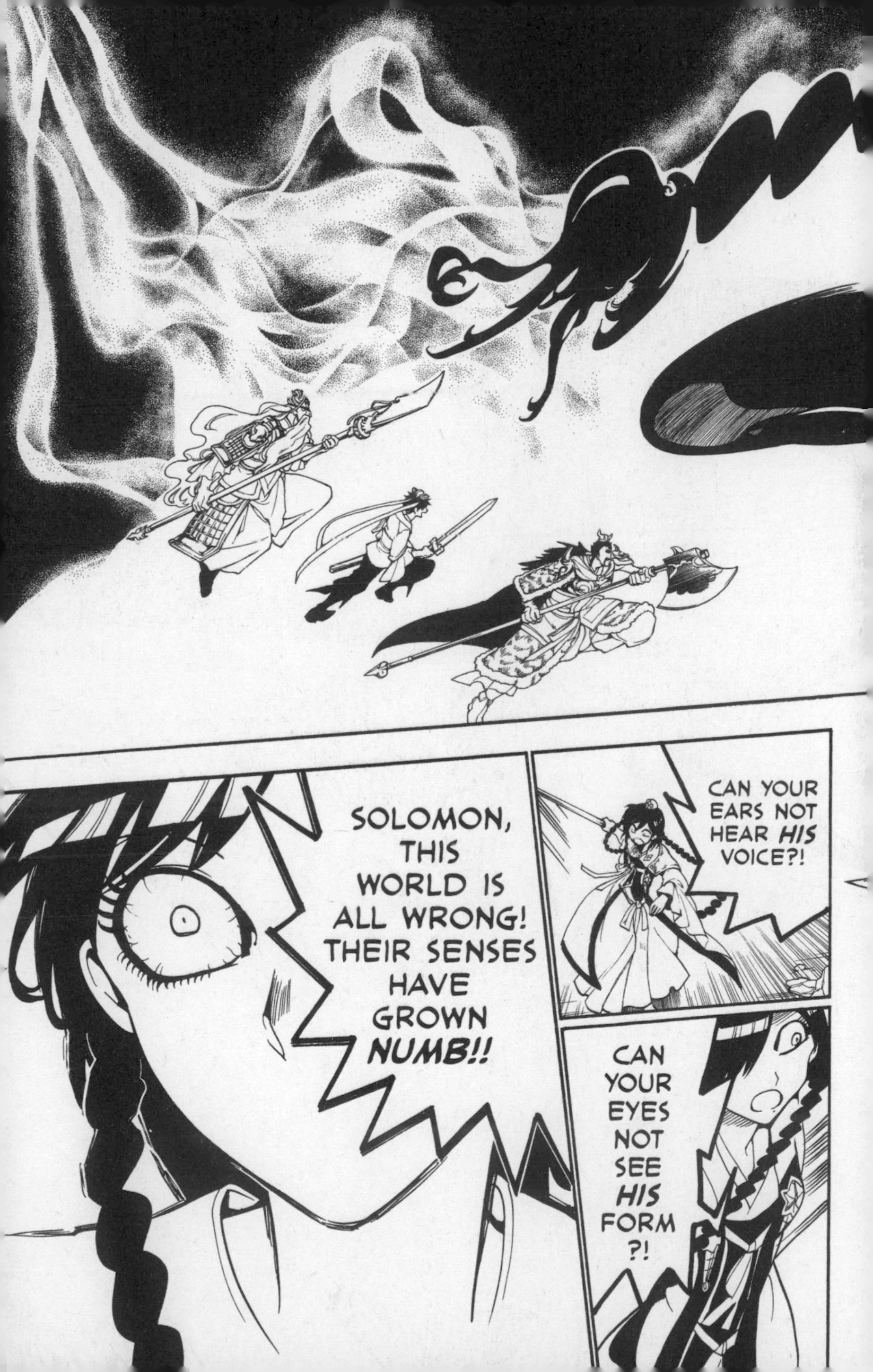
CAN YOUR EARS NOT HEAR HIS VOICE?!
CAN YOUR EYES NOT SEE HIS FORM?!
SOLOMON, THIS WORLD IS ALL WRONG! THEIR SENSES HAVE GROWN NUMB!!

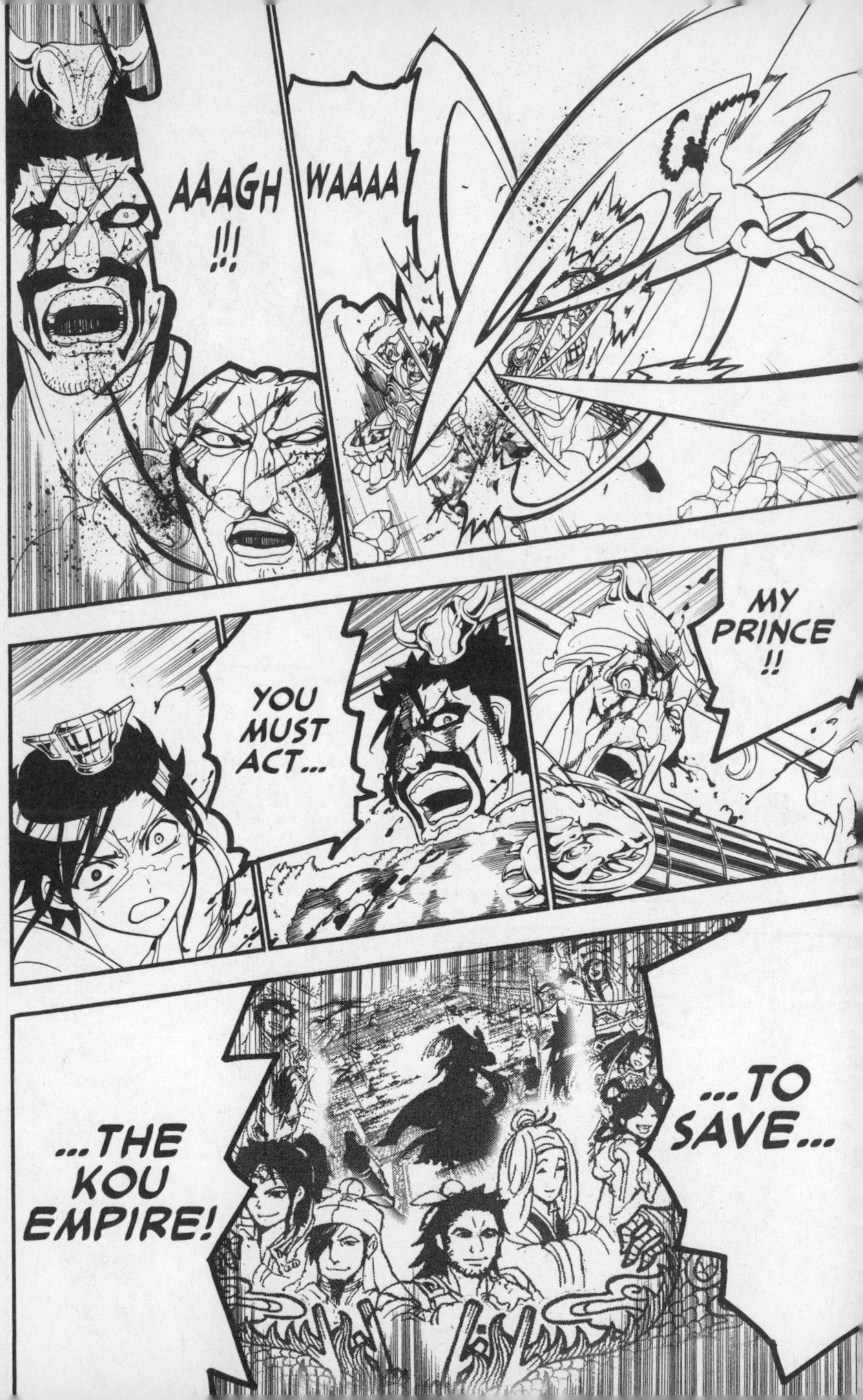
WAAAA
AAAGH !!!
MY PRINCE !!
YOU MUST ACT...
...TO SAVE...
...THE KOU EMPIRE!

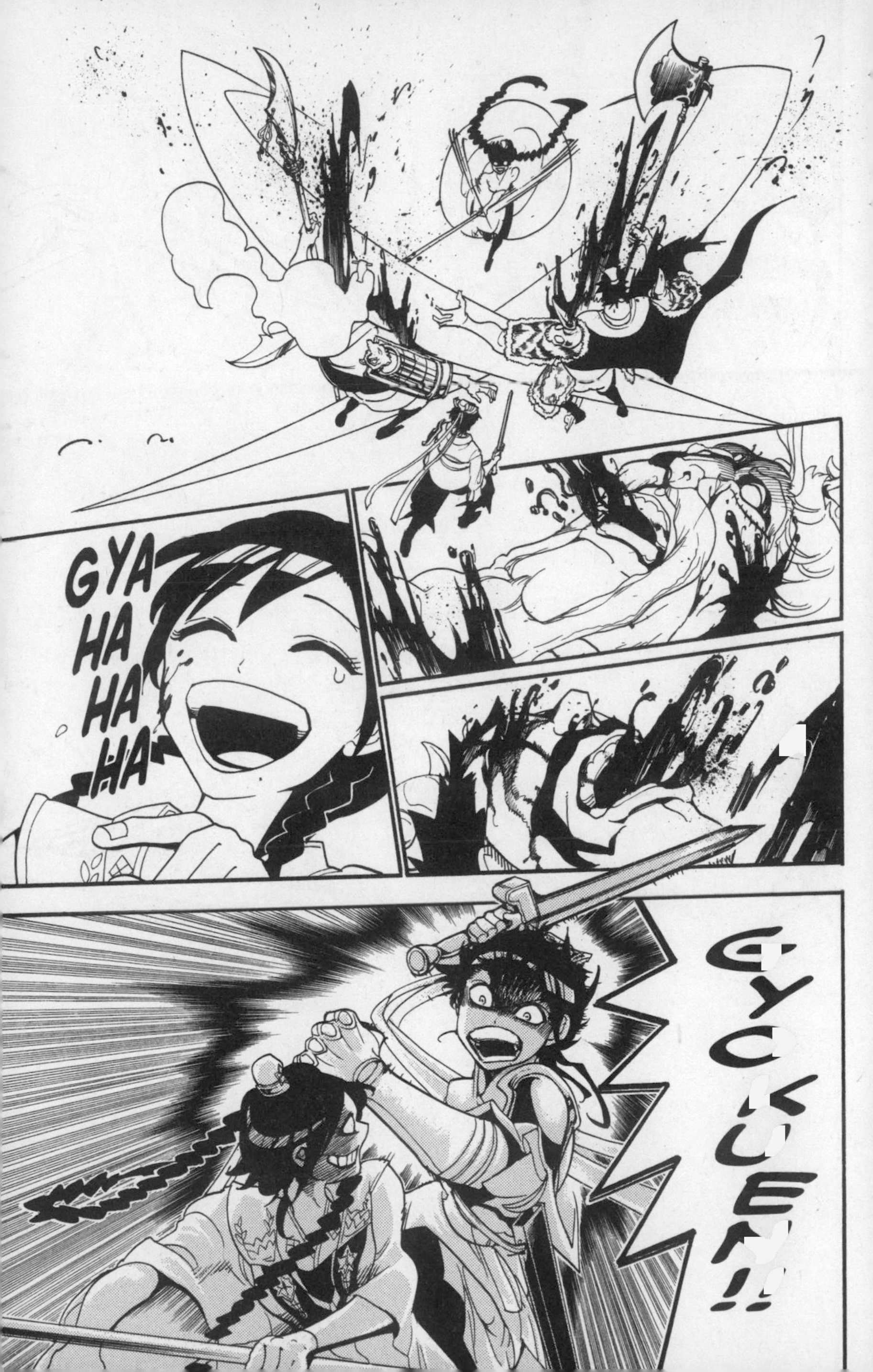
GYA HA HA HA HA
GYOKUEN!!

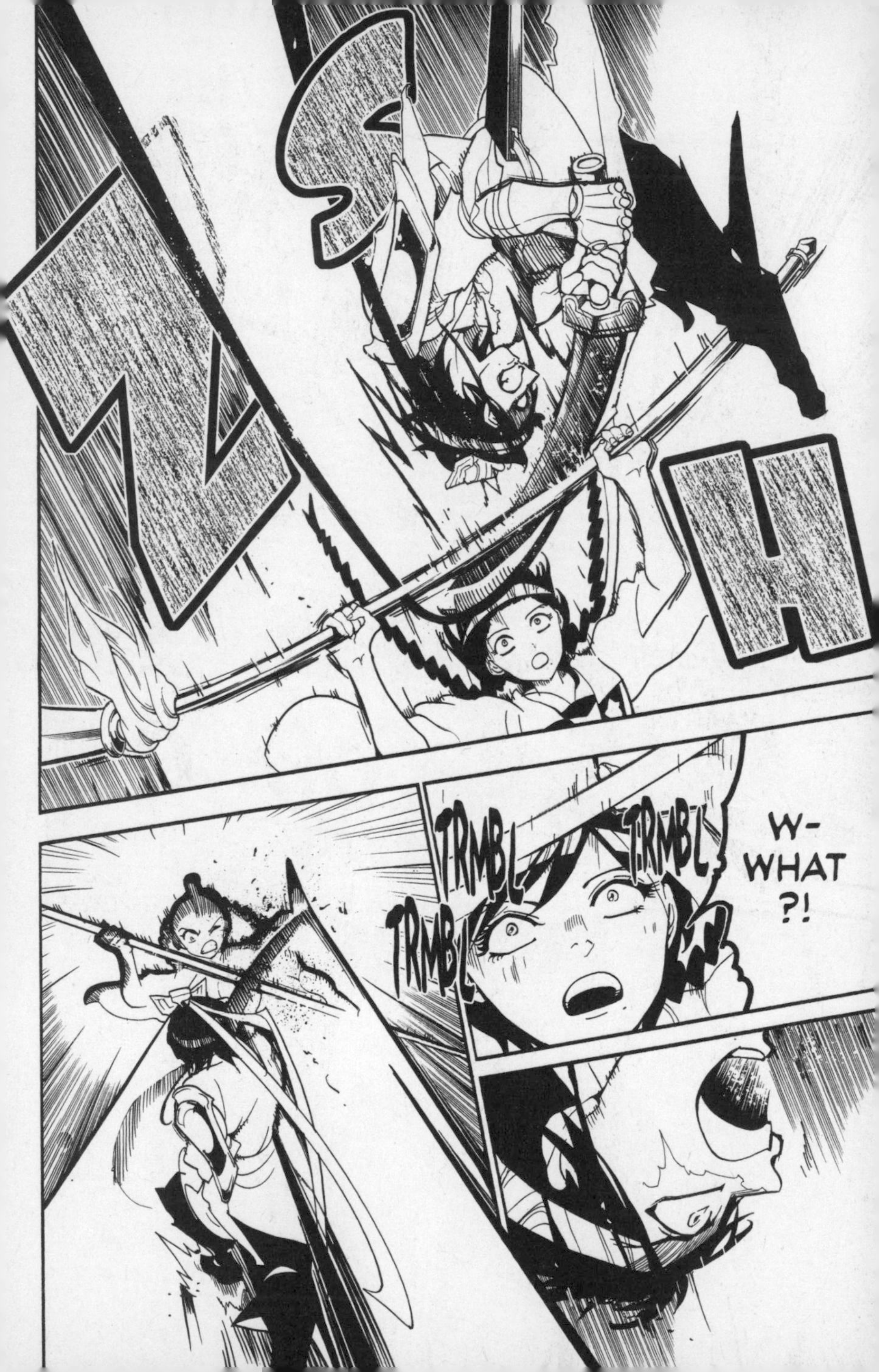
TRMBL
TRMBL
W-
WHAT
?!
TRMBL

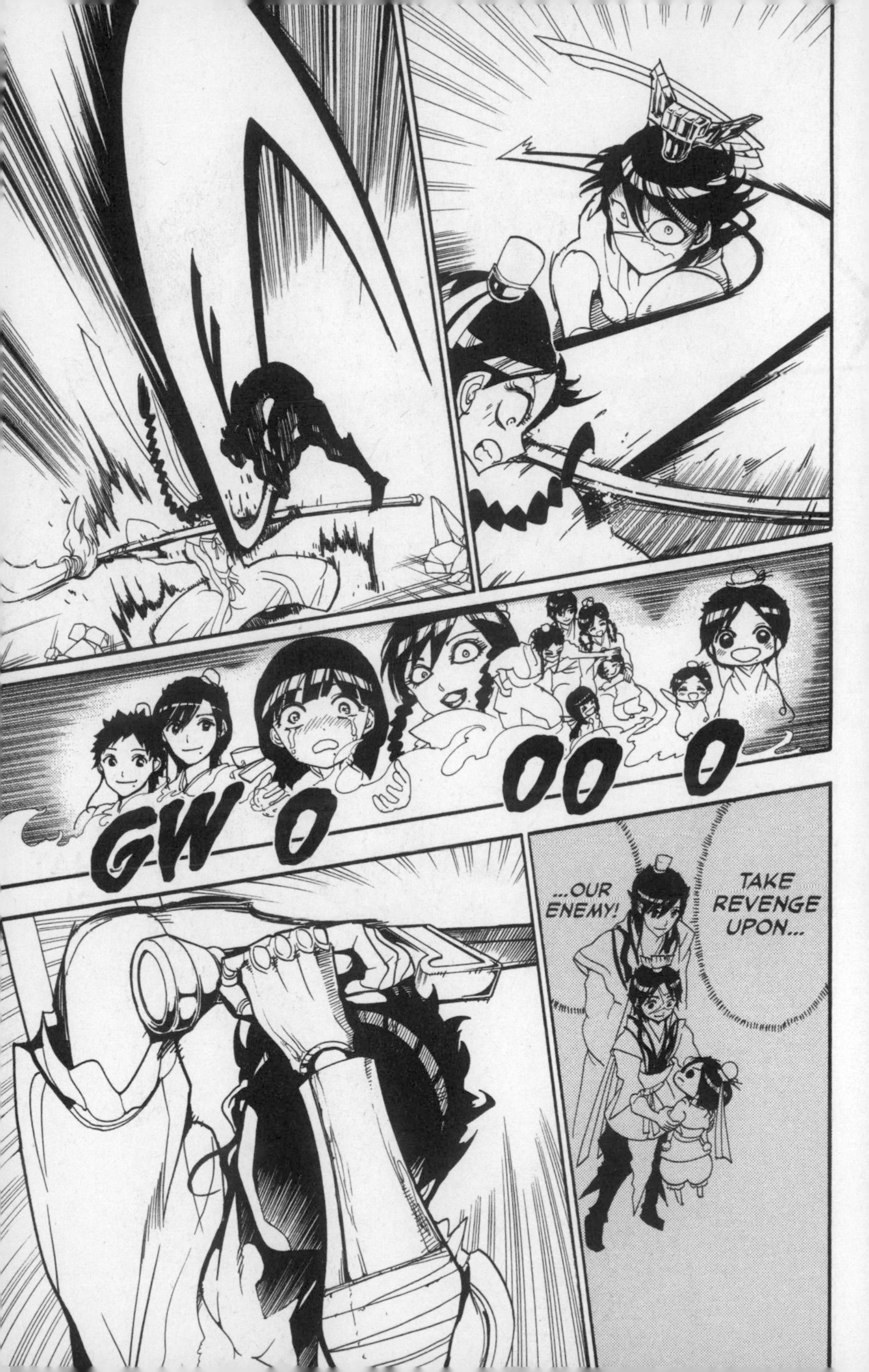
GWOOOO
TAKE REVENGE UPON...
...OUR ENEMY!

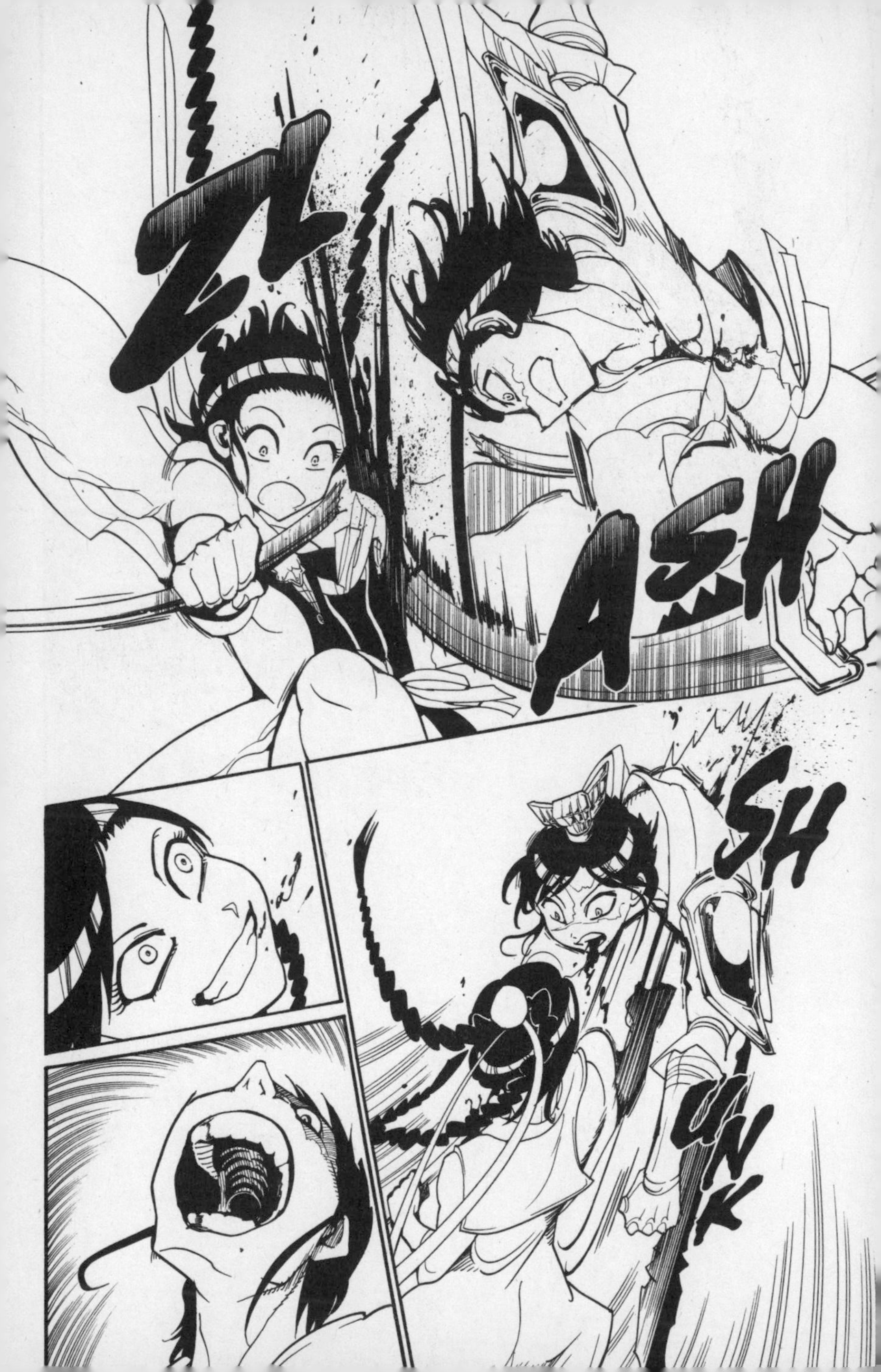
ZASH
SH
UNK

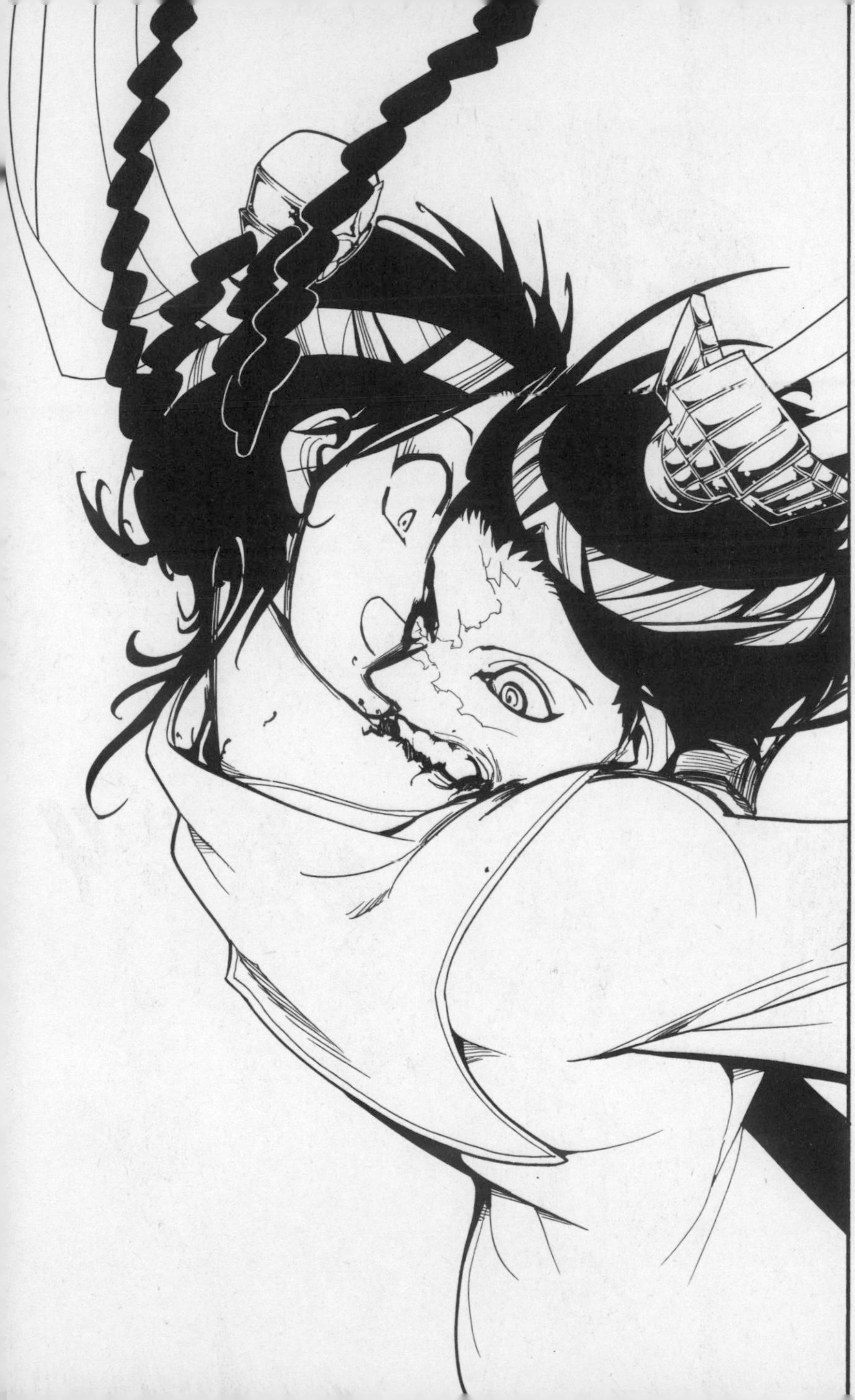

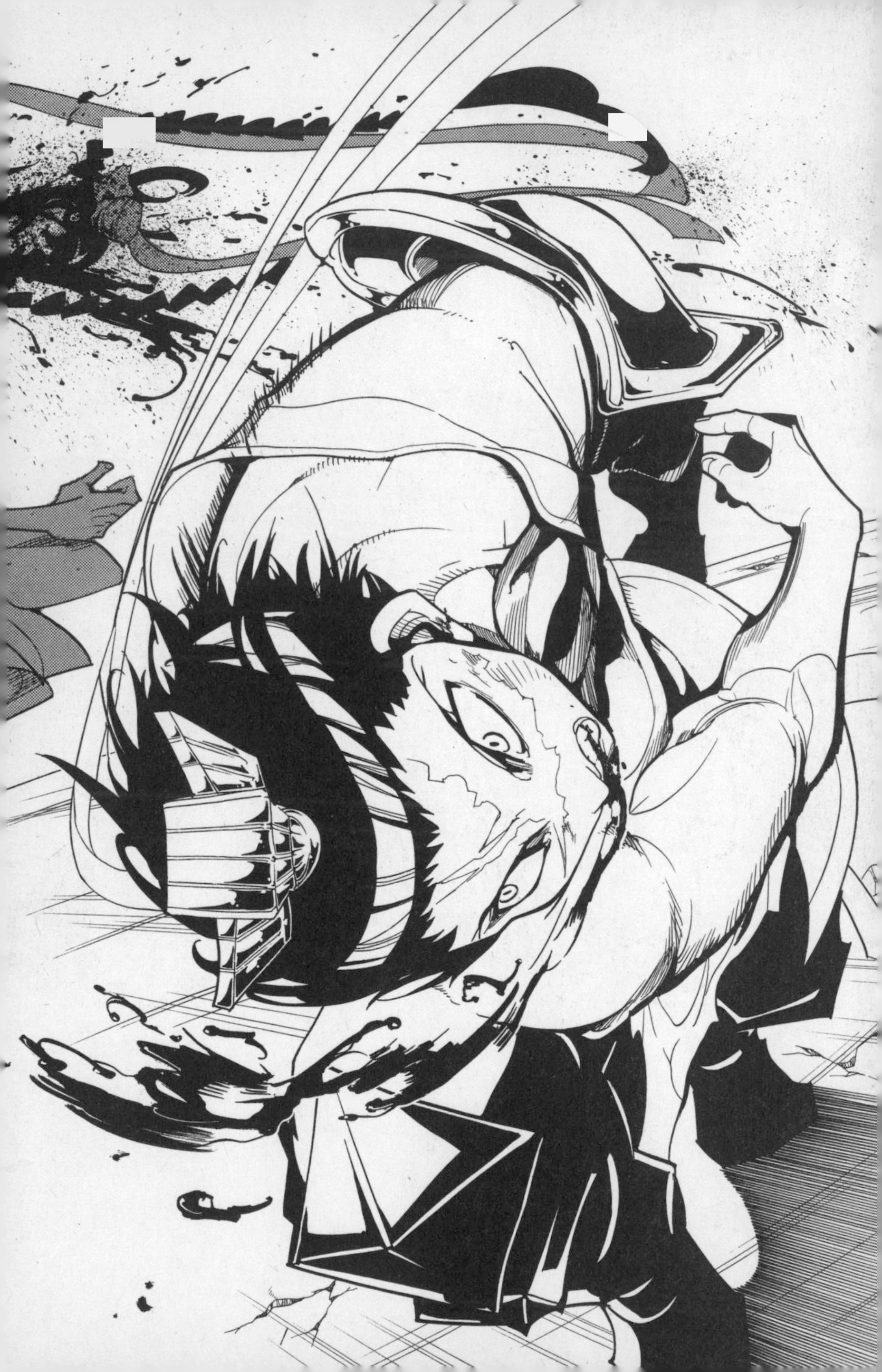

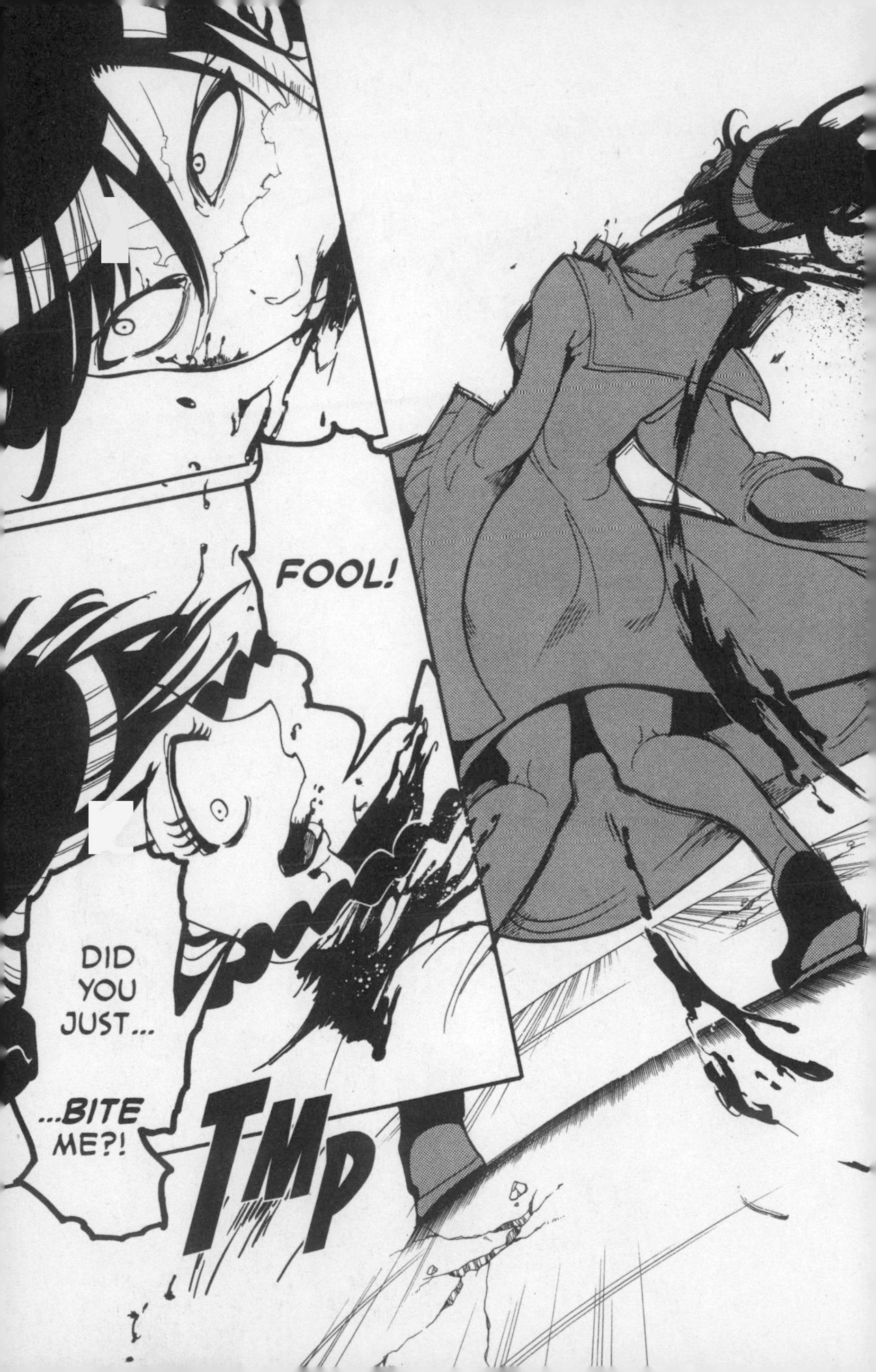
FOOL!
DID YOU JUST...
...BITE ME?!
TMP

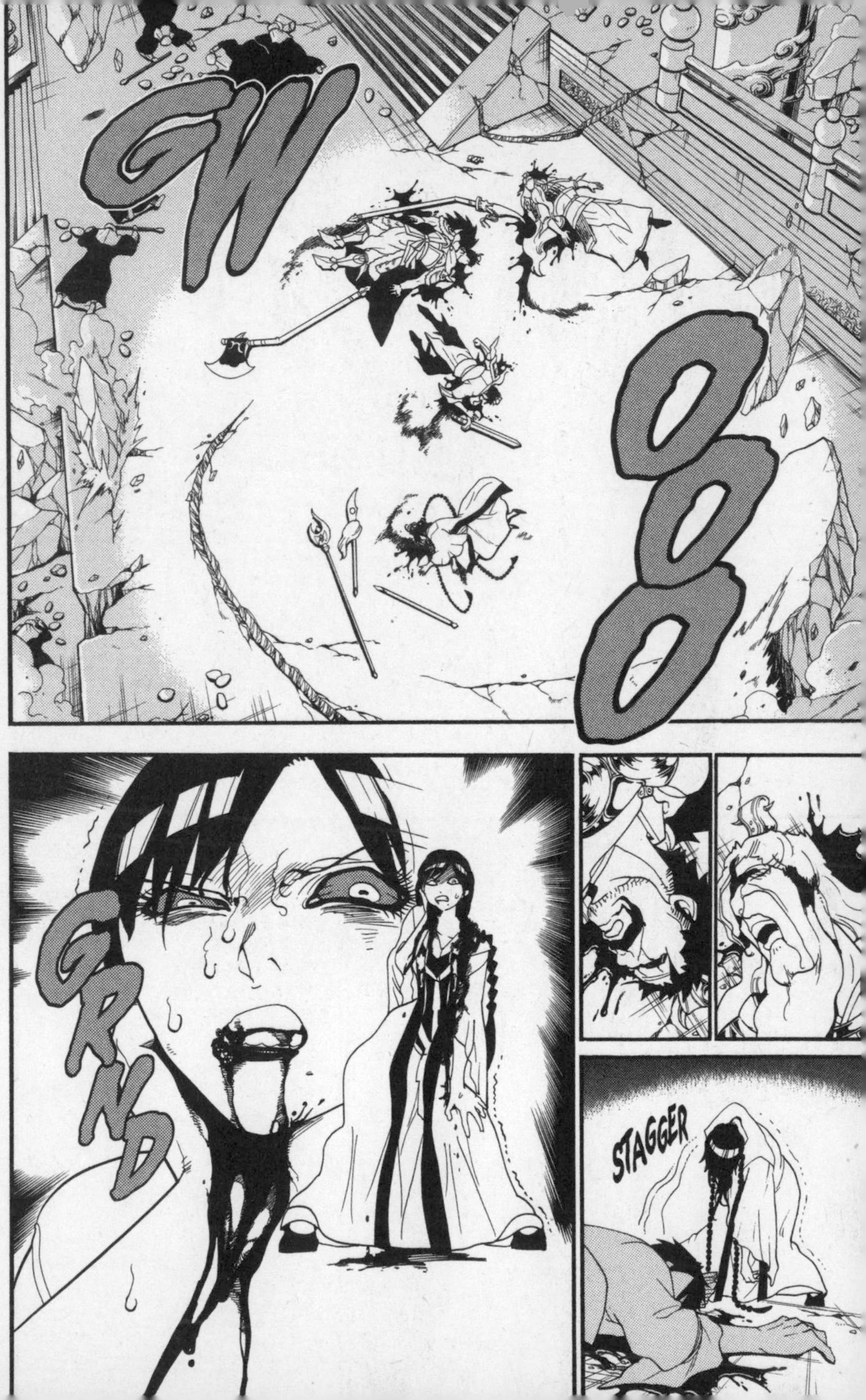
GWOOO
STAGGER
GRND

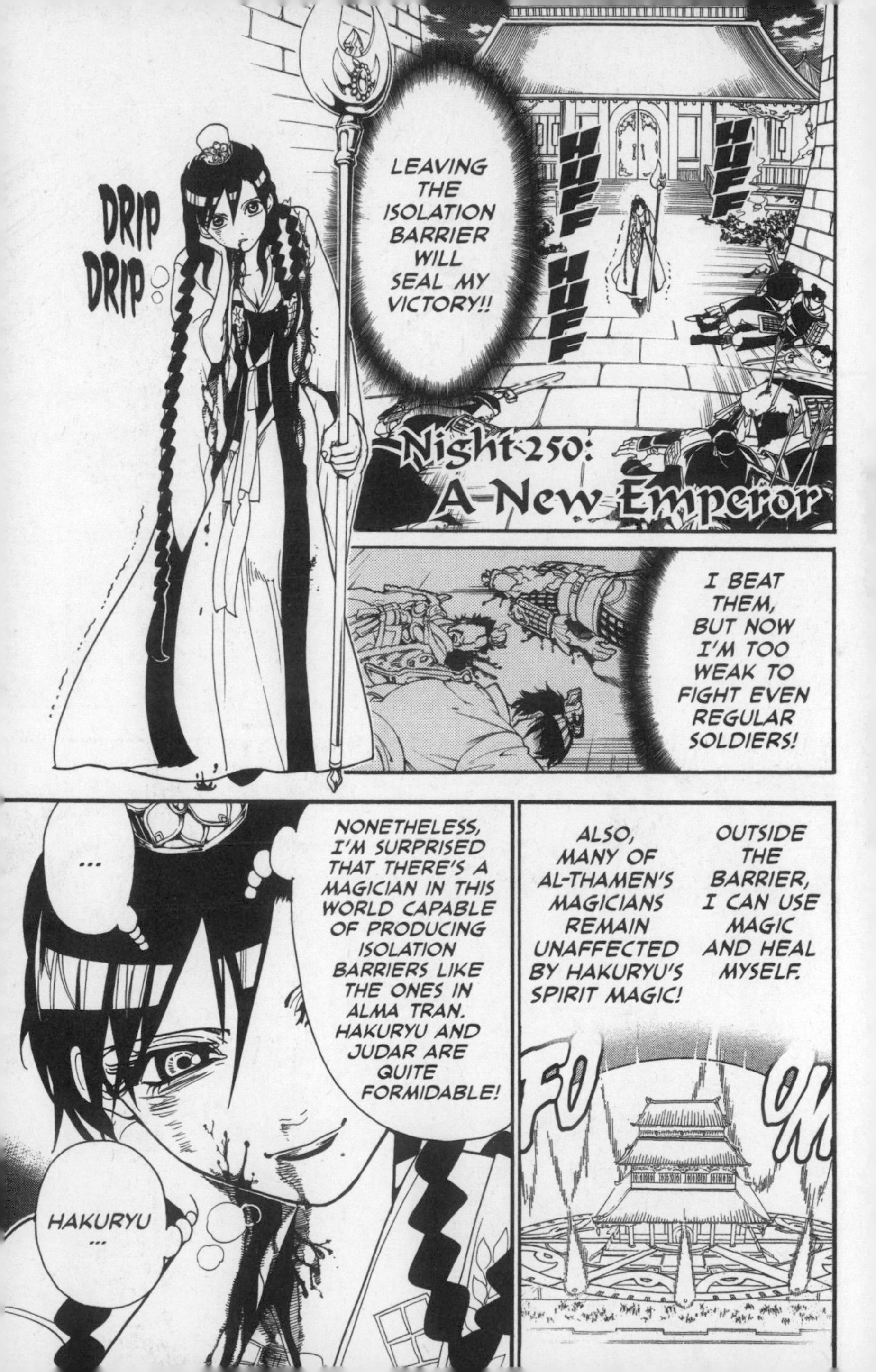
HUFF HUFF
HUFF HUFF
Night 250: A New Emperor
I BEAT THEM, BUT NOW I'M TOO WEAK TO FIGHT EVEN REGULAR SOLDIERS!
LEAVING THE ISOLATION BARRIER WILL SEAL MY VICTORY!!
DRIP DRIP
OUTSIDE THE BARRIER, I CAN USE MAGIC AND HEAL MYSELF.
ALSO, MANY OF AL-THAMEN'S MAGICIANS REMAIN UNAFFECTED BY HAKURYU'S SPIRIT MAGIC!
FO OM
NONETHELESS, I'M SURPRISED THAT THERE'S A MAGICIAN IN THIS WORLD CAPABLE OF PRODUCING ISOLATION BARRIERS LIKE THE ONES IN ALMA TRAN. HAKURYU AND JUDAR ARE QUITE FORMIDABLE!
...
HAKURYU ...

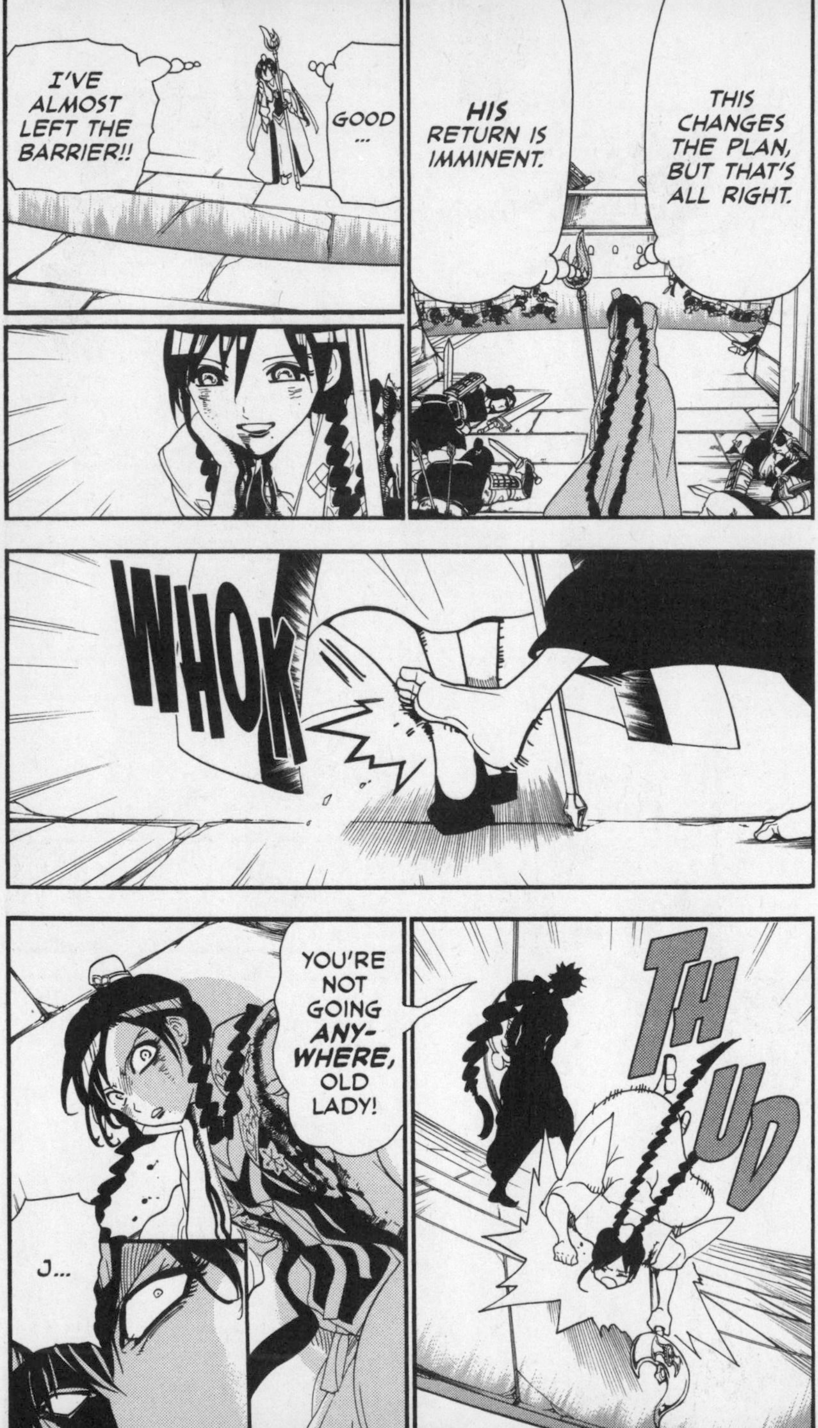
THIS CHANGES THE PLAN, BUT THAT'S ALL RIGHT.
HIS RETURN IS IMMINENT.
GOOD ...
I'VE ALMOST LEFT THE BARRIER!!
WHOK
THUD
YOU'RE NOT GOING ANYWHERE, OLD LADY!
J...

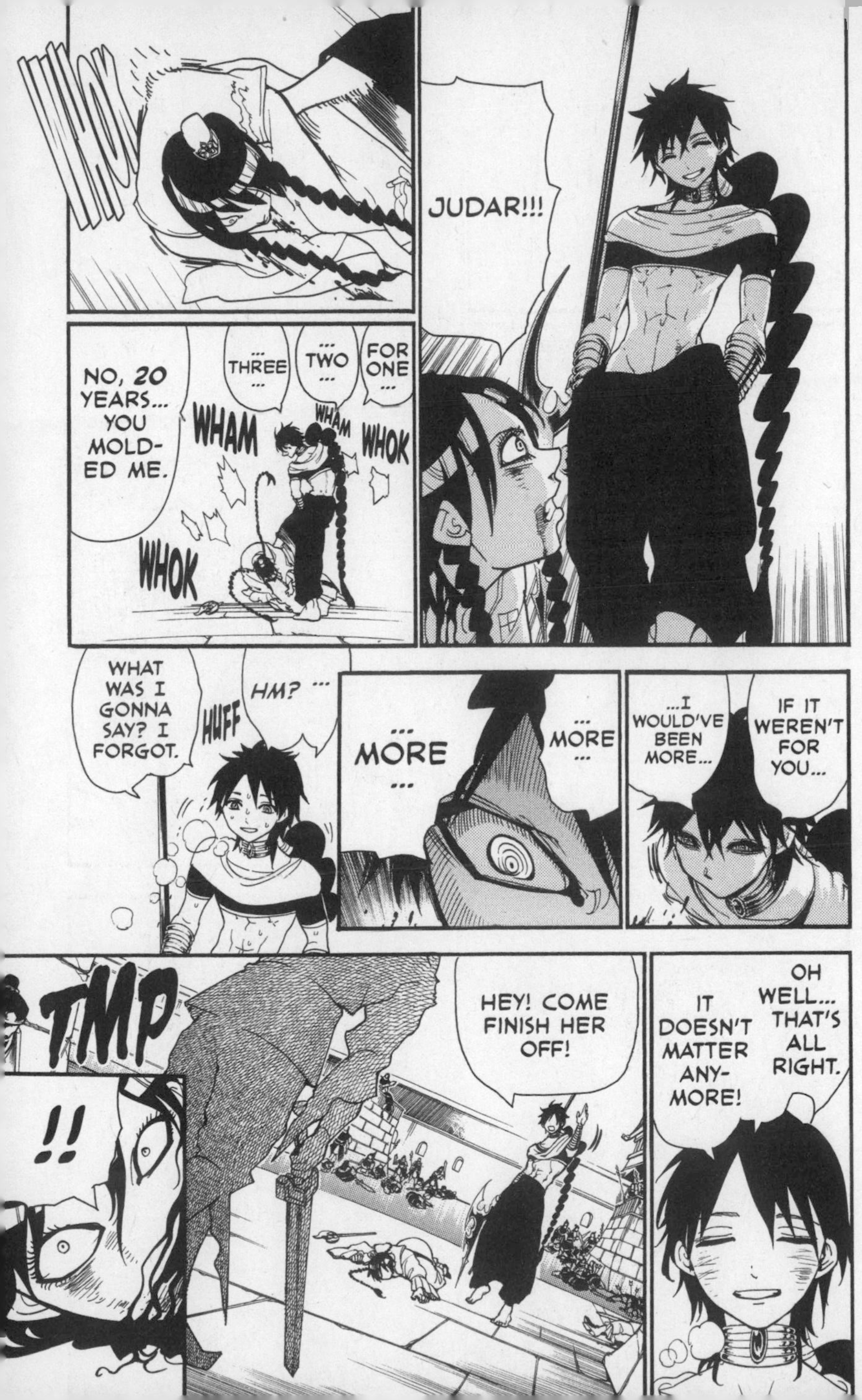
JUDAR!!!
WHOK
...FOR ONE...
...TWO...
...THREE...
WHAM
WHAM
WHOK
WHOK
NO, 20 YEARS... YOU MOLD-ED ME.
IF IT WEREN'T FOR YOU...
...I WOULD'VE BEEN MORE...
...MORE...
...MORE...
HM? ...
HUFF
WHAT WAS I GONNA SAY? I FORGOT.
OH WELL... THAT'S ALL RIGHT.
IT DOESN'T MATTER ANY-MORE!
HEY! COME FINISH HER OFF!
TMP
!!

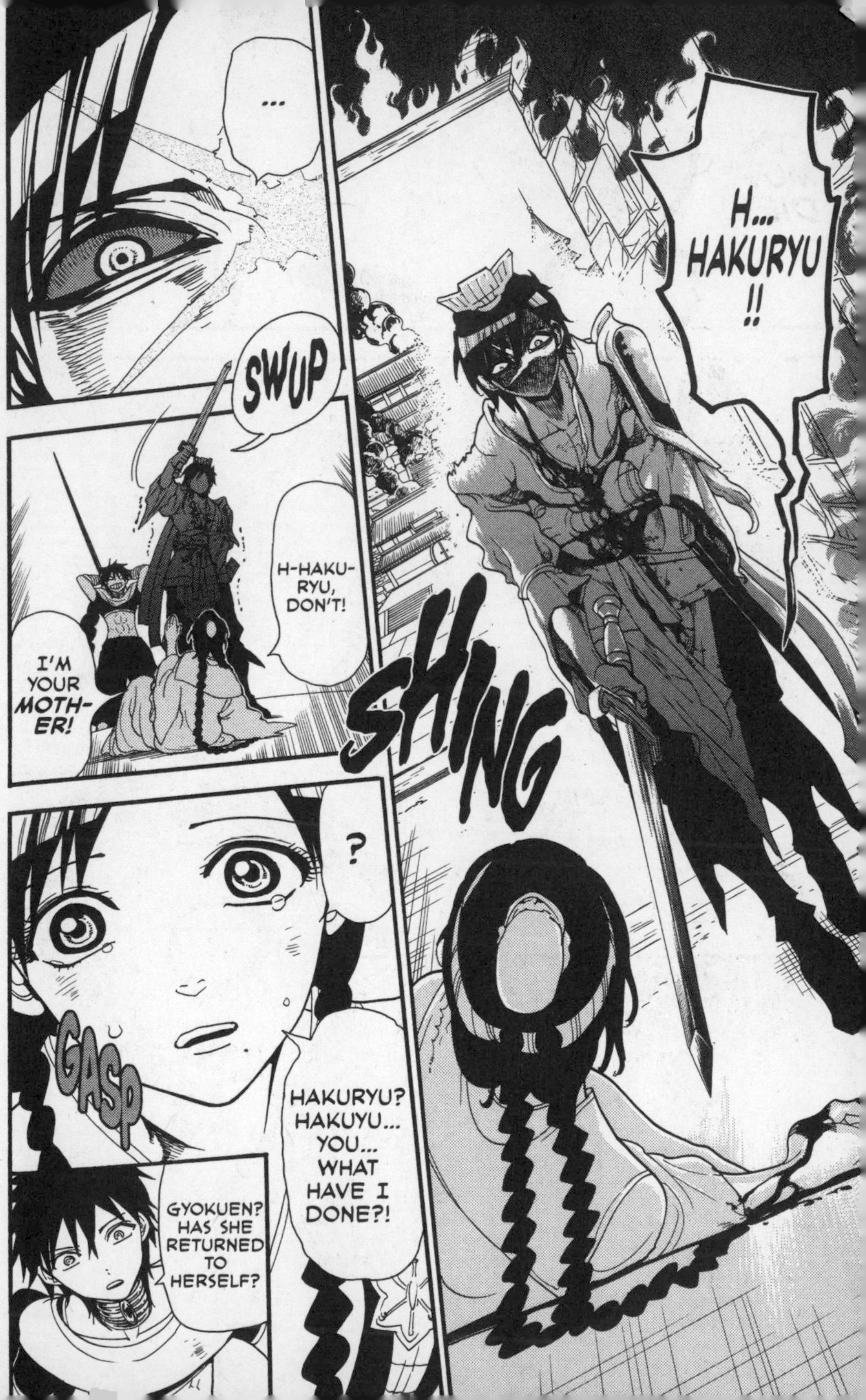
H... HAKURYU !!
SHING
...
SWUP
H-HAKU-RYU, DON'T!
I'M YOUR MOTH-ER!
?
HAKURYU? HAKUYU... YOU... WHAT HAVE I DONE?!
GASP
GYOKUEN? HAS SHE RETURNED TO HERSELF?

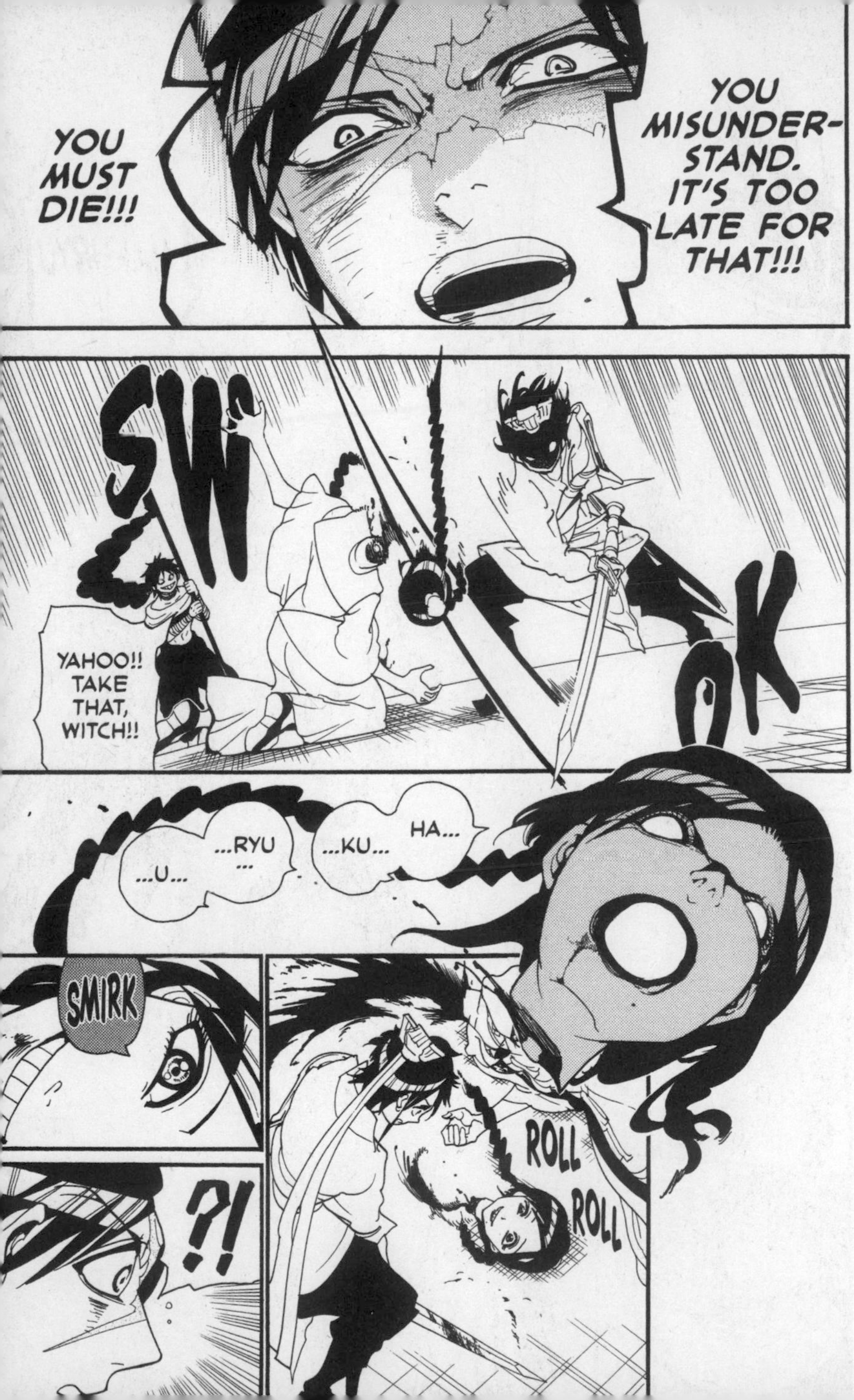
YOU MISUNDER-STAND. IT'S TOO LATE FOR THAT!!!
YOU MUST DIE!!!
SW
OK
YAHOO!! TAKE THAT, WITCH!!
HA...
...KU...
...RYU ...
...U...
ROLL ROLL
SMIRK
?!

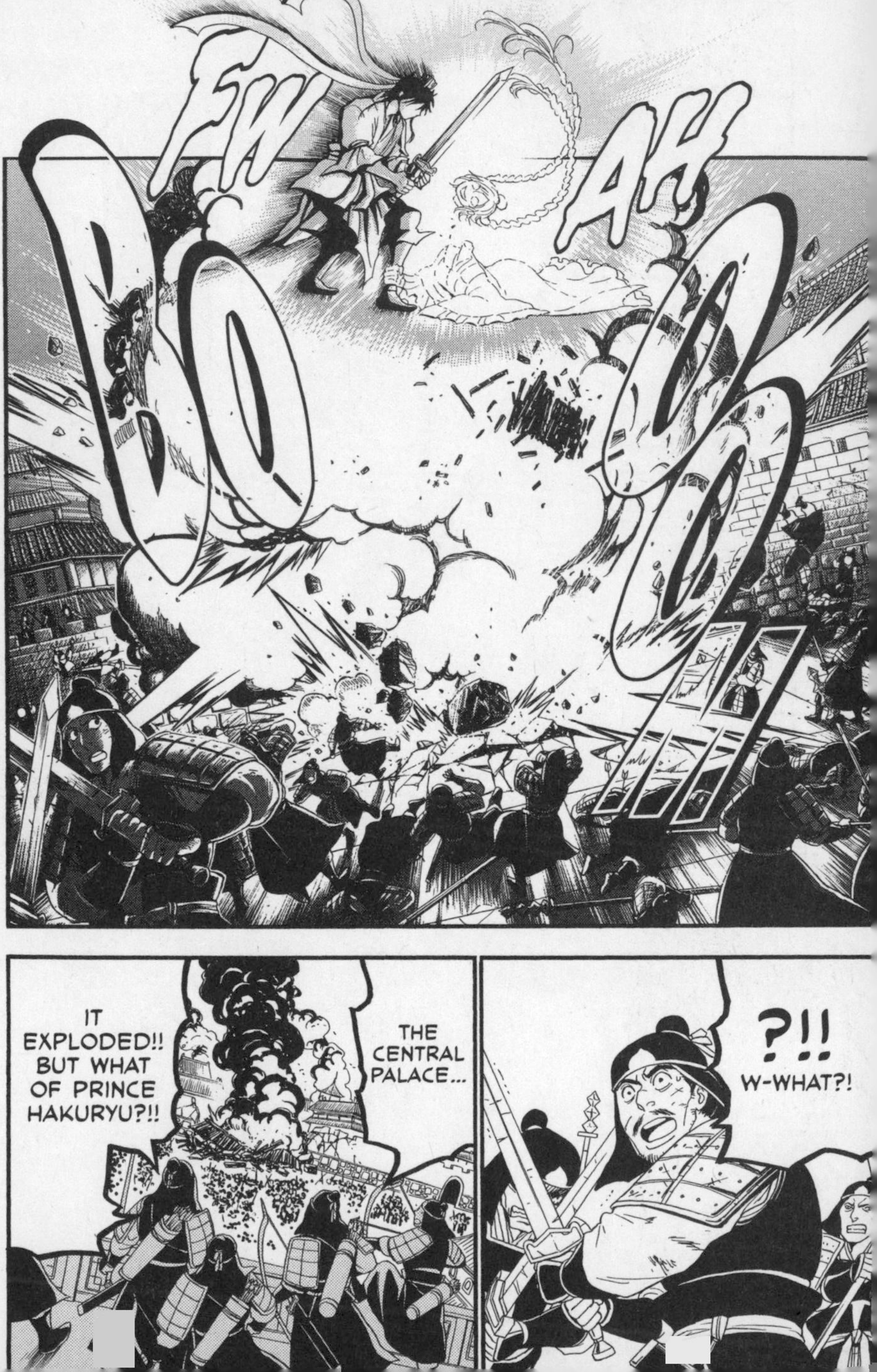
FWAH
?!!
W-WHAT?!
THE CENTRAL PALACE...
IT EXPLODED!! BUT WHAT OF PRINCE HAKURYU?!!

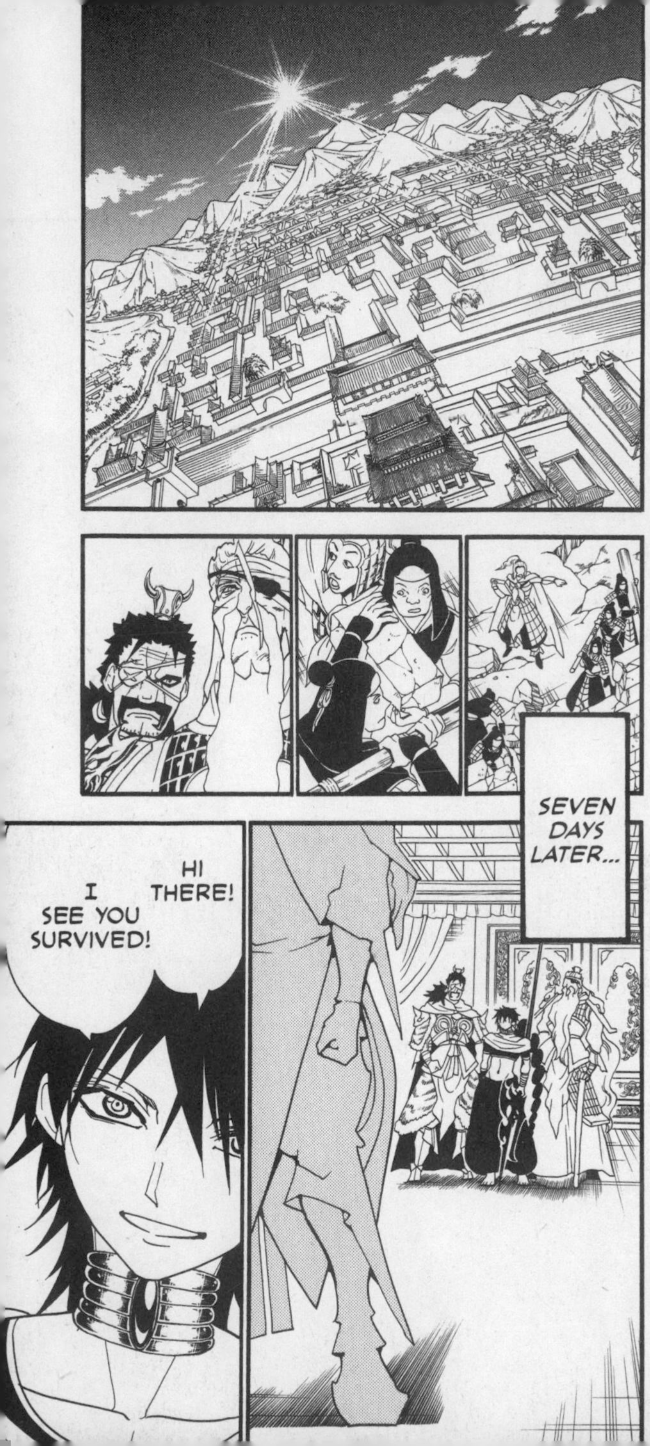
SEVEN DAYS LATER...
HI THERE! I SEE YOU SURVIVED!

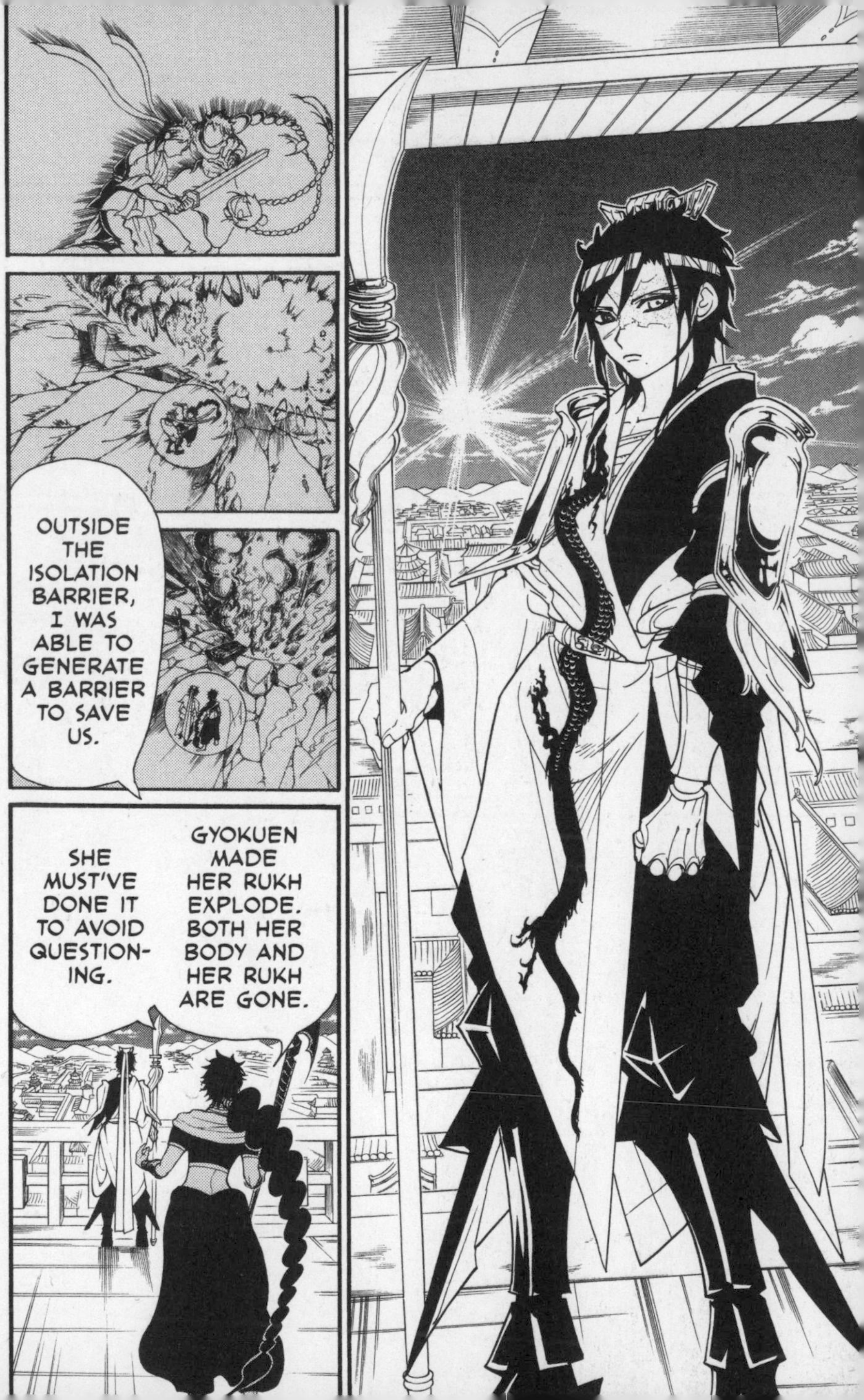
OUTSIDE THE ISOLATION BARRIER, I WAS ABLE TO GENERATE A BARRIER TO SAVE US.
GYOKUEN MADE HER RUKH EXPLODE. BOTH HER BODY AND HER RUKH ARE GONE.
SHE MUST'VE DONE IT TO AVOID QUESTIONING.

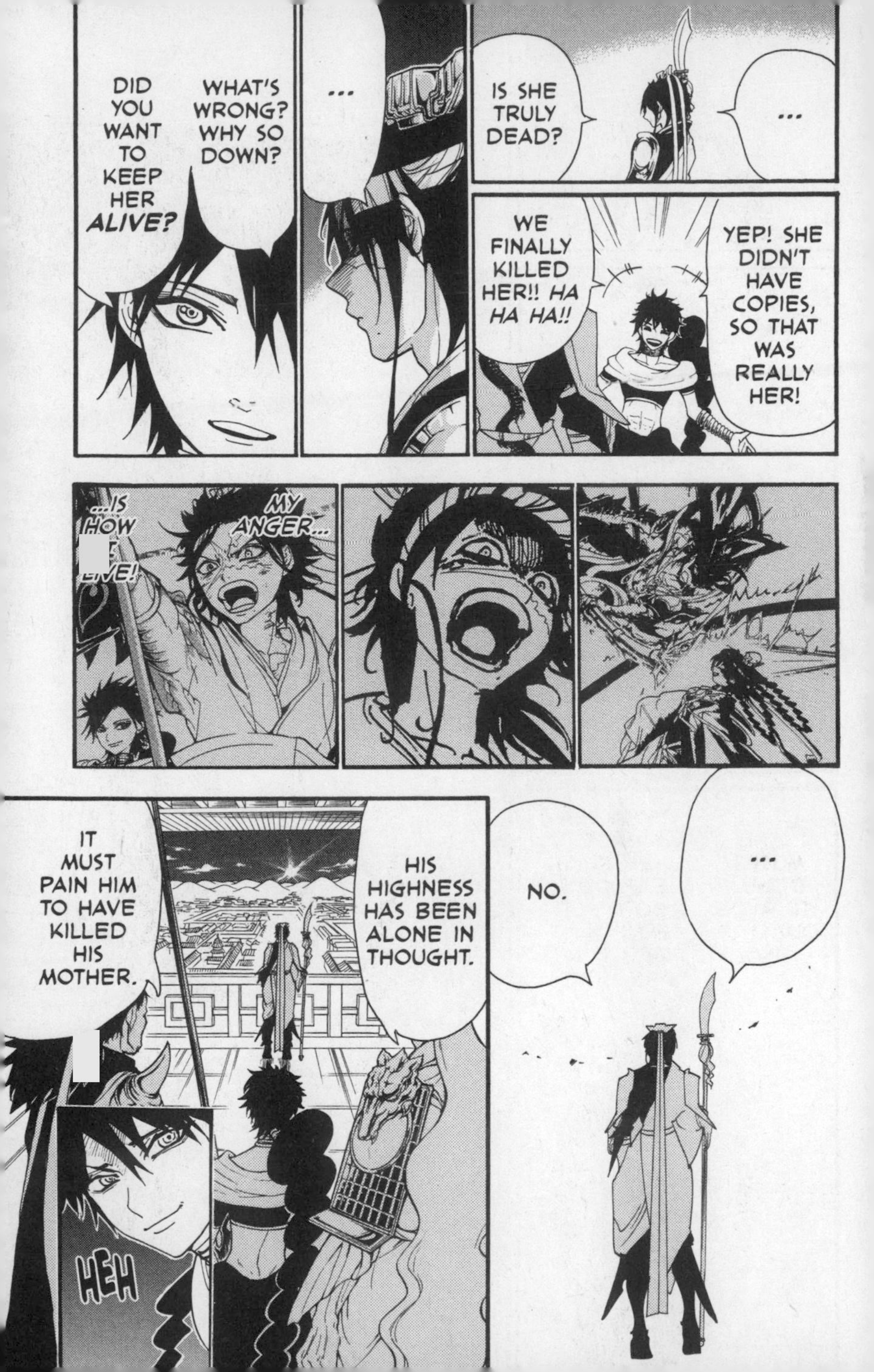
...
IS SHE TRULY DEAD?
YEP! SHE DIDN'T HAVE COPIES, SO THAT WAS REALLY HER!
WE FINALLY KILLED HER!! *HA HA HA!!*
...
WHAT'S WRONG? WHY SO DOWN?
DID YOU WANT TO KEEP HER *ALIVE?*
MY ANGER...
...IS HOW
LIVE!
...
NO.
HIS HIGHNESS HAS BEEN ALONE IN THOUGHT.
IT MUST PAIN HIM TO HAVE KILLED HIS MOTHER.
HEH

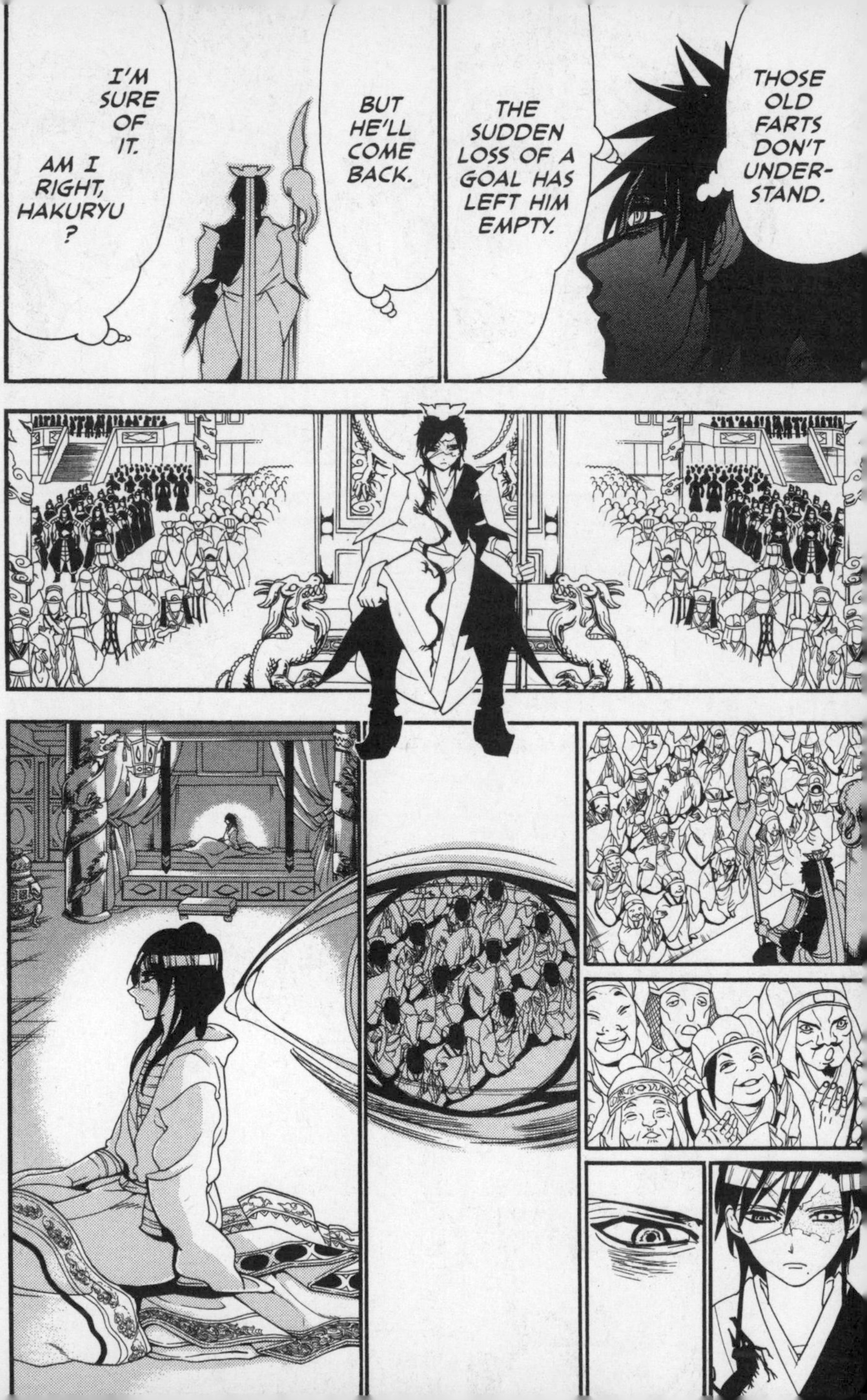
THOSE OLD FARTS DON'T UNDER-STAND.
THE SUDDEN LOSS OF A GOAL HAS LEFT HIM EMPTY.
BUT HE'LL COME BACK.
I'M SURE OF IT.
AM I RIGHT, HAKURYU?

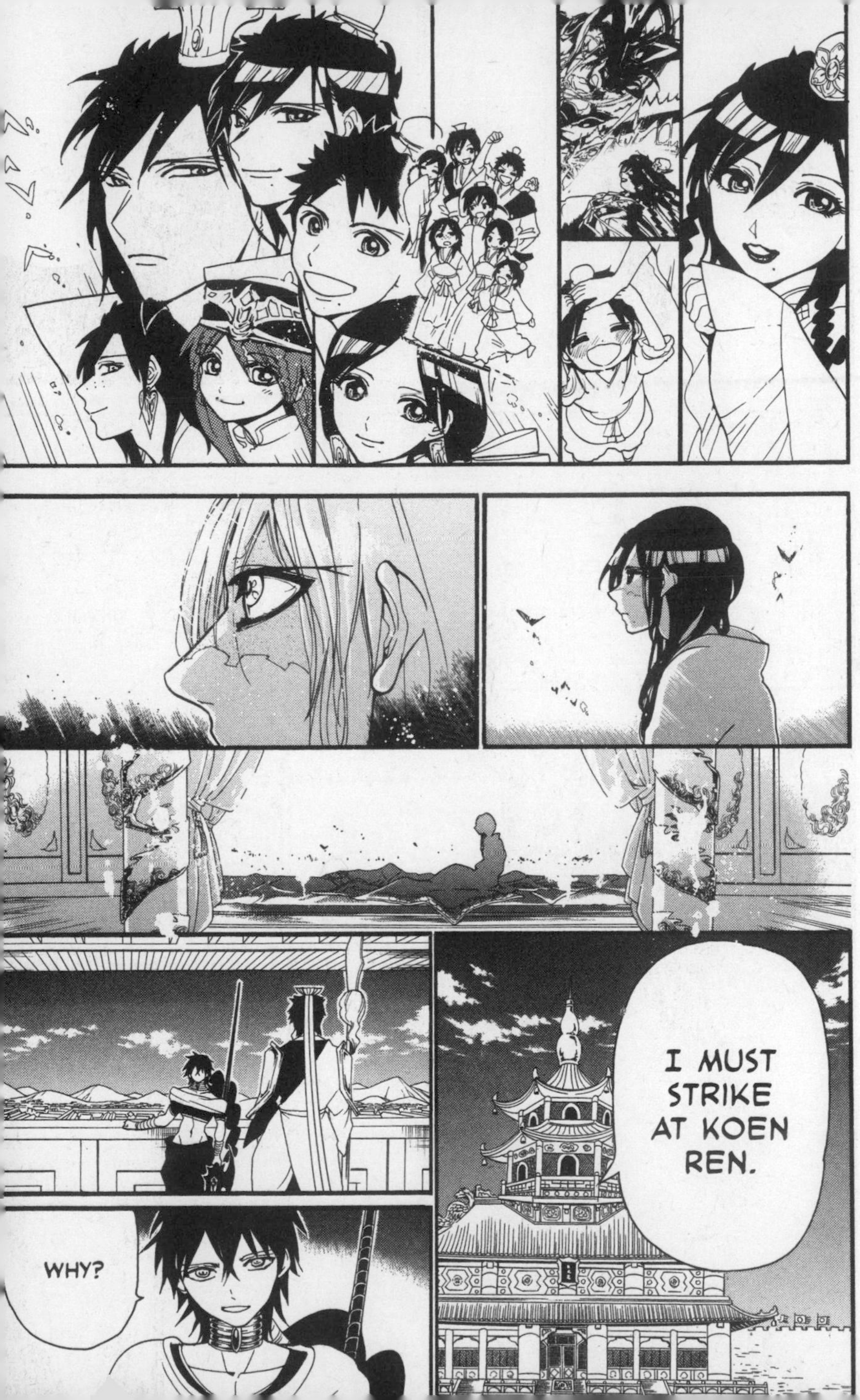
I MUST STRIKE AT KOEN REN.
WHY?

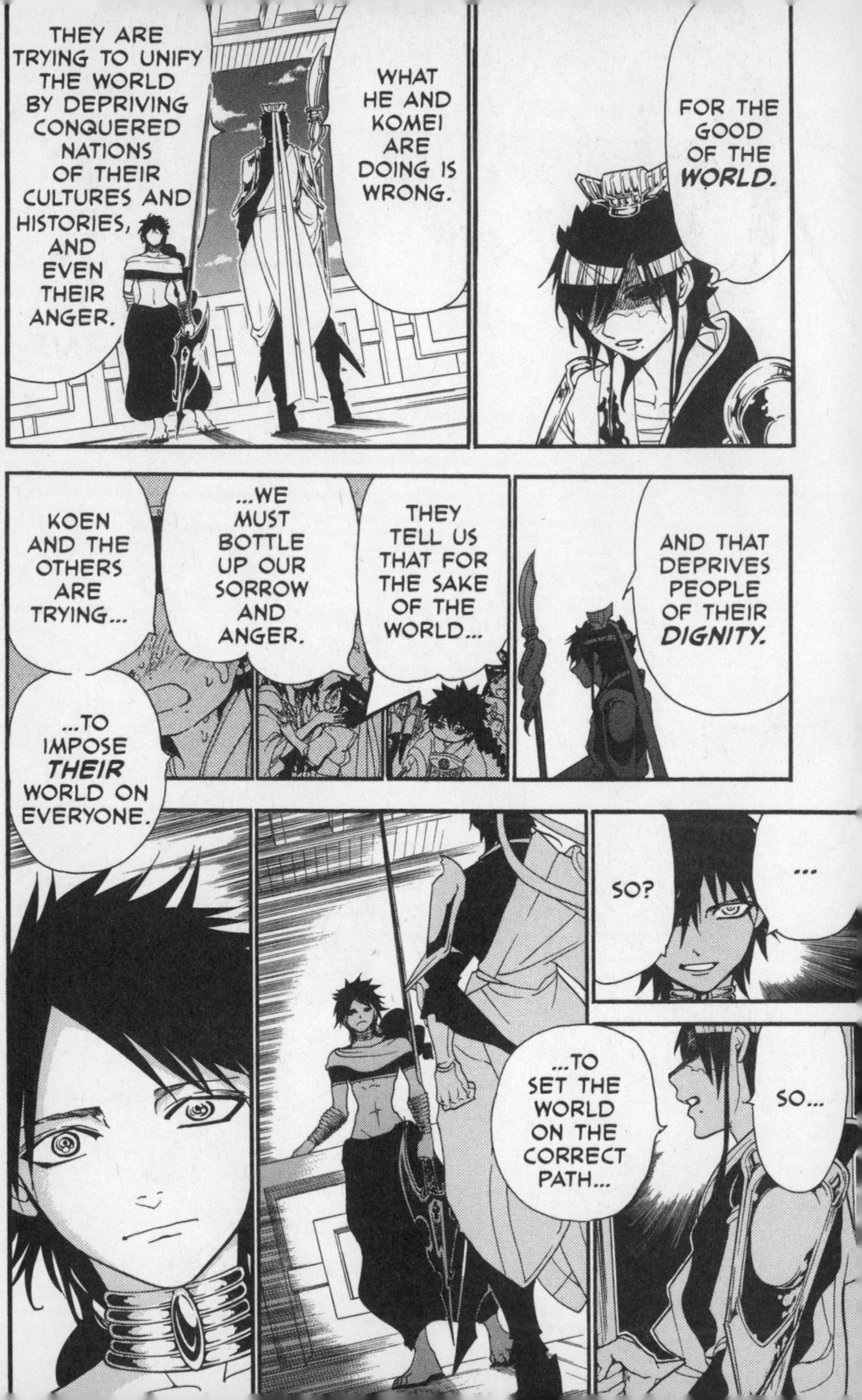

FOR THE GOOD OF THE *WORLD.*
WHAT HE AND KOMEI ARE DOING IS WRONG.
THEY ARE TRYING TO UNIFY THE WORLD BY DEPRIVING CONQUERED NATIONS OF THEIR CULTURES AND HISTORIES, AND EVEN THEIR ANGER.
AND THAT DEPRIVES PEOPLE OF THEIR *DIGNITY.*
THEY TELL US THAT FOR THE SAKE OF THE WORLD...
...WE MUST BOTTLE UP OUR SORROW AND ANGER.
KOEN AND THE OTHERS ARE TRYING...
...TO IMPOSE *THEIR* WORLD ON EVERYONE.
...
SO?
SO...
...TO SET THE WORLD ON THE CORRECT PATH...

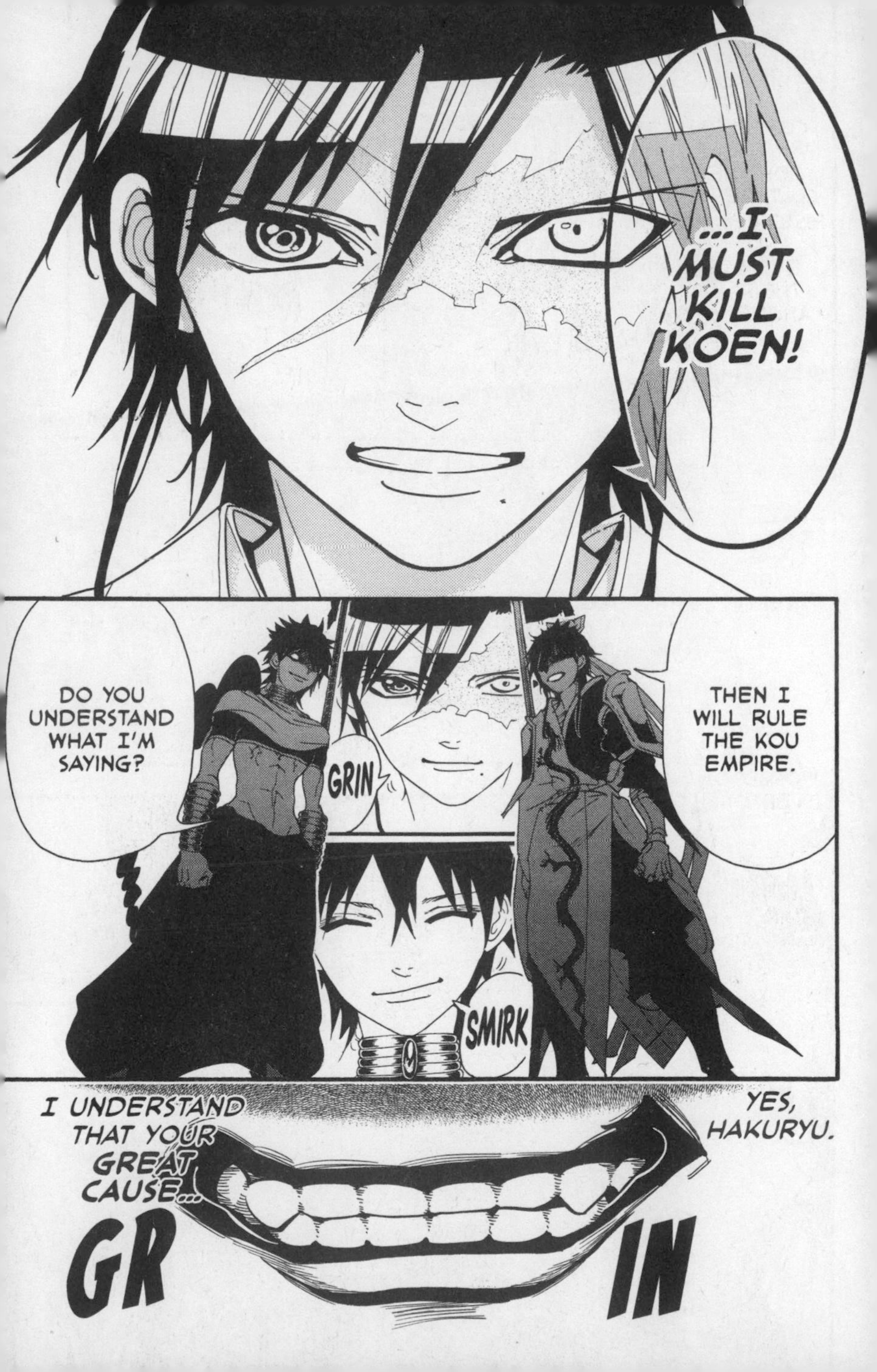
...I MUST KILL KOEN!
THEN I WILL RULE THE KOU EMPIRE.
DO YOU UNDERSTAND WHAT I'M SAYING?
GRIN
SMIRK
YES, HAKURYU.
I UNDERSTAND THAT YOUR GREAT CAUSE...
GR IN

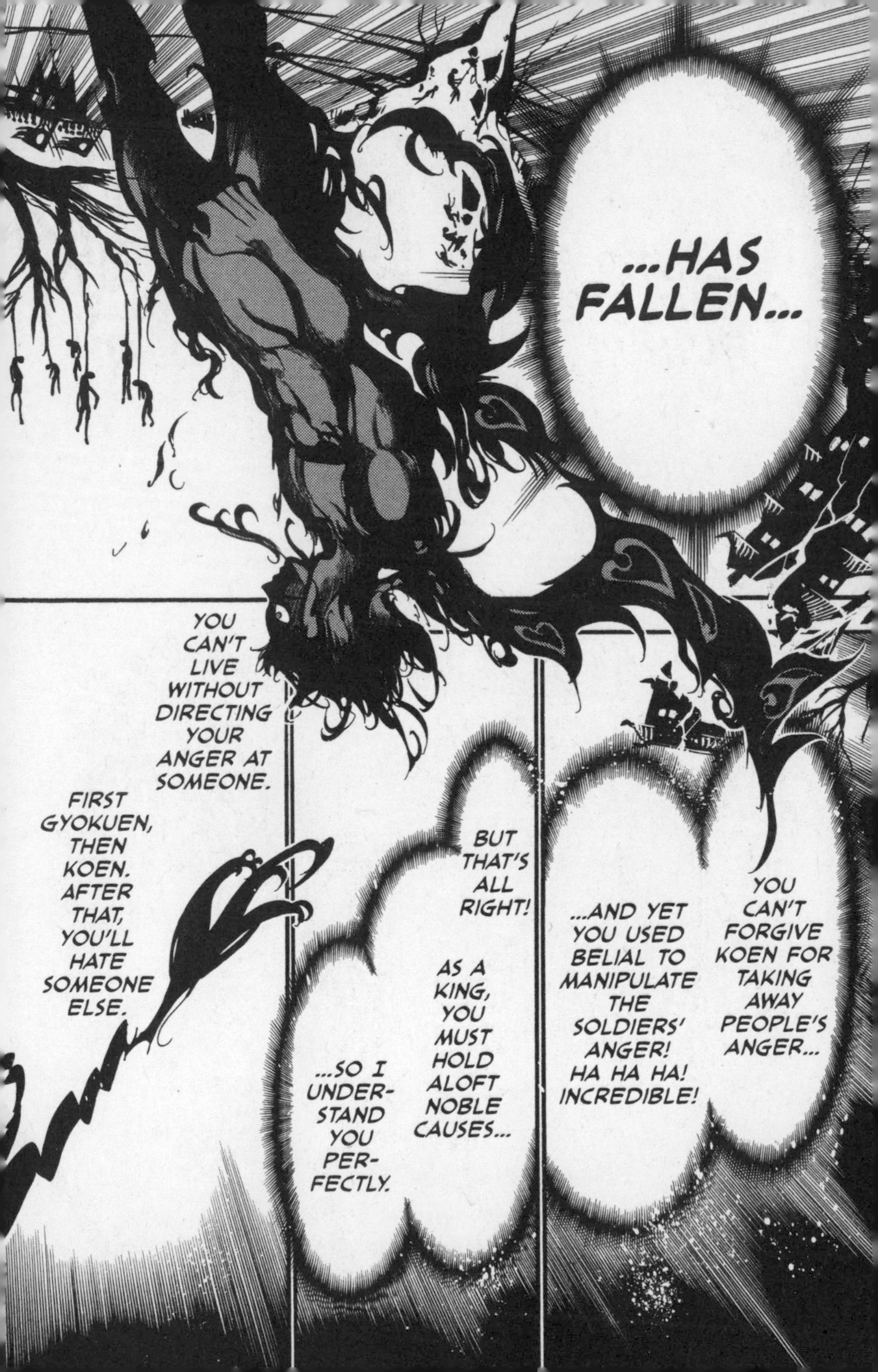
...HAS FALLEN...
YOU CAN'T FORGIVE KOEN FOR TAKING AWAY PEOPLE'S ANGER...
...AND YET YOU USED BELIAL TO MANIPULATE THE SOLDIERS' ANGER! HA HA HA! INCREDIBLE!
BUT THAT'S ALL RIGHT!
AS A KING, YOU MUST HOLD ALOFT NOBLE CAUSES...
...SO I UNDER-STAND YOU PER-FECTLY.
YOU CAN'T LIVE WITHOUT DIRECTING YOUR ANGER AT SOMEONE.
FIRST GYOKUEN, THEN KOEN. AFTER THAT, YOU'LL HATE SOMEONE ELSE.

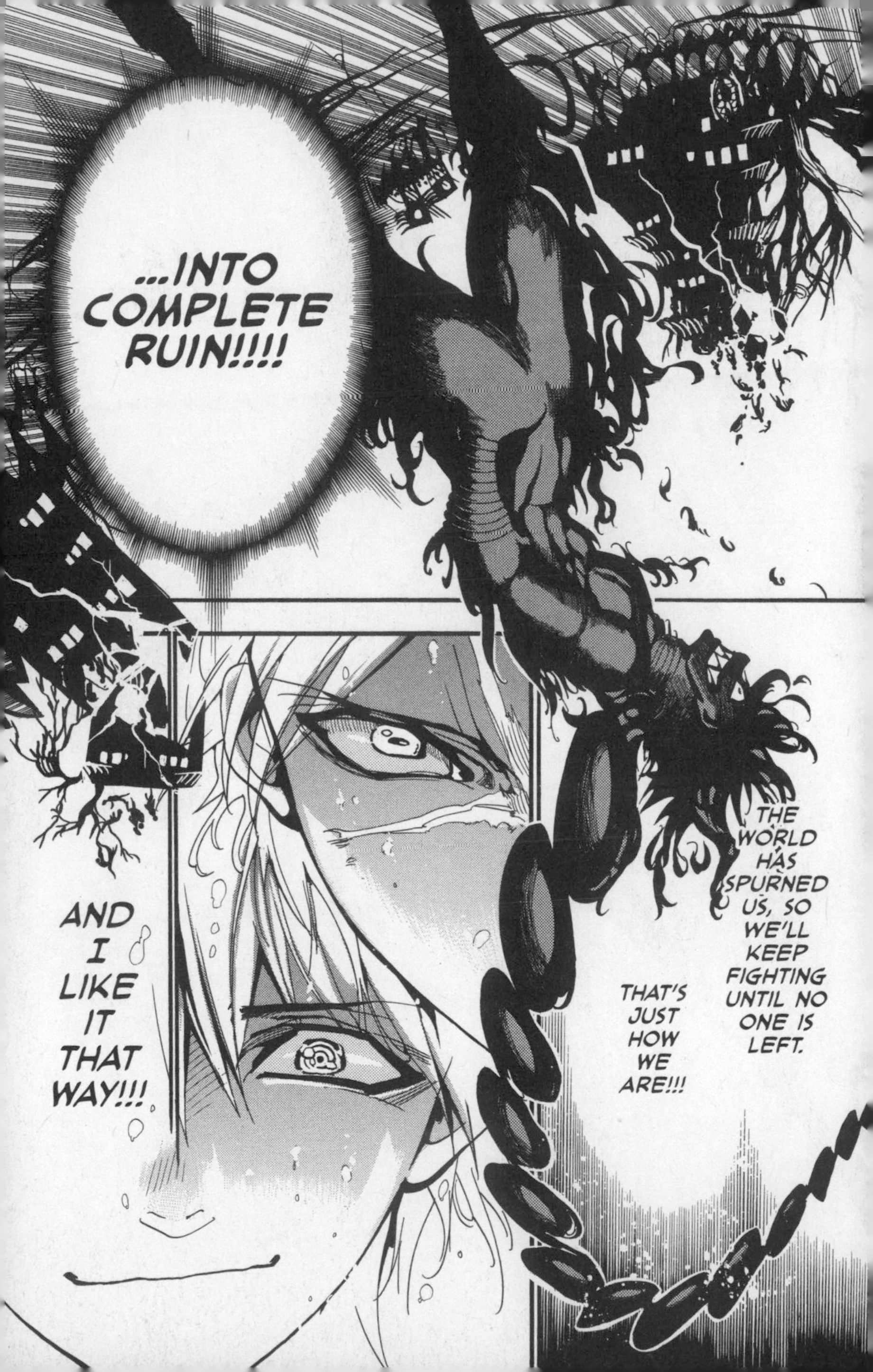
...INTO COMPLETE RUIN!!!!
THE WORLD HAS SPURNED US, SO WE'LL KEEP FIGHTING UNTIL NO ONE IS LEFT.
THAT'S JUST HOW WE ARE!!!
AND I LIKE IT THAT WAY!!!

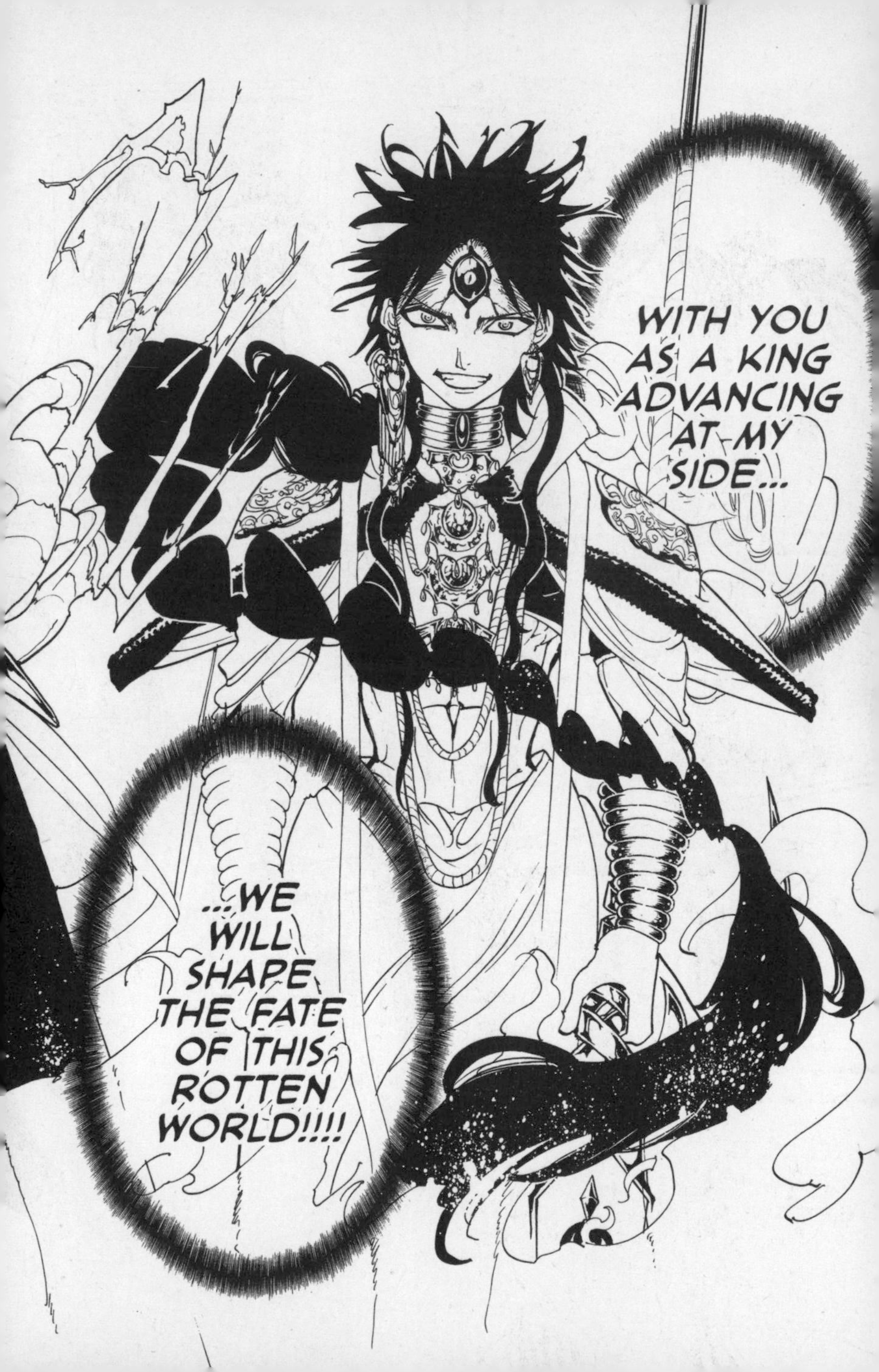
WITH YOU AS A KING ADVANCING AT MY SIDE...
...WE WILL SHAPE THE FATE OF THIS ROTTEN WORLD!!!!

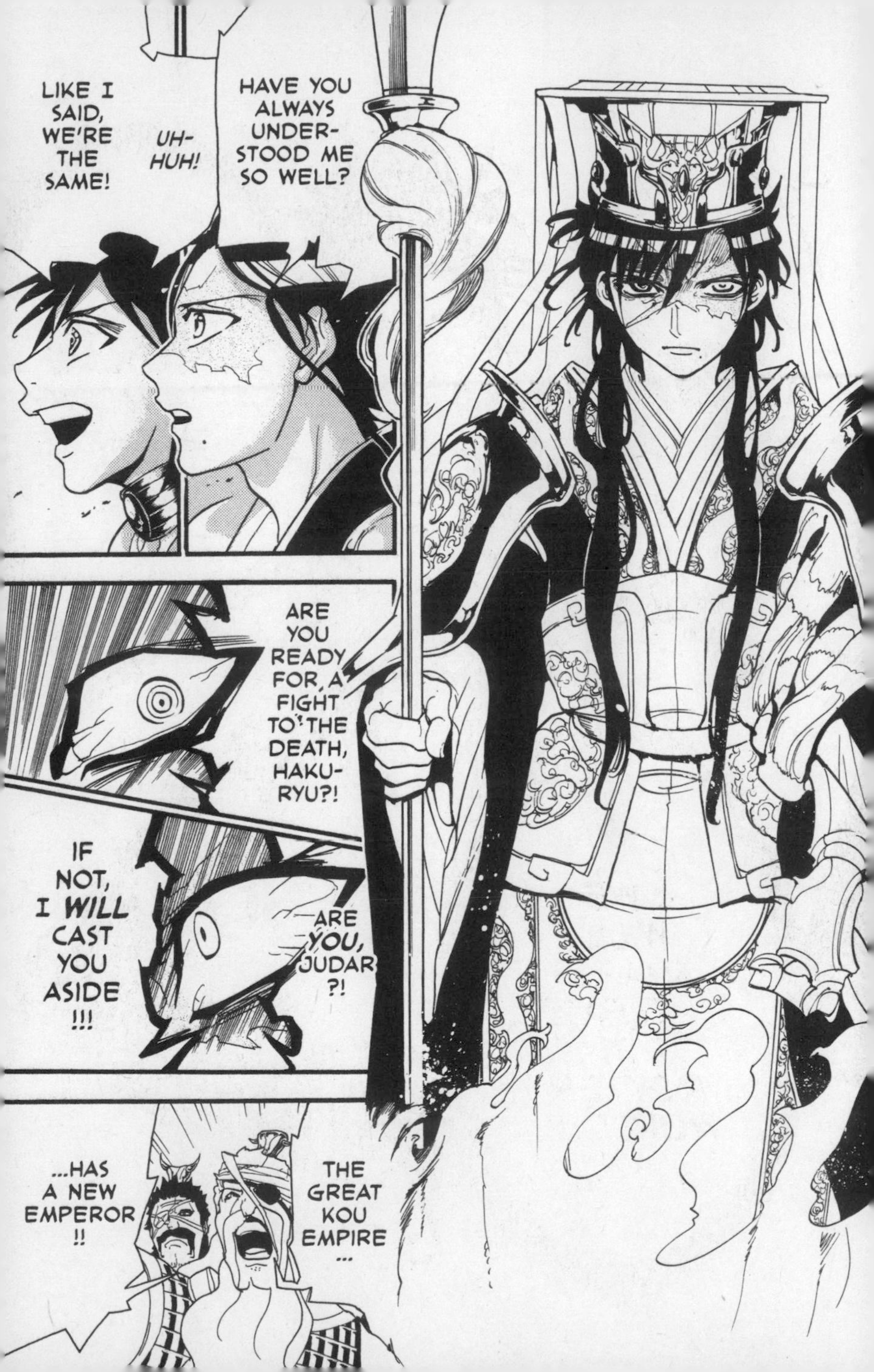
HAVE YOU ALWAYS UNDERSTOOD ME SO WELL?
UH-HUH!
LIKE I SAID, WE'RE THE SAME!
ARE YOU READY FOR A FIGHT TO THE DEATH, HAKURYU?!
ARE YOU, JUDAR?!
IF NOT, I WILL CAST YOU ASIDE!!!
THE GREAT KOU EMPIRE...
...HAS A NEW EMPEROR!!

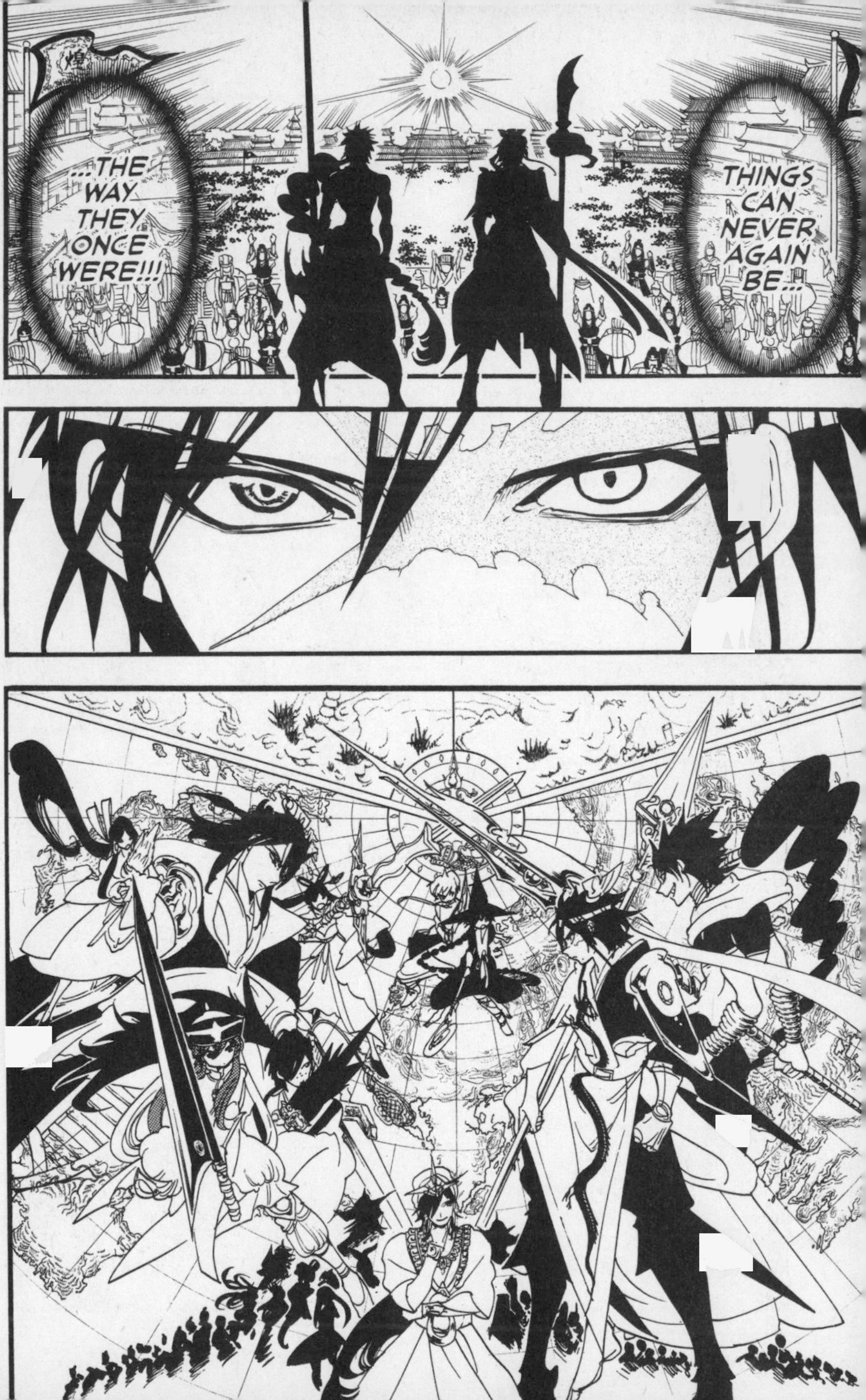
THINGS CAN NEVER AGAIN BE...
...THE WAY THEY ONCE WERE!!!
煌

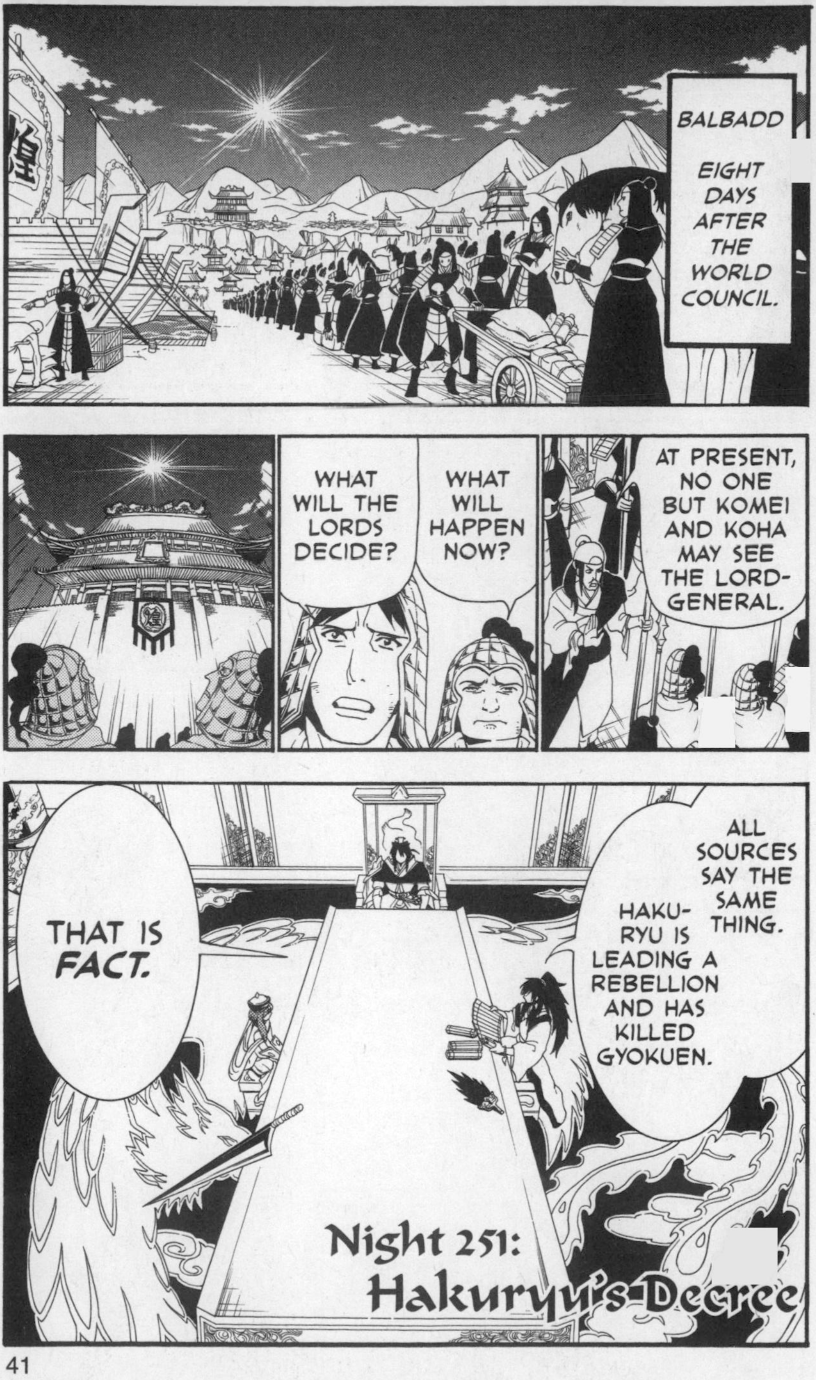
BALBADD
EIGHT DAYS AFTER THE WORLD COUNCIL.
AT PRESENT, NO ONE BUT KOMEI AND KOHA MAY SEE THE LORD-GENERAL.
WHAT WILL HAPPEN NOW?
WHAT WILL THE LORDS DECIDE?
ALL SOURCES SAY THE SAME THING. HAKURYU IS LEADING A REBELLION AND HAS KILLED GYOKUEN.
THAT IS *FACT.*
Night 251: Hakuryu's Decree

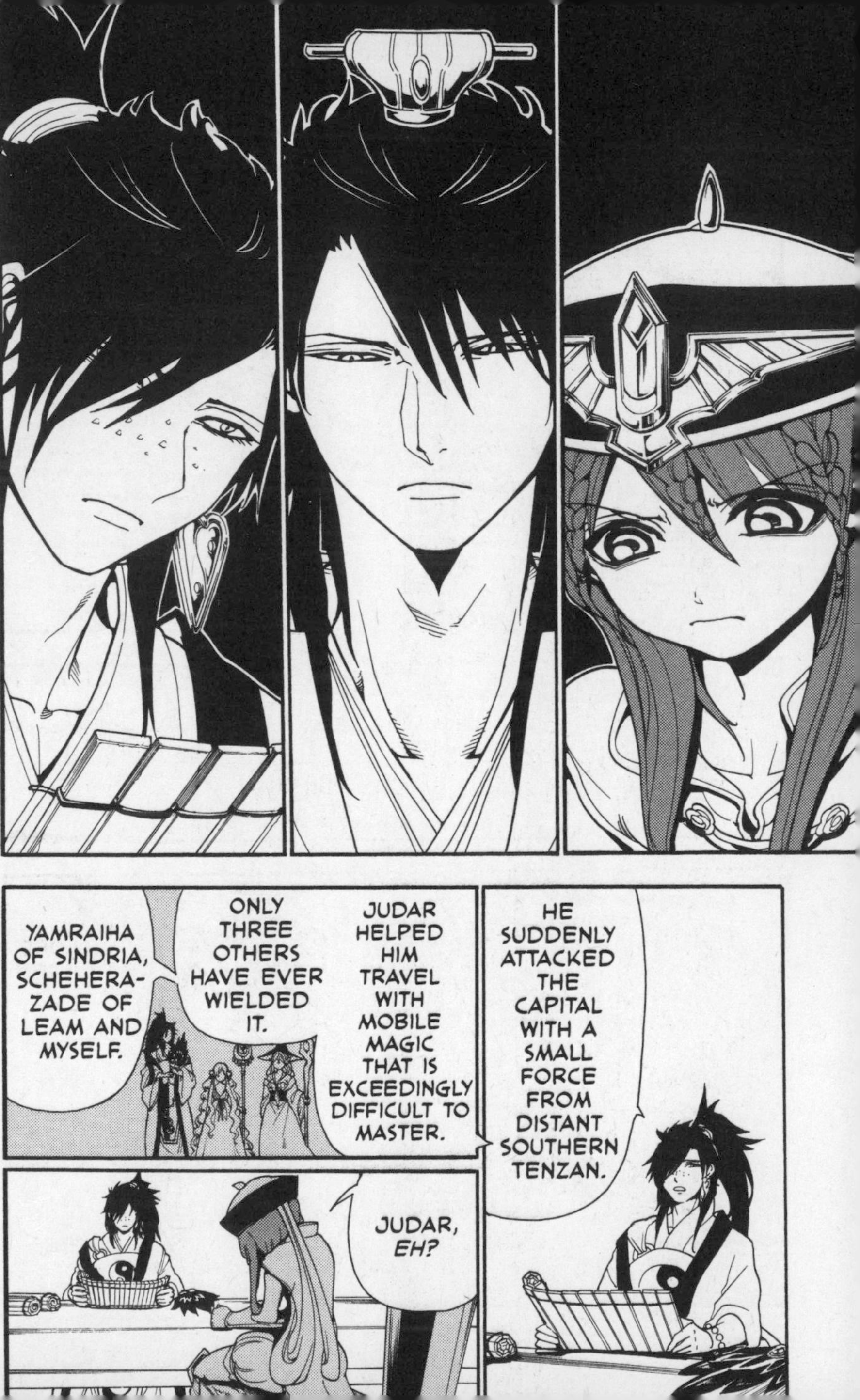
HE SUDDENLY ATTACKED THE CAPITAL WITH A SMALL FORCE FROM DISTANT SOUTHERN TENZAN.
JUDAR HELPED HIM TRAVEL WITH MOBILE MAGIC THAT IS EXCEEDINGLY DIFFICULT TO MASTER.
ONLY THREE OTHERS HAVE EVER WIELDED IT.
YAMRAIHA OF SINDRIA, SCHEHERAZADE OF LEAM AND MYSELF.
JUDAR, *EH?*

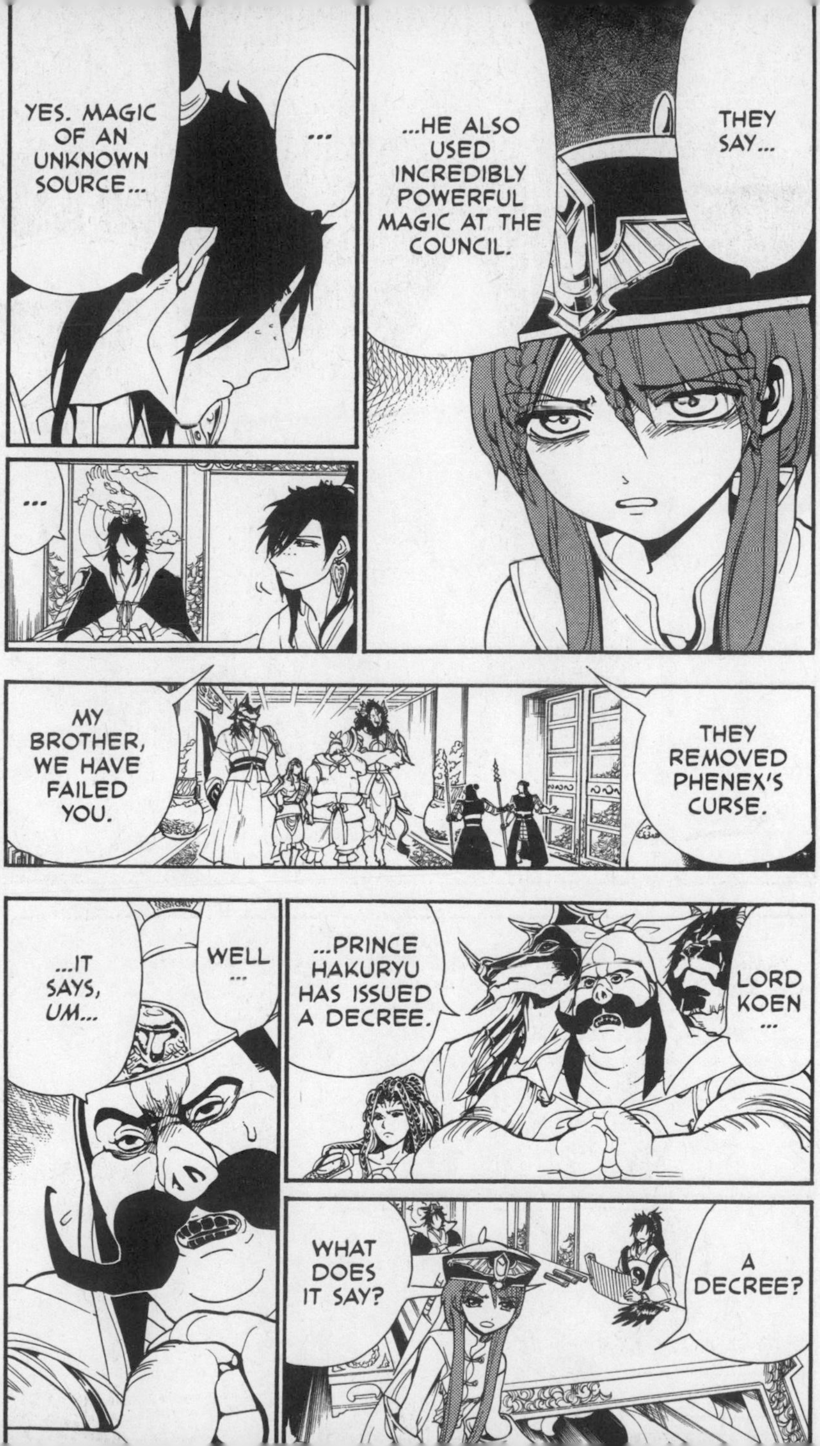
THEY SAY...
...HE ALSO USED INCREDIBLY POWERFUL MAGIC AT THE COUNCIL.
...
YES. MAGIC OF AN UNKNOWN SOURCE...
...
THEY REMOVED PHENEX'S CURSE.
MY BROTHER, WE HAVE FAILED YOU.
LORD KOEN...
...PRINCE HAKURYU HAS ISSUED A DECREE.
A DECREE?
WHAT DOES IT SAY?
WELL...
...IT SAYS, UM...

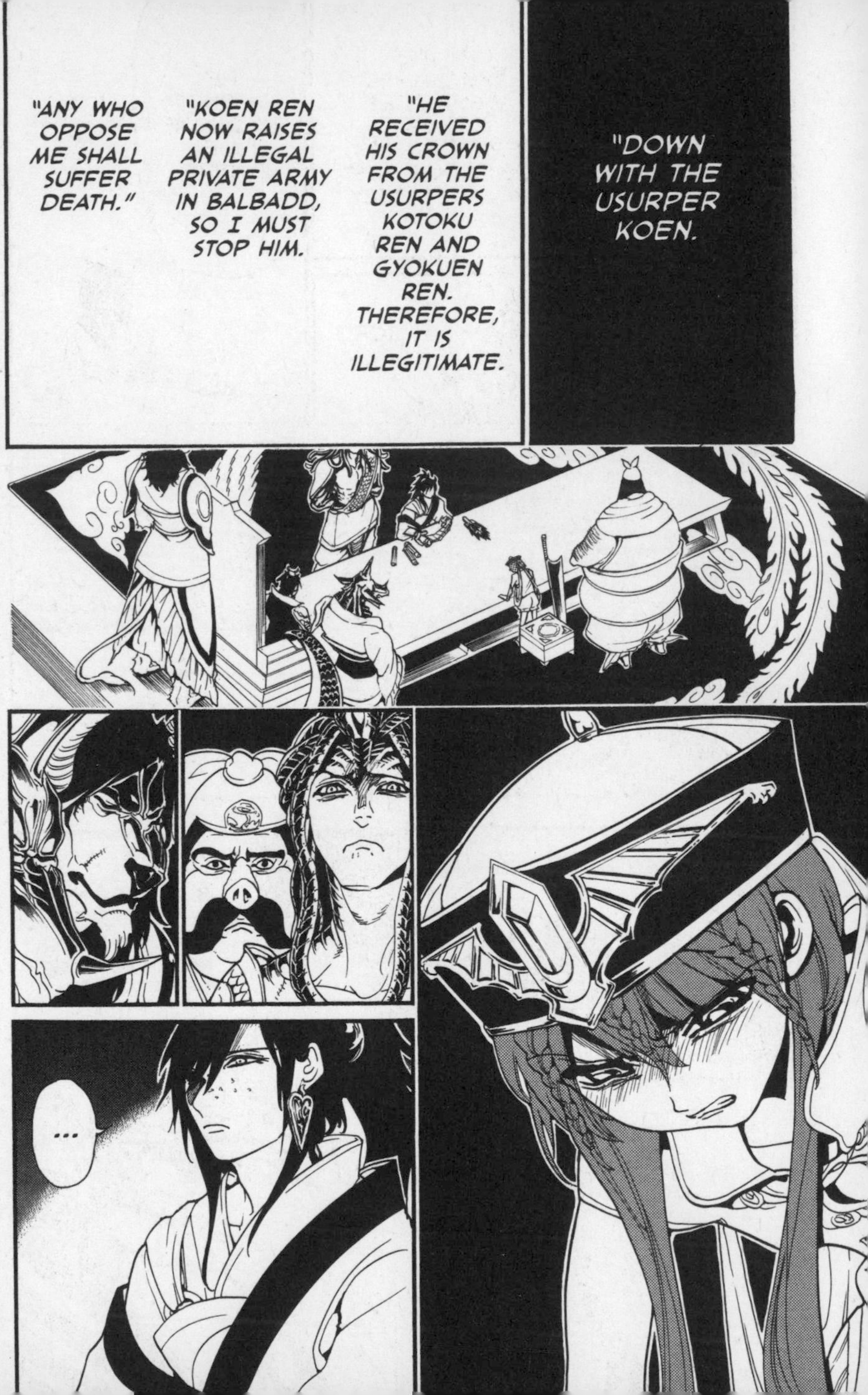
"DOWN WITH THE USURPER KOEN.
"HE RECEIVED HIS CROWN FROM THE USURPERS KOTOKU REN AND GYOKUEN REN. THEREFORE, IT IS ILLEGITIMATE.
"KOEN REN NOW RAISES AN ILLEGAL PRIVATE ARMY IN BALBADD, SO I MUST STOP HIM.
"ANY WHO OPPOSE ME SHALL SUFFER DEATH."
...

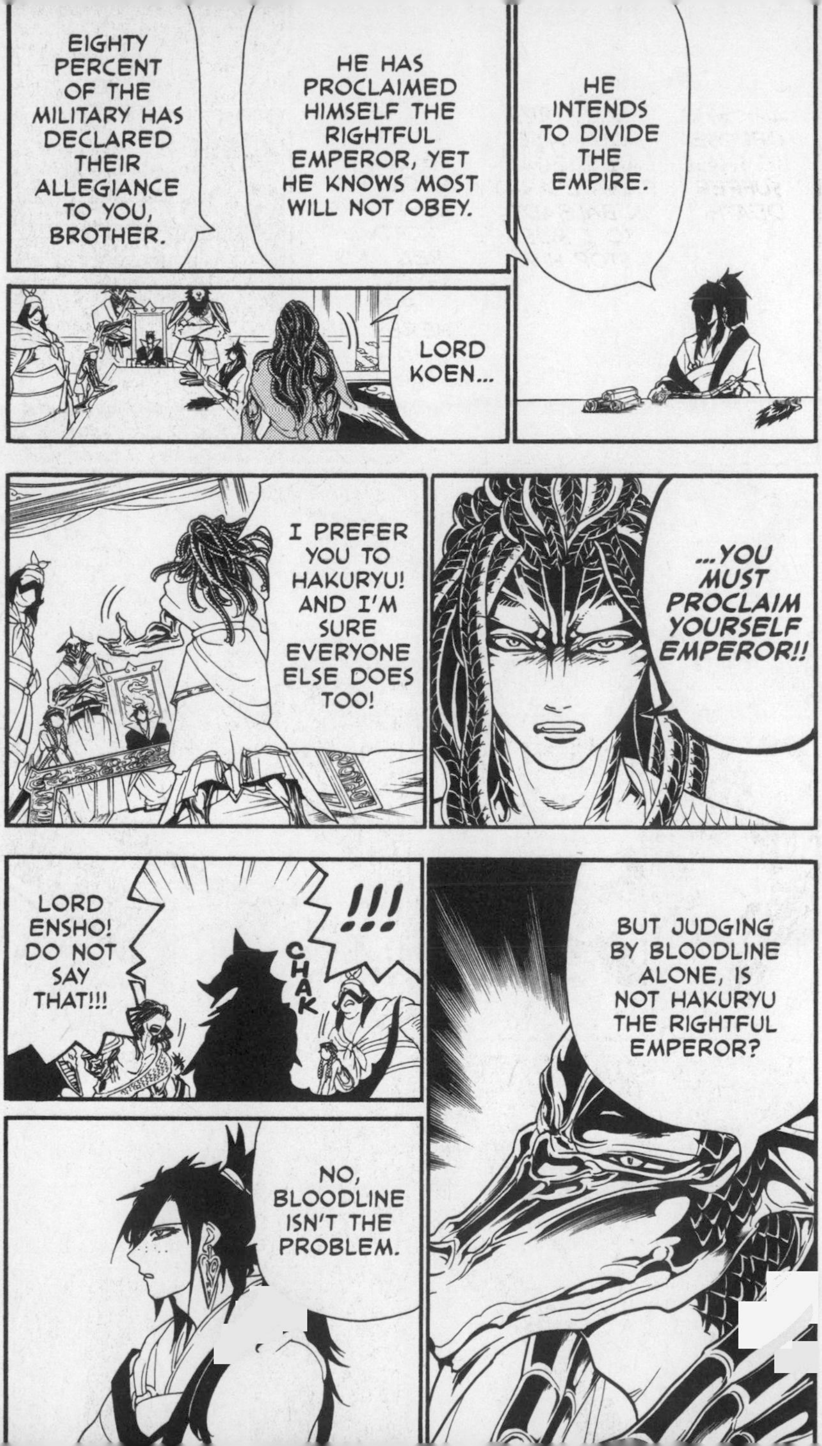
HE INTENDS TO DIVIDE THE EMPIRE.
HE HAS PROCLAIMED HIMSELF THE RIGHTFUL EMPEROR, YET HE KNOWS MOST WILL NOT OBEY.
EIGHTY PERCENT OF THE MILITARY HAS DECLARED THEIR ALLEGIANCE TO YOU, BROTHER.
LORD KOEN...
...YOU MUST PROCLAIM YOURSELF EMPEROR!!
I PREFER YOU TO HAKURYU! AND I'M SURE EVERYONE ELSE DOES TOO!
BUT JUDGING BY BLOODLINE ALONE, IS NOT HAKURYU THE RIGHTFUL EMPEROR?
!!!
CHAK
LORD ENSHO! DO NOT SAY THAT!!!
NO, BLOODLINE ISN'T THE PROBLEM.

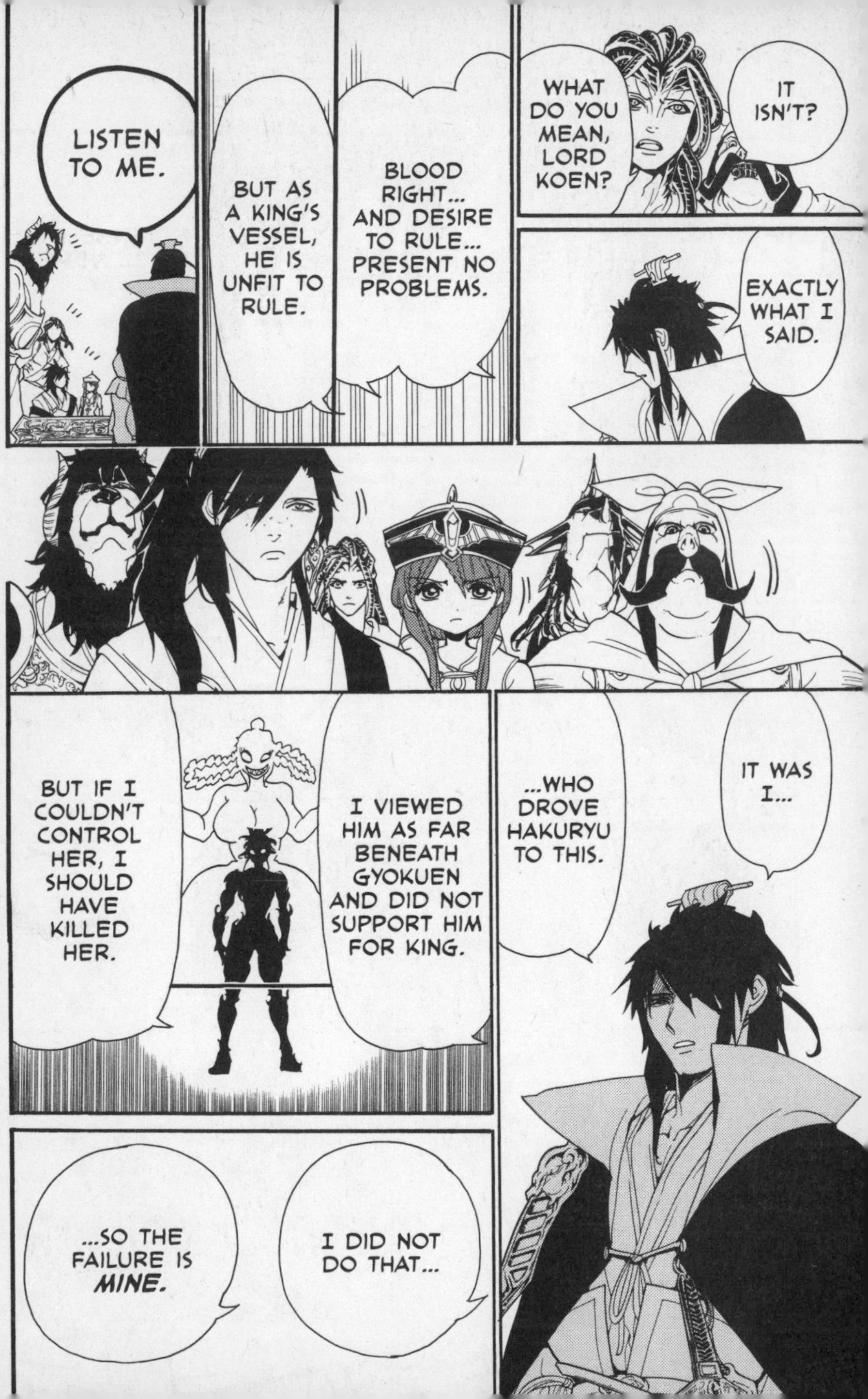
IT ISN'T?
WHAT DO YOU MEAN, LORD KOEN?
EXACTLY WHAT I SAID.
BLOOD RIGHT... AND DESIRE TO RULE... PRESENT NO PROBLEMS.
BUT AS A KING'S VESSEL, HE IS UNFIT TO RULE.
LISTEN TO ME.
IT WAS I...
...WHO DROVE HAKURYU TO THIS.
I VIEWED HIM AS FAR BENEATH GYOKUEN AND DID NOT SUPPORT HIM FOR KING.
BUT IF I COULDN'T CONTROL HER, I SHOULD HAVE KILLED HER.
I DID NOT DO THAT...
...SO THE FAILURE IS *MINE.*

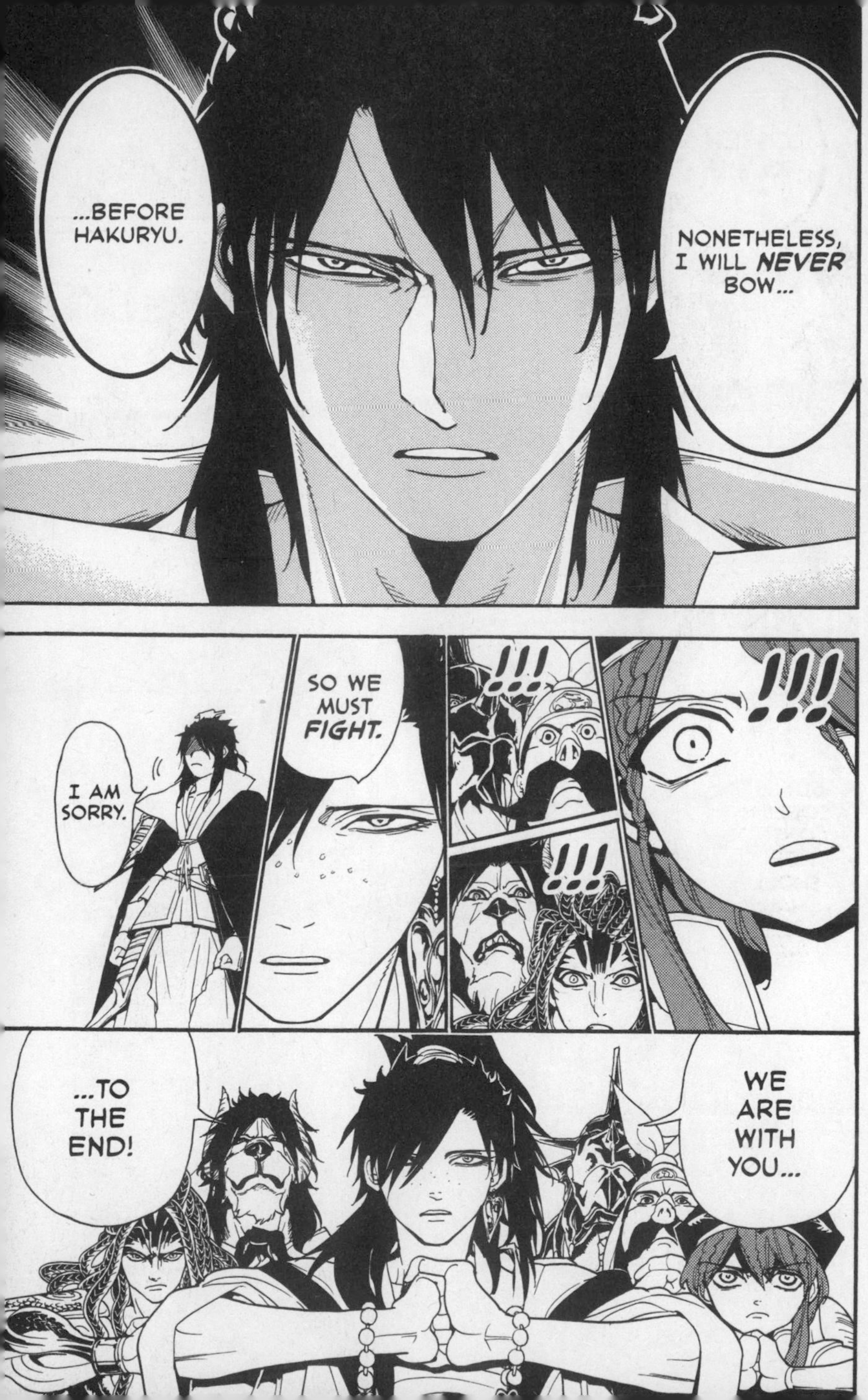
NONETHELESS, I WILL *NEVER* BOW...
...BEFORE HAKURYU.
!!!
!!!
!!!
SO WE MUST *FIGHT.*
I AM SORRY.
WE ARE WITH YOU...
...TO THE END!

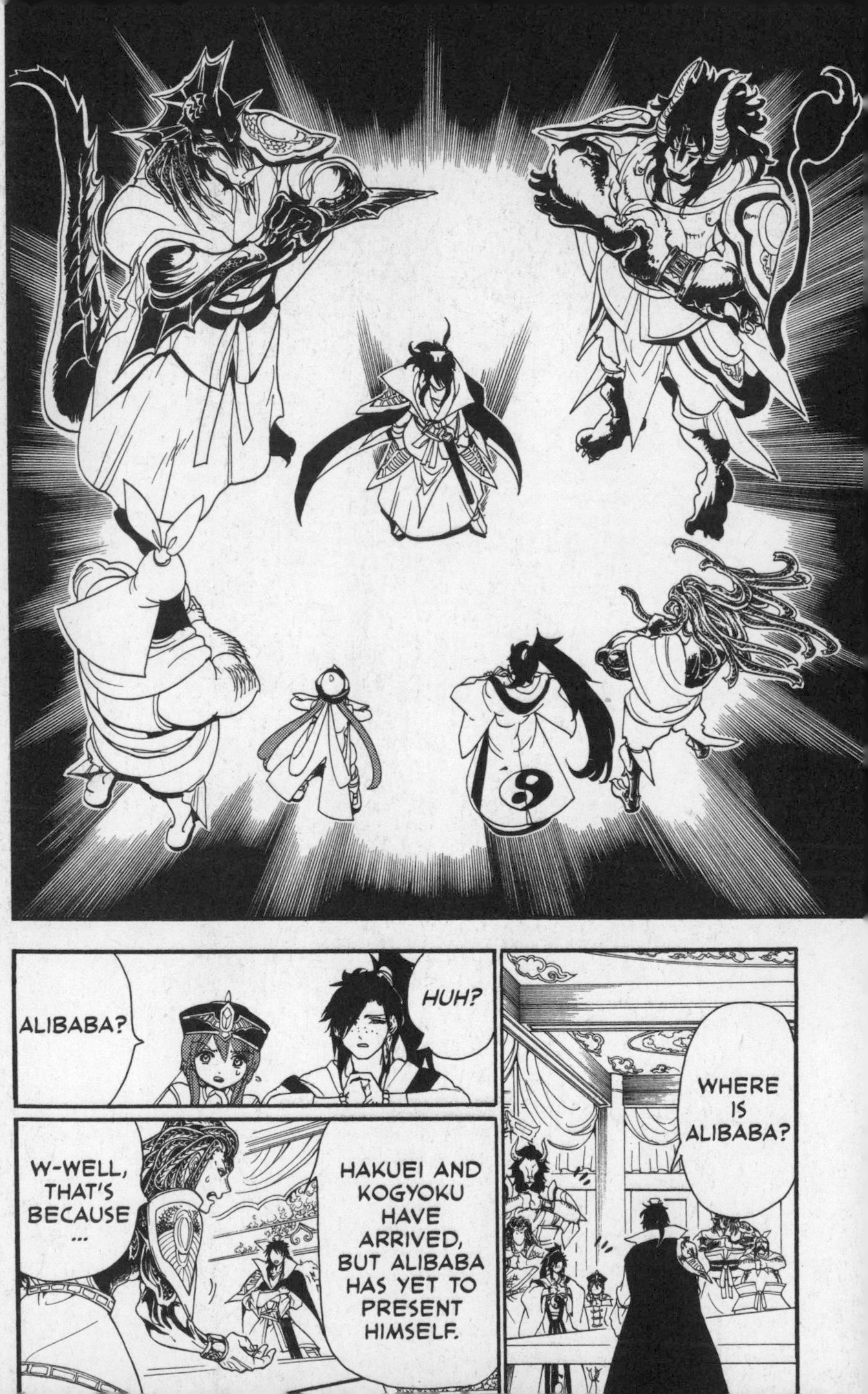
WHERE IS ALIBABA?
HUH?
ALIBABA?
HAKUEI AND KOGYOKU HAVE ARRIVED, BUT ALIBABA HAS YET TO PRESENT HIMSELF.
W-WELL, THAT'S BECAUSE ...

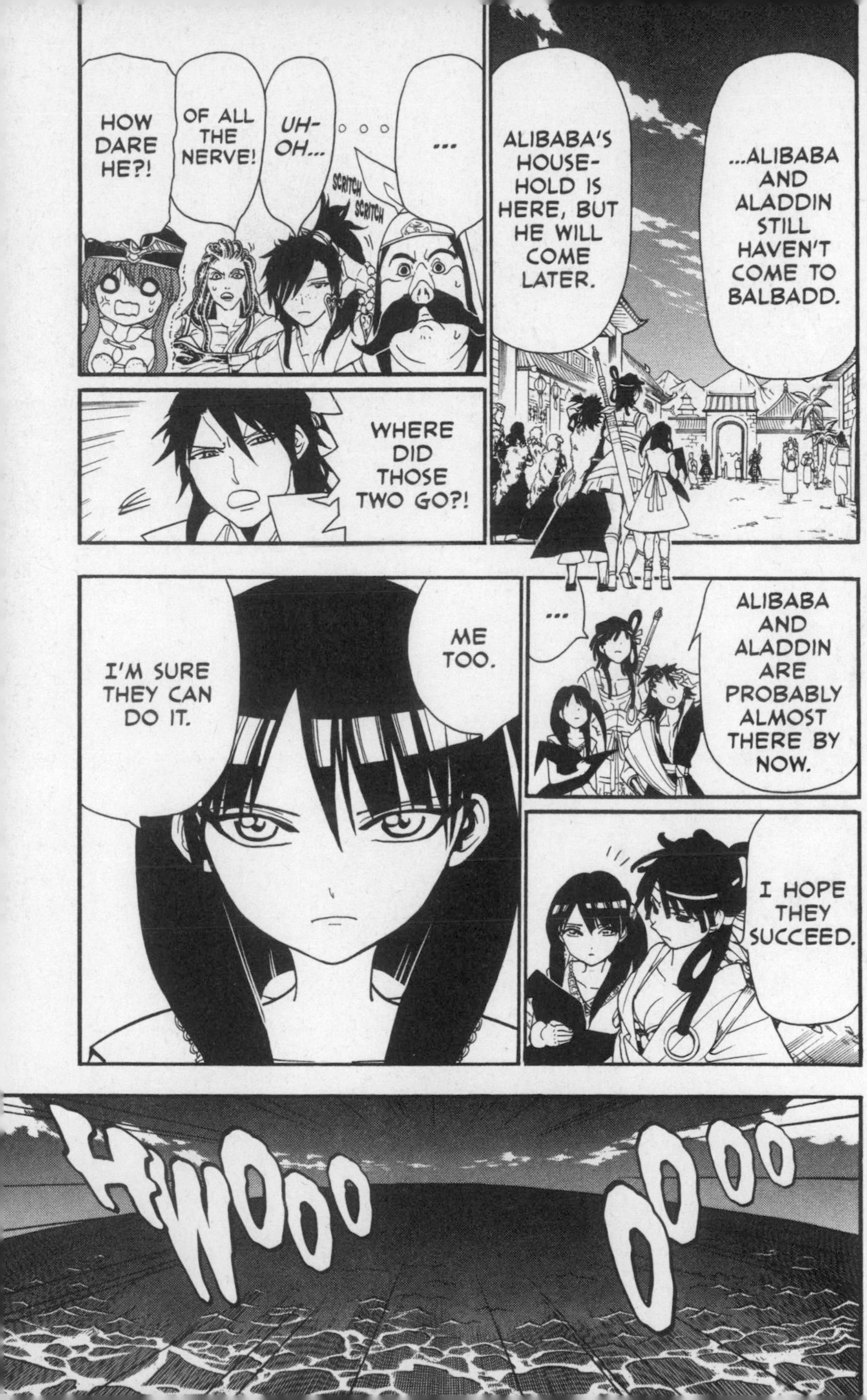
...ALIBABA AND ALADDIN STILL HAVEN'T COME TO BALBADD.
ALIBABA'S HOUSE-HOLD IS HERE, BUT HE WILL COME LATER.
...
UH-OH...
SCRITCH SCRITCH
OF ALL THE NERVE!
HOW DARE HE?!
WHERE DID THOSE TWO GO?!
ALIBABA AND ALADDIN ARE PROBABLY ALMOST THERE BY NOW.
...
I HOPE THEY SUCCEED.
ME TOO.
I'M SURE THEY CAN DO IT.
HWOOOOOOO

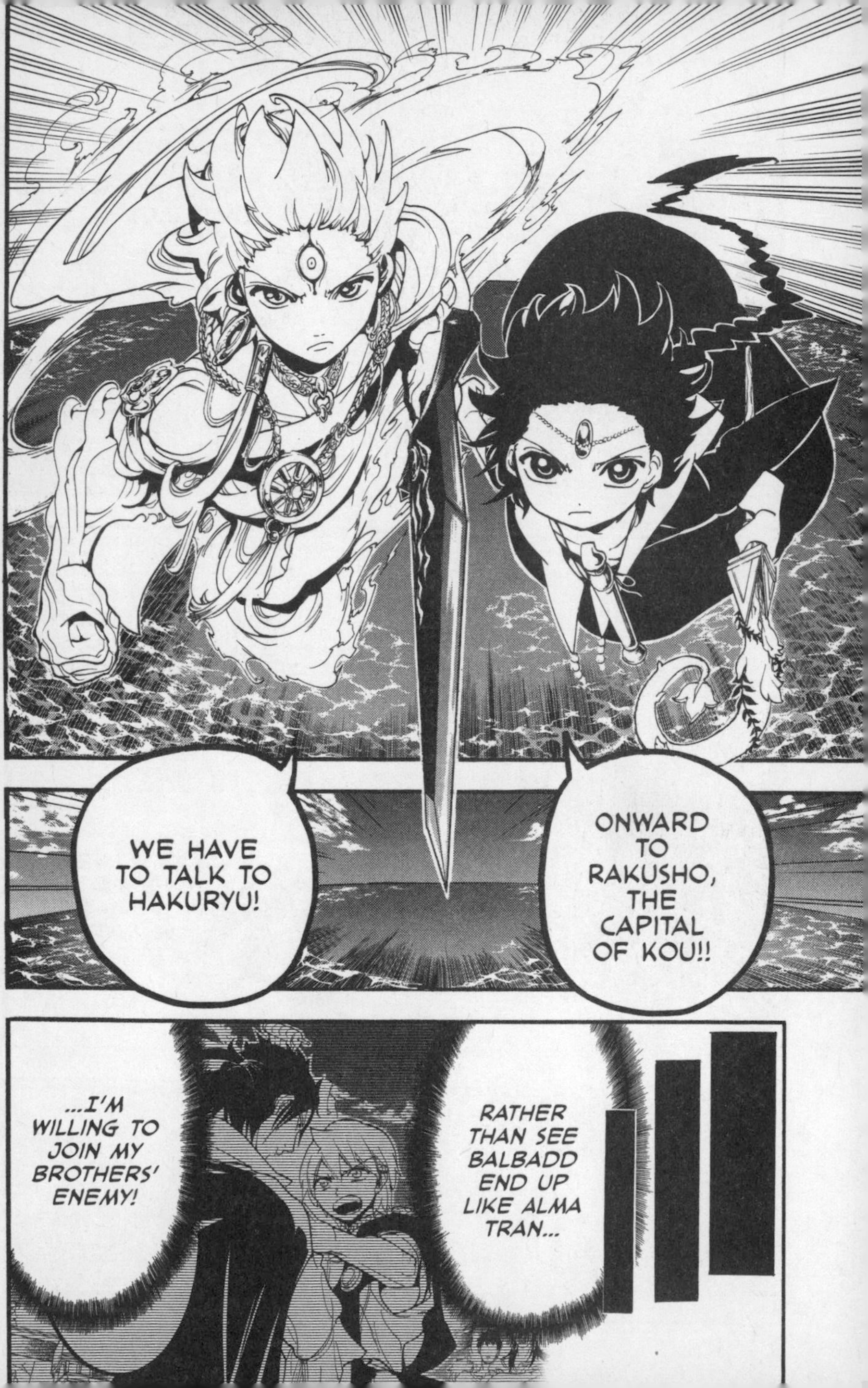
ONWARD TO RAKUSHO, THE CAPITAL OF KOU!!
WE HAVE TO TALK TO HAKURYU!
RATHER THAN SEE BALBADD END UP LIKE ALMA TRAN...
...I'M WILLING TO JOIN MY BROTHERS' ENEMY!

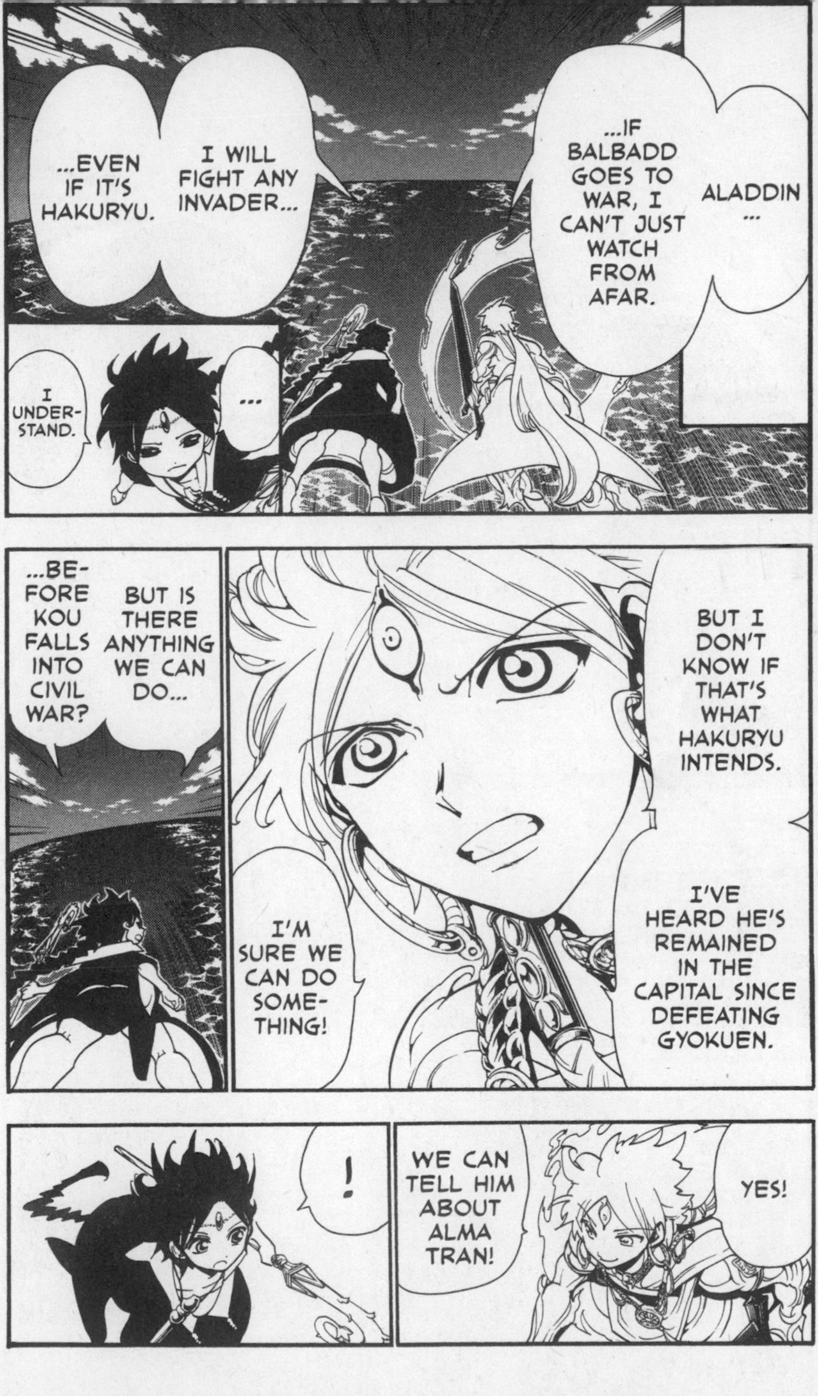
ALADDIN...
...IF BALBADD GOES TO WAR, I CAN'T JUST WATCH FROM AFAR.
I WILL FIGHT ANY INVADER...
...EVEN IF IT'S HAKURYU.
...
I UNDERSTAND.
BUT I DON'T KNOW IF THAT'S WHAT HAKURYU INTENDS.
I'VE HEARD HE'S REMAINED IN THE CAPITAL SINCE DEFEATING GYOKUEN.
I'M SURE WE CAN DO SOMETHING!
BUT IS THERE ANYTHING WE CAN DO...
...BEFORE KOU FALLS INTO CIVIL WAR?
YES!
WE CAN TELL HIM ABOUT ALMA TRAN!
!

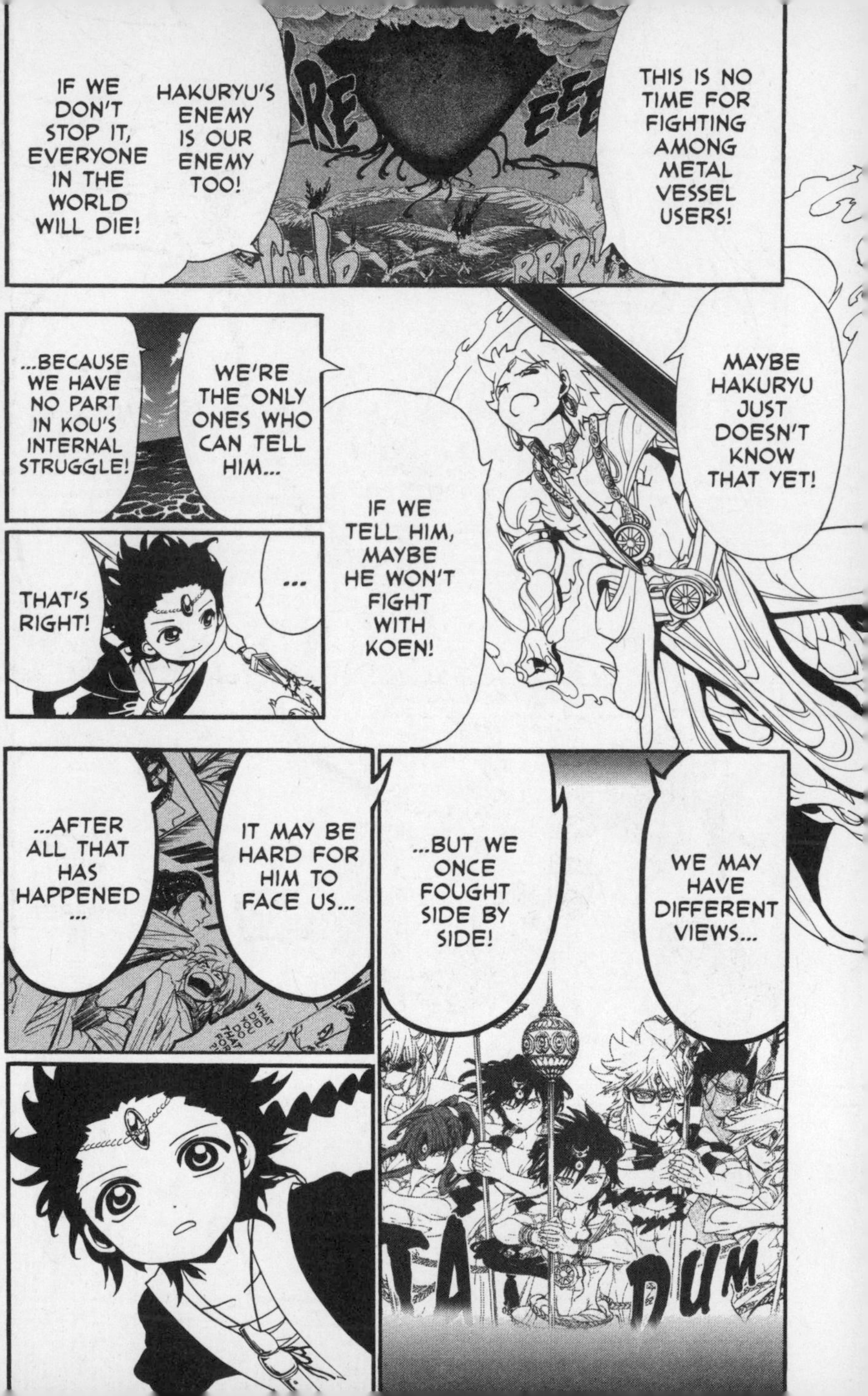
THIS IS NO TIME FOR FIGHTING AMONG METAL VESSEL USERS!
HAKURYU'S ENEMY IS OUR ENEMY TOO!
IF WE DON'T STOP IT, EVERYONE IN THE WORLD WILL DIE!
MAYBE HAKURYU JUST DOESN'T KNOW THAT YET!
IF WE TELL HIM, MAYBE HE WON'T FIGHT WITH KOEN!
WE'RE THE ONLY ONES WHO CAN TELL HIM...
...BECAUSE WE HAVE NO PART IN KOU'S INTERNAL STRUGGLE!
...
THAT'S RIGHT!
WE MAY HAVE DIFFERENT VIEWS...
...BUT WE ONCE FOUGHT SIDE BY SIDE!
TA DUM
IT MAY BE HARD FOR HIM TO FACE US...
...AFTER ALL THAT HAS HAPPENED ...

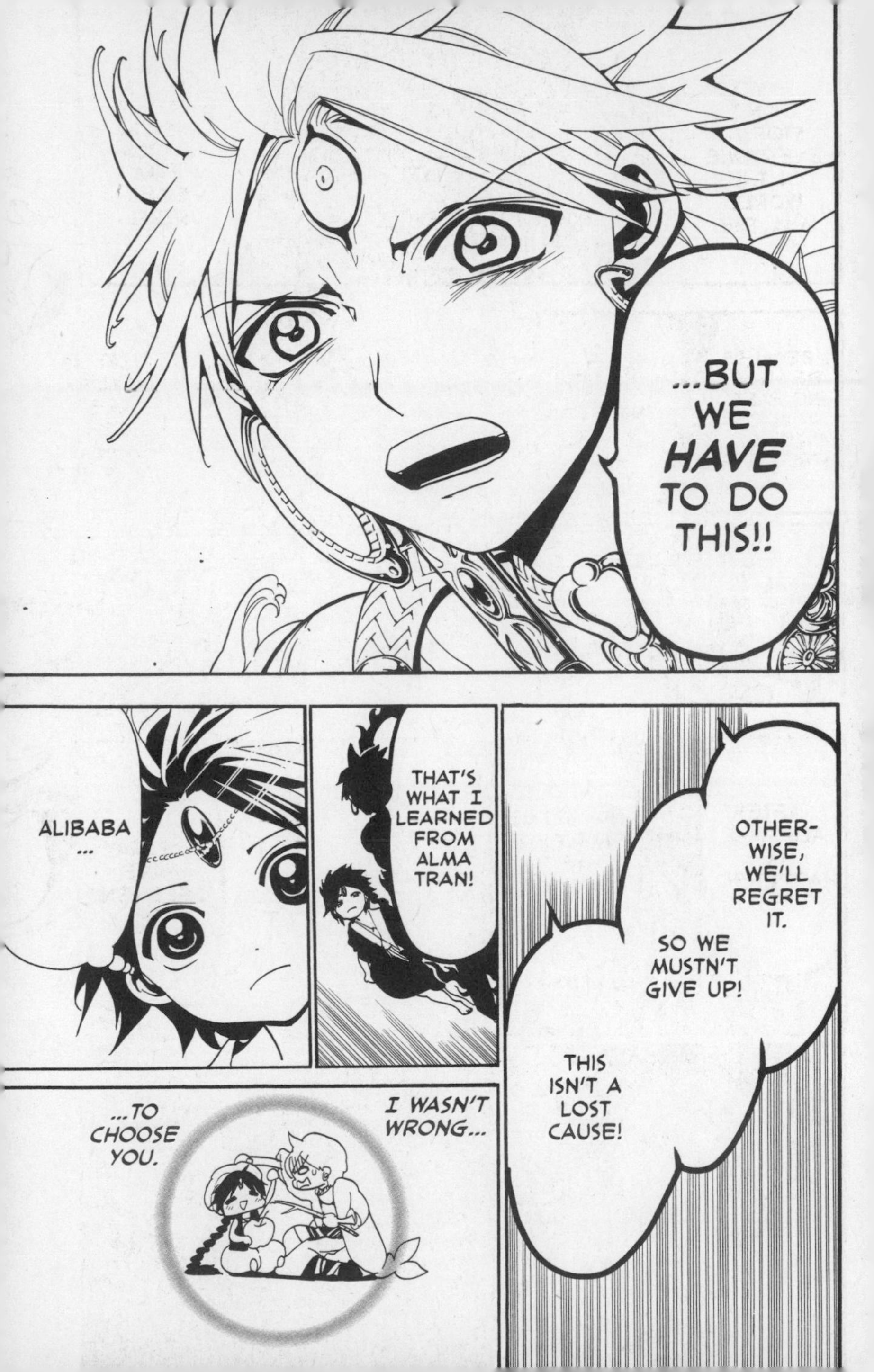
...BUT WE *HAVE* TO DO THIS!!
OTHER-WISE, WE'LL REGRET IT.
SO WE MUSTN'T GIVE UP!
THIS ISN'T A LOST CAUSE!
THAT'S WHAT I LEARNED FROM ALMA TRAN!
ALIBABA ...
I WASN'T WRONG...
...TO CHOOSE YOU.

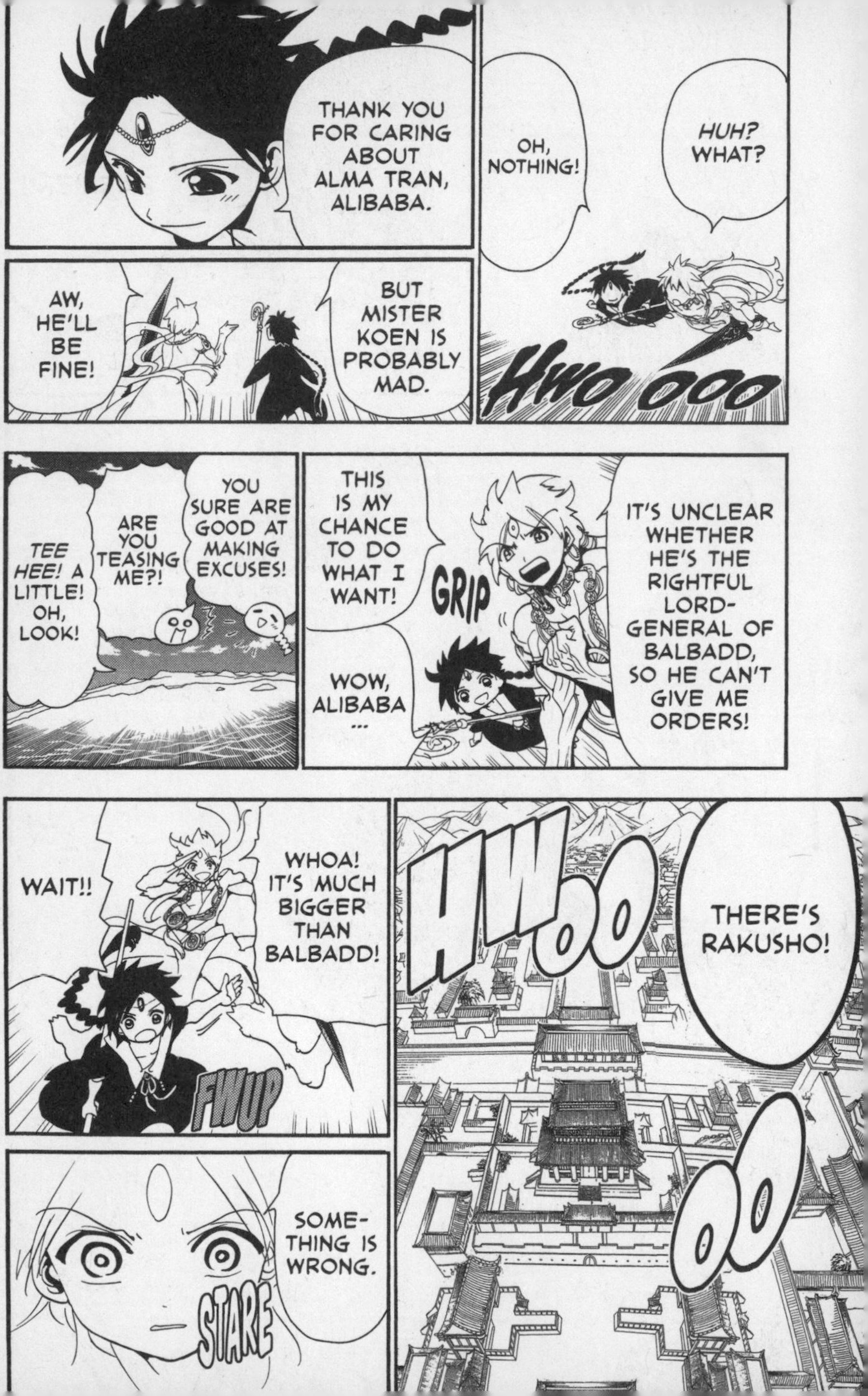
HUH? WHAT?
OH, NOTHING!
HWO OOO
THANK YOU FOR CARING ABOUT ALMA TRAN, ALIBABA.
BUT MISTER KOEN IS PROBABLY MAD.
AW, HE'LL BE FINE!
IT'S UNCLEAR WHETHER HE'S THE RIGHTFUL LORD-GENERAL OF BALBADD, SO HE CAN'T GIVE ME ORDERS!
GRIP
THIS IS MY CHANCE TO DO WHAT I WANT!
WOW, ALIBABA...
YOU SURE ARE GOOD AT MAKING EXCUSES!
ARE YOU TEASING ME?!
TEE HEE! A LITTLE! OH, LOOK!
THERE'S RAKUSHO!
HWOOOOO
WHOA! IT'S MUCH BIGGER THAN BALBADD!
WAIT!!
FWUP
SOMETHING IS WRONG.
STARE

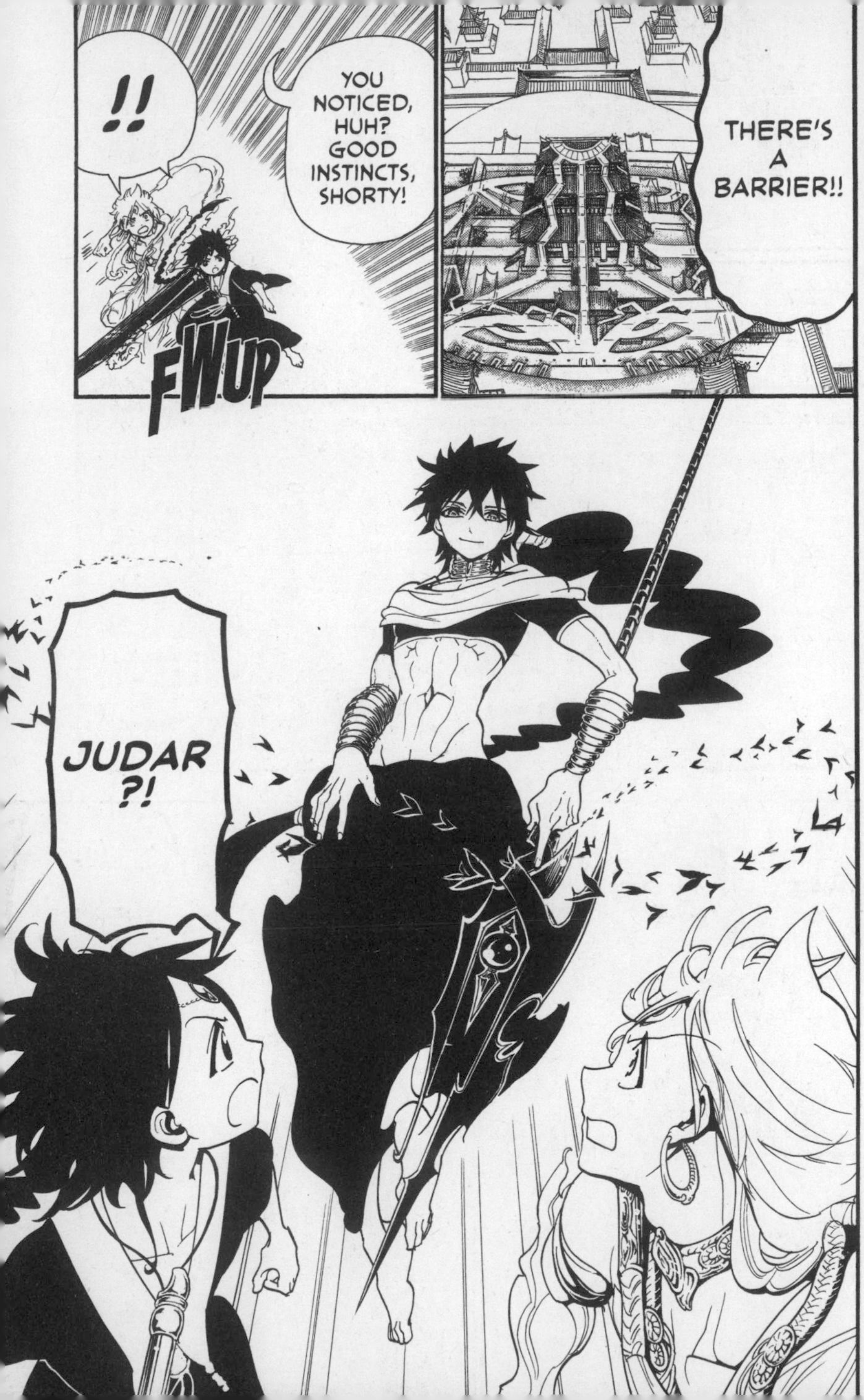
THERE'S A BARRIER!!
YOU NOTICED, HUH? GOOD INSTINCTS, SHORTY!
!!
FWUP
JUDAR ?!

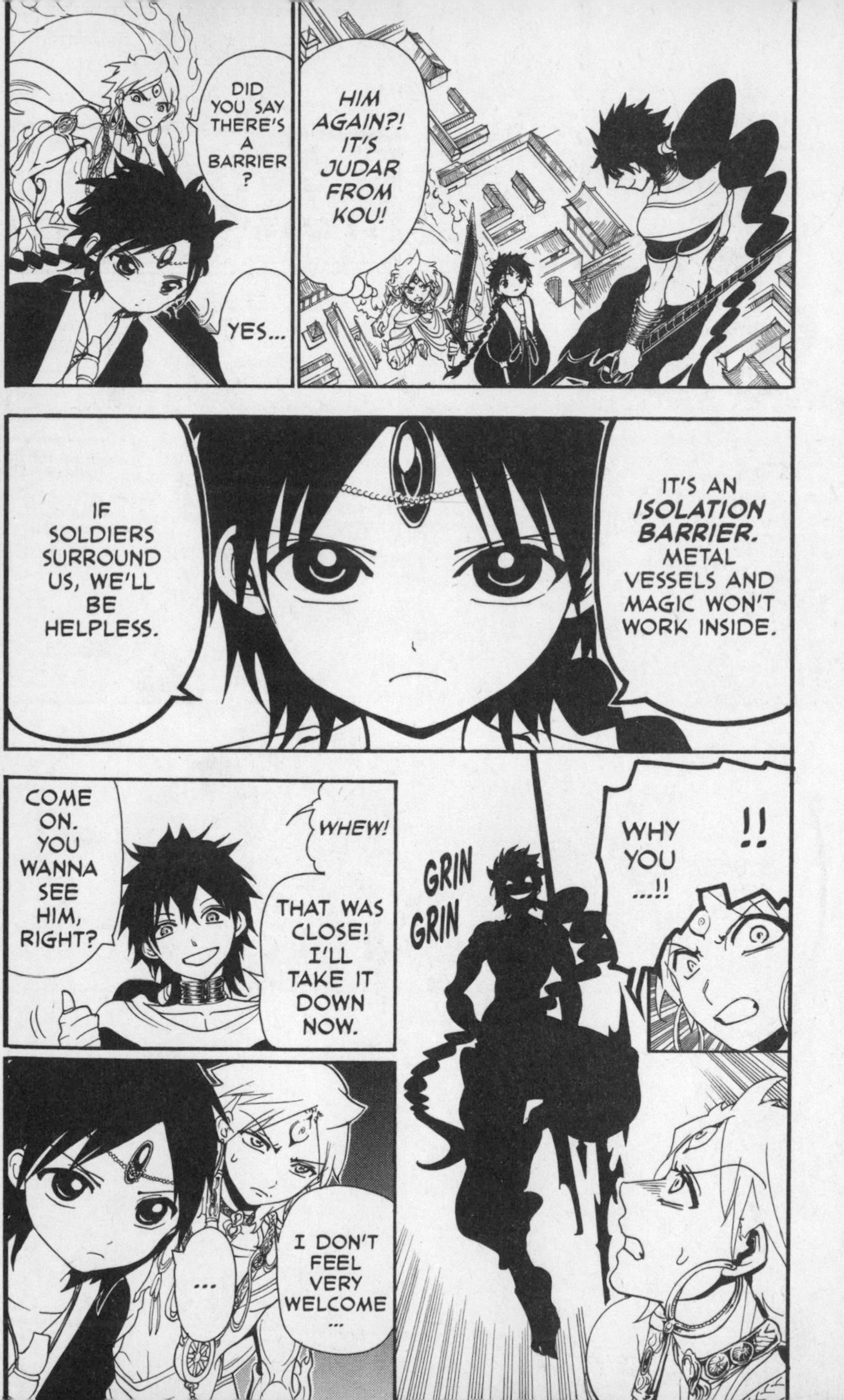
HIM AGAIN?! IT'S JUDAR FROM KOU!
DID YOU SAY THERE'S A BARRIER?
YES...
IT'S AN ISOLATION BARRIER. METAL VESSELS AND MAGIC WON'T WORK INSIDE.
IF SOLDIERS SURROUND US, WE'LL BE HELPLESS.
!!
WHY YOU ...!!
GRIN GRIN
WHEW! THAT WAS CLOSE! I'LL TAKE IT DOWN NOW.
COME ON. YOU WANNA SEE HIM, RIGHT?
I DON'T FEEL VERY WELCOME ...
...

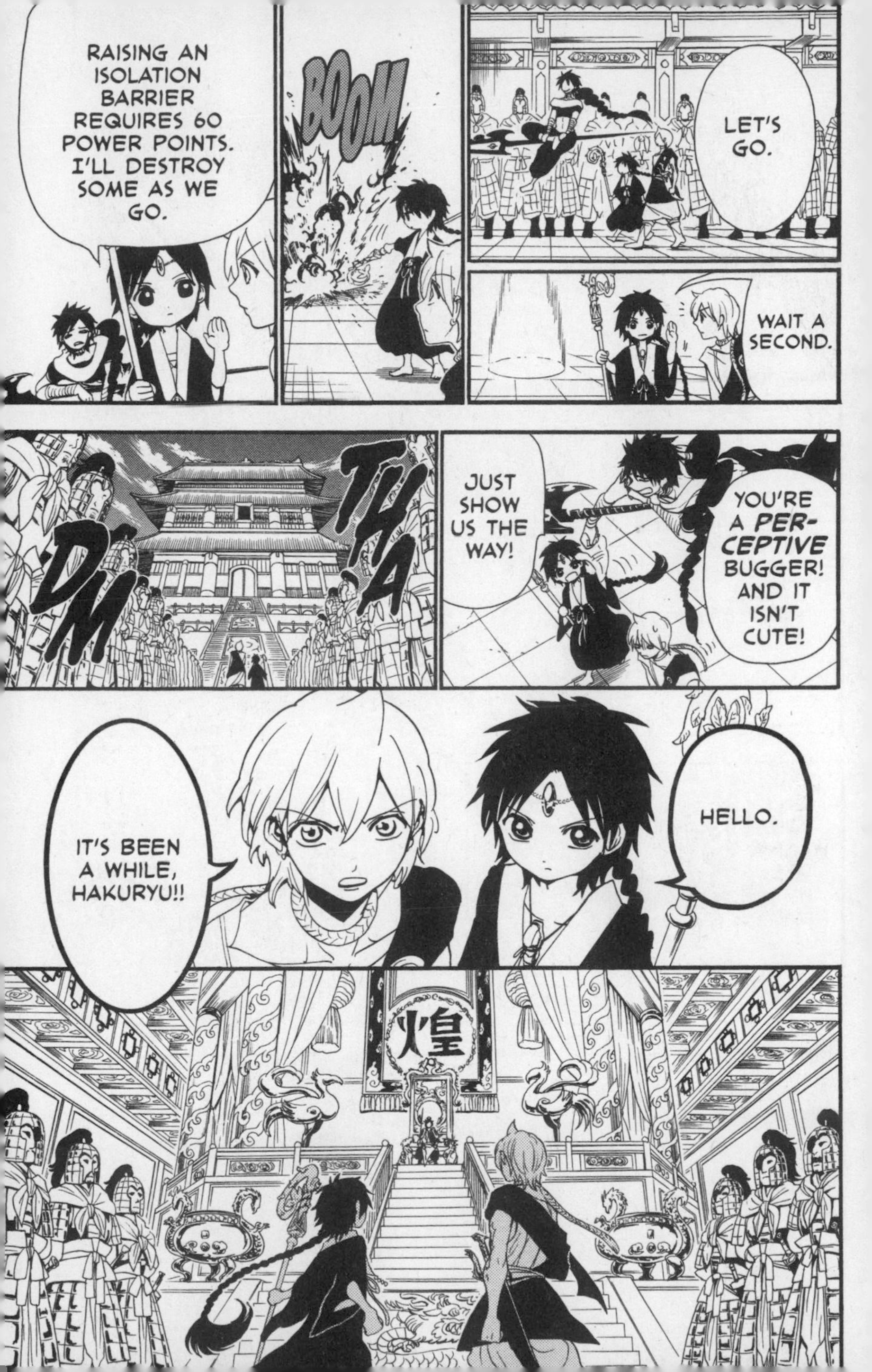
LET'S GO.
WAIT A SECOND.
BOOM
RAISING AN ISOLATION BARRIER REQUIRES 60 POWER POINTS. I'LL DESTROY SOME AS WE GO.
YOU'RE A *PERCEPTIVE* BUGGER! AND IT ISN'T CUTE!
JUST SHOW US THE WAY!
THA
DM
HELLO.
IT'S BEEN A WHILE, HAKURYU!!
煌

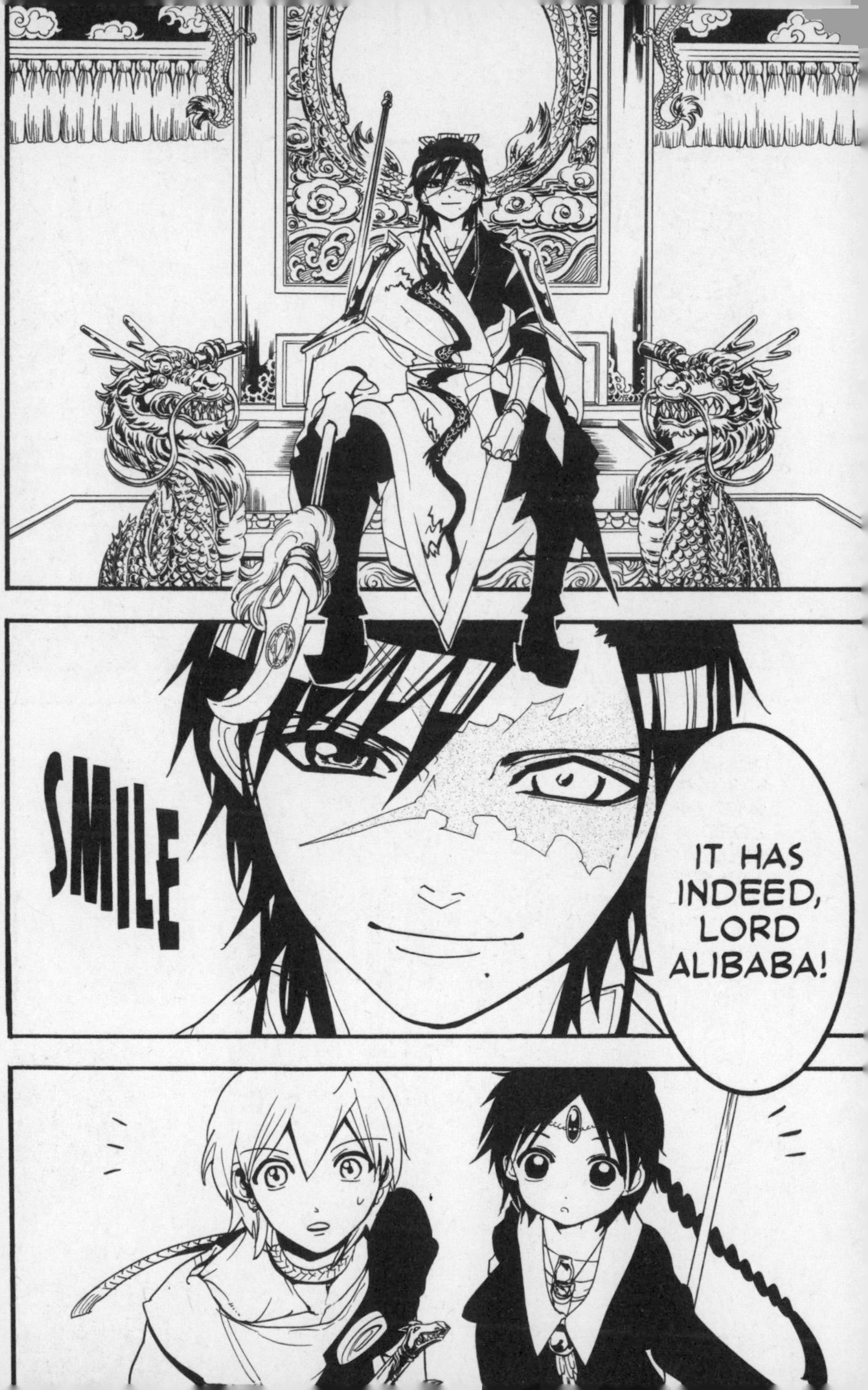
SMILE
IT HAS INDEED, LORD ALIBABA!

Night 252: Reunion of King's Vessels

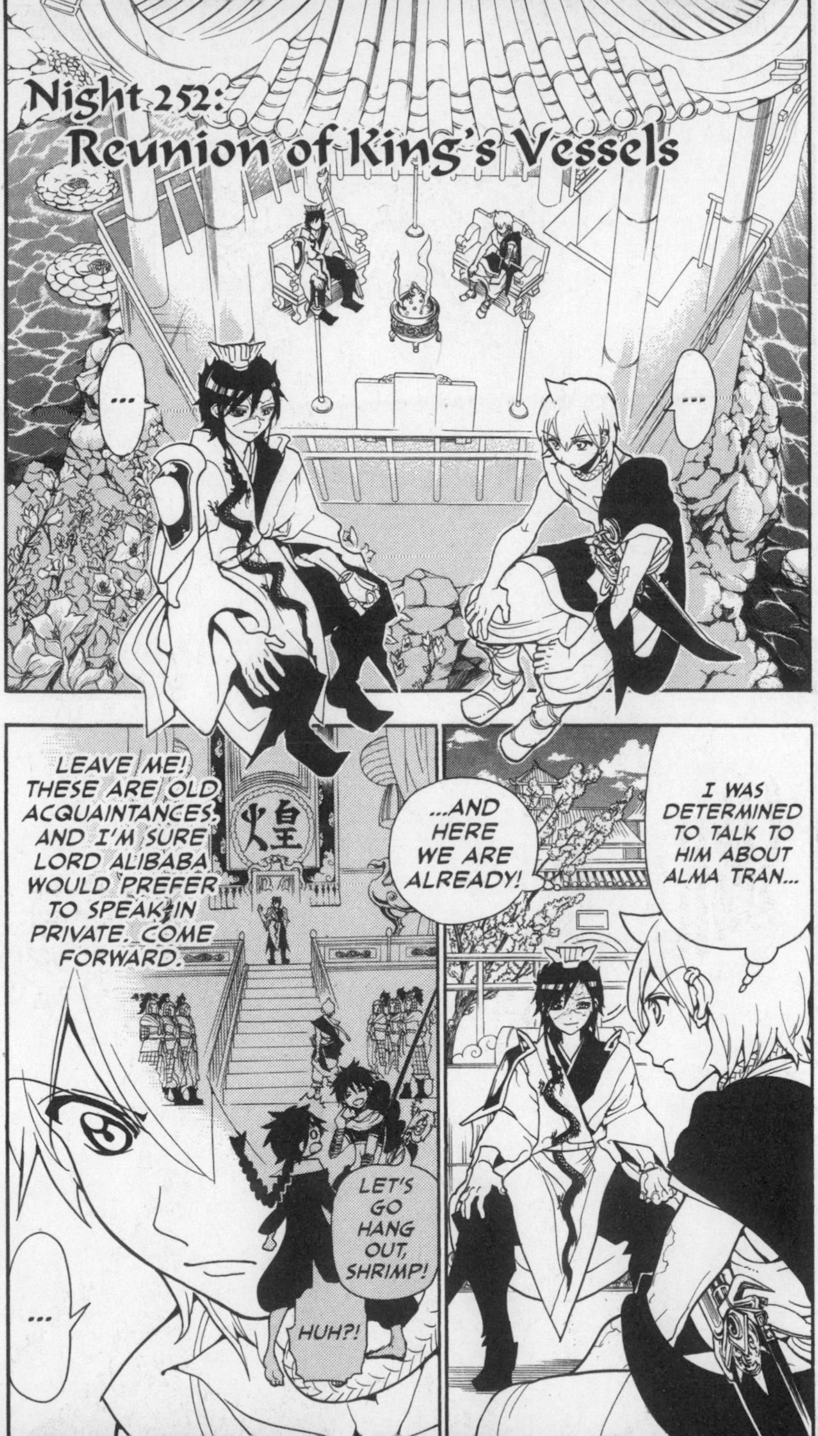
...
...
I WAS DETERMINED TO TALK TO HIM ABOUT ALMA TRAN...
...AND HERE WE ARE ALREADY!
LEAVE ME! THESE ARE OLD ACQUAINTANCES, AND I'M SURE LORD ALIBABA WOULD PREFER TO SPEAK IN PRIVATE. COME FORWARD.
LET'S GO HANG OUT, SHRIMP!
HUH?!
...

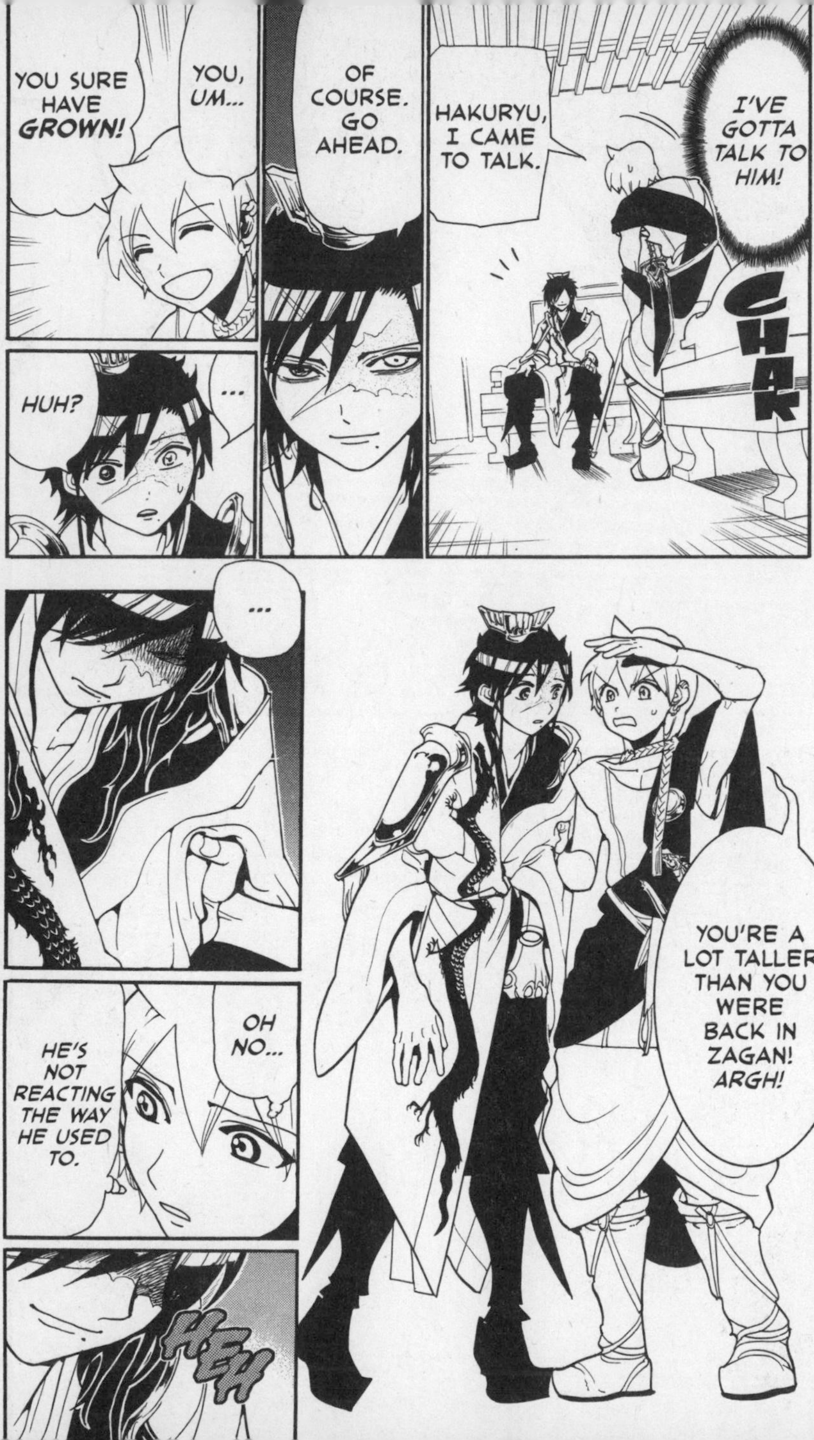
I'VE GOTTA TALK TO HIM!
CHAK
HAKURYU, I CAME TO TALK.
OF COURSE. GO AHEAD.
YOU, UM...
YOU SURE HAVE GROWN!
...
HUH?
YOU'RE A LOT TALLER THAN YOU WERE BACK IN ZAGAN! ARGH!
...
OH NO...
HE'S NOT REACTING THE WAY HE USED TO.
HEH

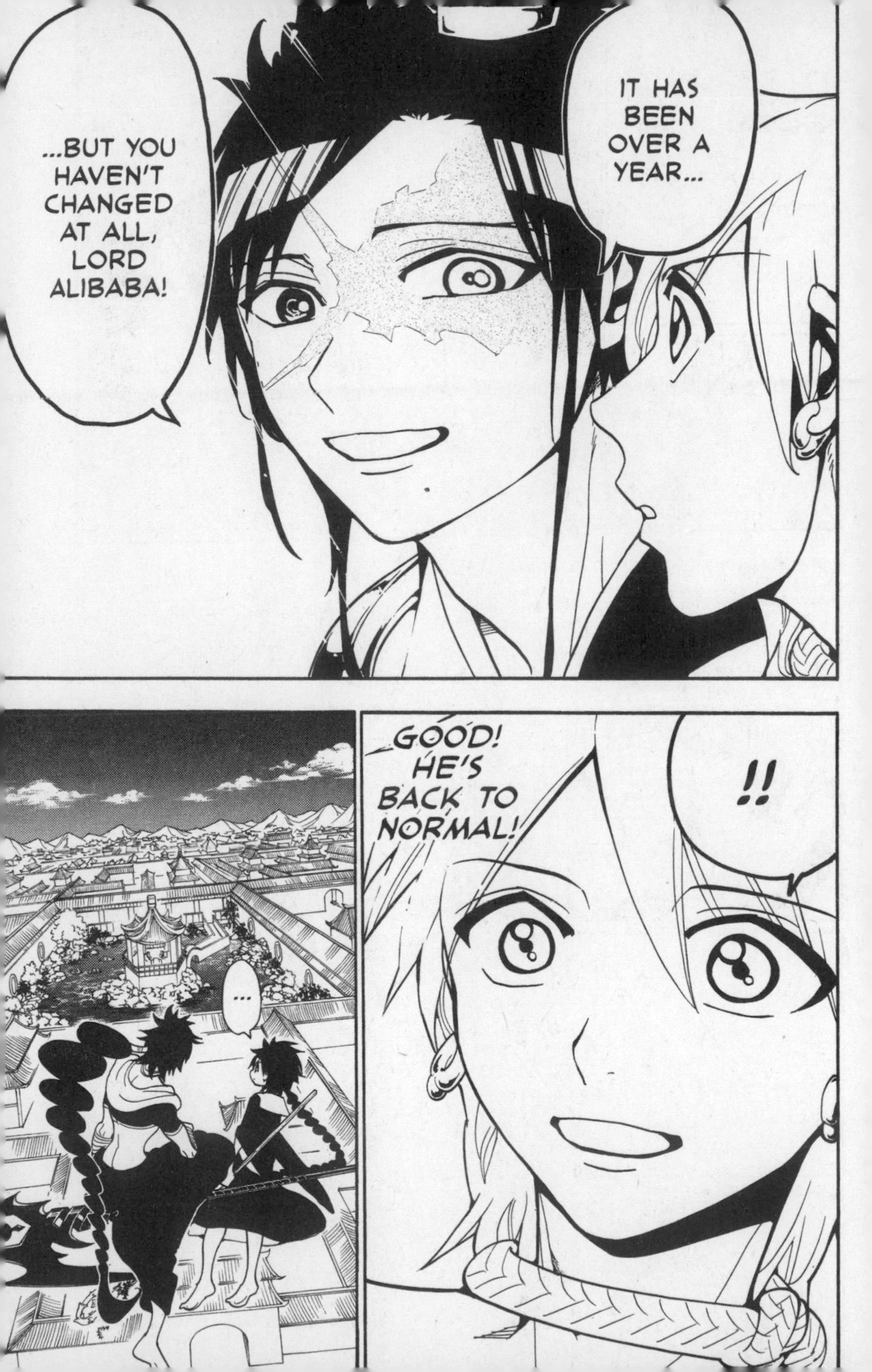
IT HAS BEEN OVER A YEAR...
...BUT YOU HAVEN'T CHANGED AT ALL, LORD ALIBABA!
!!
GOOD! HE'S BACK TO NORMAL!
...

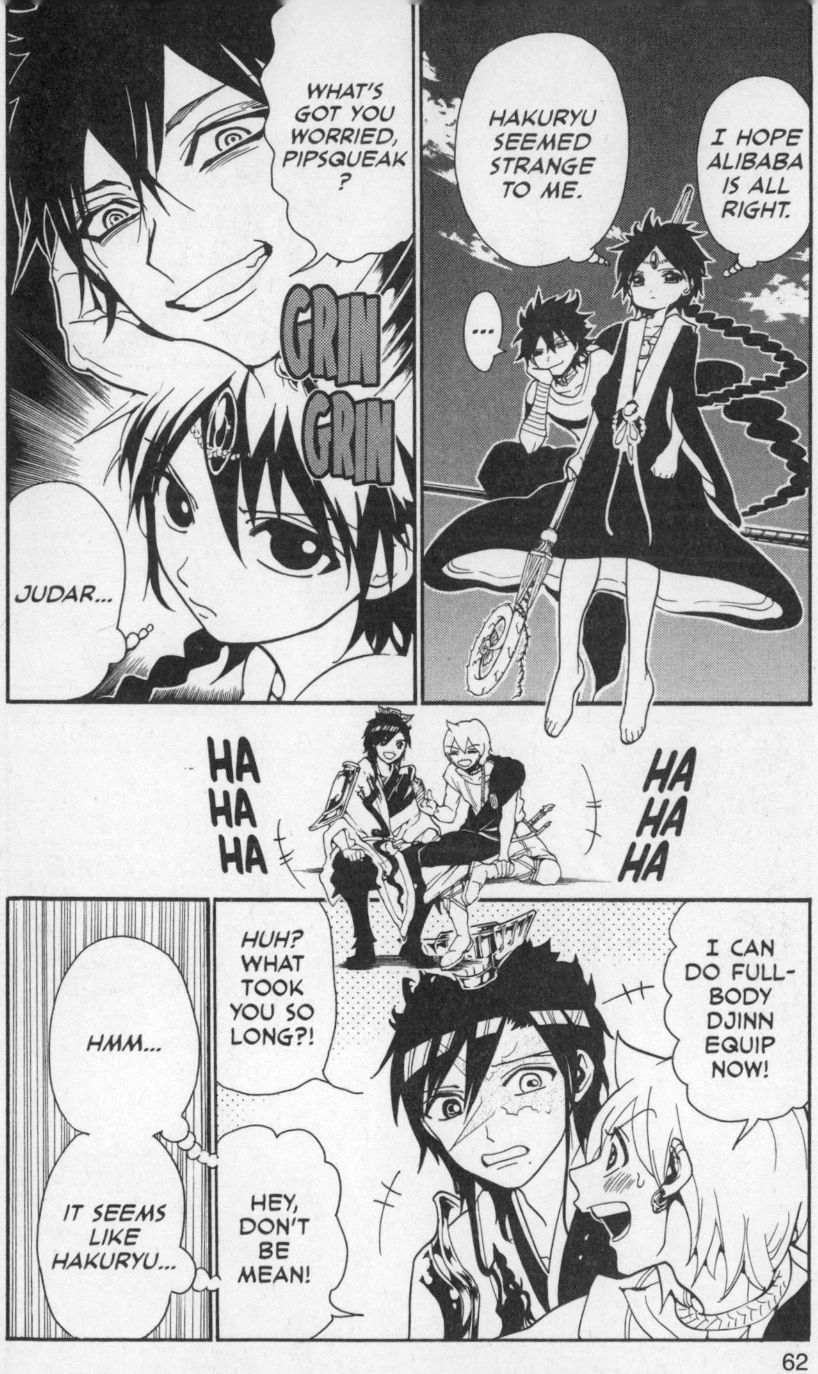
I HOPE ALIBABA IS ALL RIGHT.
HAKURYU SEEMED STRANGE TO ME.
...
WHAT'S GOT YOU WORRIED, PIPSQUEAK?
GRIN GRIN
JUDAR...
HA HA HA
HA HA HA
I CAN DO FULL-BODY DJINN EQUIP NOW!
HUH? WHAT TOOK YOU SO LONG?!
HEY, DON'T BE MEAN!
HMM...
IT SEEMS LIKE HAKURYU...

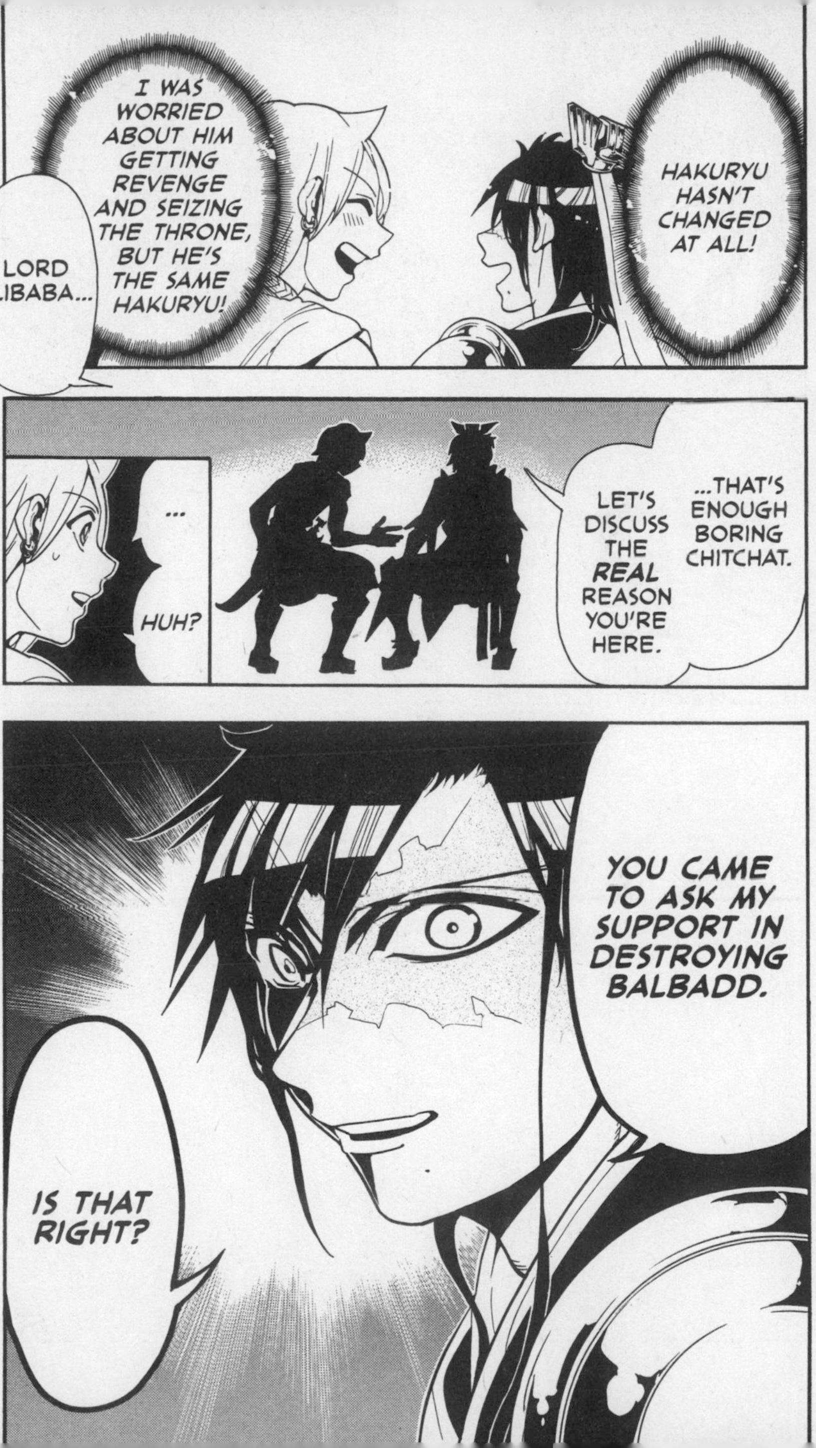
HAKURYU HASN'T CHANGED AT ALL!
I WAS WORRIED ABOUT HIM GETTING REVENGE AND SEIZING THE THRONE, BUT HE'S THE SAME HAKURYU!
LORD ALIBABA...
...THAT'S ENOUGH BORING CHITCHAT.
LET'S DISCUSS THE *REAL* REASON YOU'RE HERE.
...
HUH?
YOU CAME TO ASK MY SUPPORT IN DESTROYING BALBADD.
IS THAT RIGHT?

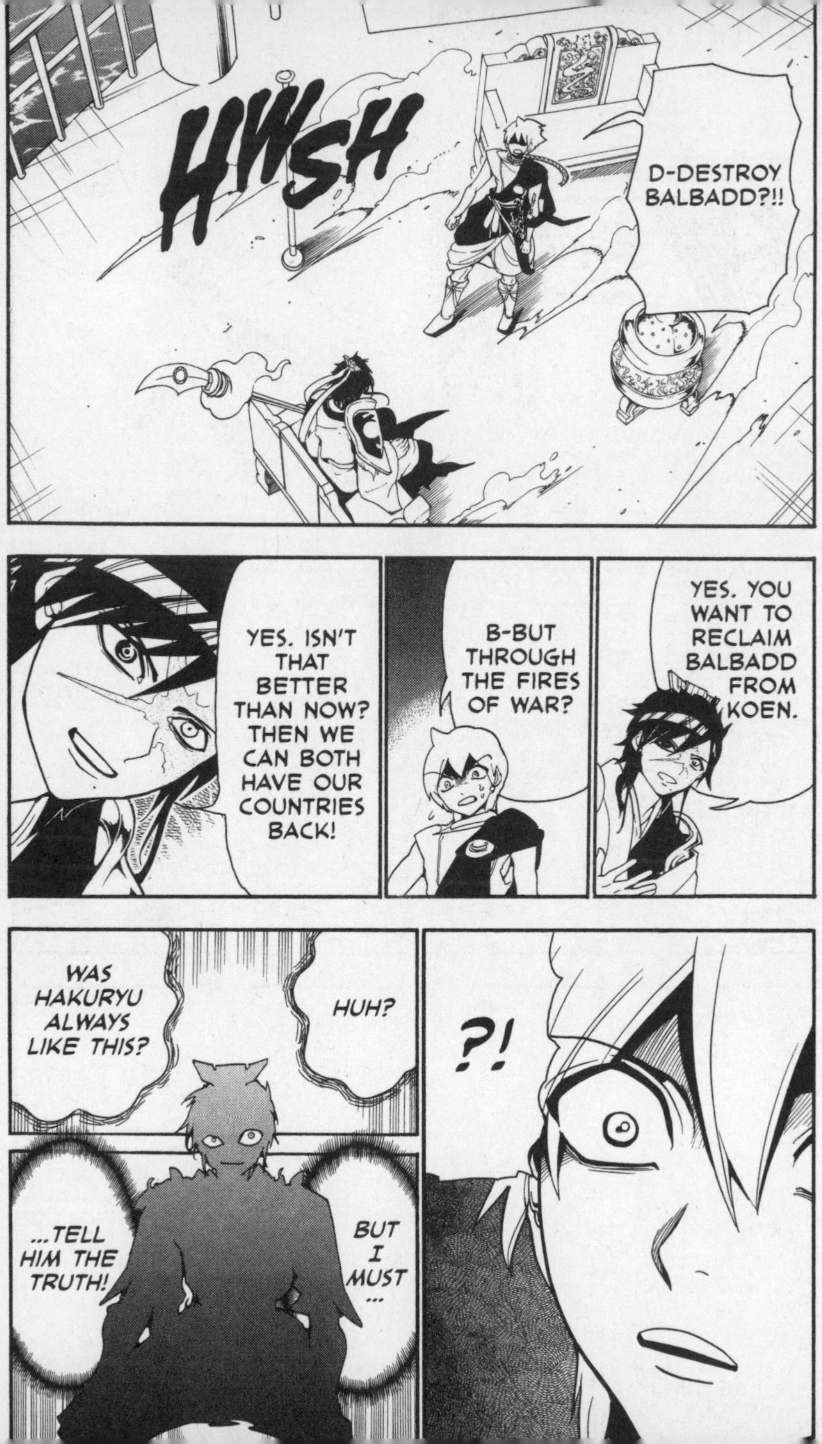
HWSH
D-DESTROY BALBADD?!!
YES. YOU WANT TO RECLAIM BALBADD FROM KOEN.
B-BUT THROUGH THE FIRES OF WAR?
YES. ISN'T THAT BETTER THAN NOW? THEN WE CAN BOTH HAVE OUR COUNTRIES BACK!
?!
HUH?
WAS HAKURYU ALWAYS LIKE THIS?
BUT I MUST ...
...TELL HIM THE TRUTH!

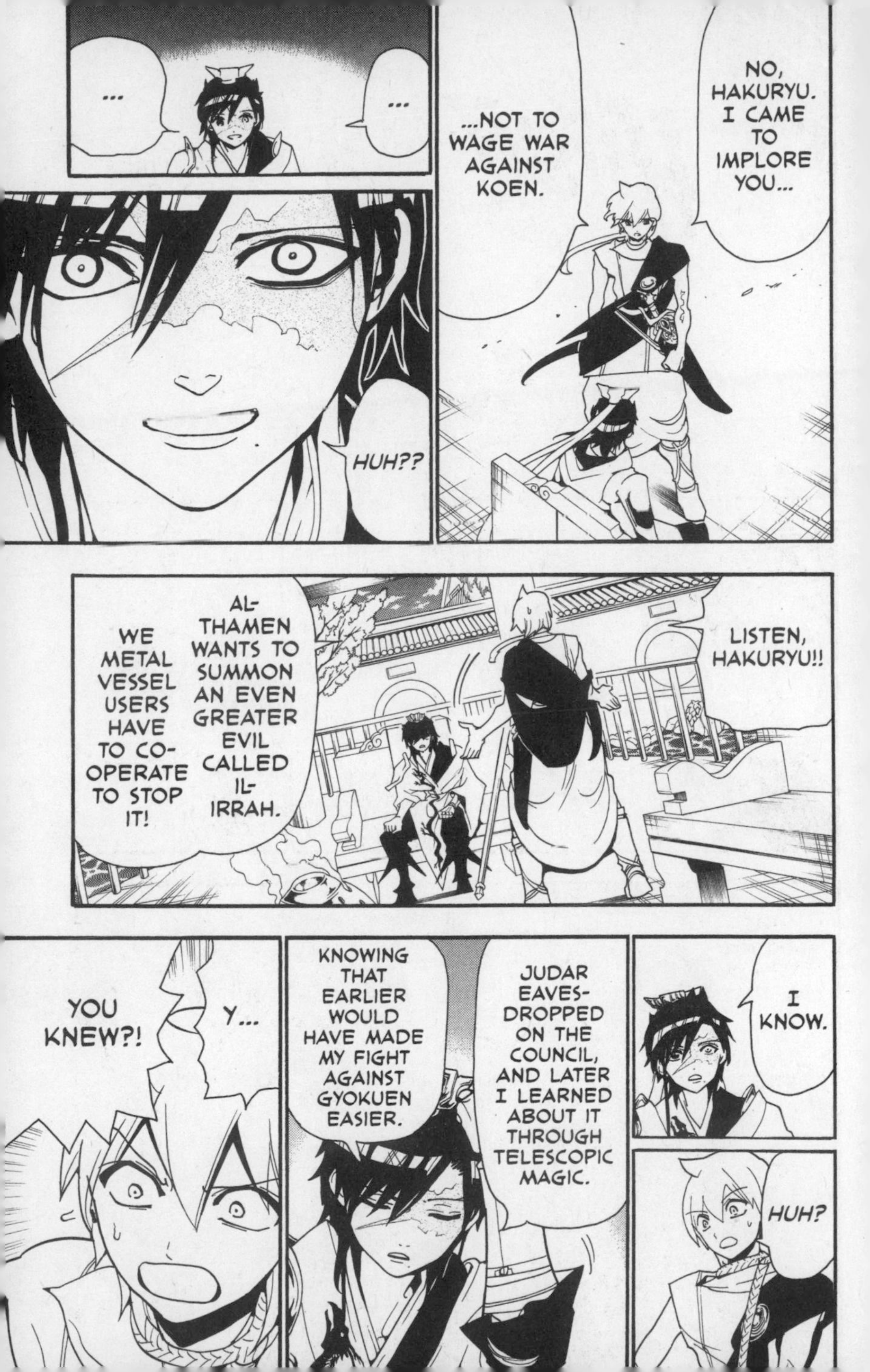
NO, HAKURYU. I CAME TO IMPLORE YOU...
...NOT TO WAGE WAR AGAINST KOEN.
...
...
HUH??
LISTEN, HAKURYU!!
AL-THAMEN WANTS TO SUMMON AN EVEN GREATER EVIL CALLED IL-IRRAH.
WE METAL VESSEL USERS HAVE TO CO-OPERATE TO STOP IT!
I KNOW.
HUH?
JUDAR EAVES-DROPPED ON THE COUNCIL, AND LATER I LEARNED ABOUT IT THROUGH TELESCOPIC MAGIC.
KNOWING THAT EARLIER WOULD HAVE MADE MY FIGHT AGAINST GYOKUEN EASIER.
Y...
YOU KNEW?!

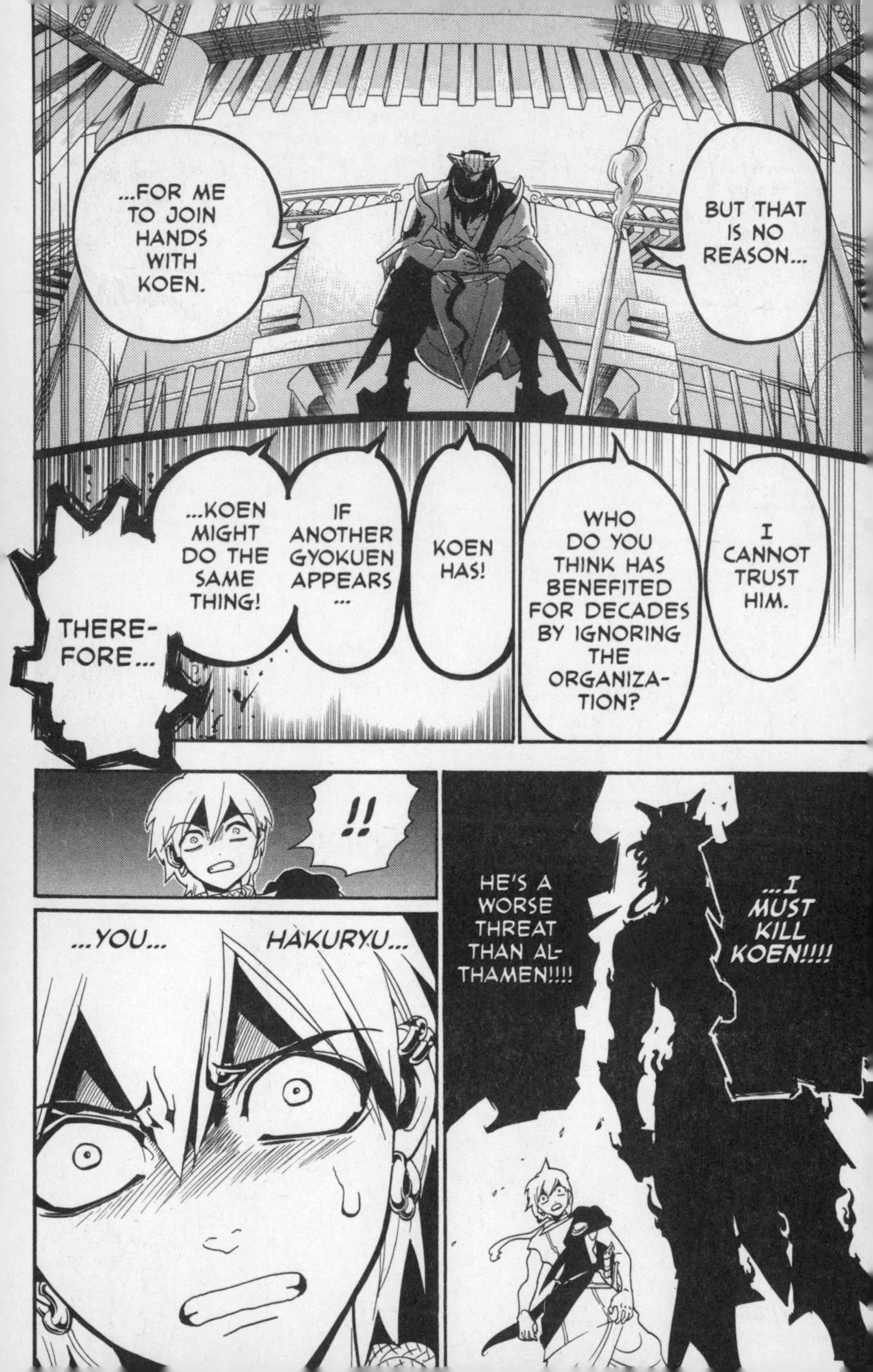
BUT THAT IS NO REASON...
...FOR ME TO JOIN HANDS WITH KOEN.
I CANNOT TRUST HIM.
WHO DO YOU THINK HAS BENEFITED FOR DECADES BY IGNORING THE ORGANIZATION?
KOEN HAS!
IF ANOTHER GYOKUEN APPEARS...
...KOEN MIGHT DO THE SAME THING!
THEREFORE...
...I MUST KILL KOEN!!!!
HE'S A WORSE THREAT THAN AL-THAMEN!!!!
!!
HAKURYU...
...YOU...

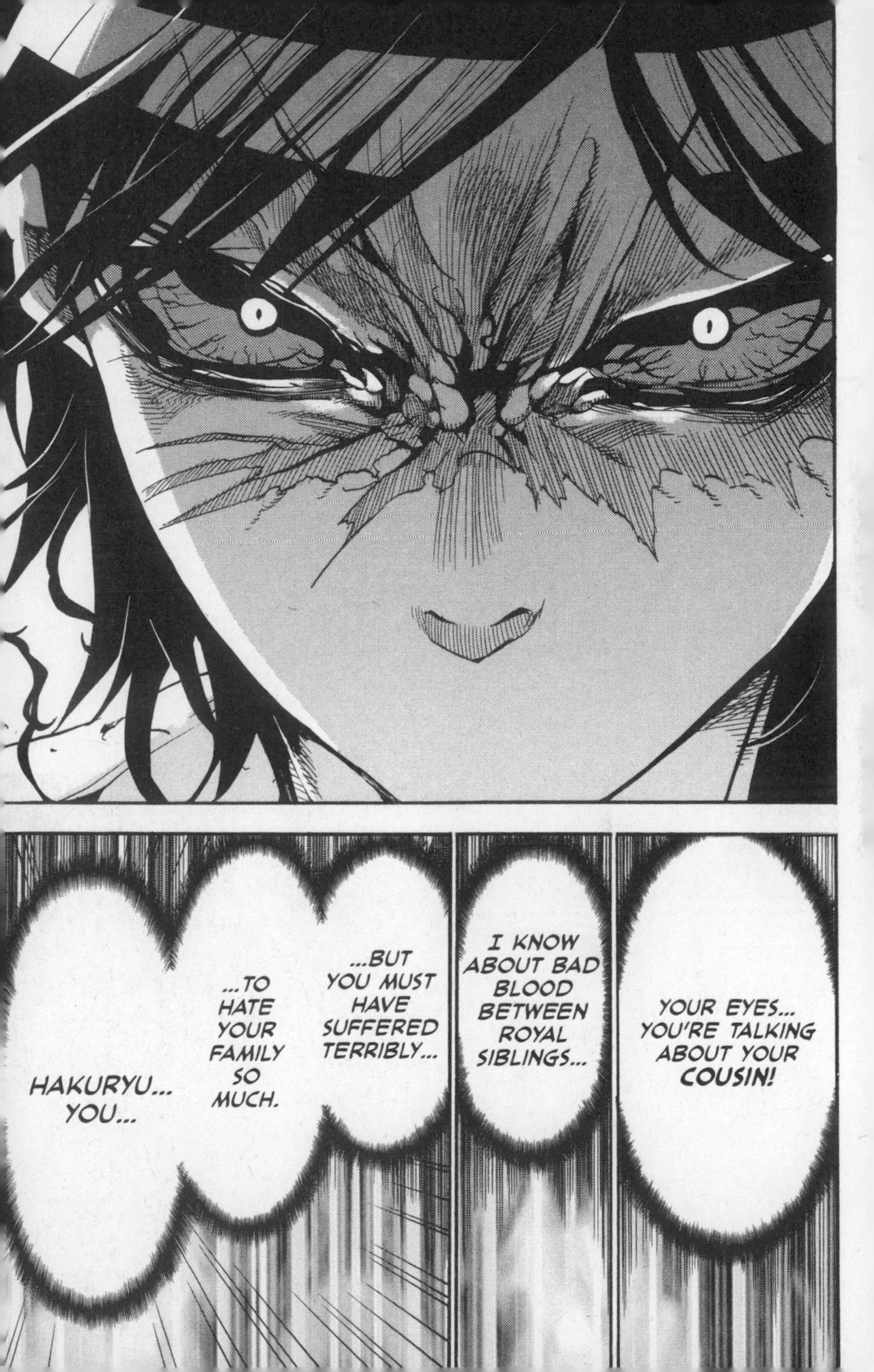
YOUR EYES... YOU'RE TALKING ABOUT YOUR COUSIN!
I KNOW ABOUT BAD BLOOD BETWEEN ROYAL SIBLINGS...
...BUT YOU MUST HAVE SUFFERED TERRIBLY...
...TO HATE YOUR FAMILY SO MUCH.
HAKURYU... YOU...

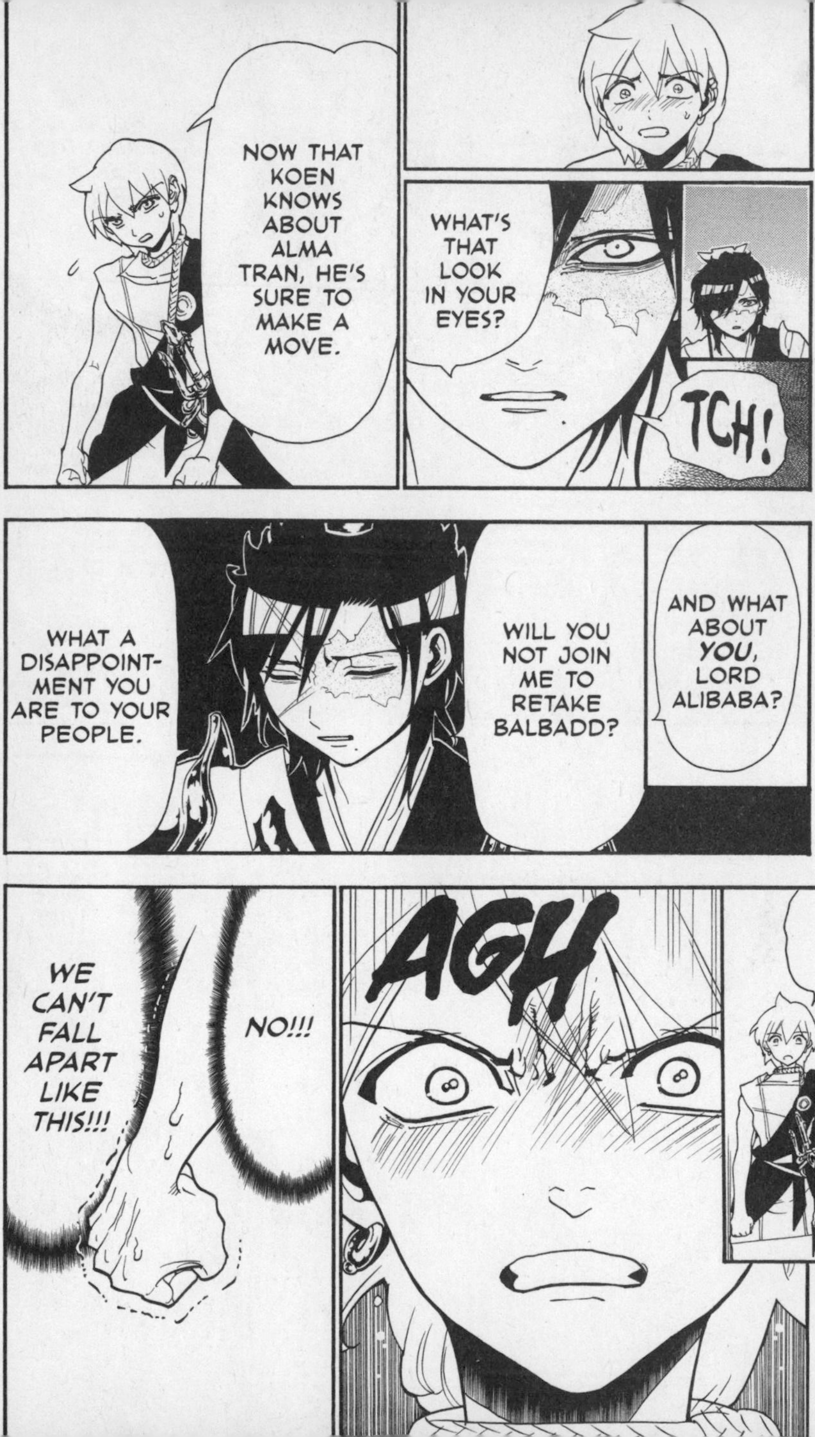
WHAT'S THAT LOOK IN YOUR EYES?
TCH!
NOW THAT KOEN KNOWS ABOUT ALMA TRAN, HE'S SURE TO MAKE A MOVE.
AND WHAT ABOUT *YOU*, LORD ALIBABA?
WILL YOU NOT JOIN ME TO RETAKE BALBADD?
WHAT A DISAPPOINTMENT YOU ARE TO YOUR PEOPLE.
...
AGH
NO!!!
WE CAN'T FALL APART LIKE THIS!!!

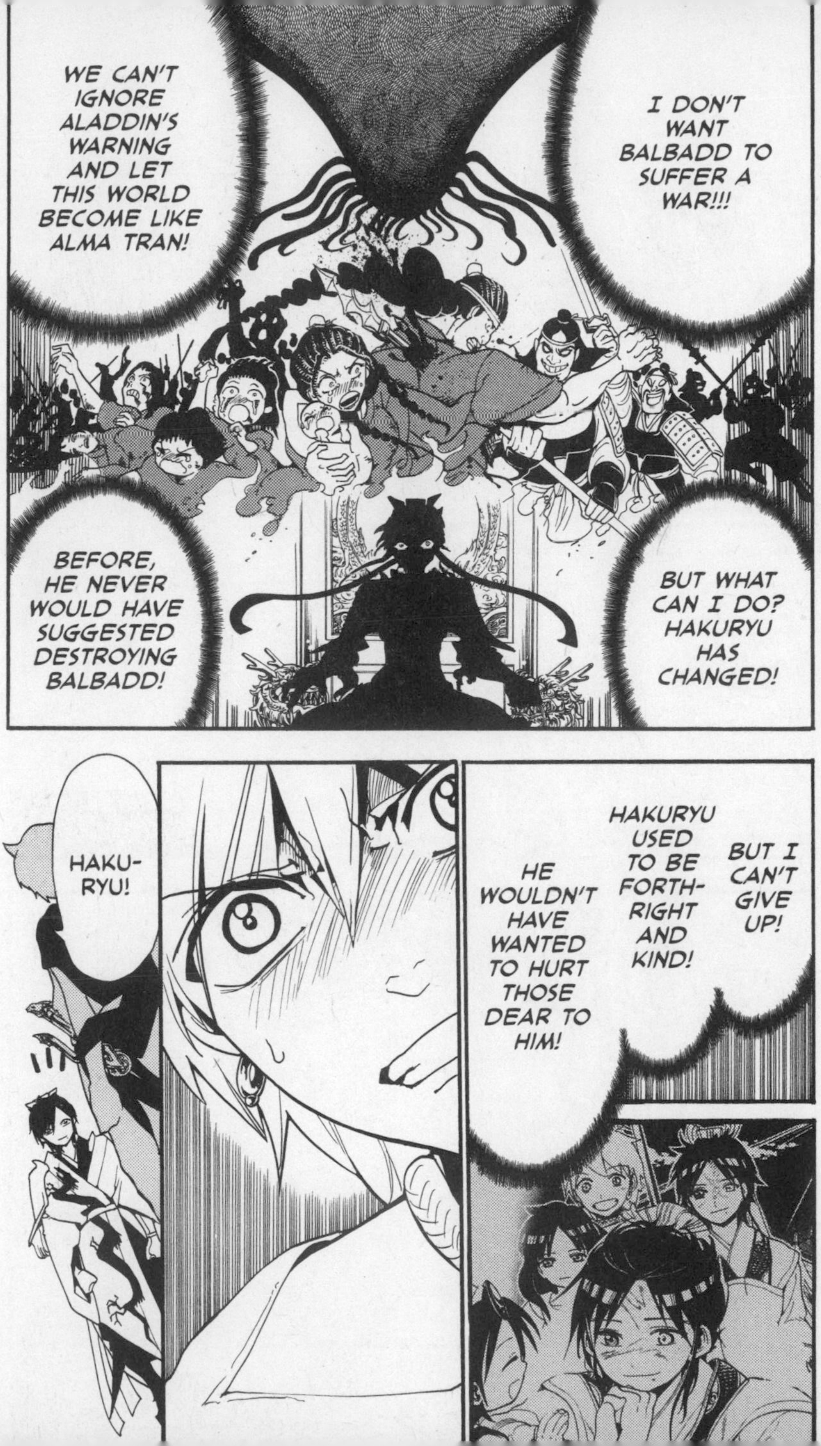
I DON'T WANT BALBADD TO SUFFER A WAR!!!
WE CAN'T IGNORE ALADDIN'S WARNING AND LET THIS WORLD BECOME LIKE ALMA TRAN!
BUT WHAT CAN I DO? HAKURYU HAS CHANGED!
BEFORE, HE NEVER WOULD HAVE SUGGESTED DESTROYING BALBADD!
BUT I CAN'T GIVE UP!
HAKURYU USED TO BE FORTH-RIGHT AND KIND!
HE WOULDN'T HAVE WANTED TO HURT THOSE DEAR TO HIM!
HAKU-RYU!

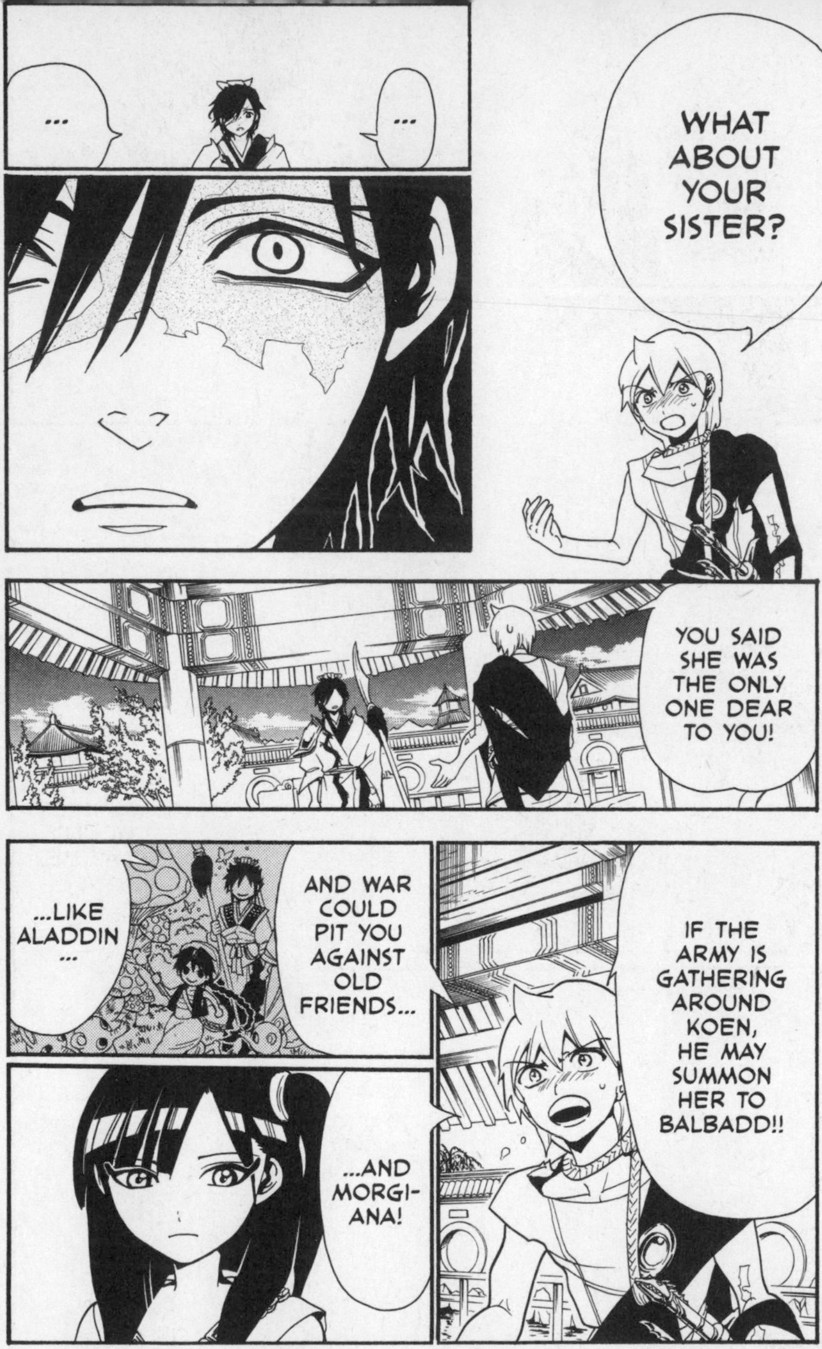
WHAT ABOUT YOUR SISTER?
...
...
YOU SAID SHE WAS THE ONLY ONE DEAR TO YOU!
IF THE ARMY IS GATHERING AROUND KOEN, HE MAY SUMMON HER TO BALBADD!!
AND WAR COULD PIT YOU AGAINST OLD FRIENDS...
...LIKE ALADDIN ...
...AND MORGI-ANA!

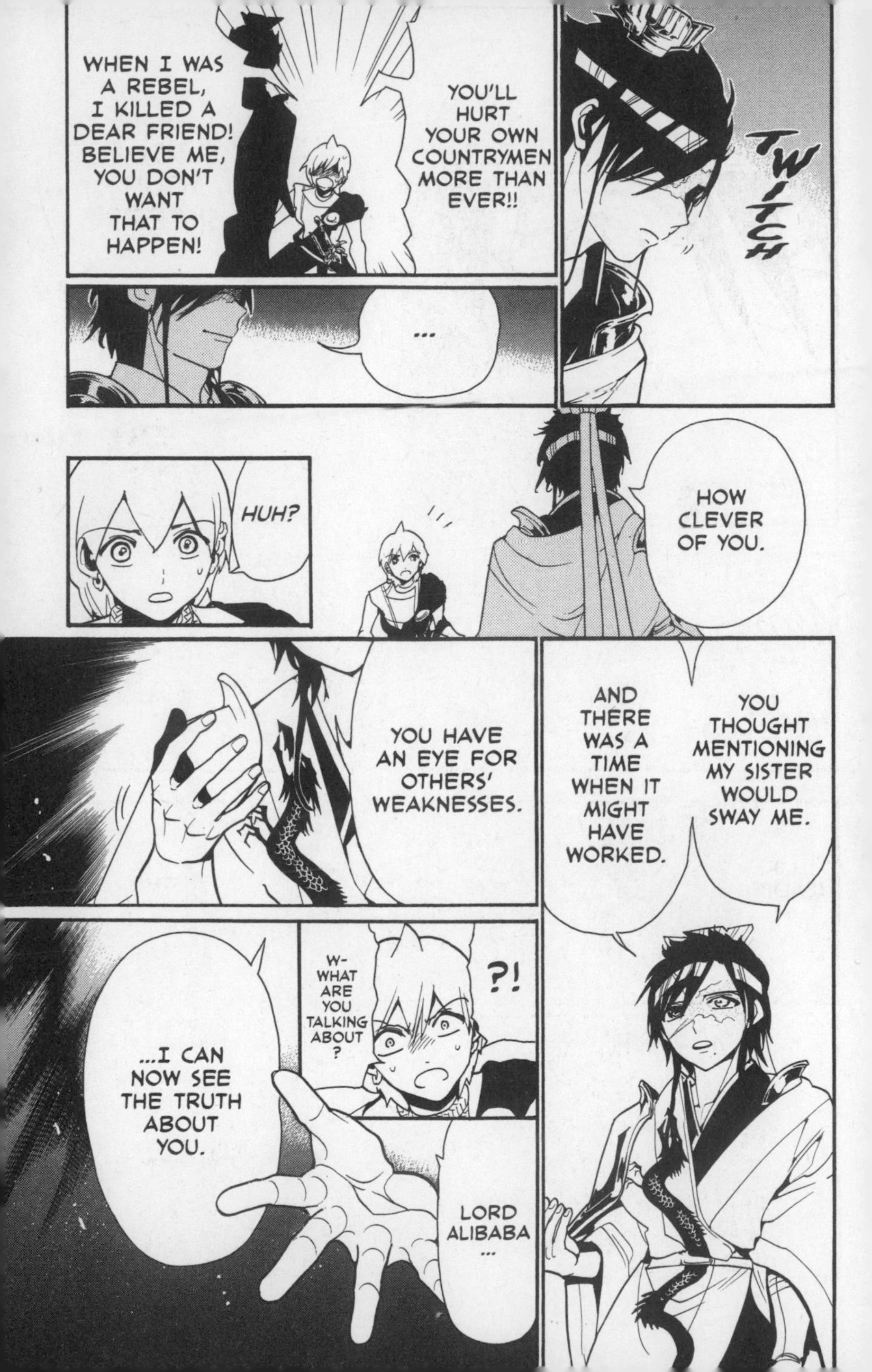
TWITCH
YOU'LL HURT YOUR OWN COUNTRYMEN MORE THAN EVER!!
WHEN I WAS A REBEL, I KILLED A DEAR FRIEND! BELIEVE ME, YOU DON'T WANT THAT TO HAPPEN!
...
HOW CLEVER OF YOU.
HUH?
YOU THOUGHT MENTIONING MY SISTER WOULD SWAY ME.
AND THERE WAS A TIME WHEN IT MIGHT HAVE WORKED.
YOU HAVE AN EYE FOR OTHERS' WEAKNESSES.
?!
W-WHAT ARE YOU TALKING ABOUT?
LORD ALIBABA...
...I CAN NOW SEE THE TRUTH ABOUT YOU.

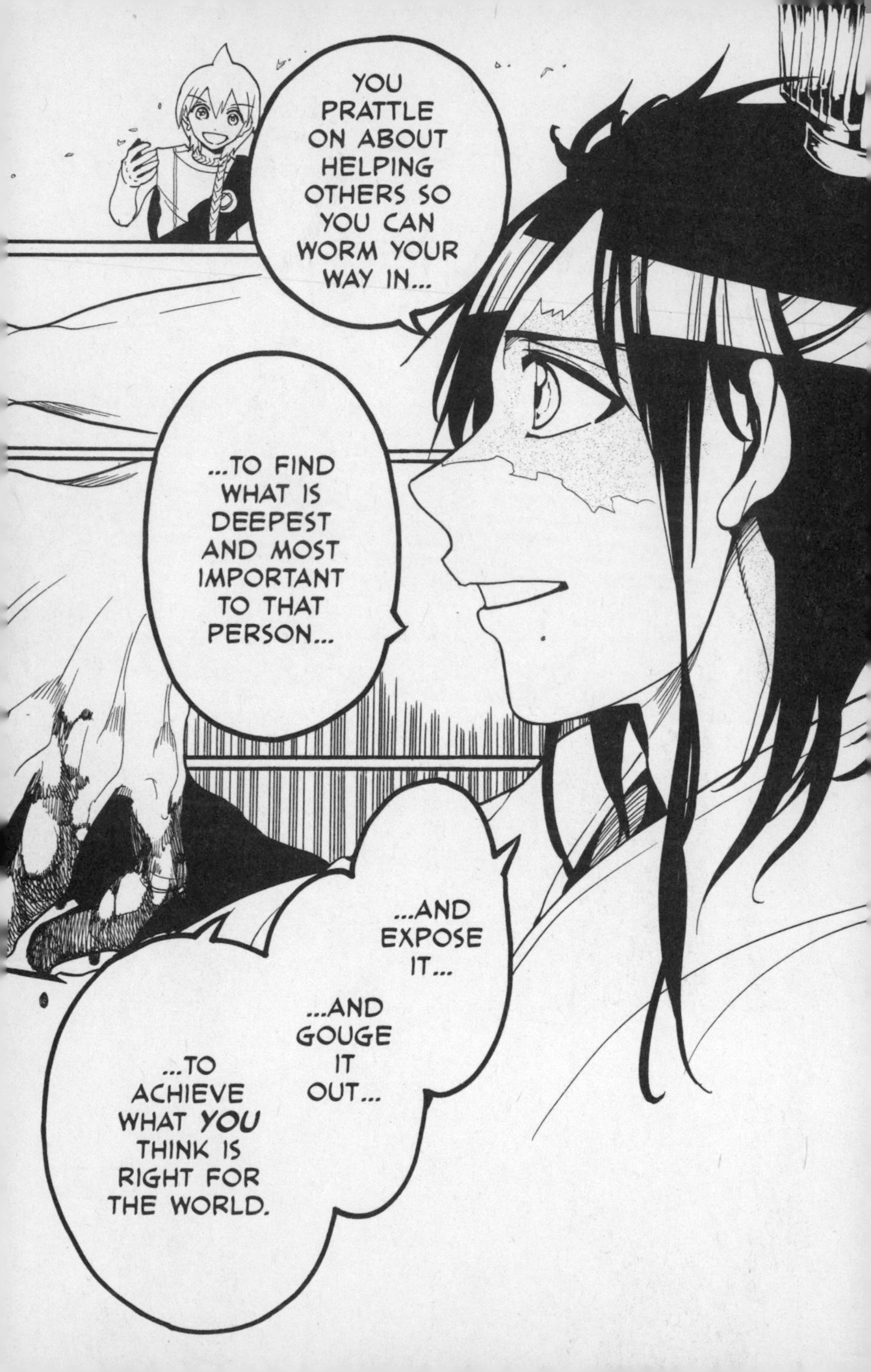
YOU PRATTLE ON ABOUT HELPING OTHERS SO YOU CAN WORM YOUR WAY IN...
...TO FIND WHAT IS DEEPEST AND MOST IMPORTANT TO THAT PERSON...
...AND EXPOSE IT...
...AND GOUGE IT OUT...
...TO ACHIEVE WHAT *YOU* THINK IS RIGHT FOR THE WORLD.

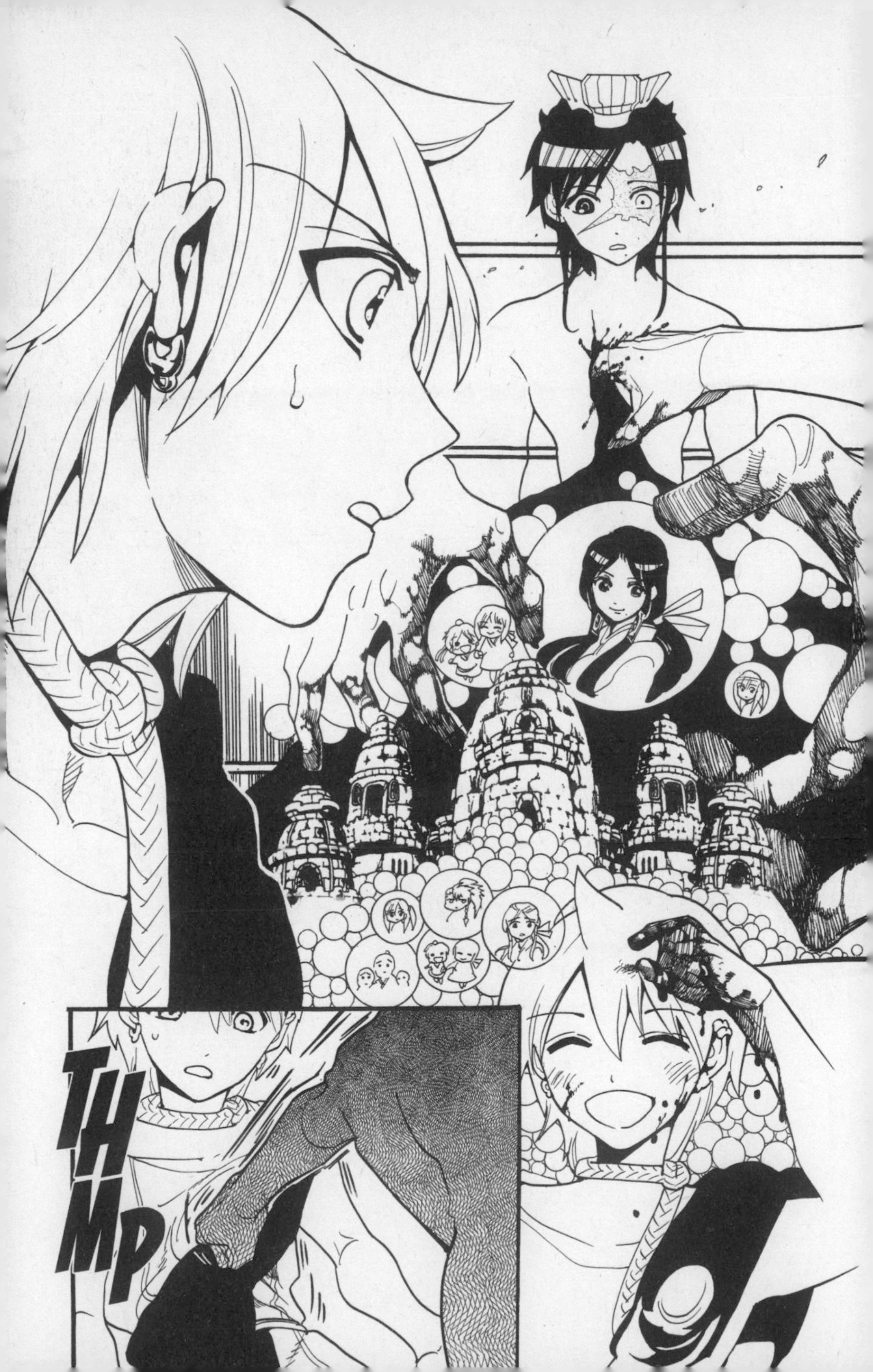
THUMP

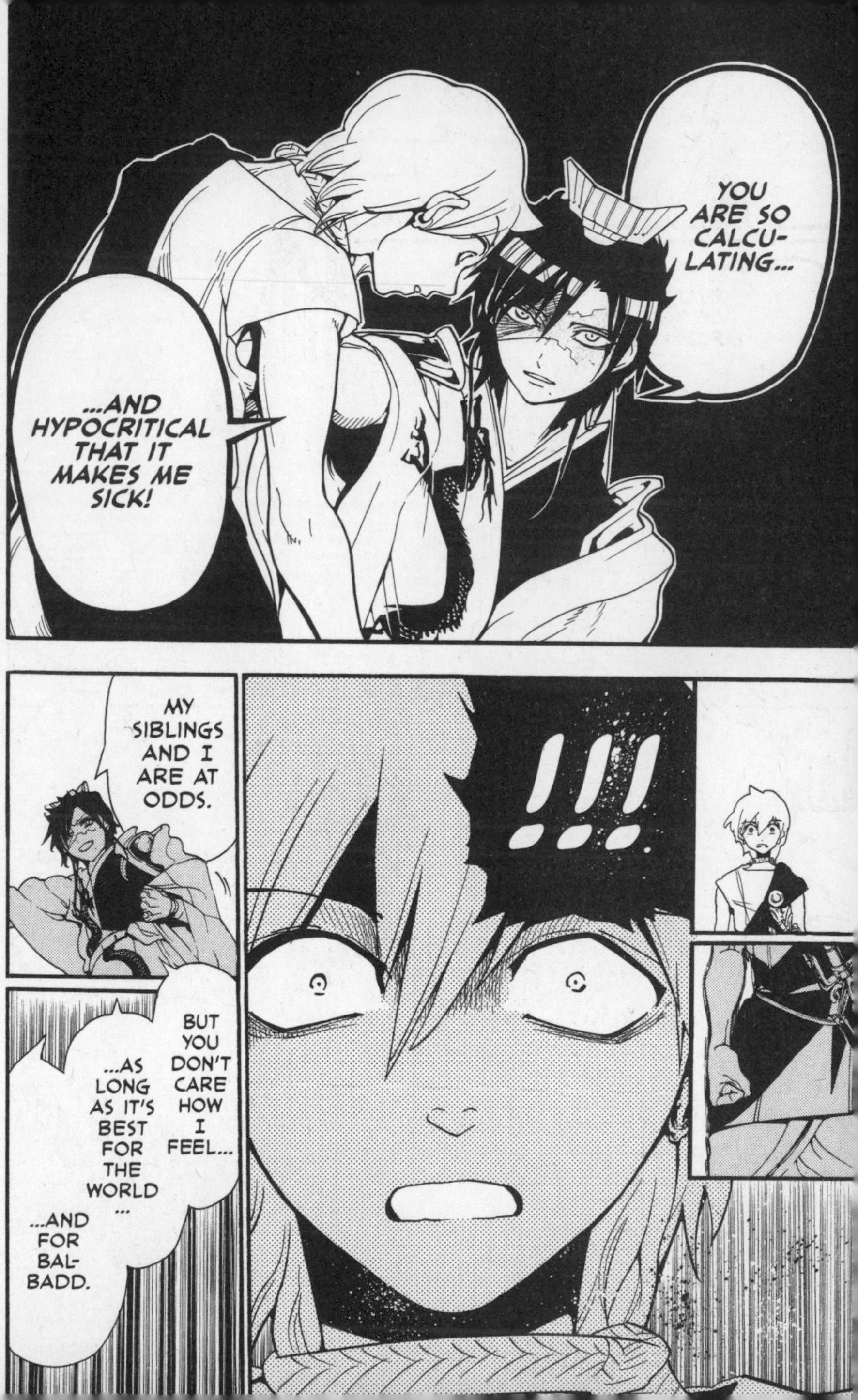
YOU ARE SO CALCU-LATING...
...AND HYPOCRITICAL THAT IT MAKES ME SICK!
!!!
MY SIBLINGS AND I ARE AT ODDS.
BUT YOU DON'T CARE HOW I FEEL...
...AS LONG AS IT'S BEST FOR THE WORLD...
...AND FOR BAL-BADD.

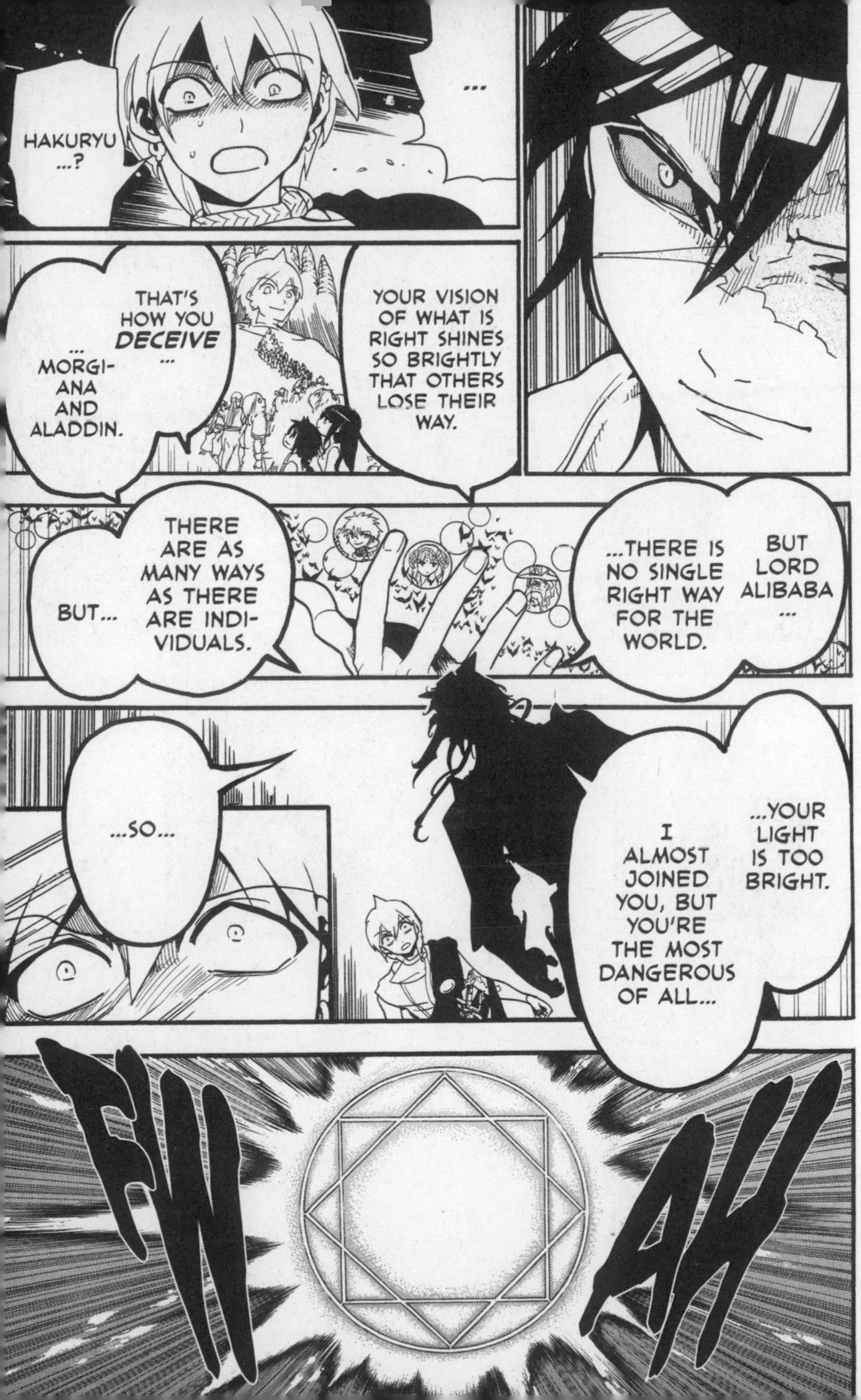
...
HAKURYU ...?
YOUR VISION OF WHAT IS RIGHT SHINES SO BRIGHTLY THAT OTHERS LOSE THEIR WAY.
THAT'S HOW YOU DECEIVE ...
... MORGI-ANA AND ALADDIN.
BUT LORD ALIBABA ...
...THERE IS NO SINGLE RIGHT WAY FOR THE WORLD.
THERE ARE AS MANY WAYS AS THERE ARE INDI-VIDUALS.
BUT...
...YOUR LIGHT IS TOO BRIGHT.
I ALMOST JOINED YOU, BUT YOU'RE THE MOST DANGEROUS OF ALL...
...SO...
FWAH

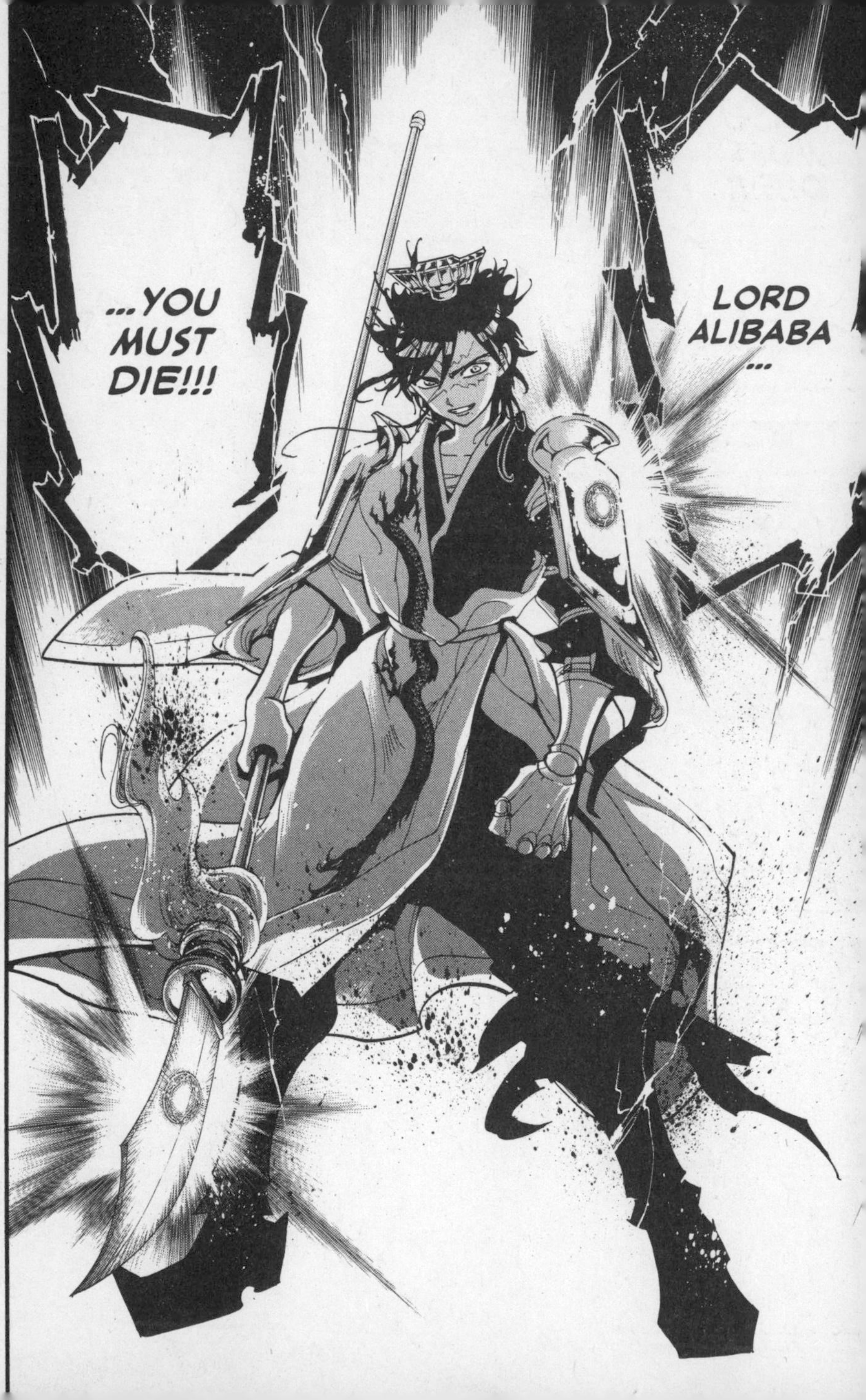
LORD ALIBABA ...
...YOU MUST DIE!!!

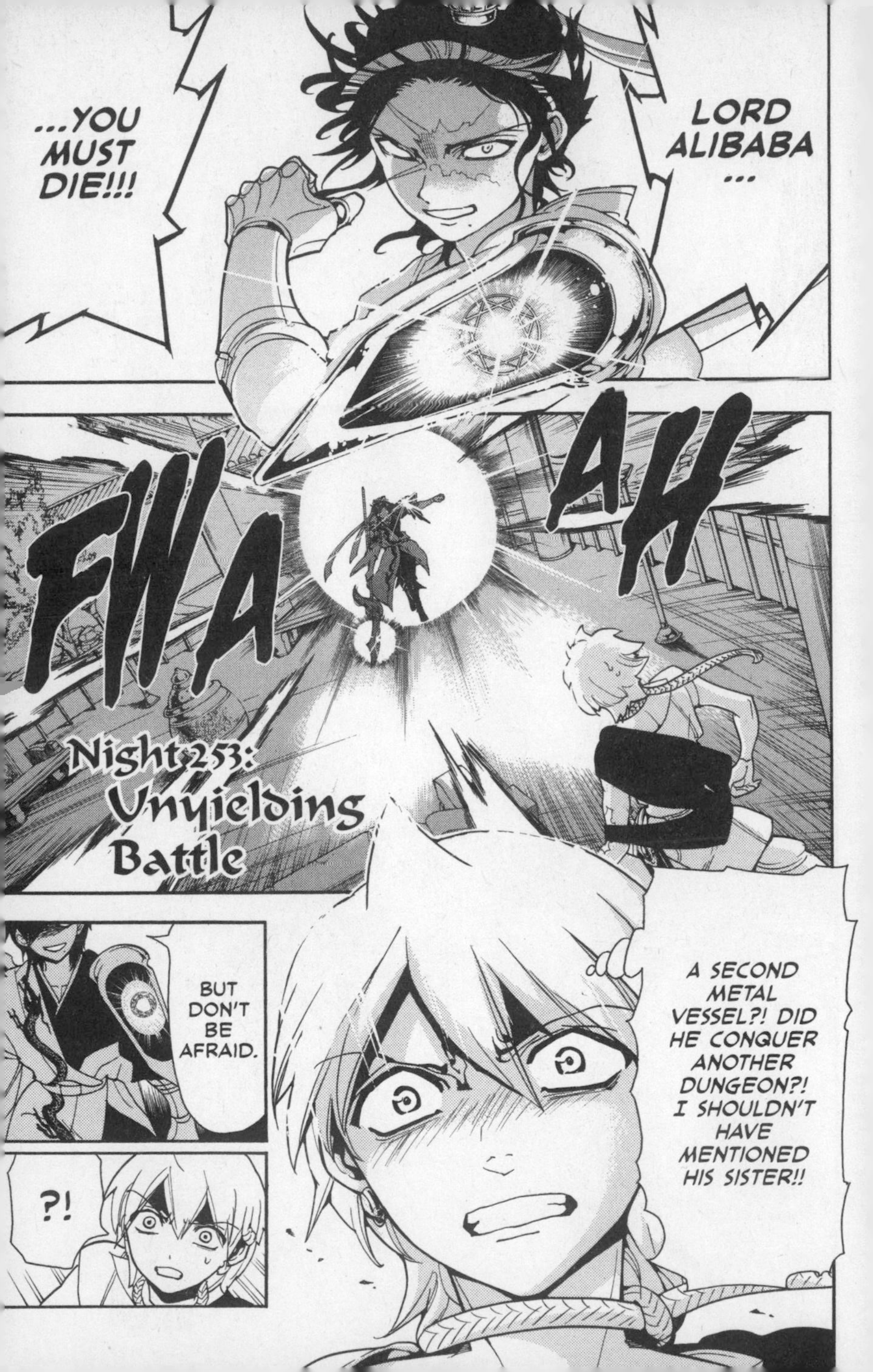
LORD ALIBABA ...
...YOU MUST DIE!!!
FWAAH
Night 253: Unyielding Battle
A SECOND METAL VESSEL?! DID HE CONQUER ANOTHER DUNGEON?! I SHOULDN'T HAVE MENTIONED HIS SISTER!!
BUT DON'T BE AFRAID.
?!

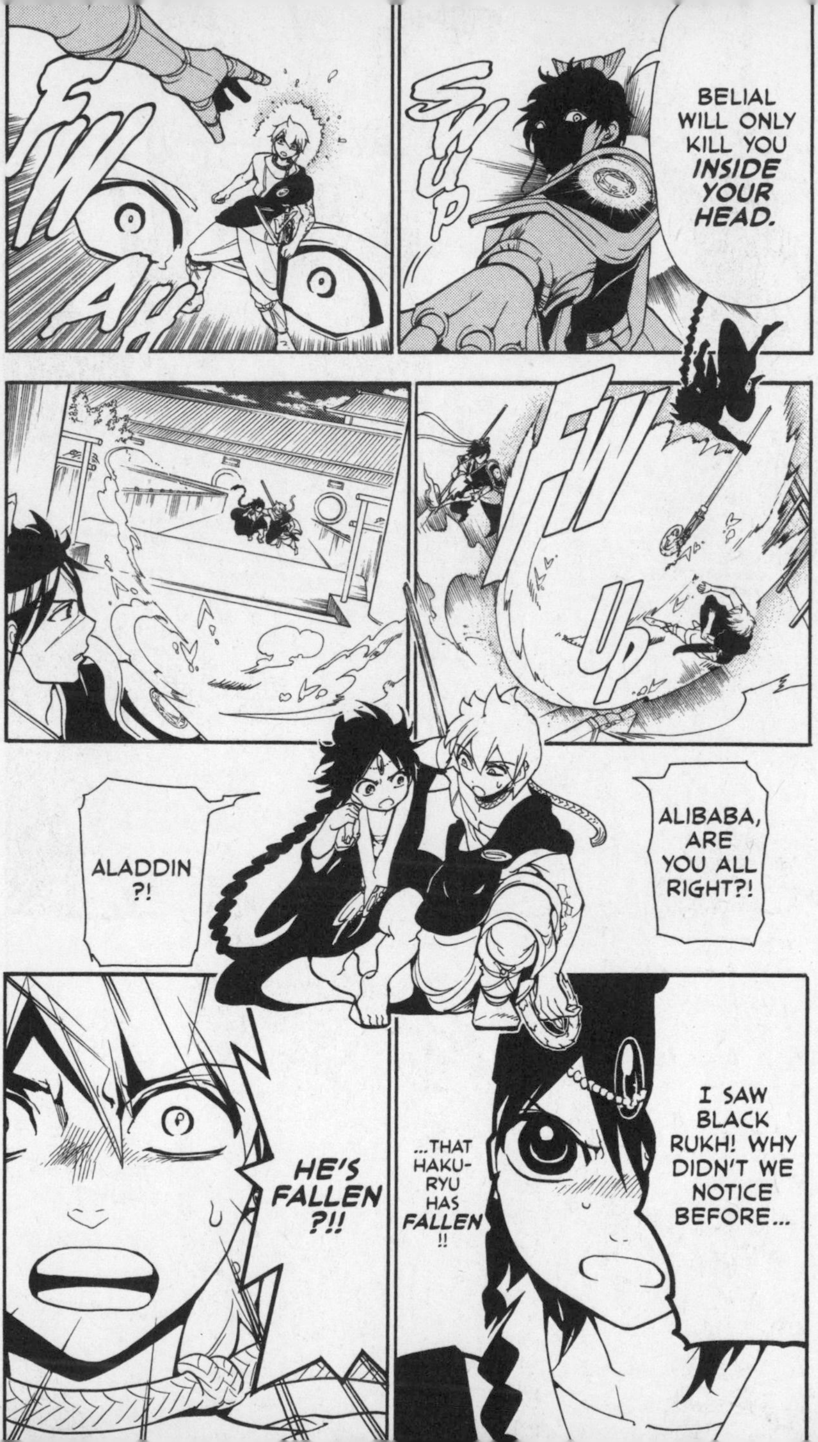
SWUP
BELIAL WILL ONLY KILL YOU INSIDE YOUR HEAD.
FWAH!!
FWUP
ALIBABA, ARE YOU ALL RIGHT?!
ALADDIN ?!
I SAW BLACK RUKH! WHY DIDN'T WE NOTICE BEFORE...
...THAT HAKU-RYU HAS FALLEN !!
HE'S FALLEN ?!!

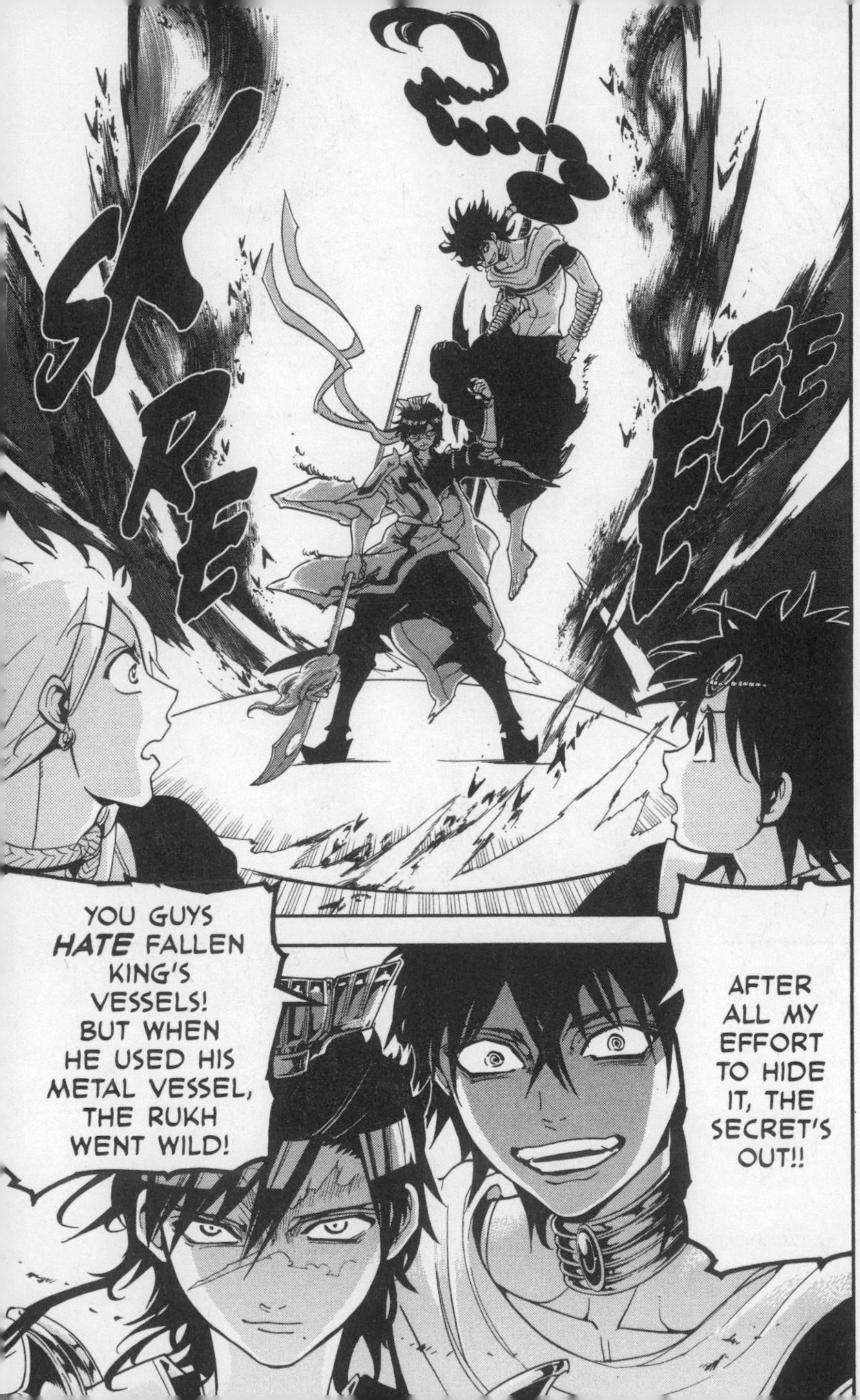
AFTER ALL MY EFFORT TO HIDE IT, THE SECRET'S OUT!!
YOU GUYS *HATE* FALLEN KING'S VESSELS! BUT WHEN HE USED HIS METAL VESSEL, THE RUKH WENT WILD!

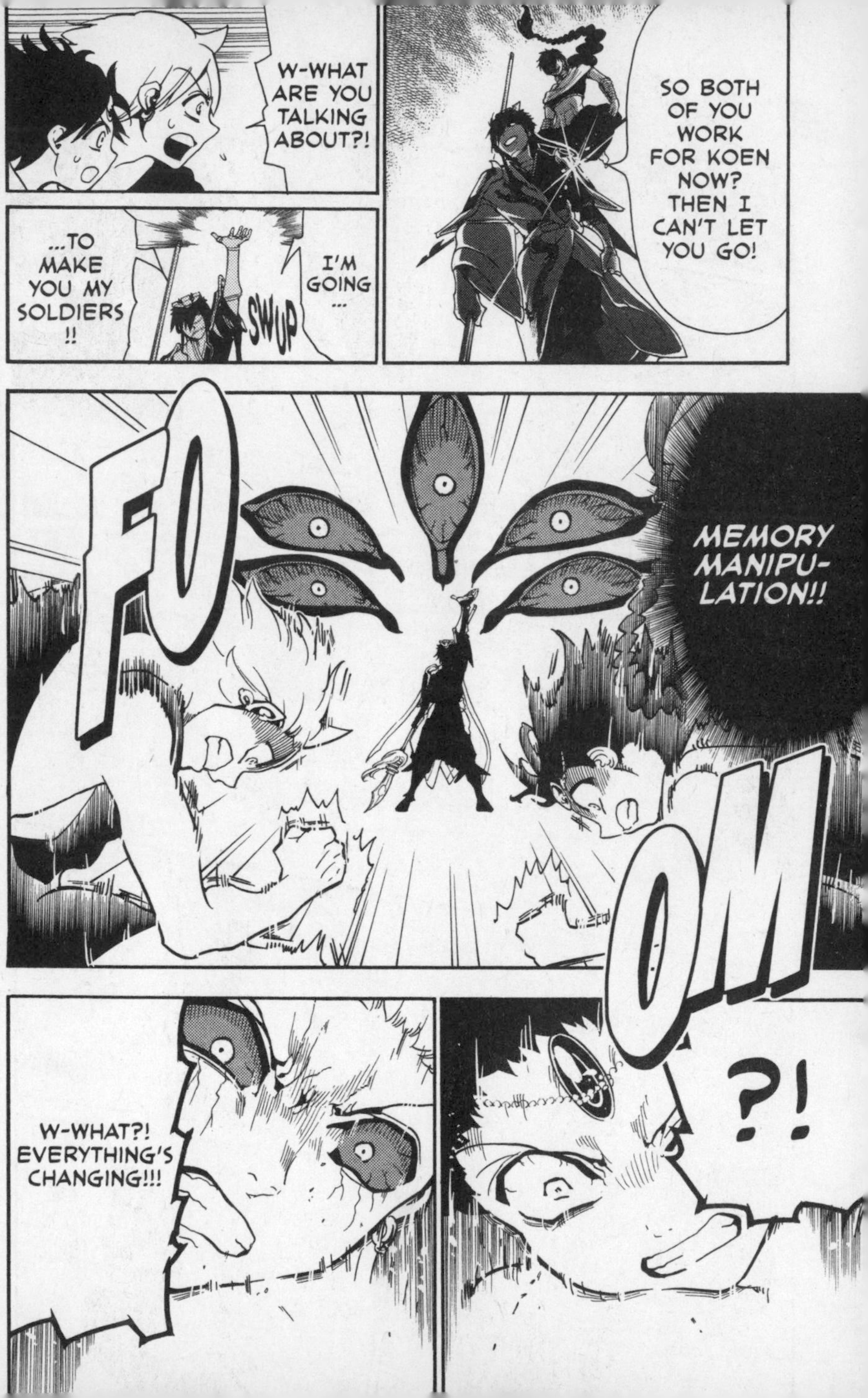
SO BOTH OF YOU WORK FOR KOEN NOW? THEN I CAN'T LET YOU GO!
W-WHAT ARE YOU TALKING ABOUT?!
I'M GOING ...
SWUP
...TO MAKE YOU MY SOLDIERS !!
MEMORY MANIPU-LATION!!
FO
OM
?!
W-WHAT?! EVERYTHING'S CHANGING!!!

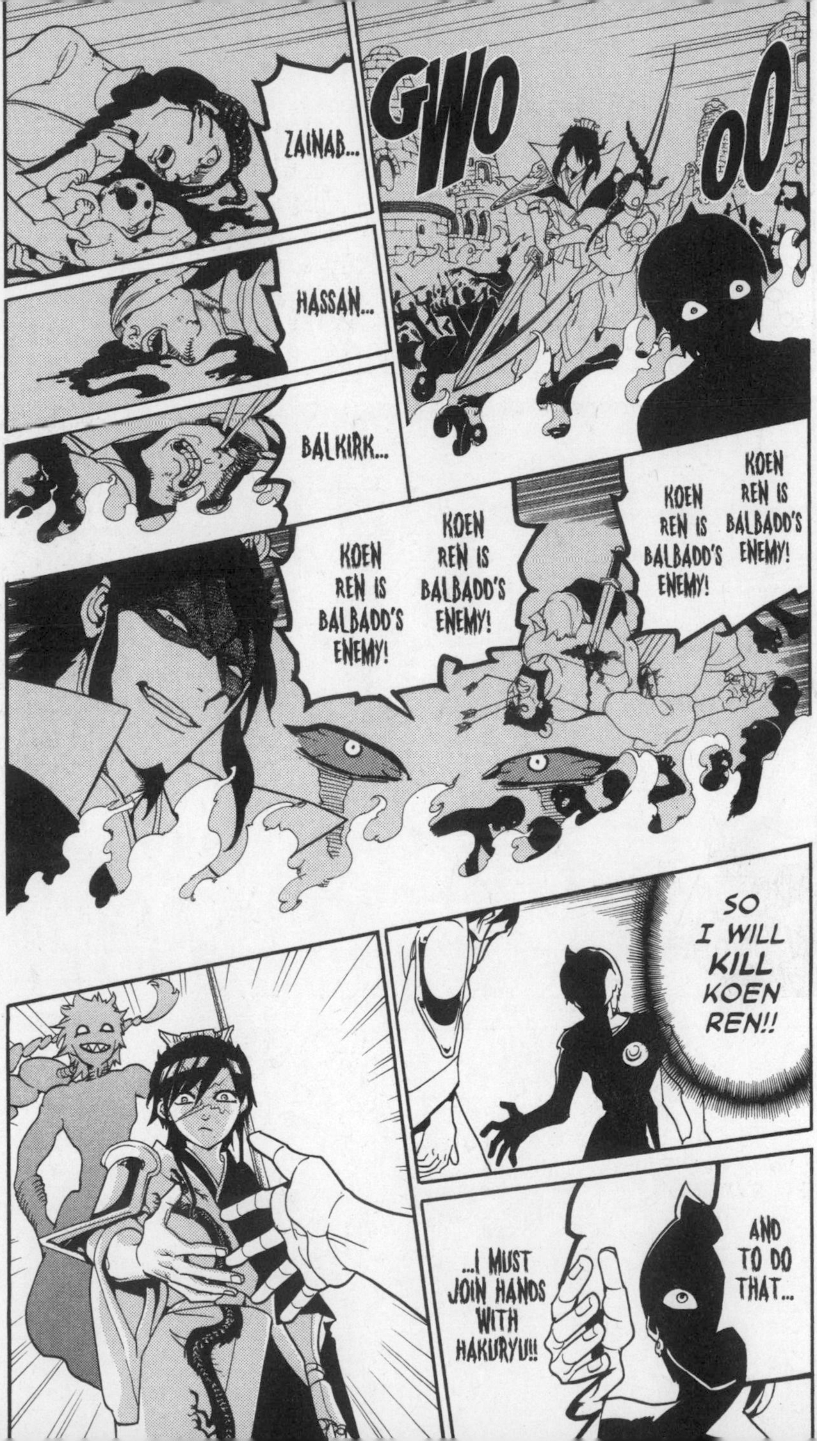
GWOOO
ZAINAB...
HASSAN...
BALKIRK...
KOEN REN IS BALBADD'S ENEMY!
KOEN REN IS BALBADD'S ENEMY!
KOEN REN IS BALBADD'S ENEMY!
KOEN REN IS BALBADD'S ENEMY!
SO I WILL KILL KOEN REN!!
AND TO DO THAT...
...I MUST JOIN HANDS WITH HAKURYU!!

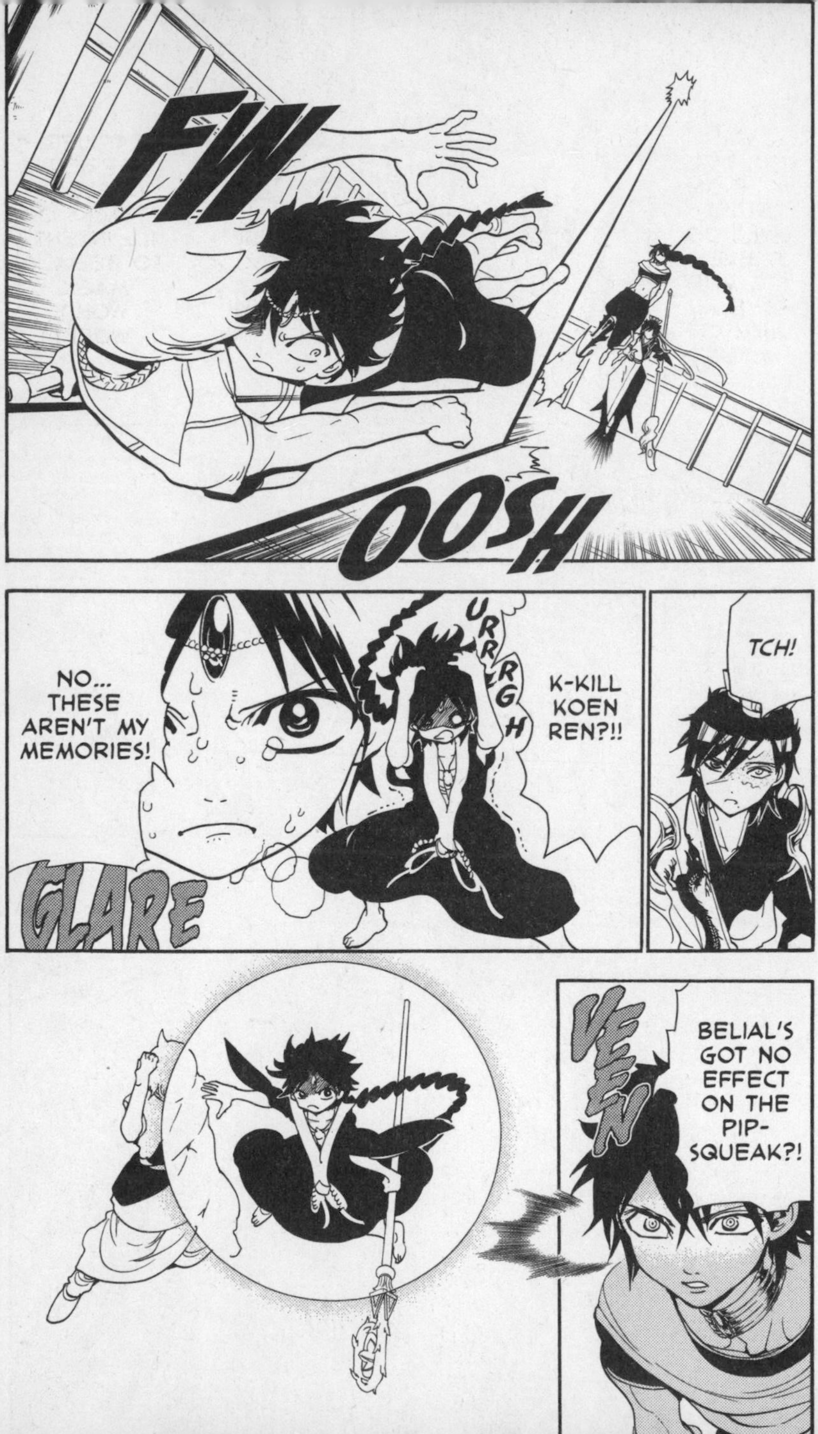
FWOOSH
TCH!
URRRGH
K-KILL KOEN REN?!!
NO... THESE AREN'T MY MEMORIES!
GLARE
VEEN
BELIAL'S GOT NO EFFECT ON THE PIP-SQUEAK?!

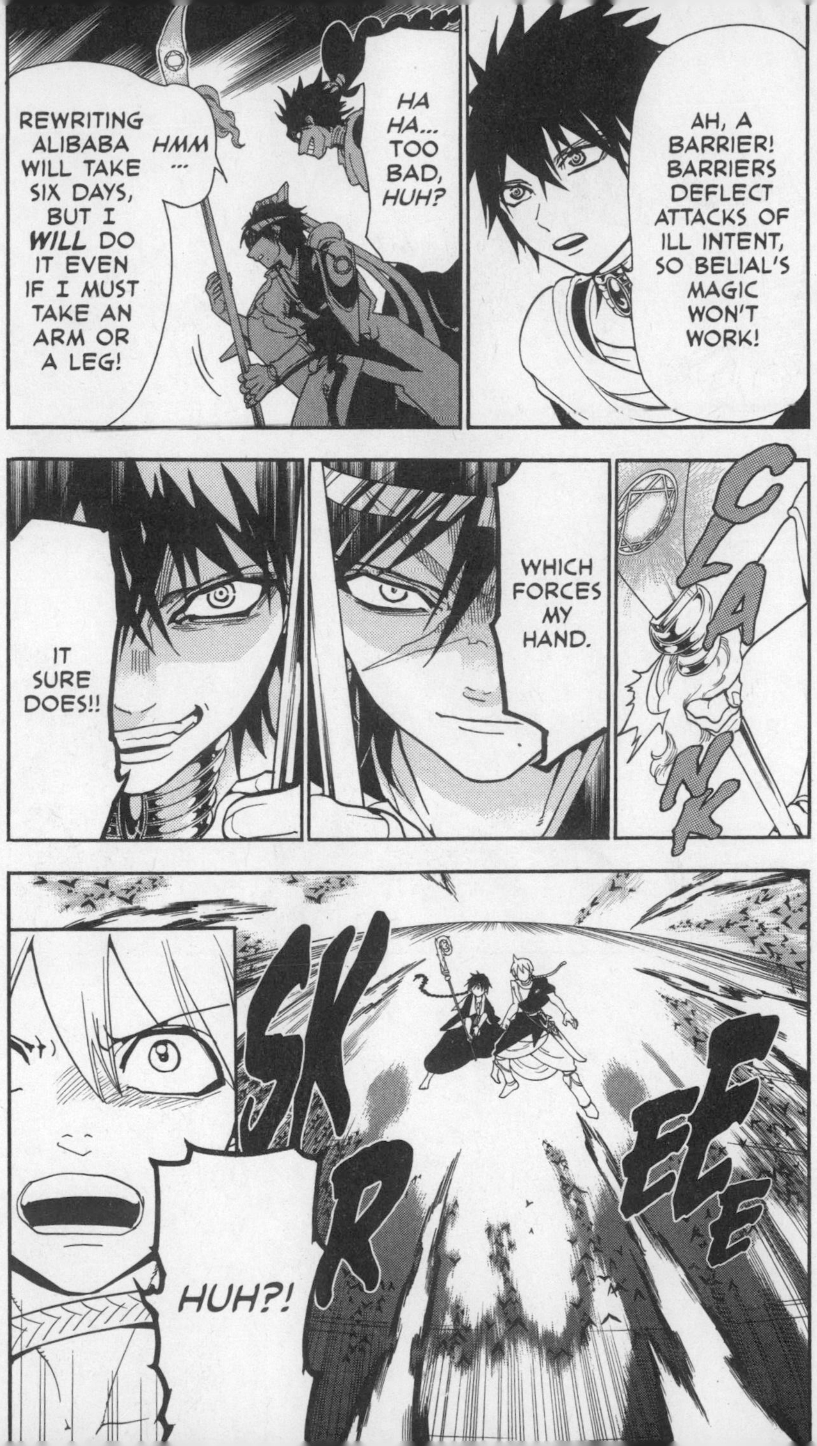
AH, A BARRIER! BARRIERS DEFLECT ATTACKS OF ILL INTENT, SO BELIAL'S MAGIC WON'T WORK!
HA HA... TOO BAD, HUH?
HMM ...
REWRITING ALIBABA WILL TAKE SIX DAYS, BUT I *WILL* DO IT EVEN IF I MUST TAKE AN ARM OR A LEG!
CLANK
WHICH FORCES MY HAND.
IT SURE DOES!!
SKREEE
HUH?!

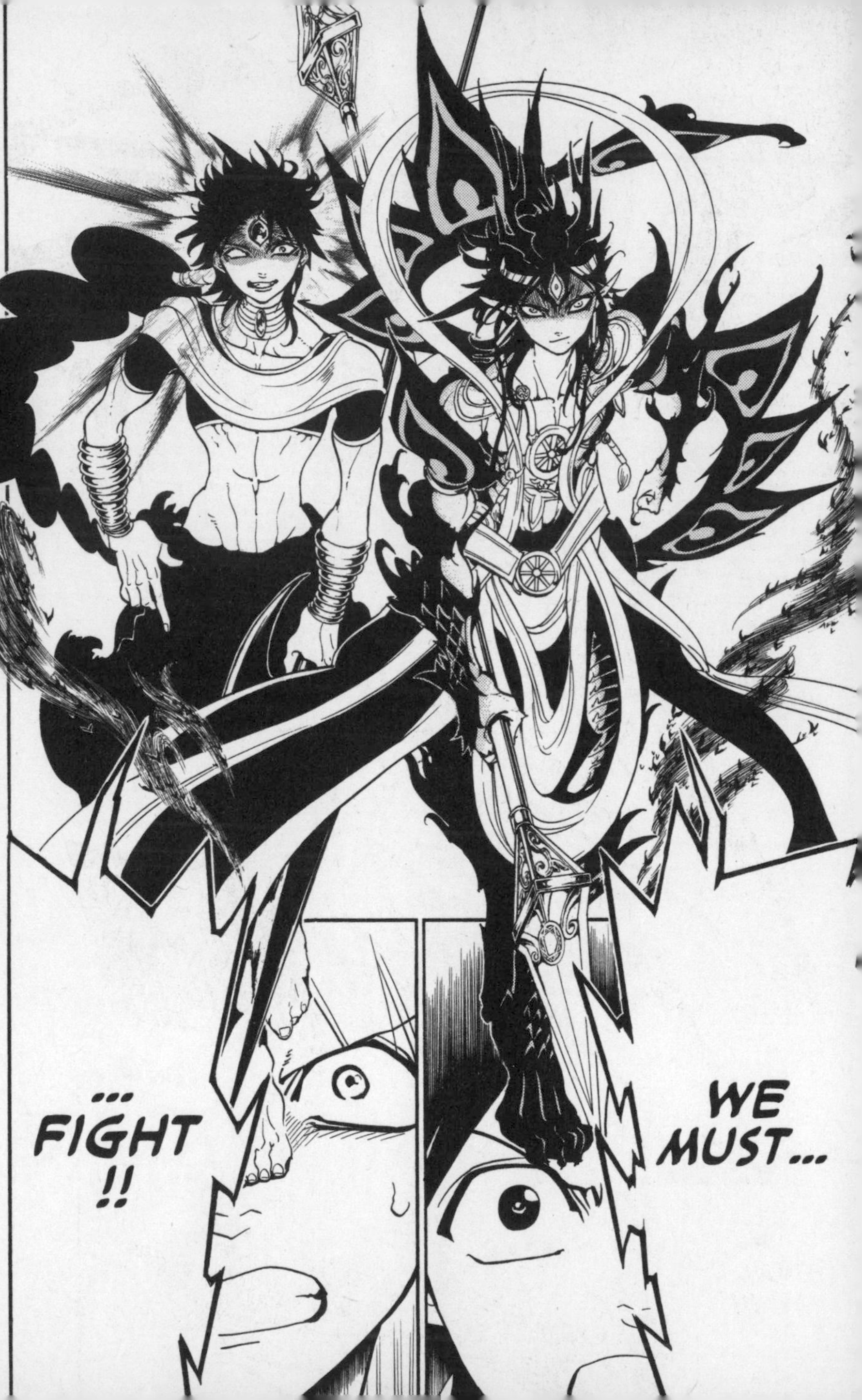
WE MUST...
...FIGHT !!

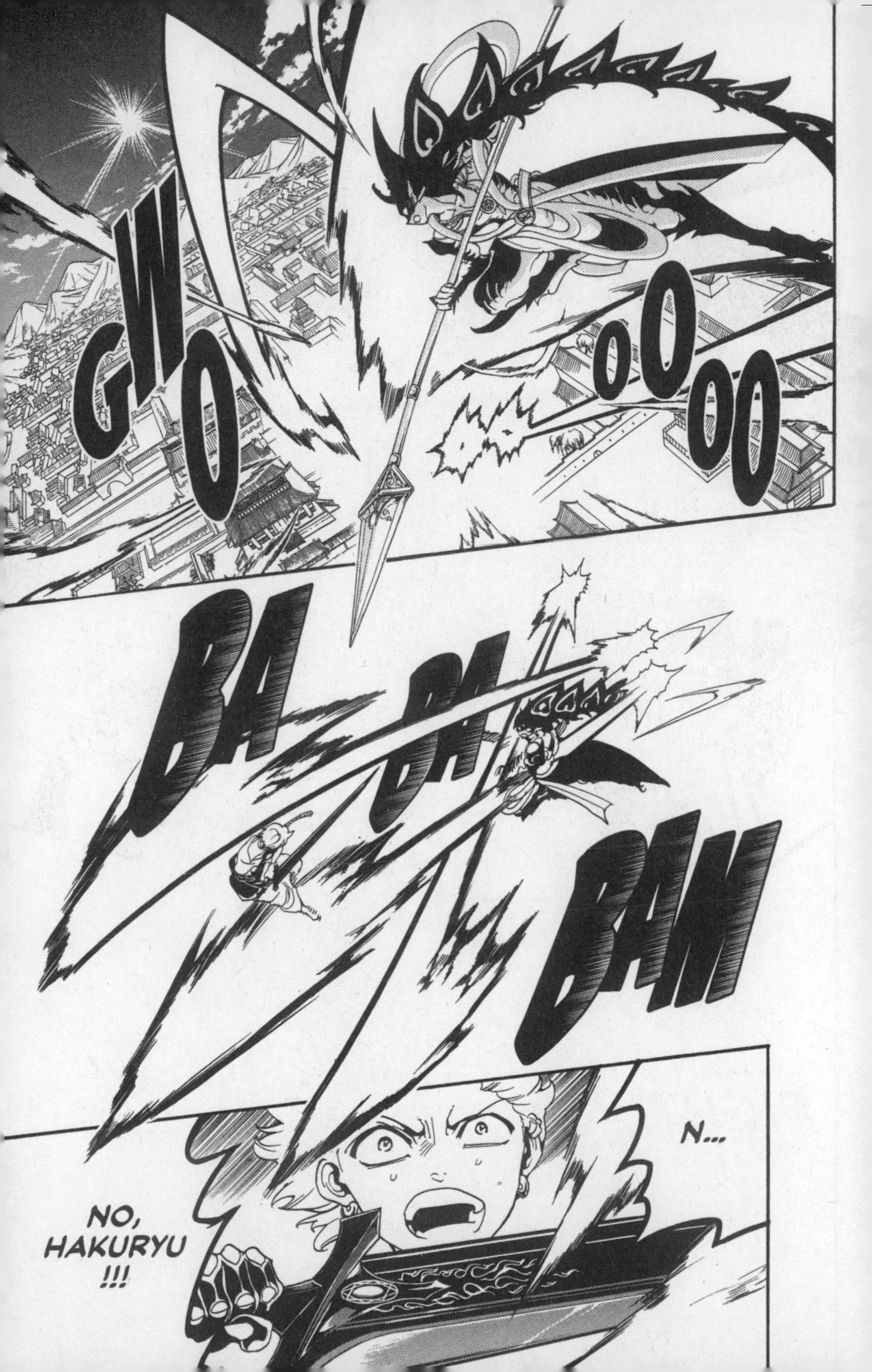
GWOOOOO
BA BA BAM
N...
NO, HAKURYU !!!

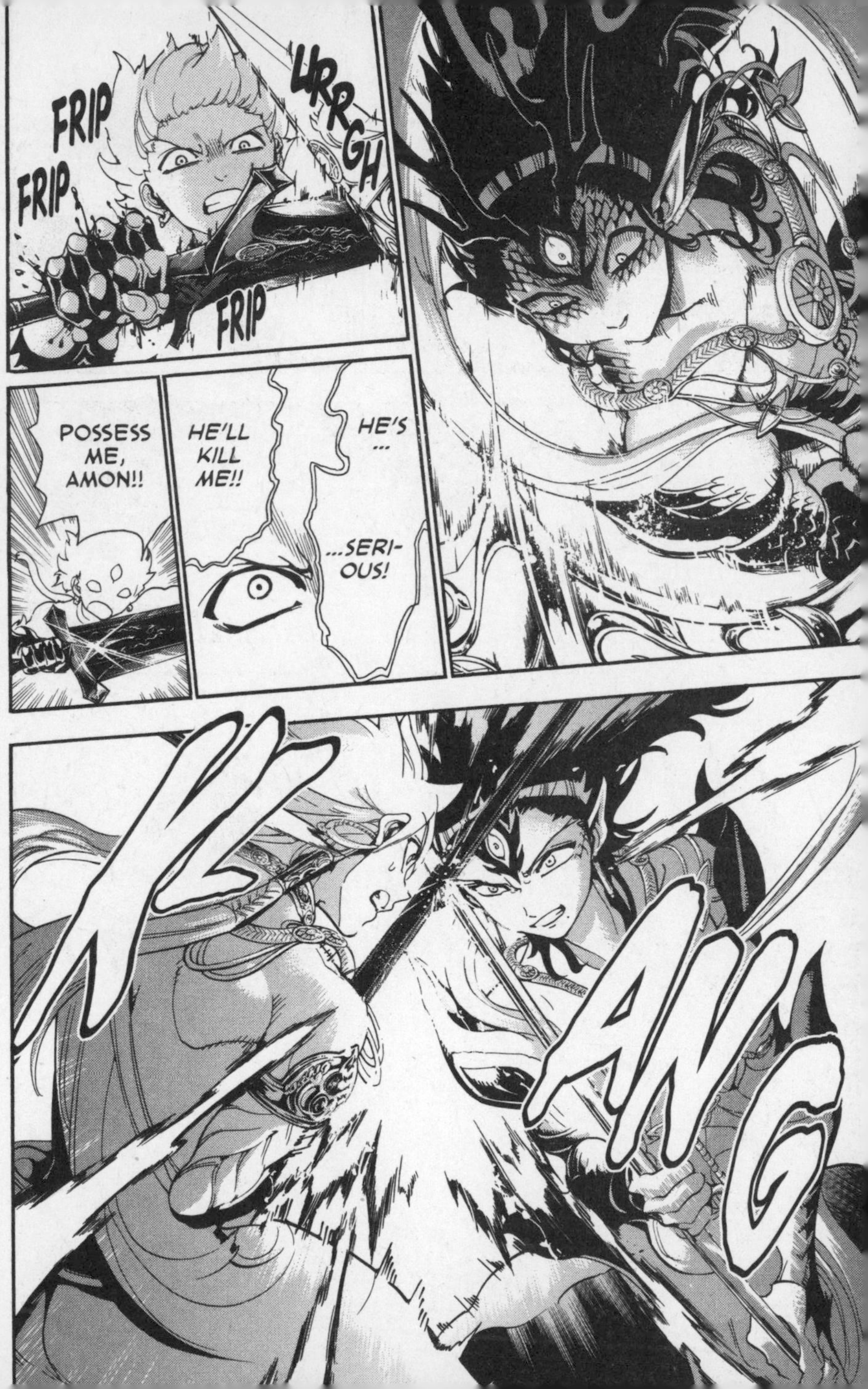
URRGH
FRIP
FRIP
FRIP
HE'S ...
...SERI-
OUS!
HE'LL
KILL
ME!!
POSSESS
ME,
AMON!!
KLANG

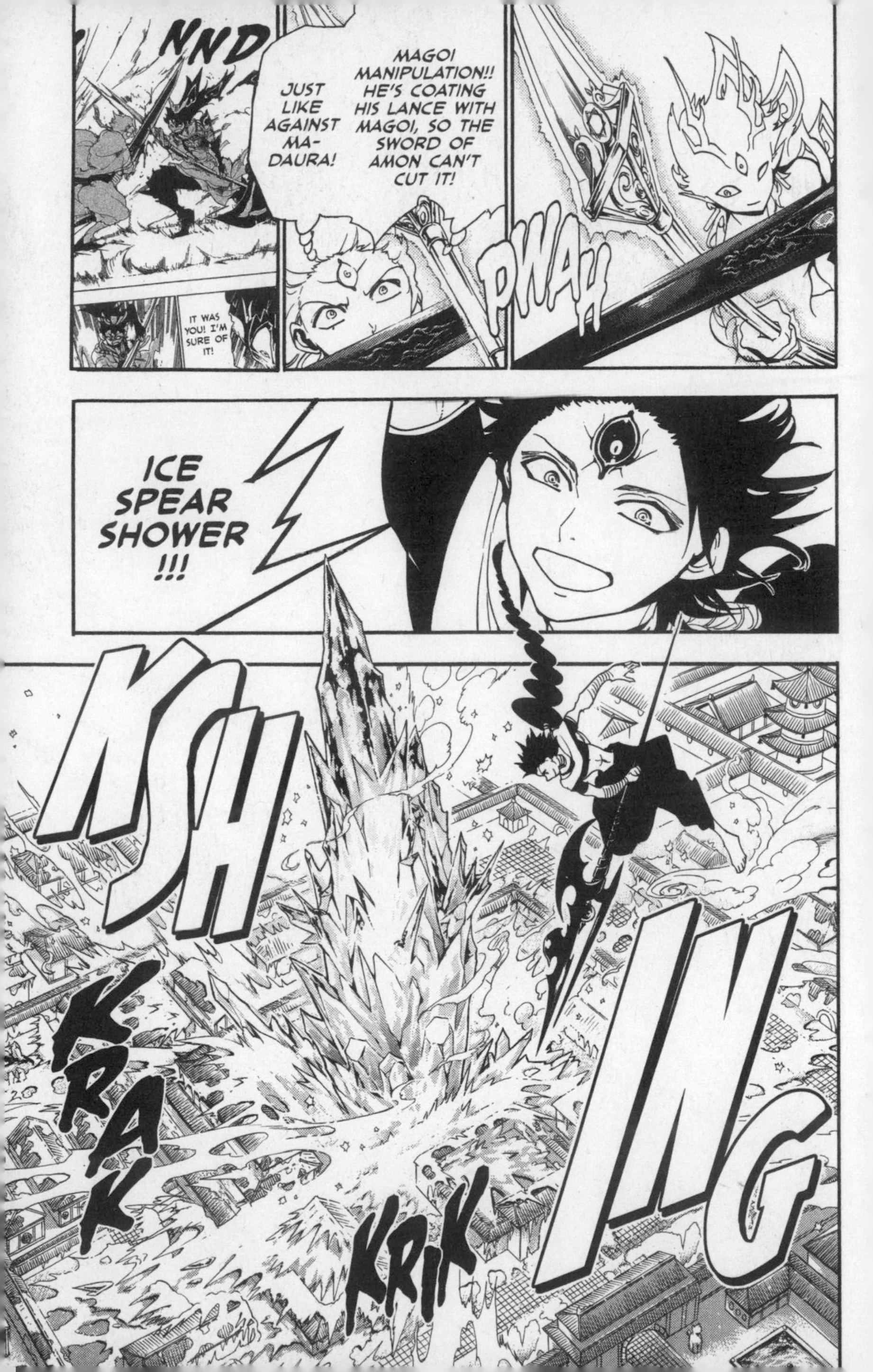
PWAH
MAGOI MANIPULATION!! HE'S COATING HIS LANCE WITH MAGOI, SO THE SWORD OF AMON CAN'T CUT IT!
JUST LIKE AGAINST MA-DAURA!
NND
IT WAS YOU! I'M SURE OF IT!
ICE SPEAR SHOWER !!!
NSH
ING
KRAK
KRIK

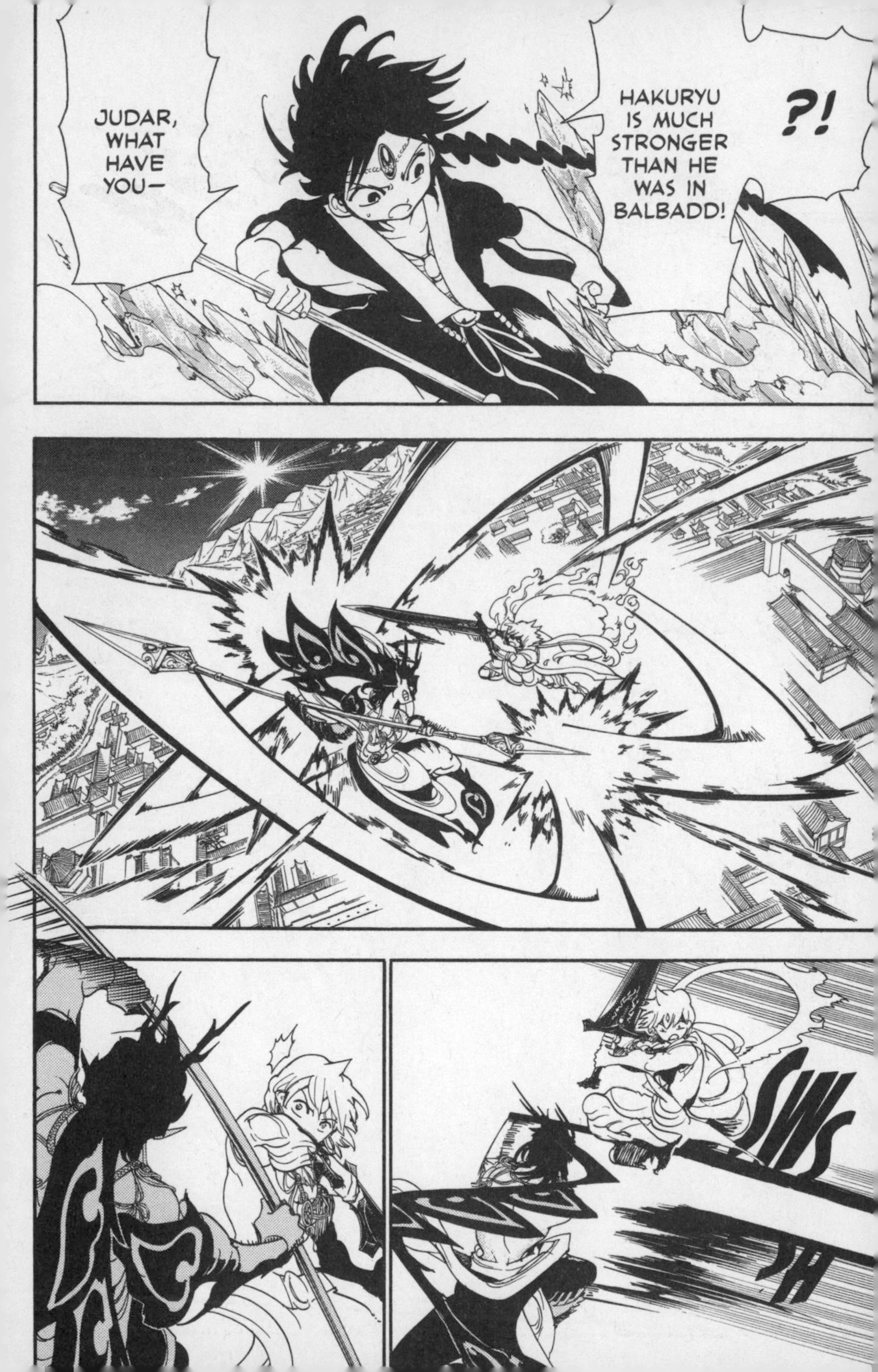
?!
HAKURYU IS MUCH STRONGER THAN HE WAS IN BALBADD!
JUDAR, WHAT HAVE YOU—

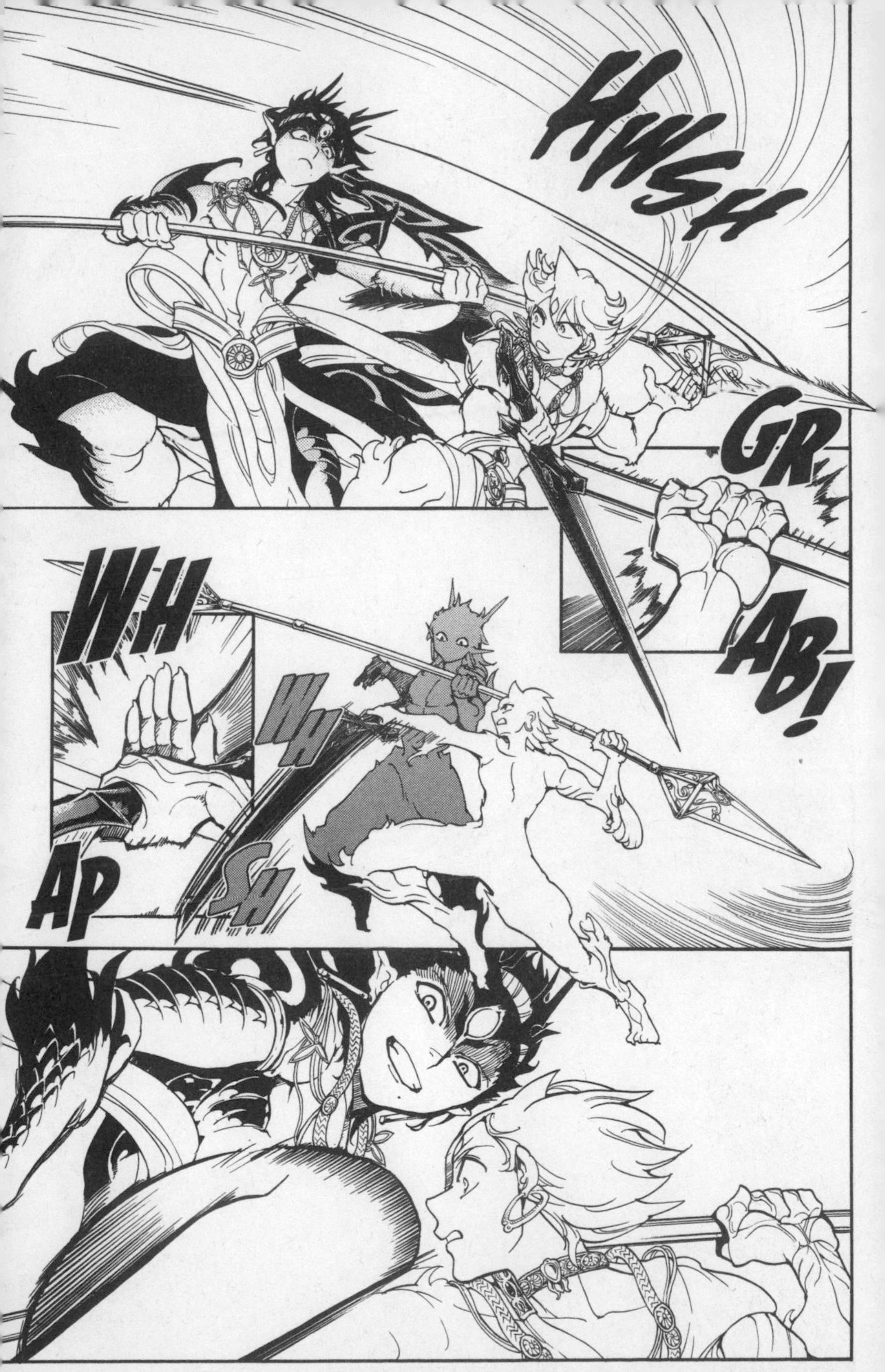
HWSH
GRAB!
WHSH
WHAP

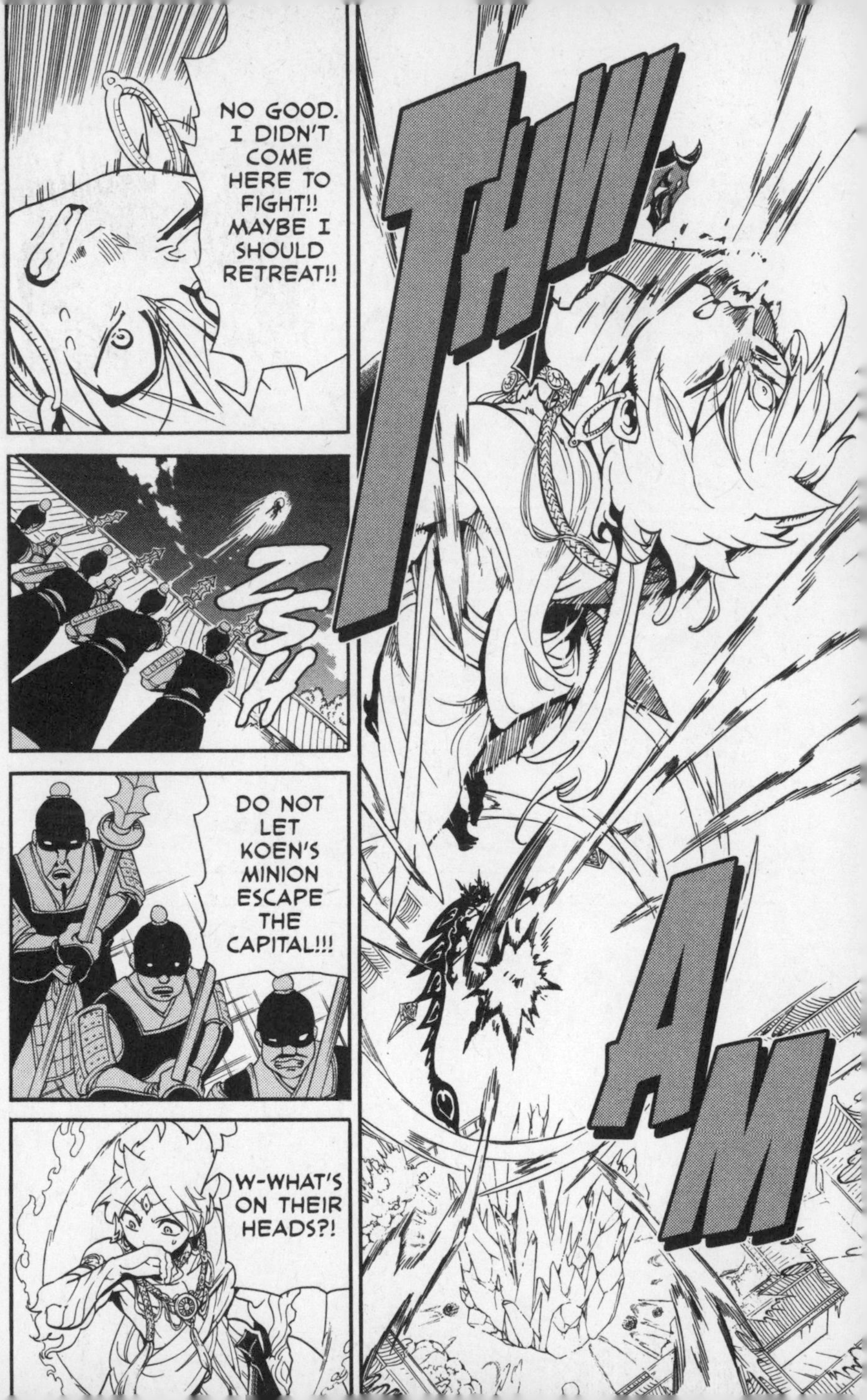
THU
AM
NO GOOD. I DIDN'T COME HERE TO FIGHT!! MAYBE I SHOULD RETREAT!!
ZWSH
DO NOT LET KOEN'S MINION ESCAPE THE CAPITAL!!!
W-WHAT'S ON THEIR HEADS?!

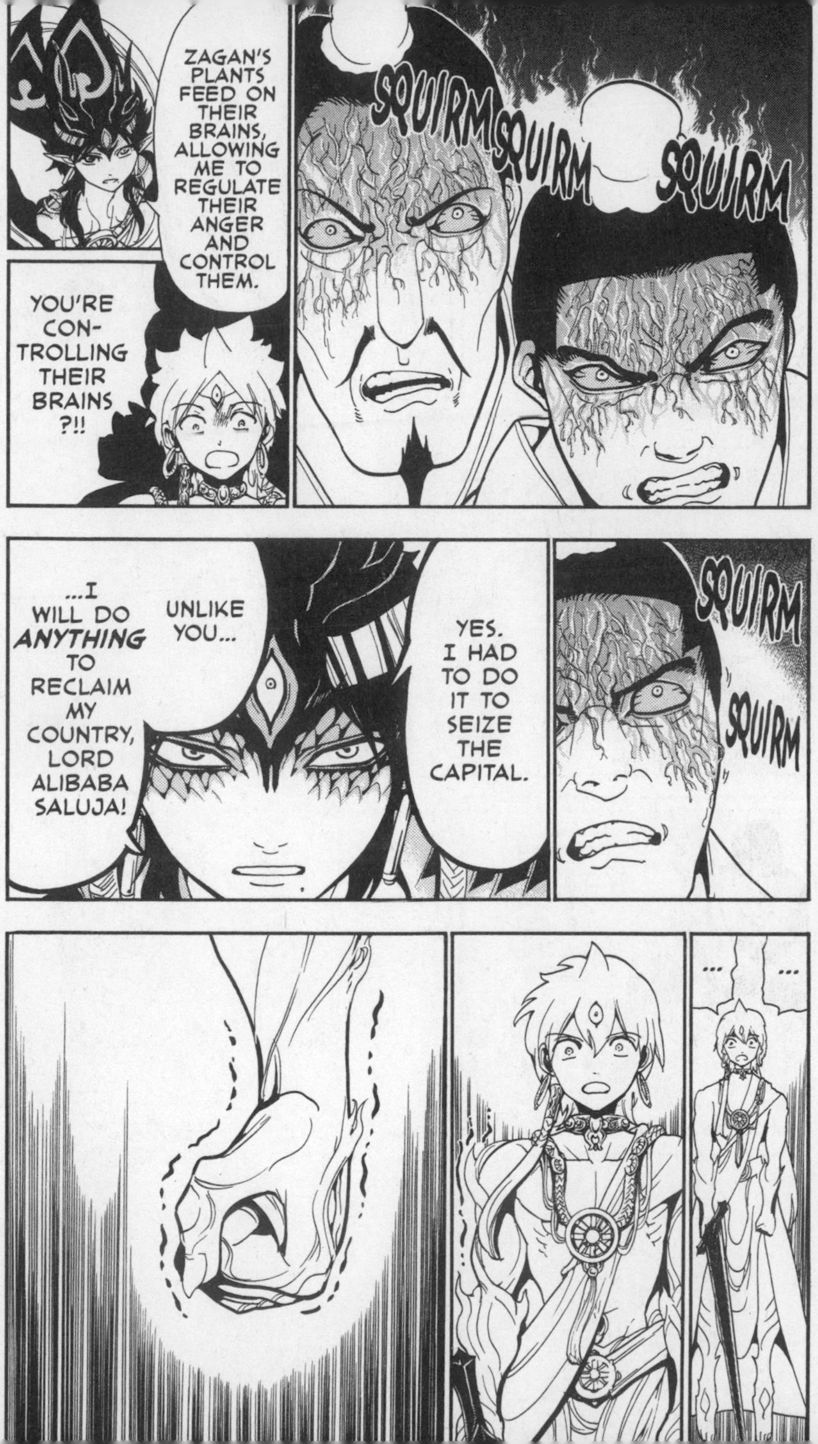
SQUIRM SQUIRM SQUIRM
ZAGAN'S PLANTS FEED ON THEIR BRAINS, ALLOWING ME TO REGULATE THEIR ANGER AND CONTROL THEM.
YOU'RE CON-TROLLING THEIR BRAINS ?!!
SQUIRM SQUIRM
YES. I HAD TO DO IT TO SEIZE THE CAPITAL.
UNLIKE YOU...
...I WILL DO ANYTHING TO RECLAIM MY COUNTRY, LORD ALIBABA SALUJA!
... ...

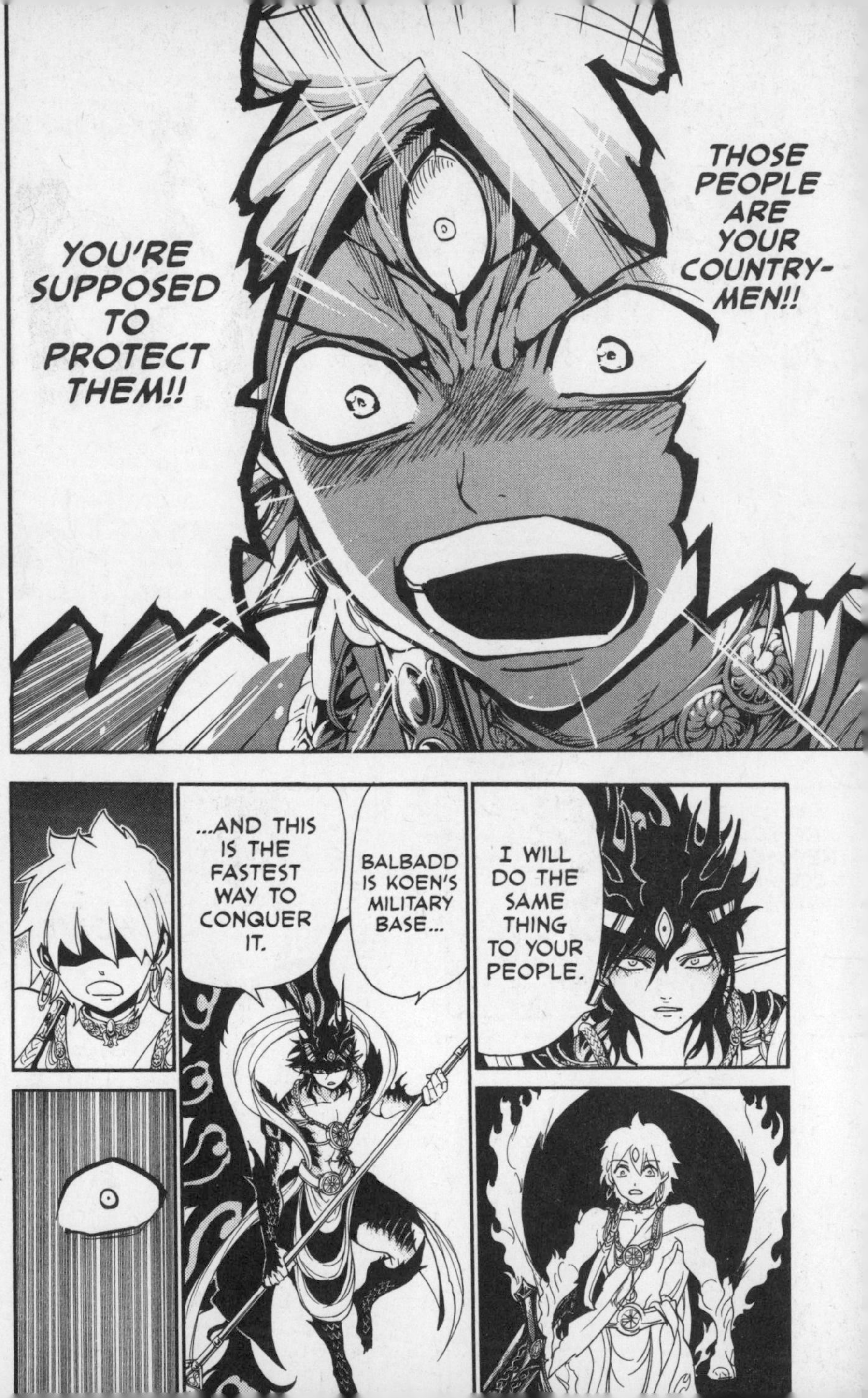
THOSE PEOPLE ARE YOUR COUNTRY-MEN!!
YOU'RE SUPPOSED TO PROTECT THEM!!
I WILL DO THE SAME THING TO YOUR PEOPLE.
BALBADD IS KOEN'S MILITARY BASE...
...AND THIS IS THE FASTEST WAY TO CONQUER IT.

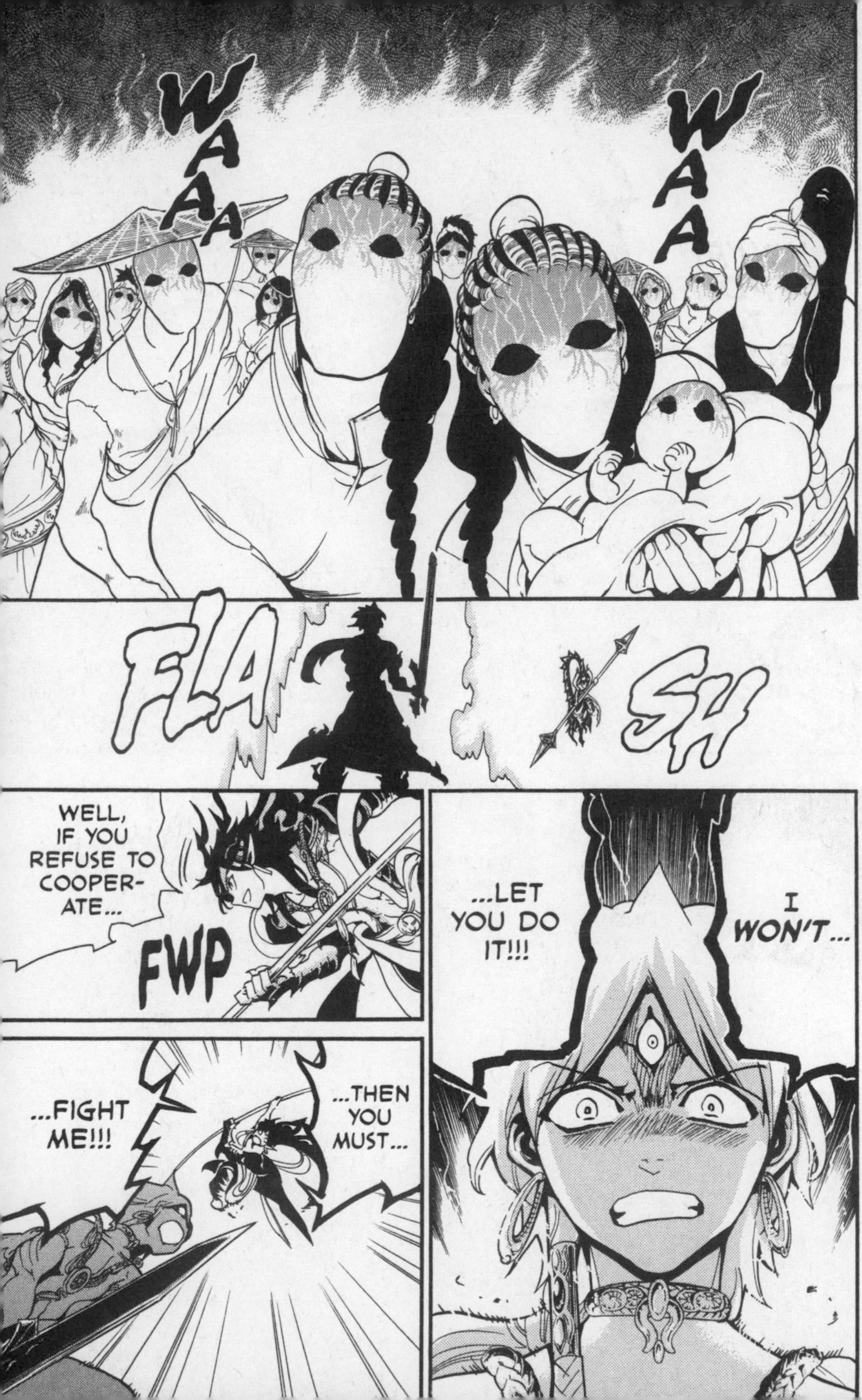
WAAA
WAAA
FLASH
I WON'T...
...LET YOU DO IT!!!
WELL, IF YOU REFUSE TO COOPER-ATE...
FWP
...THEN YOU MUST...
...FIGHT ME!!!

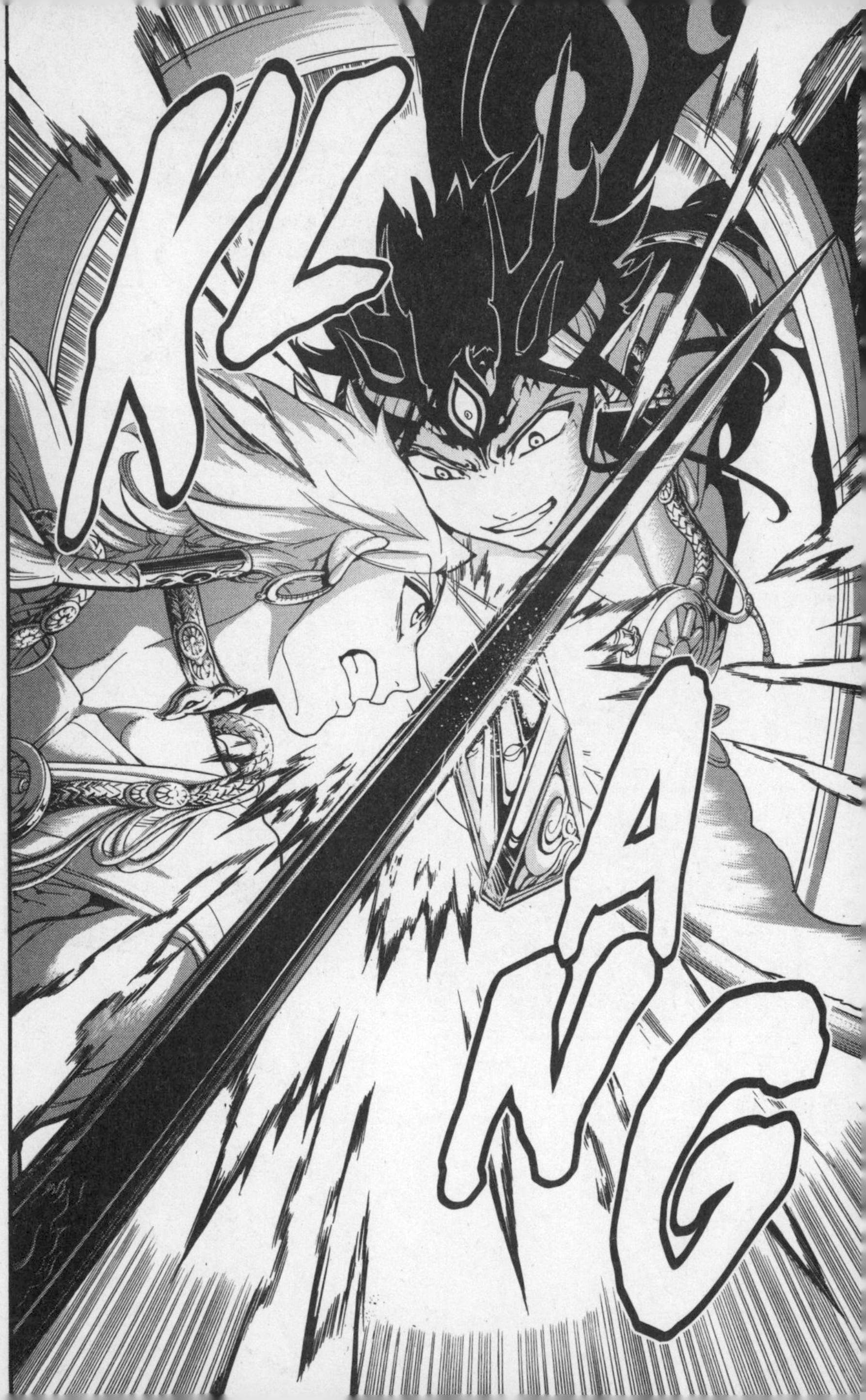
KLANG

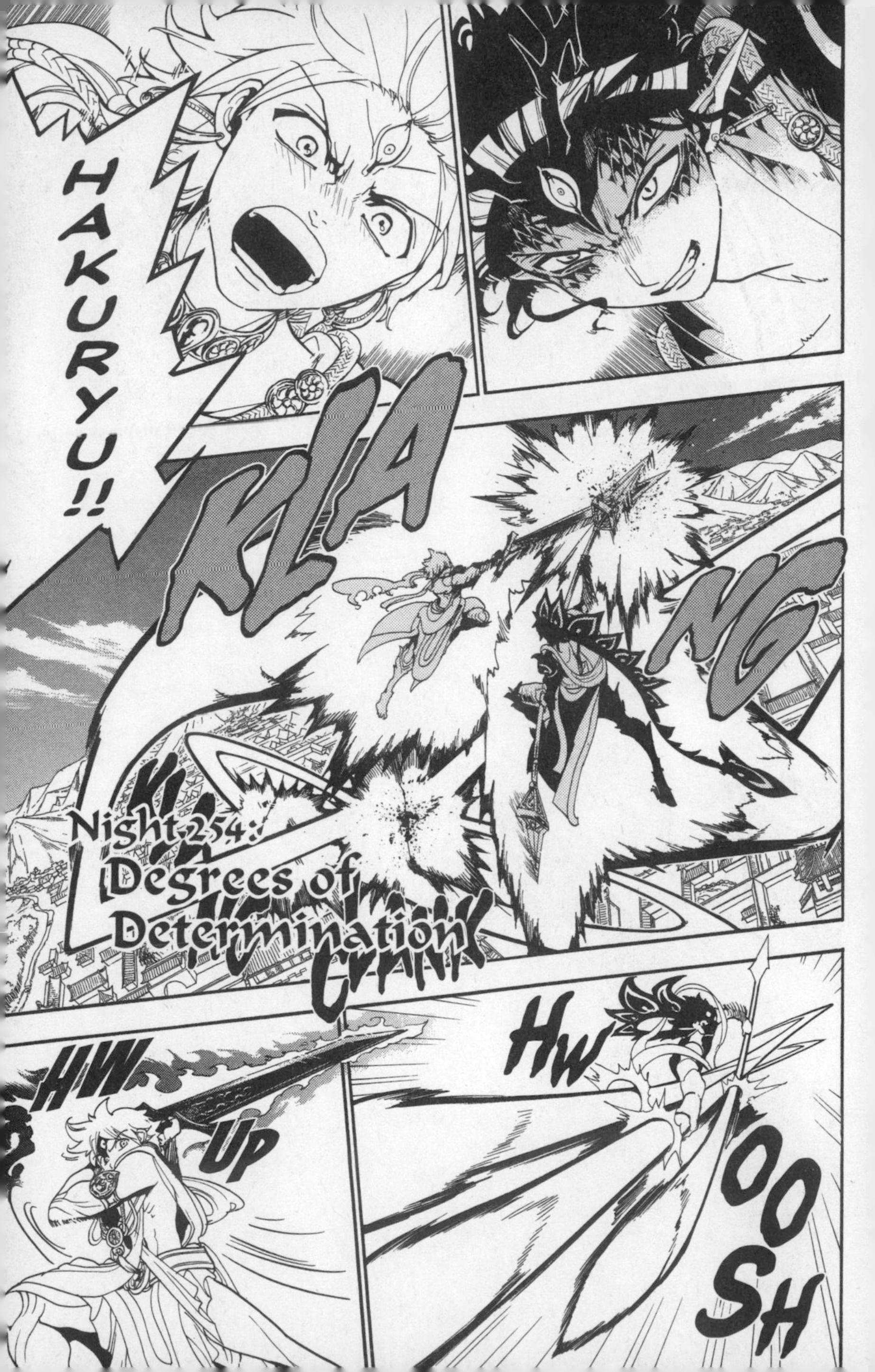

HAKURYU!!
KLANG
Night 254: Degrees of Determination
CRANK
HWOOSH
HWUP

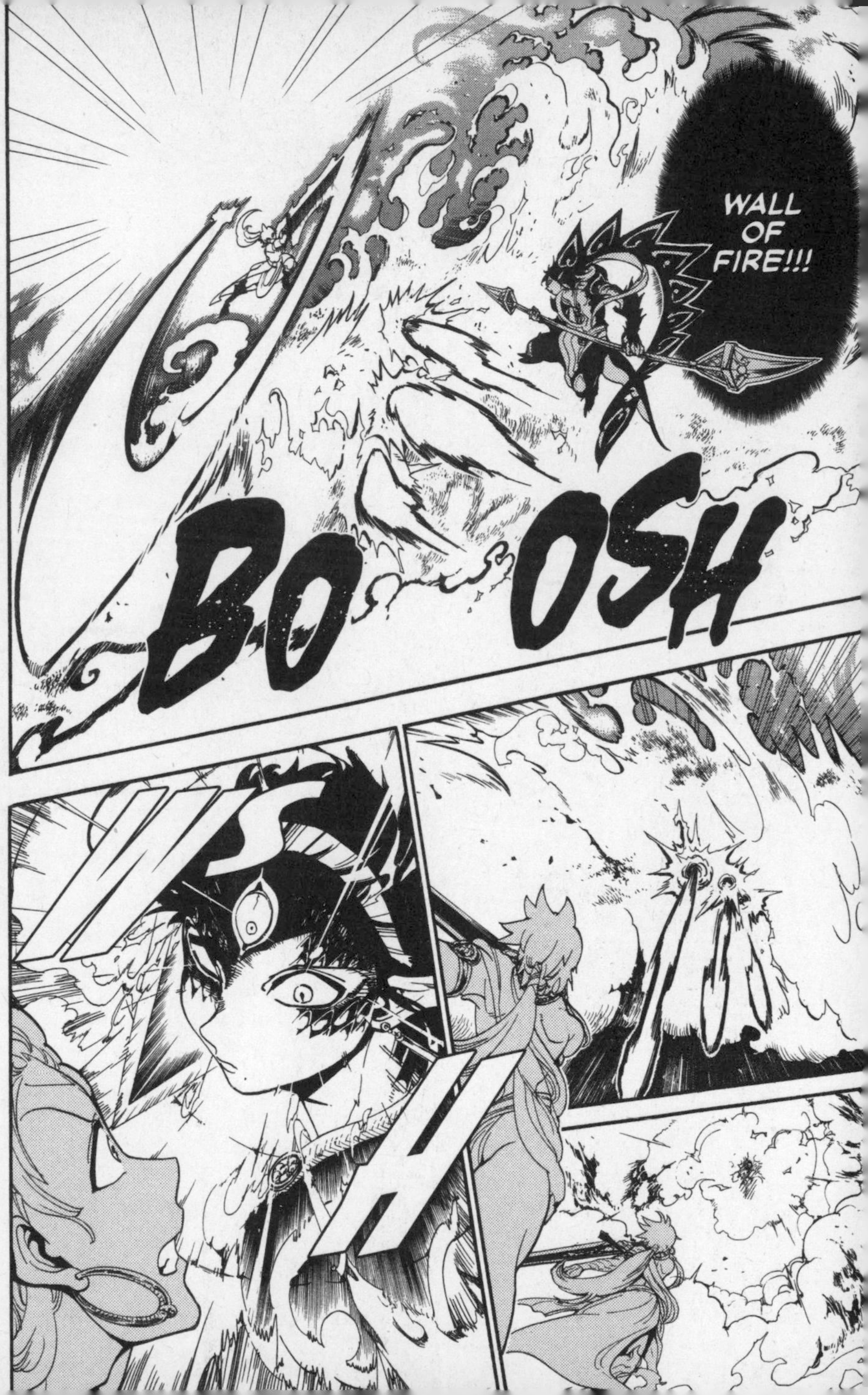
WALL OF FIRE!!!
BOOSH
WSH

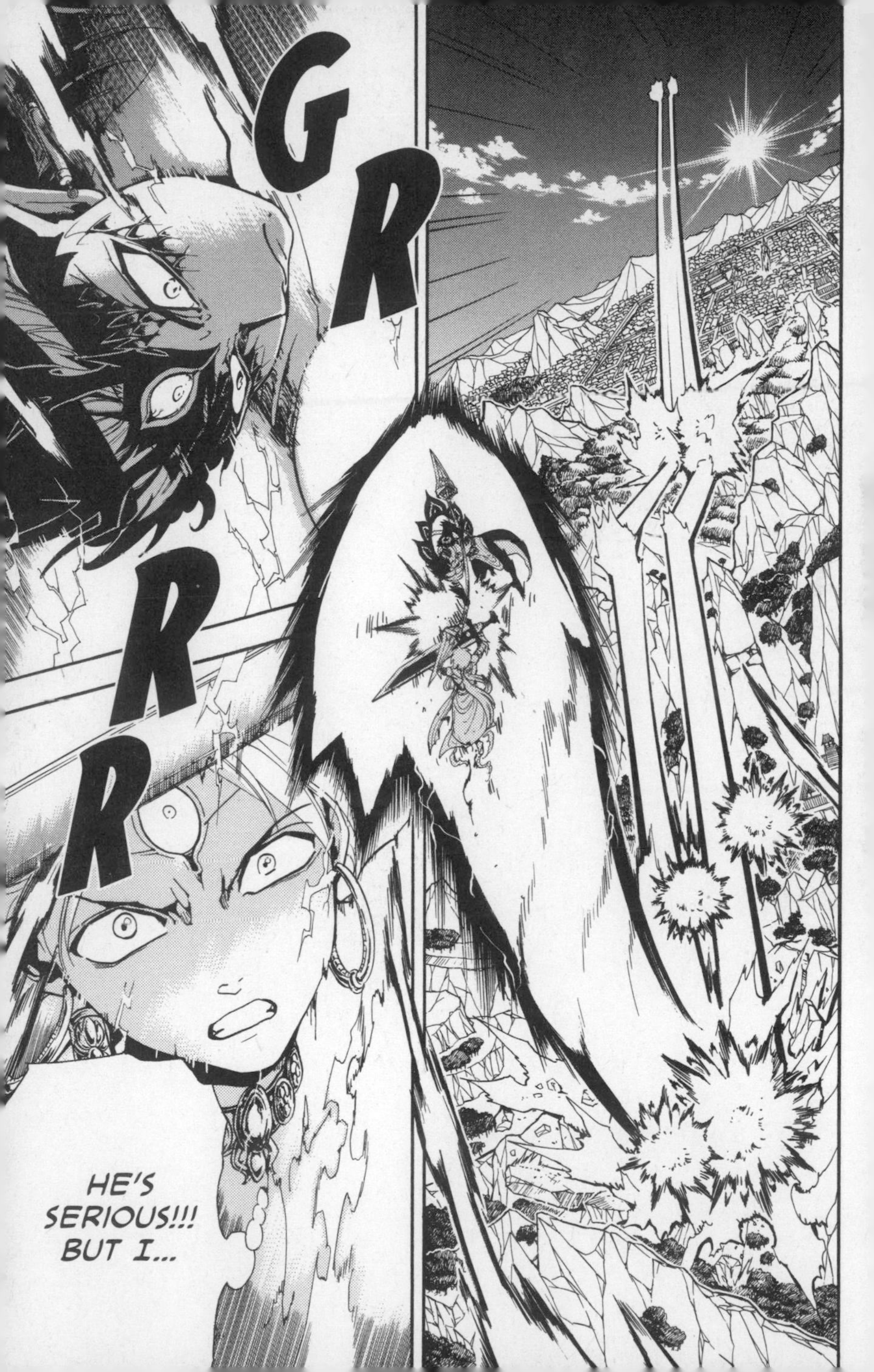
GRRRR
HE'S SERIOUS!!! BUT I...

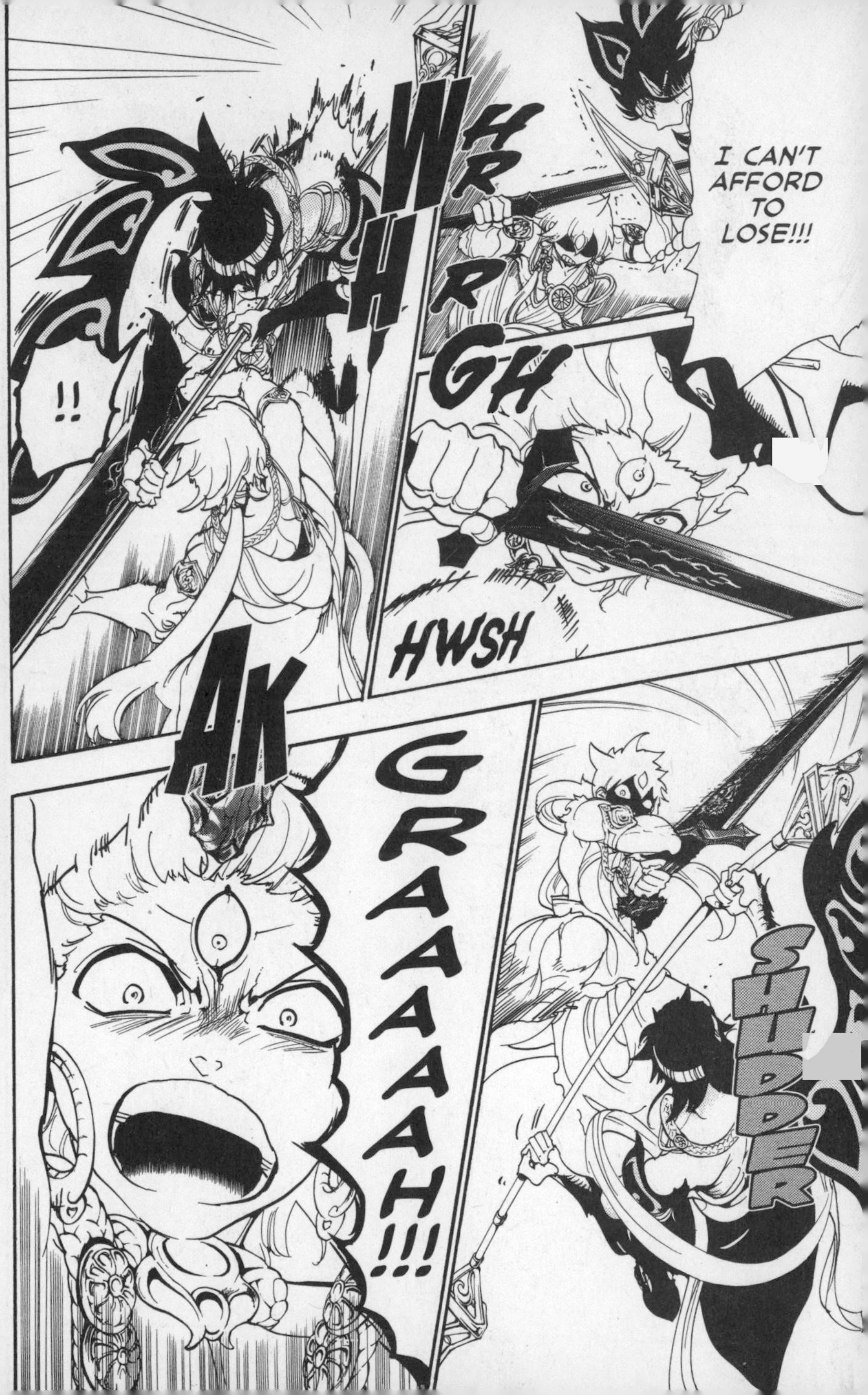
I CAN'T AFFORD TO LOSE!!!
WHH
HRRGH
!!
HWSH
AK
SHUDDER
GRAAAAH!!!

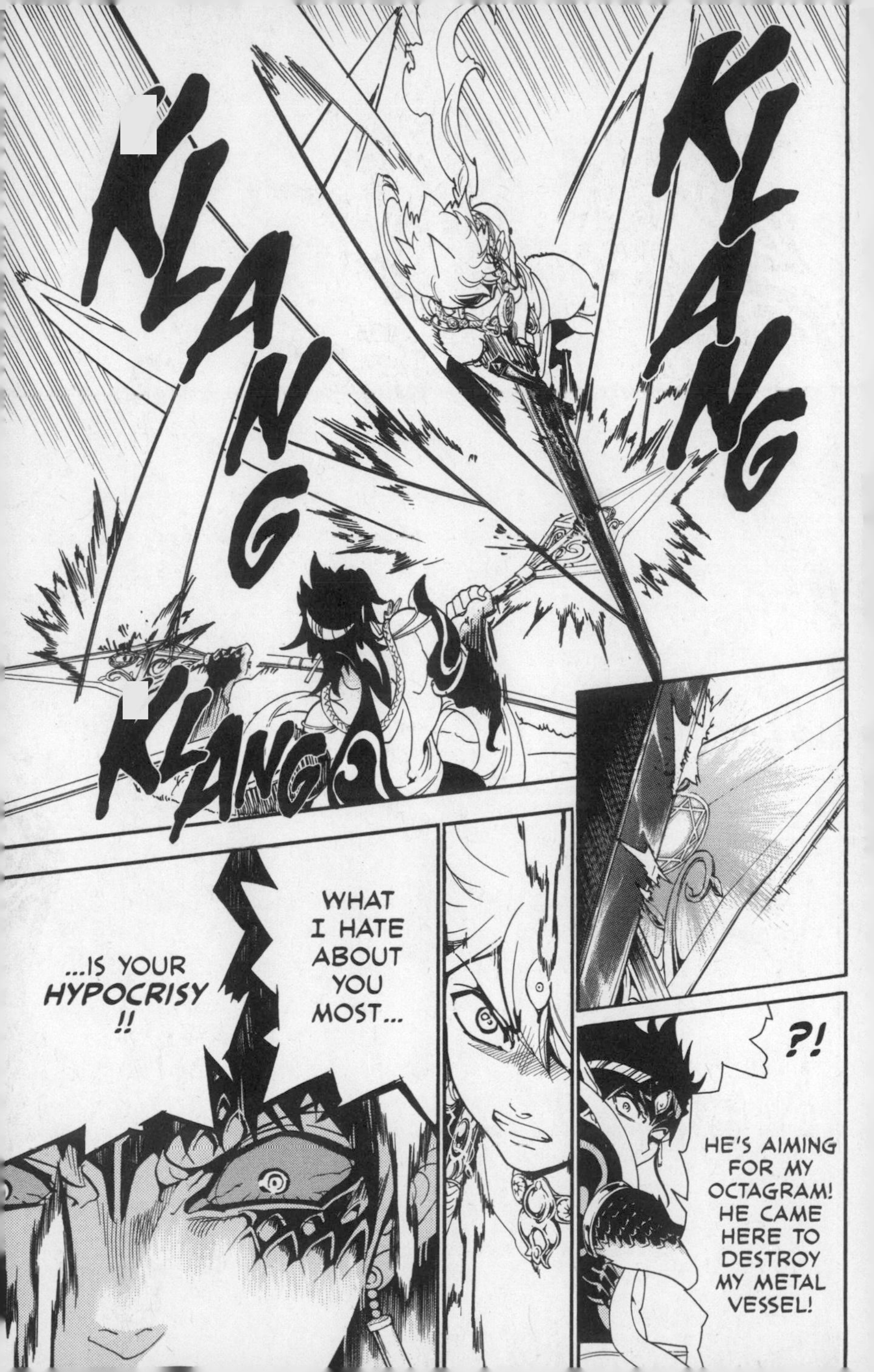
KLANG
KLANG
KLANG
?!
HE'S AIMING FOR MY OCTAGRAM! HE CAME HERE TO DESTROY MY METAL VESSEL!
WHAT I HATE ABOUT YOU MOST...
...IS YOUR *HYPOCRISY*!!

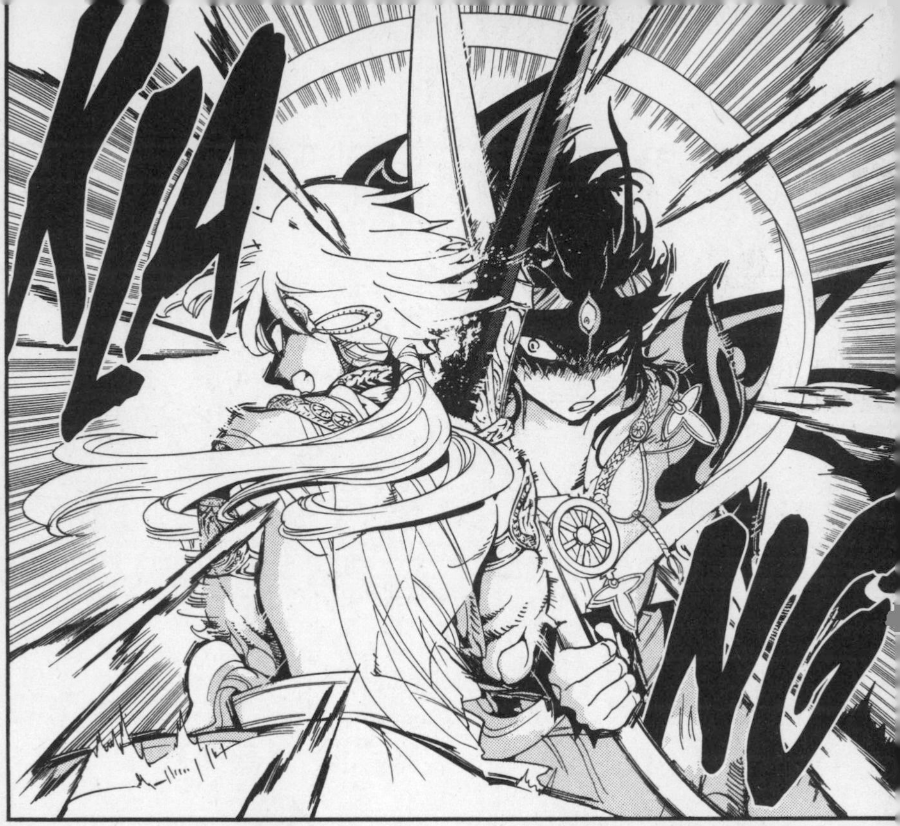

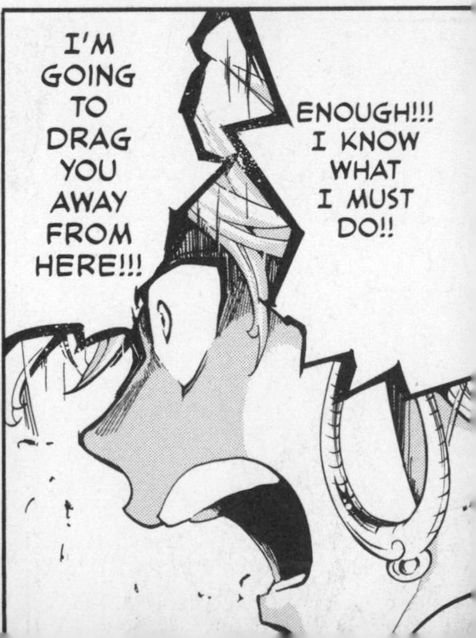
ENOUGH!!! I KNOW WHAT I MUST DO!!
I'M GOING TO DRAG YOU AWAY FROM HERE!!!

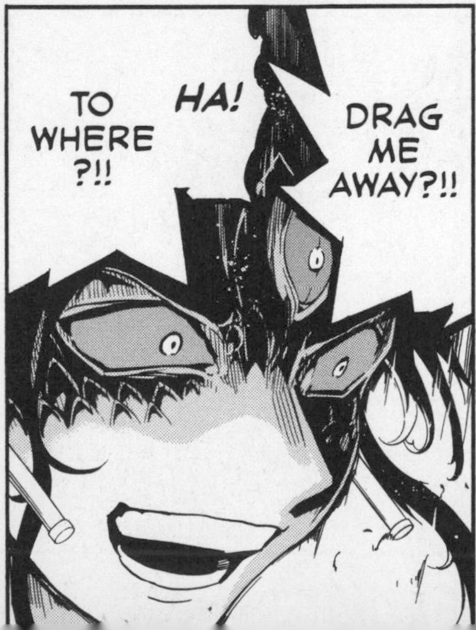
DRAG ME AWAY?!!
HA!
TO WHERE ?!!

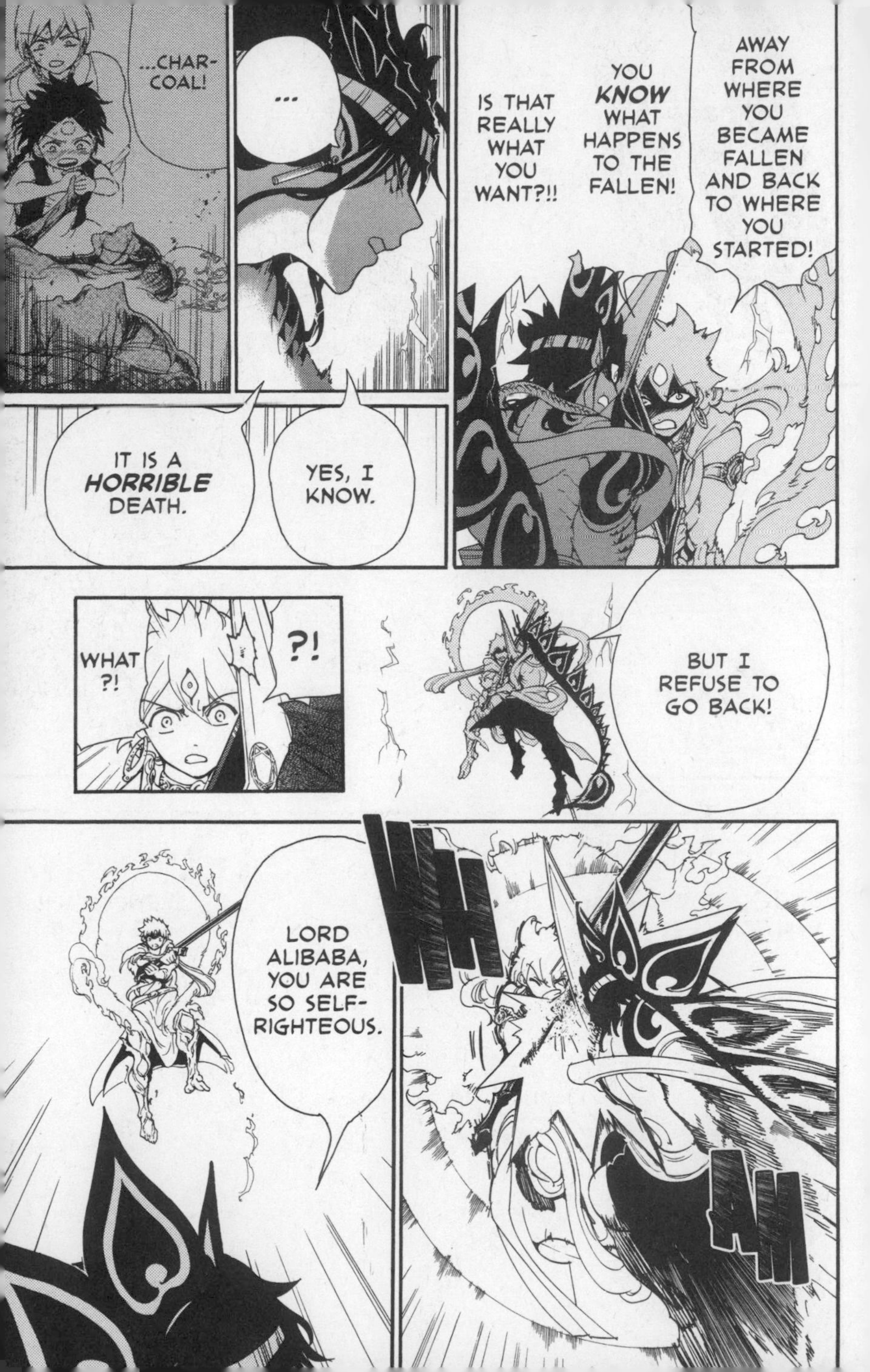

AWAY FROM WHERE YOU BECAME FALLEN AND BACK TO WHERE YOU STARTED!
YOU *KNOW* WHAT HAPPENS TO THE FALLEN!
IS THAT REALLY WHAT YOU WANT?!!
...
...CHAR-COAL!
YES, I KNOW.
IT IS A *HORRIBLE* DEATH.
BUT I REFUSE TO GO BACK!
?!
WHAT ?!
WHH
AM
LORD ALIBABA, YOU ARE SO SELF-RIGHTEOUS.

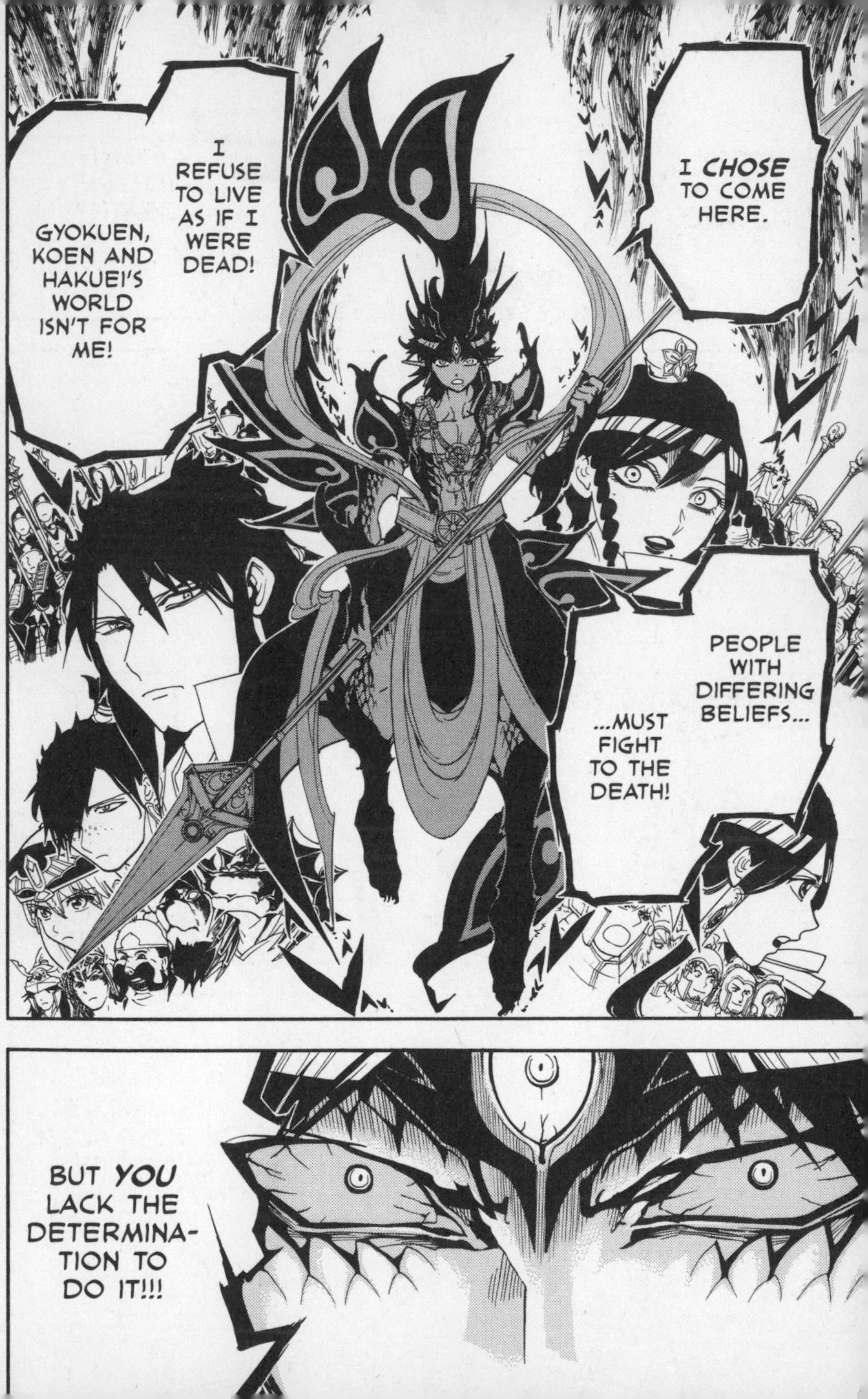
I *CHOSE* TO COME HERE.
I REFUSE TO LIVE AS IF I WERE DEAD!
GYOKUEN, KOEN AND HAKUEI'S WORLD ISN'T FOR ME!
PEOPLE WITH DIFFERING BELIEFS...
...MUST FIGHT TO THE DEATH!
BUT *YOU* LACK THE DETERMINA-TION TO DO IT!!!

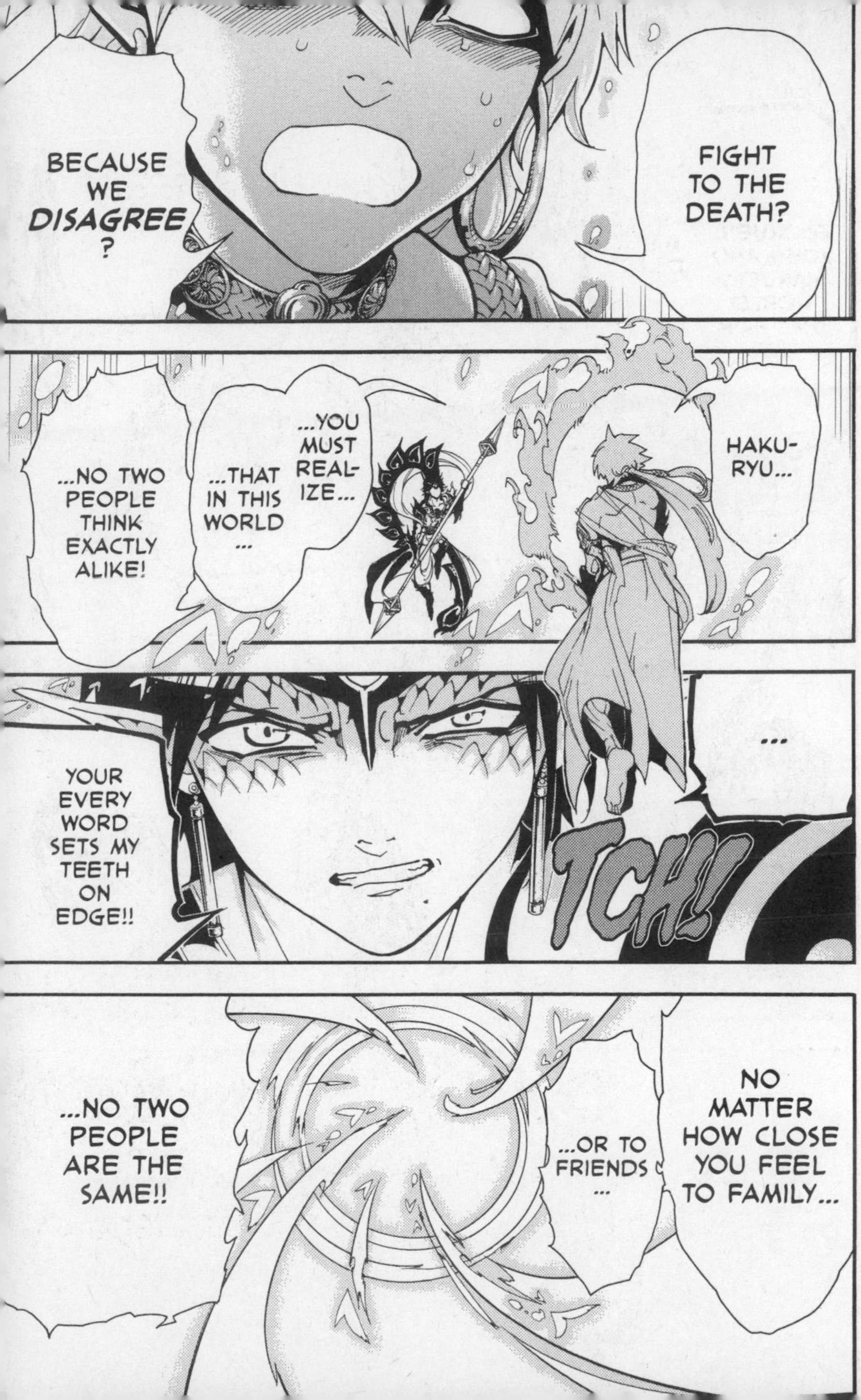
FIGHT TO THE DEATH?
BECAUSE WE DISAGREE?
HAKU-RYU...
...YOU MUST REAL-IZE...
...THAT IN THIS WORLD...
...NO TWO PEOPLE THINK EXACTLY ALIKE!
...
TCH!
YOUR EVERY WORD SETS MY TEETH ON EDGE!!
NO MATTER HOW CLOSE YOU FEEL TO FAMILY...
...OR TO FRIENDS...
...NO TWO PEOPLE ARE THE SAME!!

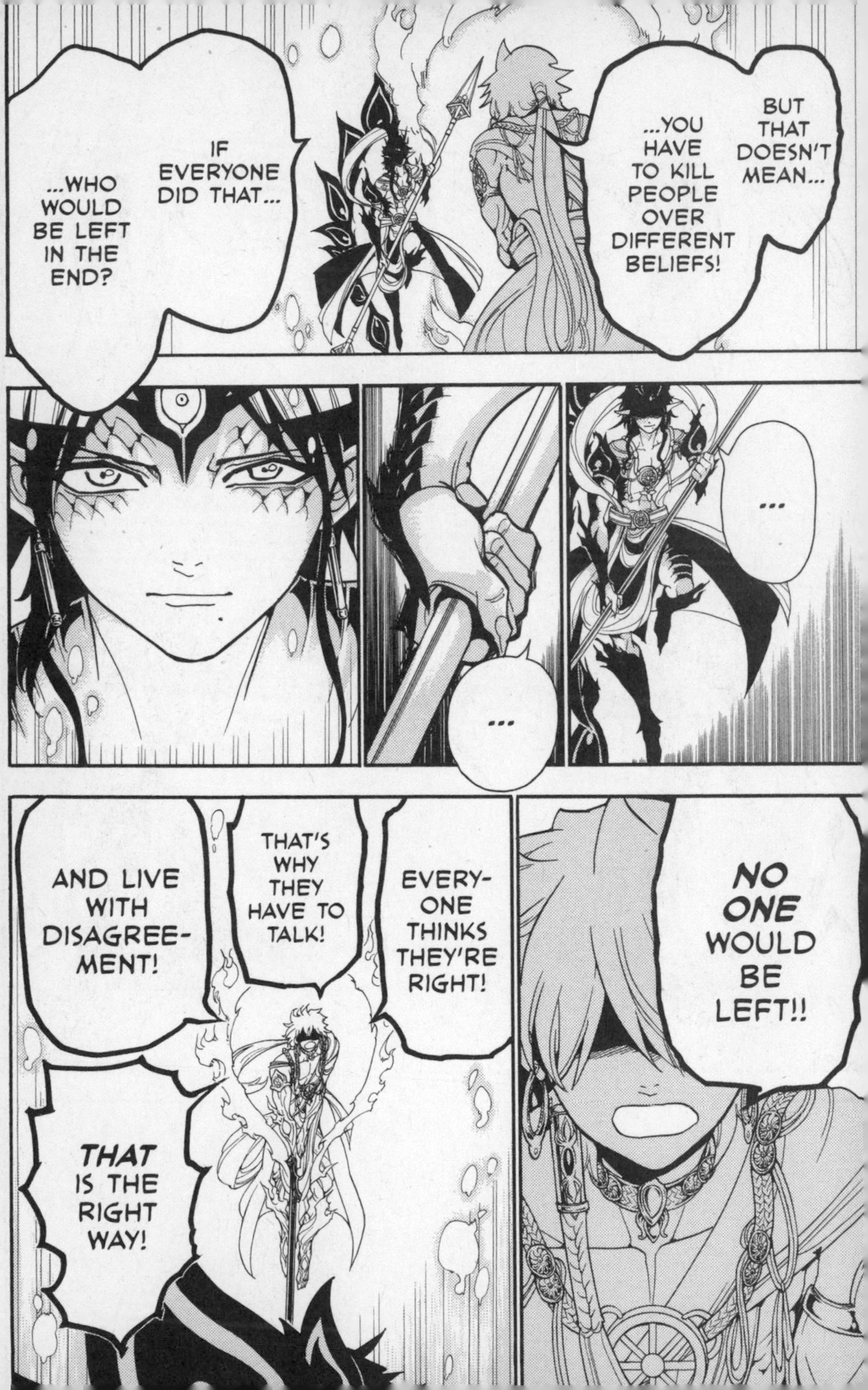
BUT THAT DOESN'T MEAN...
...YOU HAVE TO KILL PEOPLE OVER DIFFERENT BELIEFS!
IF EVERYONE DID THAT...
...WHO WOULD BE LEFT IN THE END?
...
...
NO ONE WOULD BE LEFT!!
EVERY-ONE THINKS THEY'RE RIGHT!
THAT'S WHY THEY HAVE TO TALK!
AND LIVE WITH DISAGREE-MENT!
THAT IS THE RIGHT WAY!

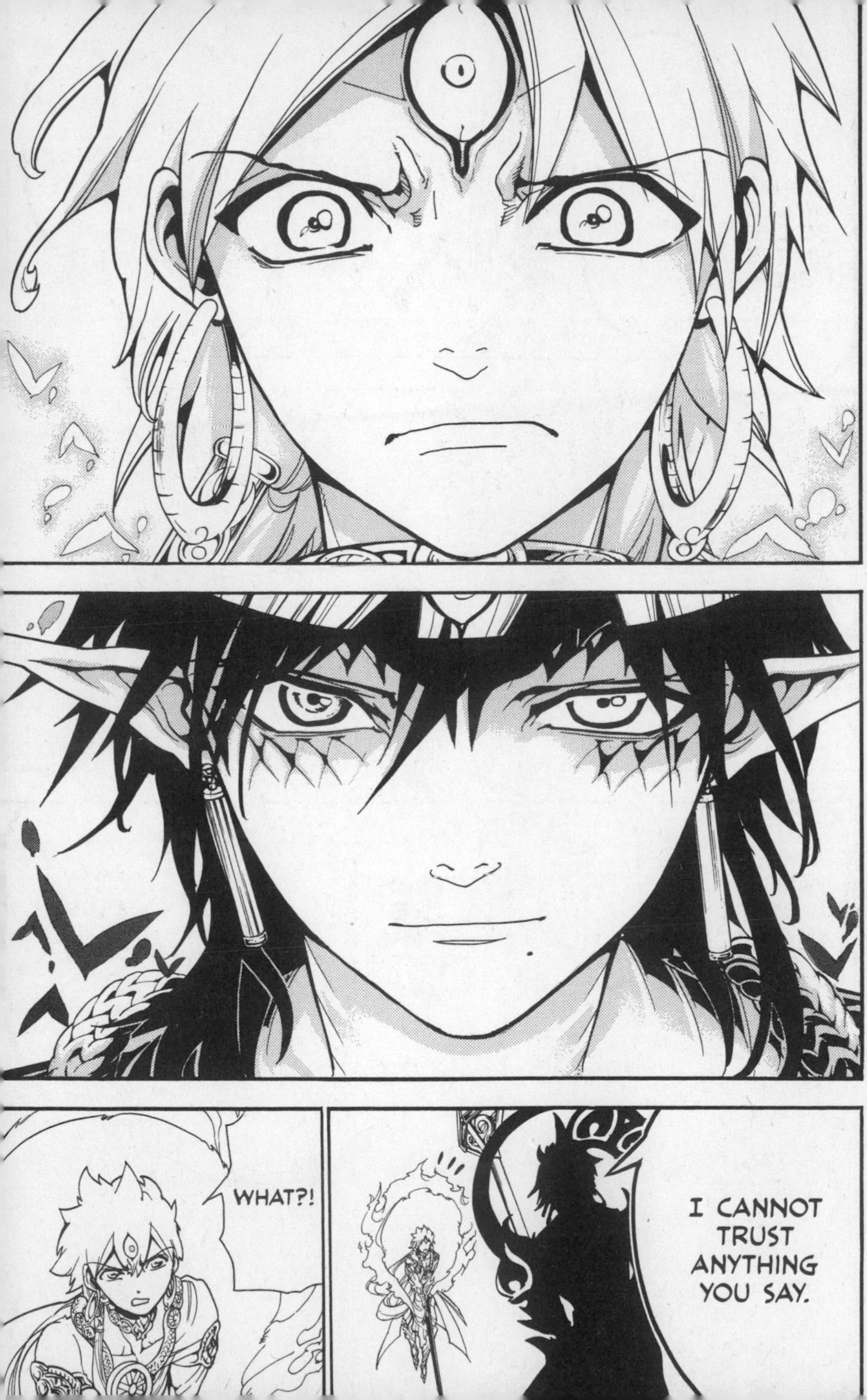
I CANNOT TRUST ANYTHING YOU SAY.
WHAT?!

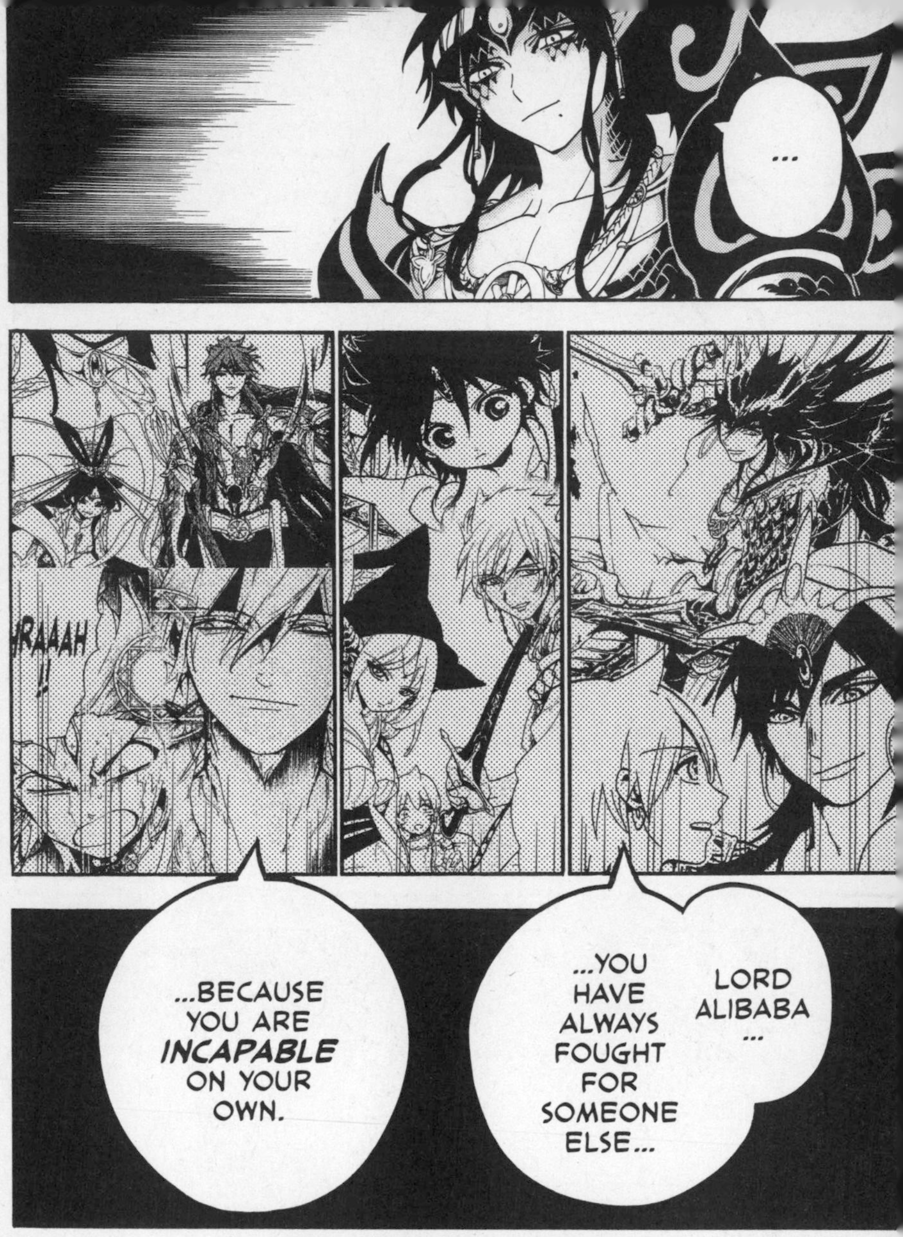
...
HRAAAH !!
LORD ALIBABA...
...YOU HAVE ALWAYS FOUGHT FOR SOMEONE ELSE...
...BECAUSE YOU ARE *INCAPABLE* ON YOUR OWN.

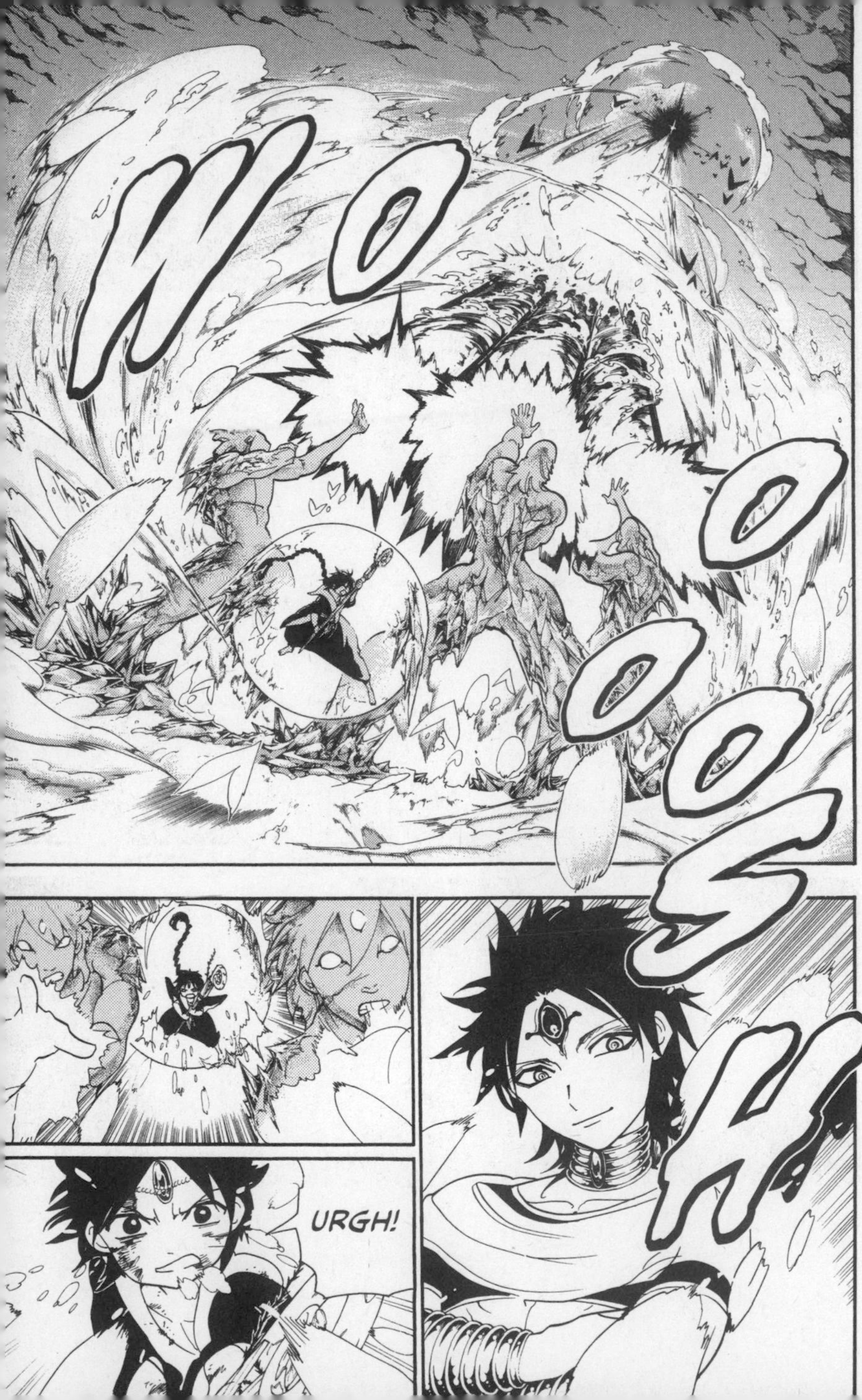
WHOOOOOSH!
URGH!

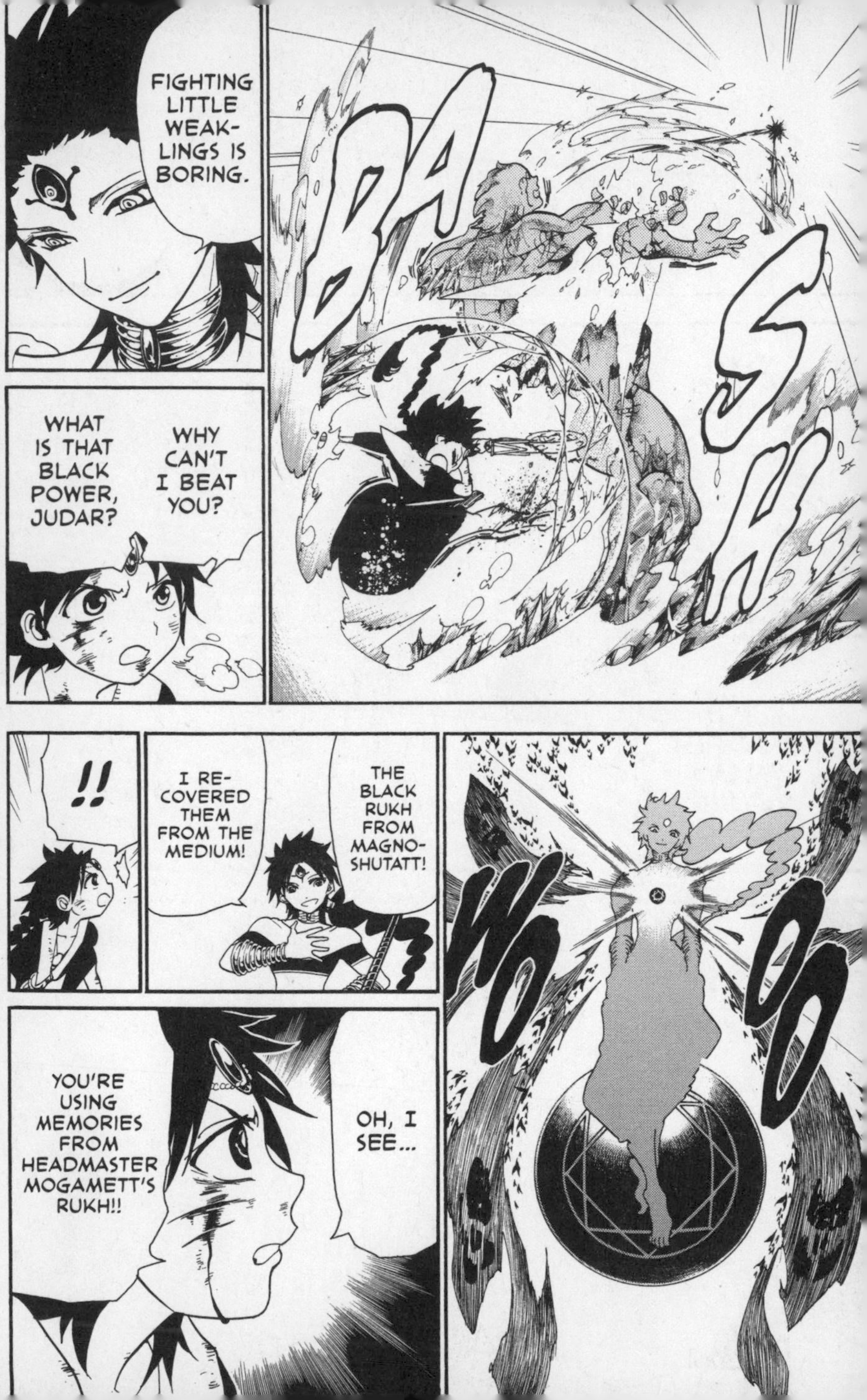
BASH
FIGHTING LITTLE WEAKLINGS IS BORING.
WHY CAN'T I BEAT YOU?
WHAT IS THAT BLACK POWER, JUDAR?
THE BLACK RUKH FROM MAGNOSHUTATT!
I RECOVERED THEM FROM THE MEDIUM!
!!
OH, I SEE...
YOU'RE USING MEMORIES FROM HEADMASTER MOGAMETT'S RUKH!!

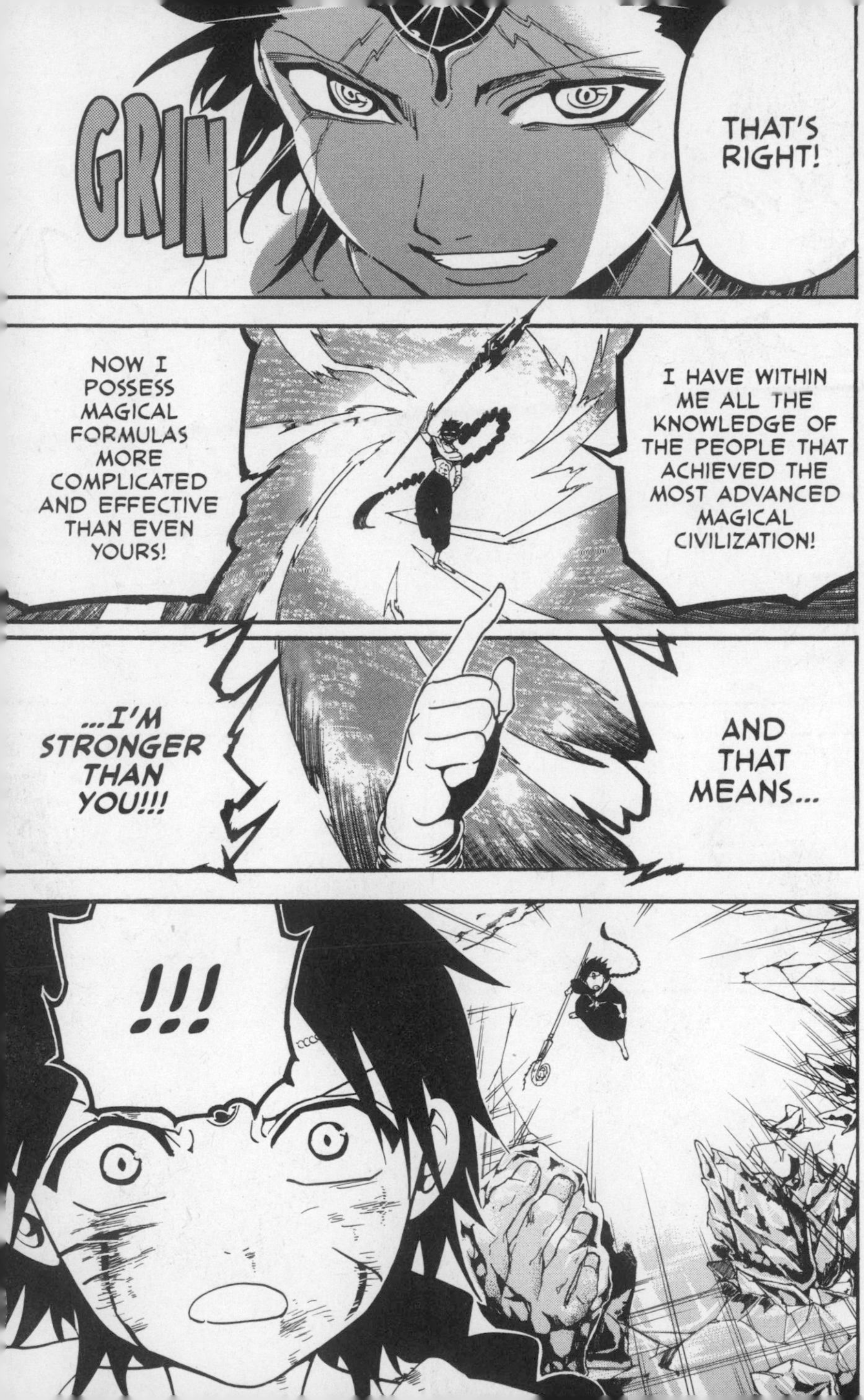
THAT'S RIGHT!
GRIN
I HAVE WITHIN ME ALL THE KNOWLEDGE OF THE PEOPLE THAT ACHIEVED THE MOST ADVANCED MAGICAL CIVILIZATION!
NOW I POSSESS MAGICAL FORMULAS MORE COMPLICATED AND EFFECTIVE THAN EVEN YOURS!
AND THAT MEANS...
...I'M STRONGER THAN YOU!!!
!!!

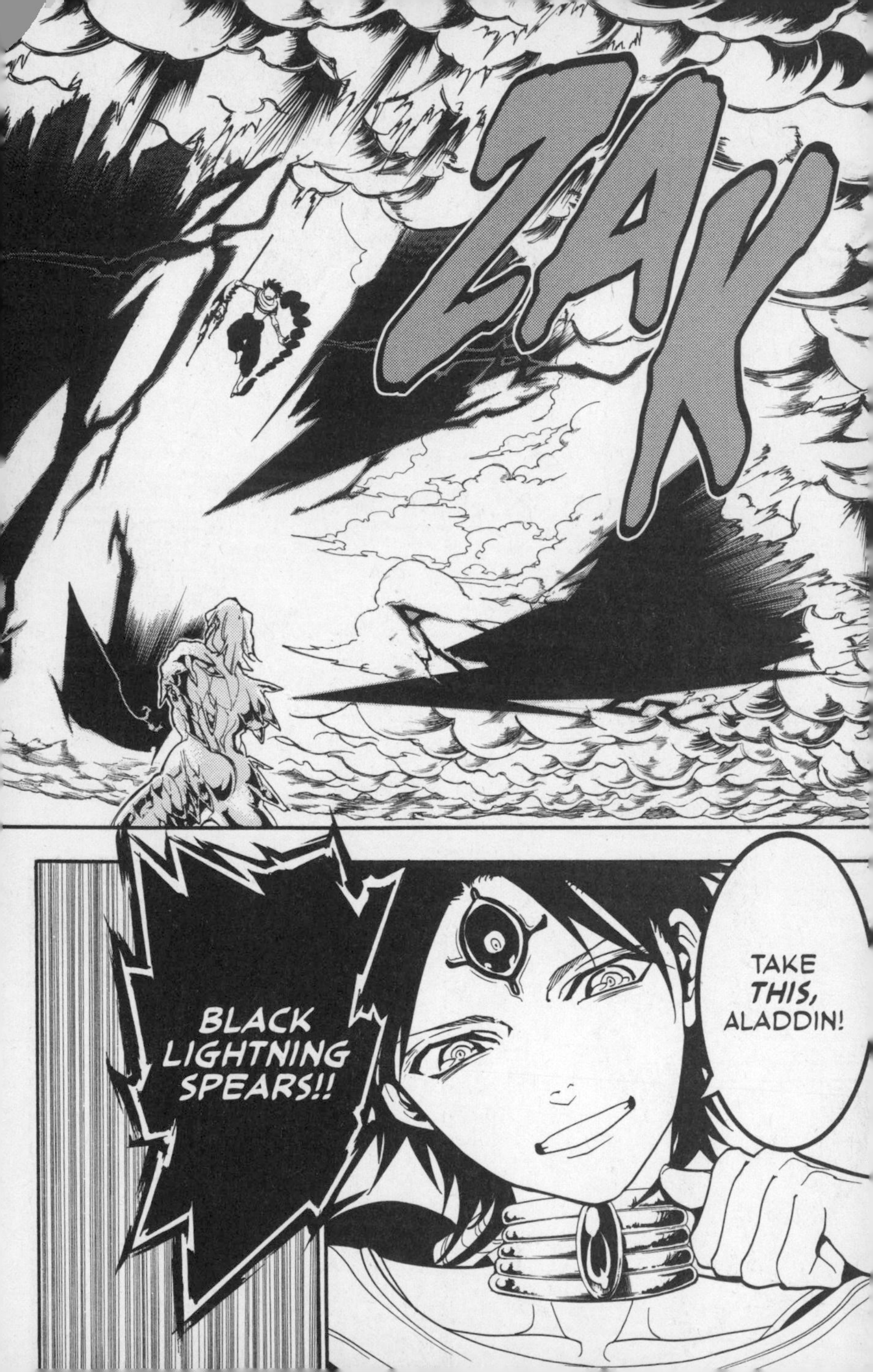
ZAK
TAKE THIS, ALADDIN!
BLACK LIGHTNING SPEARS!!

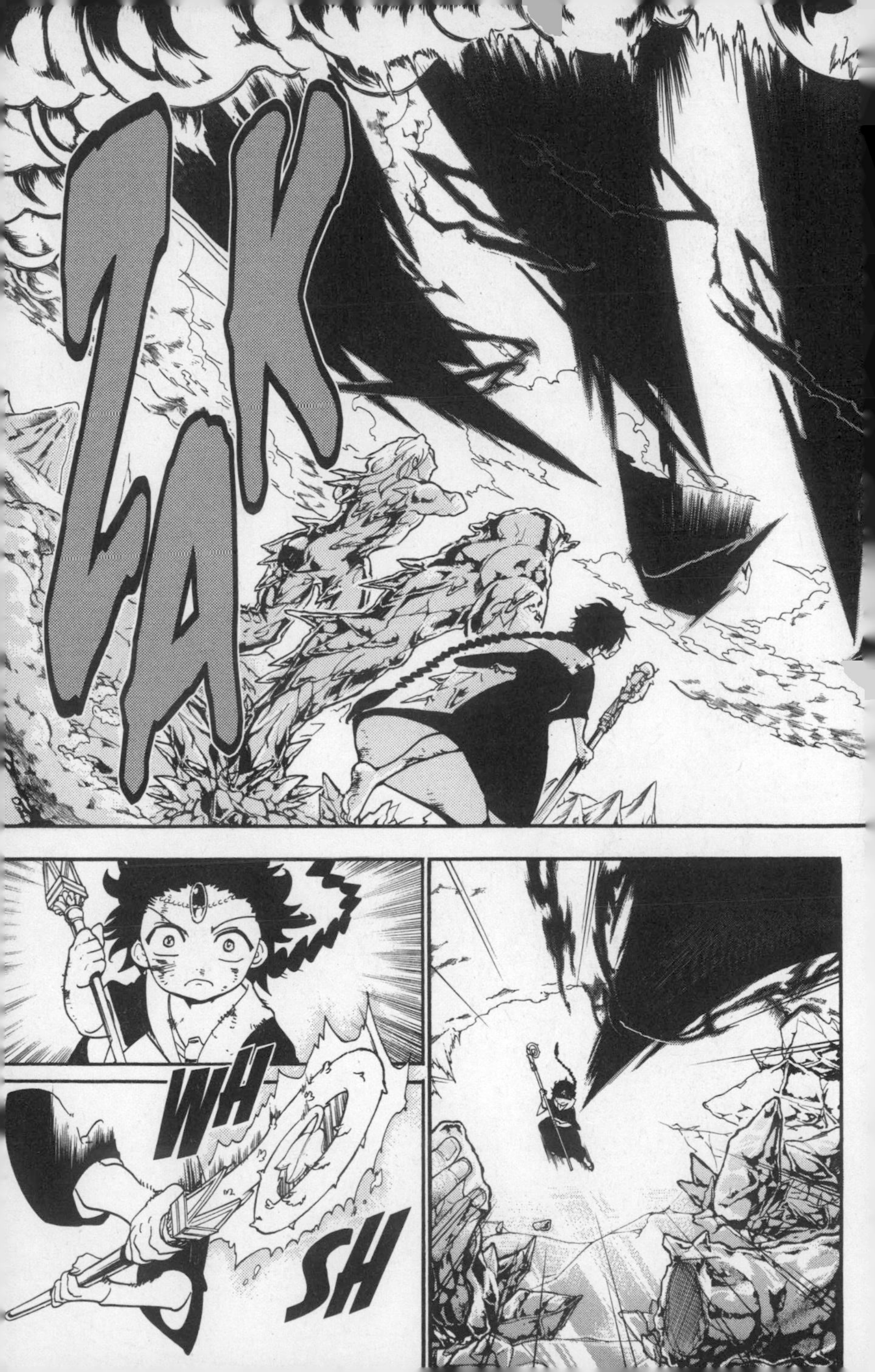
ZAK ZAK
WH
SH

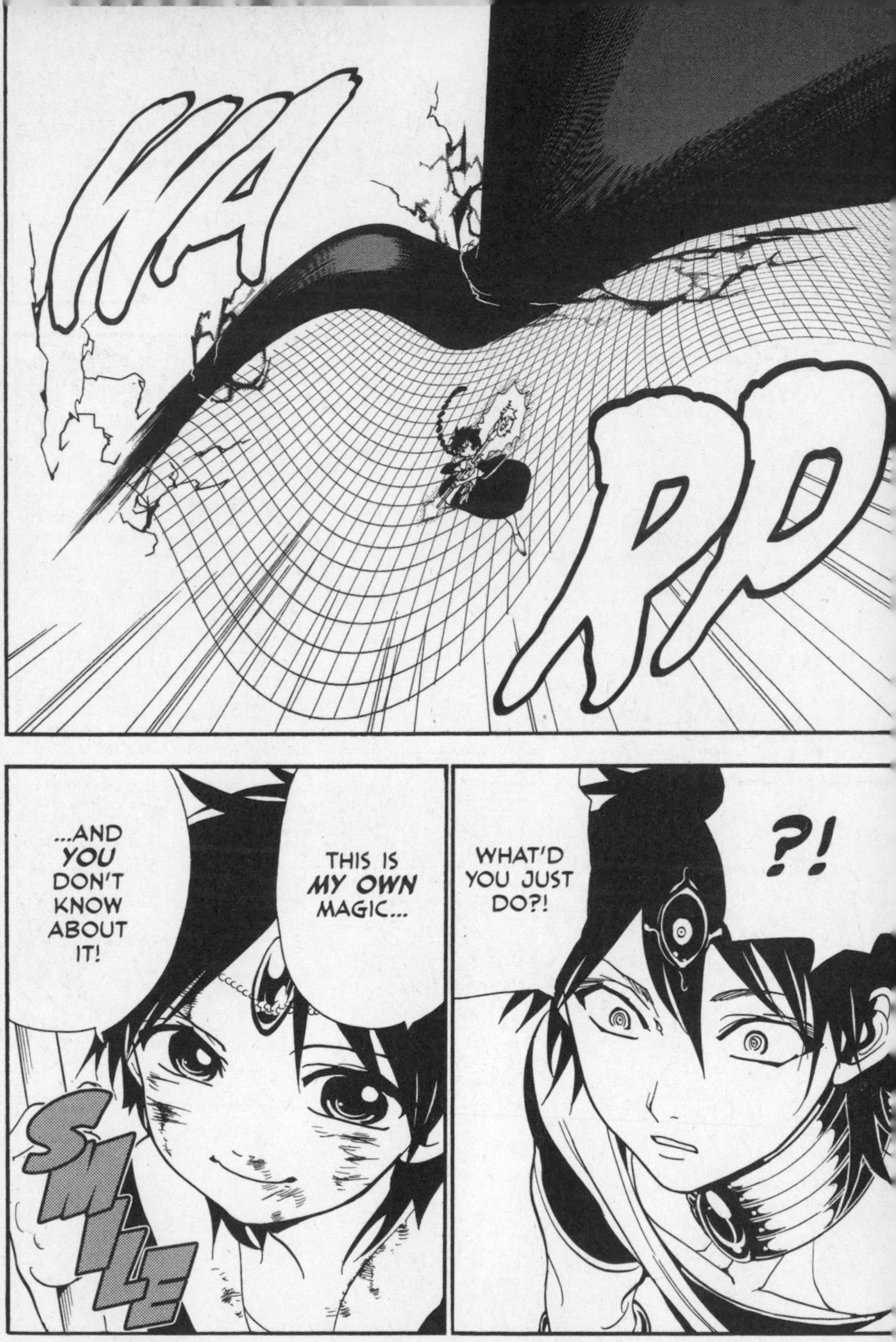
WARP
?!
WHAT'D YOU JUST DO?!
THIS IS MY OWN MAGIC...
...AND YOU DON'T KNOW ABOUT IT!
SMILE

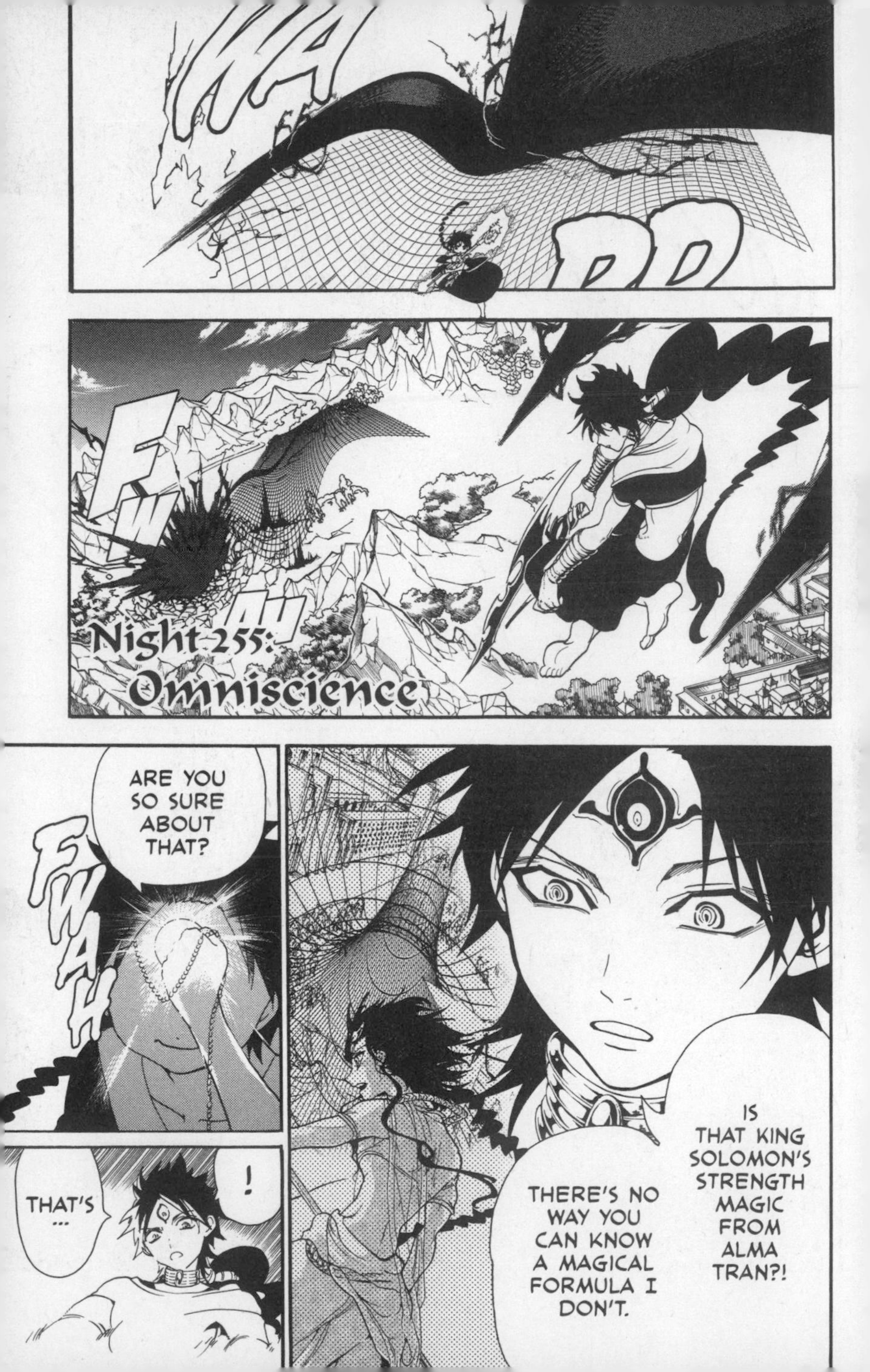
Night 255: Omniscience
IS THAT KING SOLOMON'S STRENGTH MAGIC FROM ALMA TRAN?!
THERE'S NO WAY YOU CAN KNOW A MAGICAL FORMULA I DON'T.
ARE YOU SO SURE ABOUT THAT?
FWAH
!
THAT'S ...

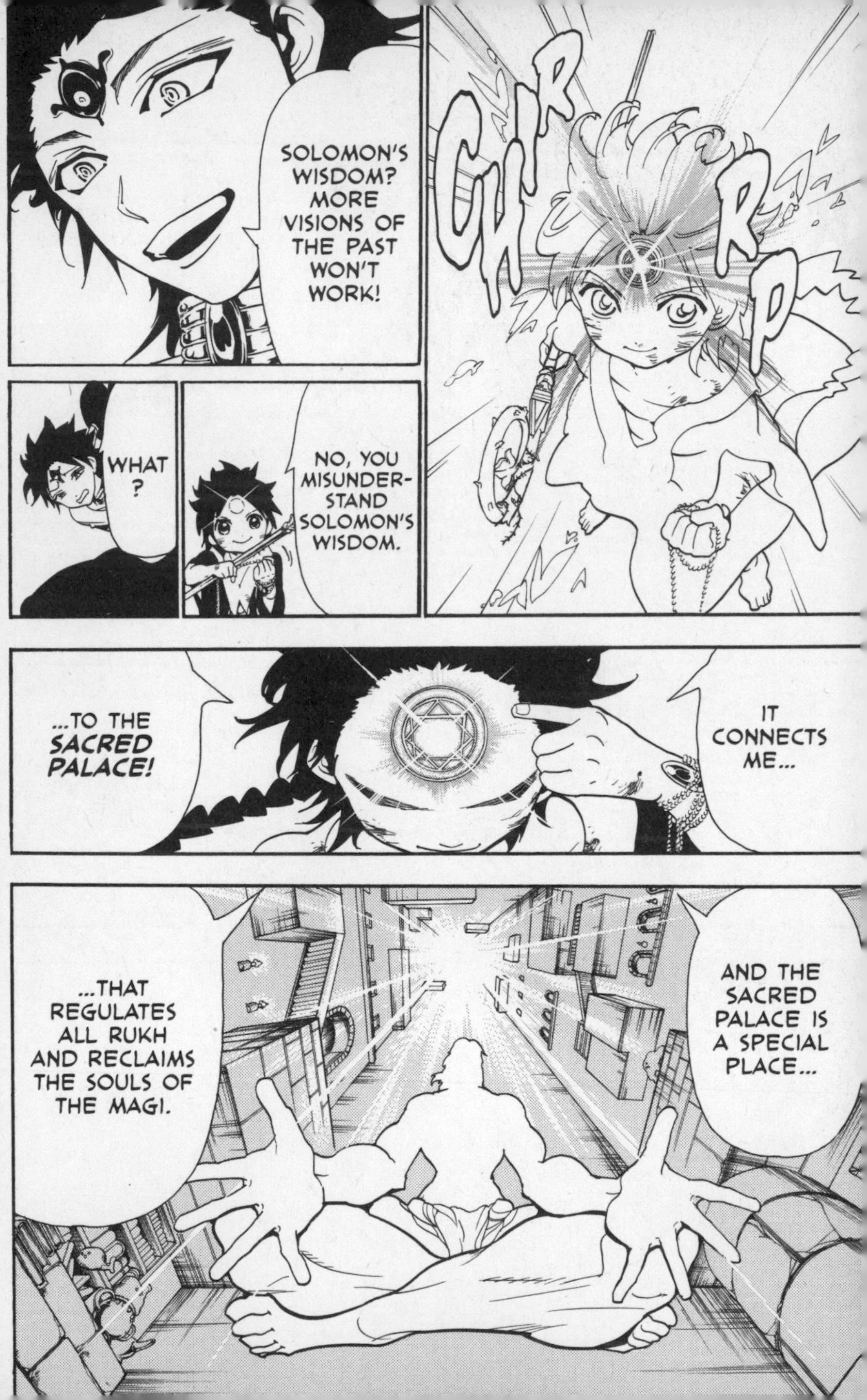
SOLOMON'S WISDOM? MORE VISIONS OF THE PAST WON'T WORK!
NO, YOU MISUNDERSTAND SOLOMON'S WISDOM.
WHAT?
IT CONNECTS ME...
...TO THE *SACRED PALACE!*
AND THE SACRED PALACE IS A SPECIAL PLACE...
...THAT REGULATES ALL RUKH AND RECLAIMS THE SOULS OF THE MAGI.

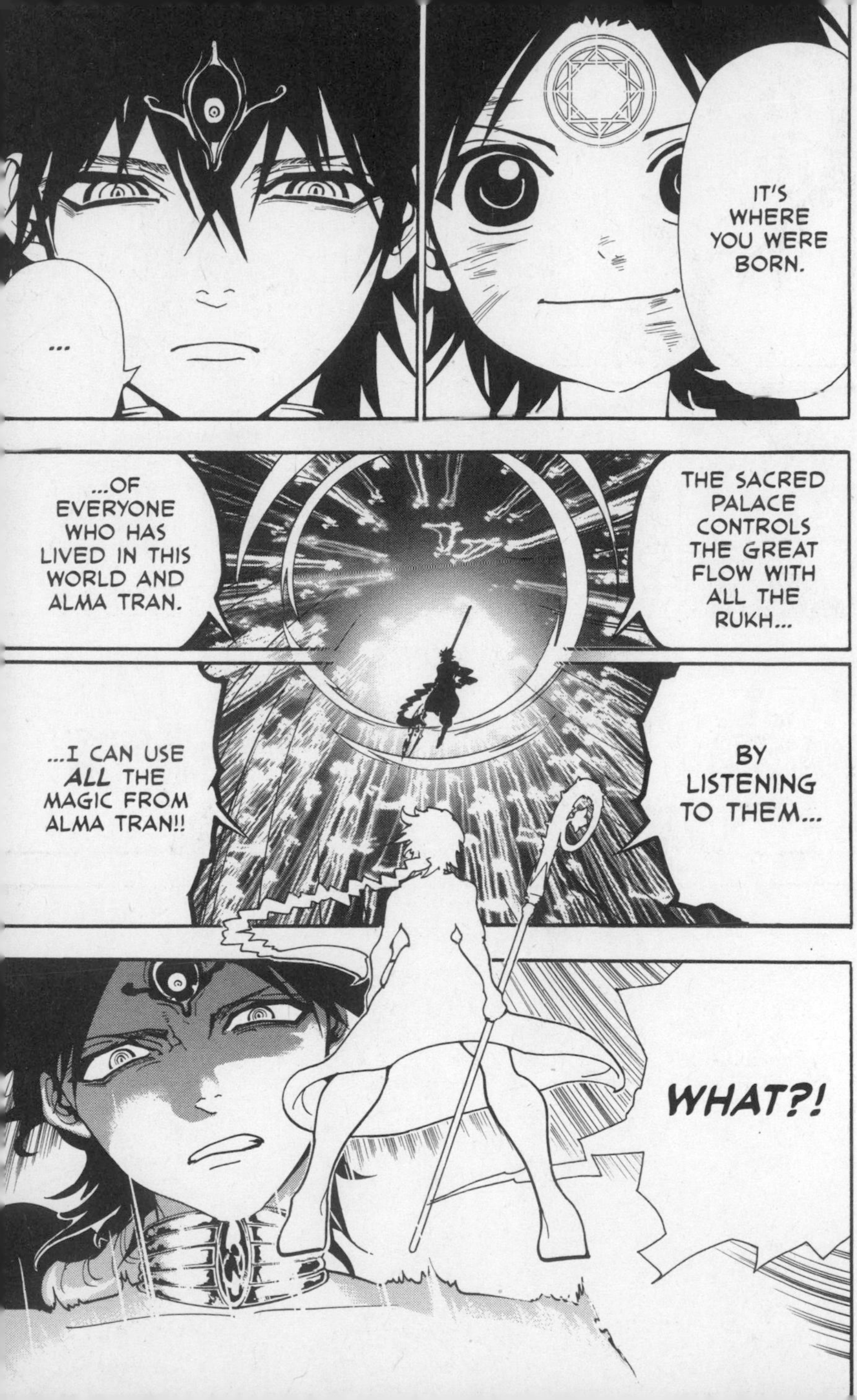
IT'S WHERE YOU WERE BORN.
...
THE SACRED PALACE CONTROLS THE GREAT FLOW WITH ALL THE RUKH...
...OF EVERYONE WHO HAS LIVED IN THIS WORLD AND ALMA TRAN.
BY LISTENING TO THEM...
...I CAN USE ALL THE MAGIC FROM ALMA TRAN!!
WHAT?!

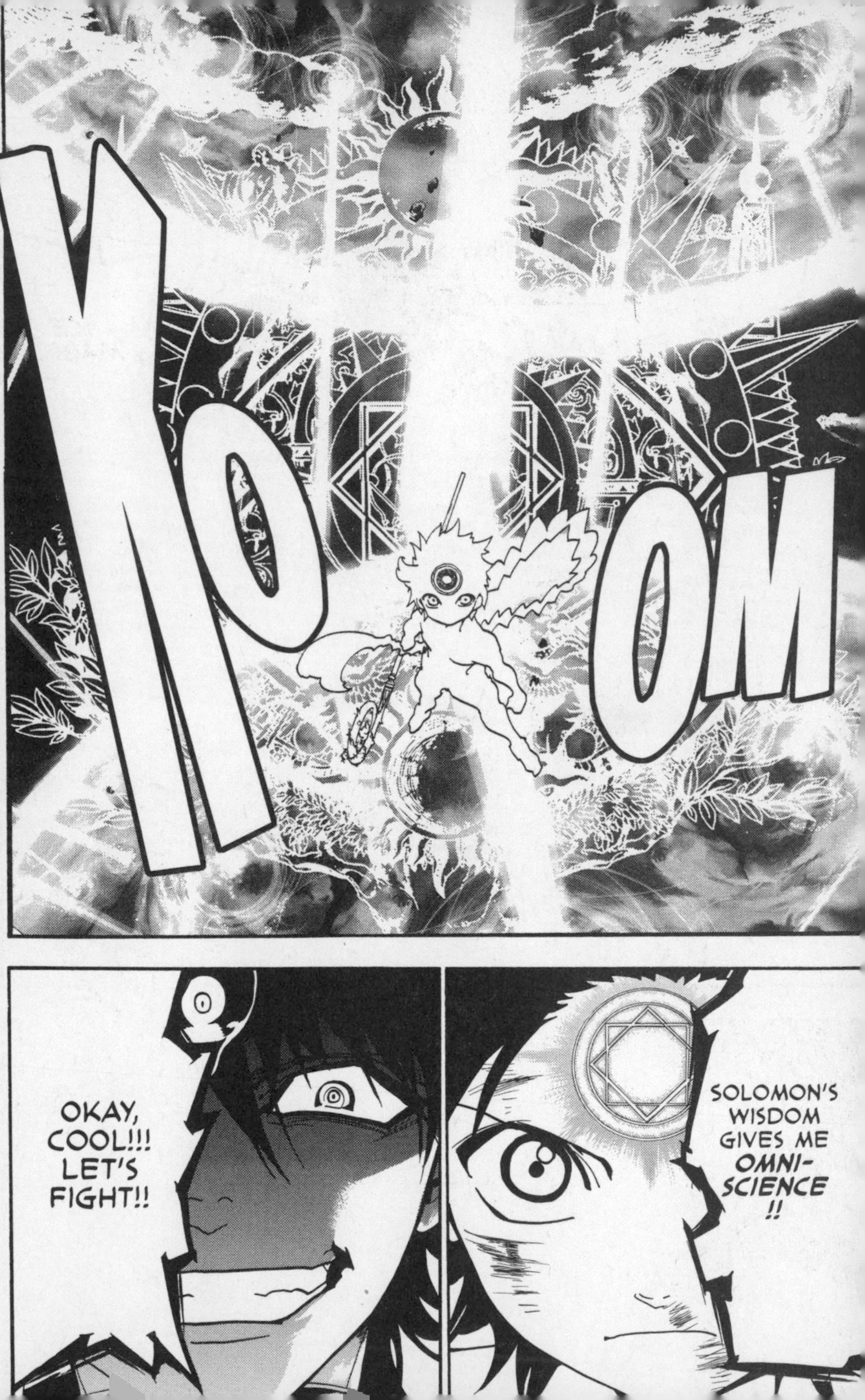
VROOM
SOLOMON'S WISDOM GIVES ME *OMNI-SCIENCE* !!
OKAY, COOL!!! LET'S FIGHT!!

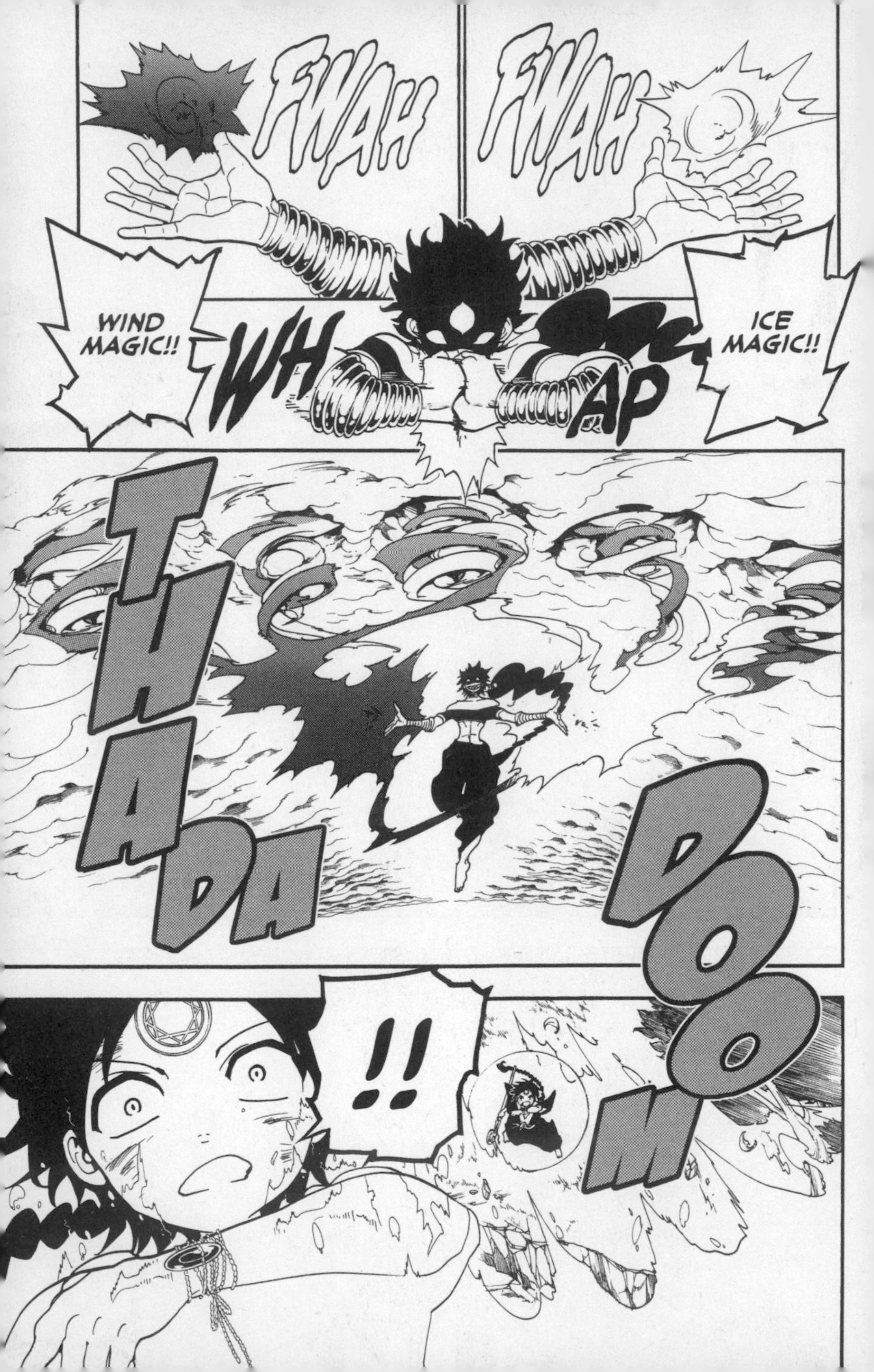
FWAH
FWAH
ICE MAGIC!!
WIND MAGIC!!
WHAP
THADA
DOOOM
!!

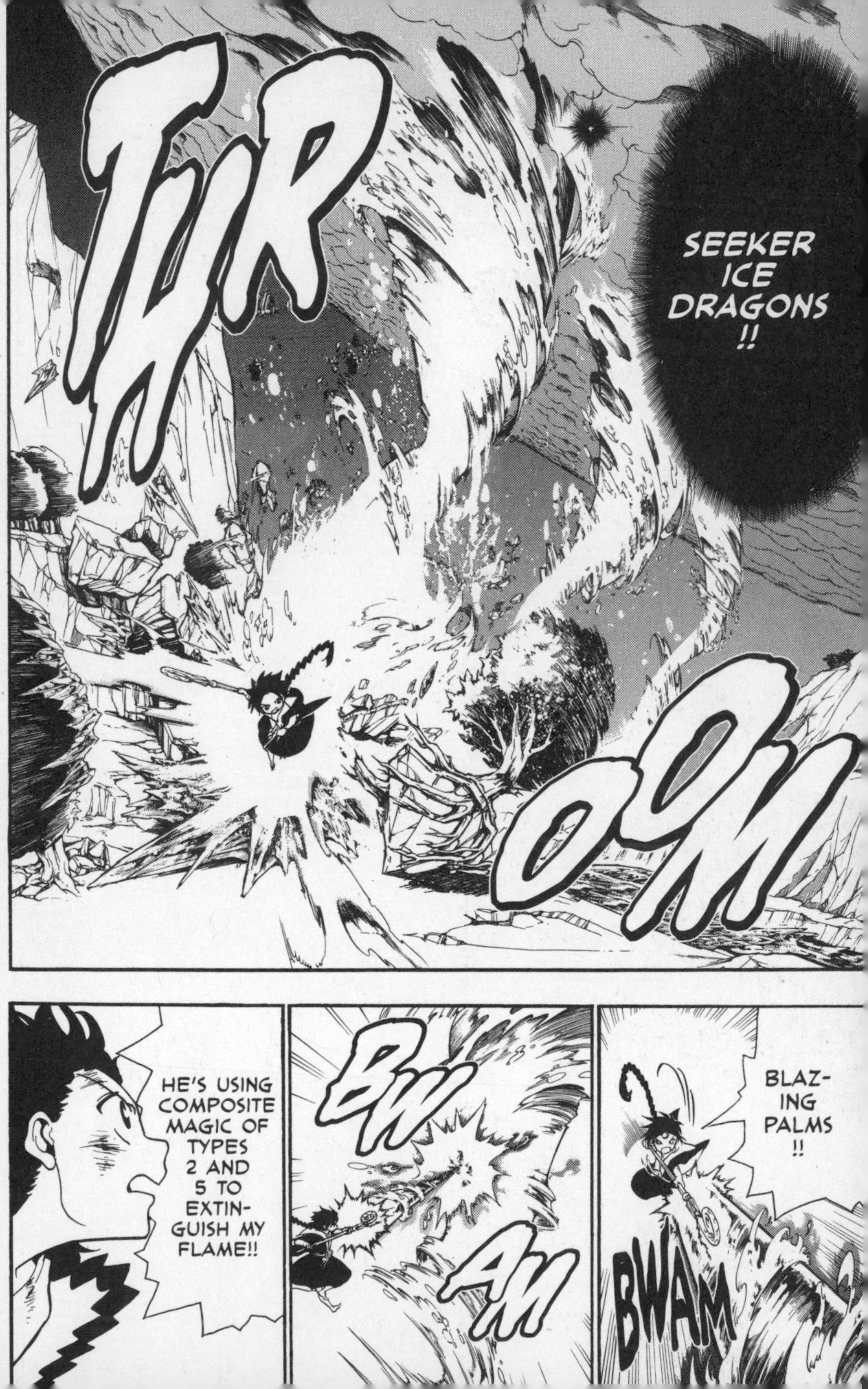
SEEKER ICE DRAGONS!!
BLAZ-ING PALMS!!
BWAM
BW
AM
HE'S USING COMPOSITE MAGIC OF TYPES 2 AND 5 TO EXTIN-GUISH MY FLAME!!

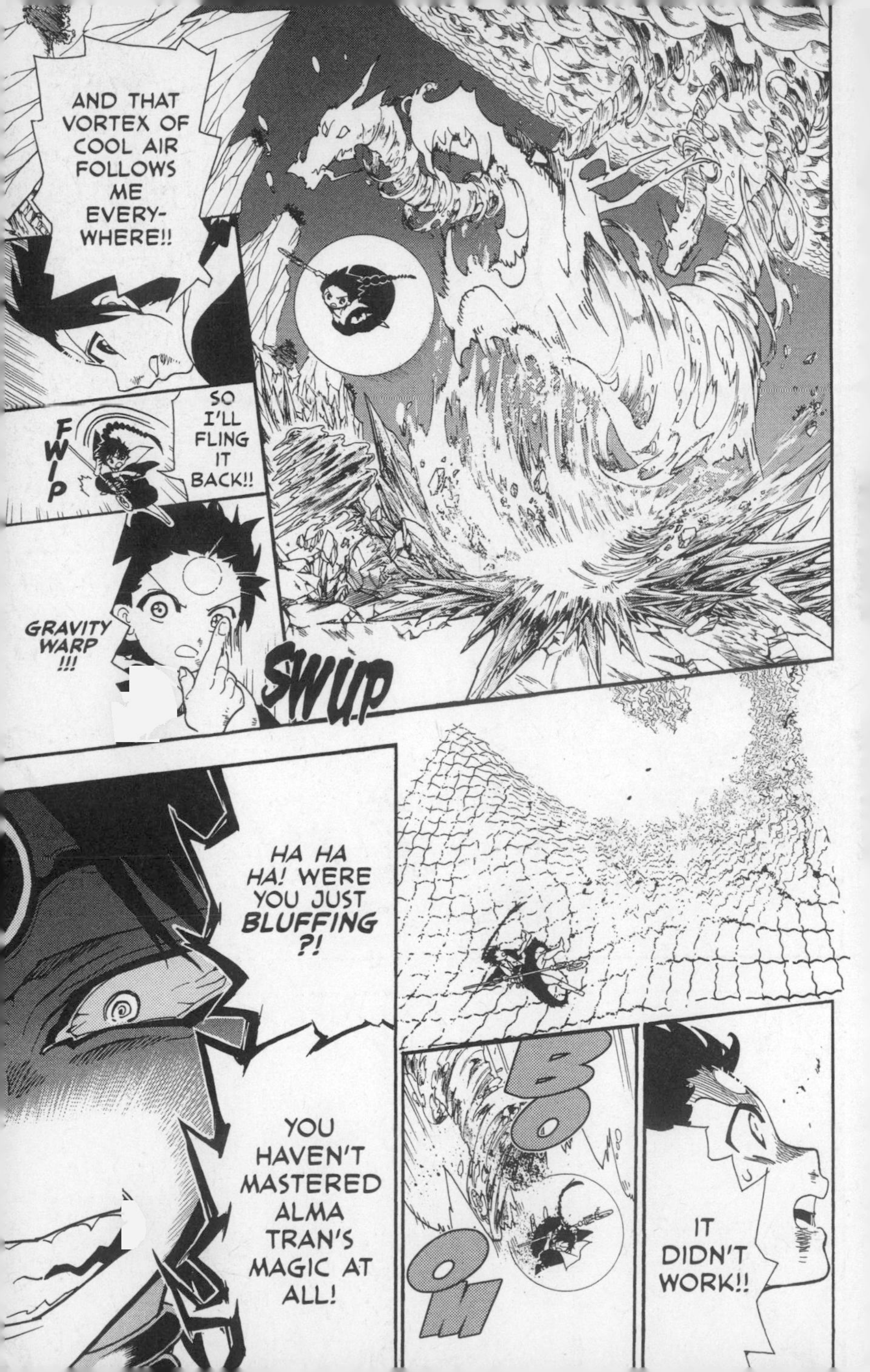
AND THAT VORTEX OF COOL AIR FOLLOWS ME EVERY-WHERE!!
FWIP
SO I'LL FLING IT BACK!!
GRAVITY WARP!!!
SWUP
IT DIDN'T WORK!!
BOOM
HA HA HA! WERE YOU JUST BLUFFING?!
YOU HAVEN'T MASTERED ALMA TRAN'S MAGIC AT ALL!

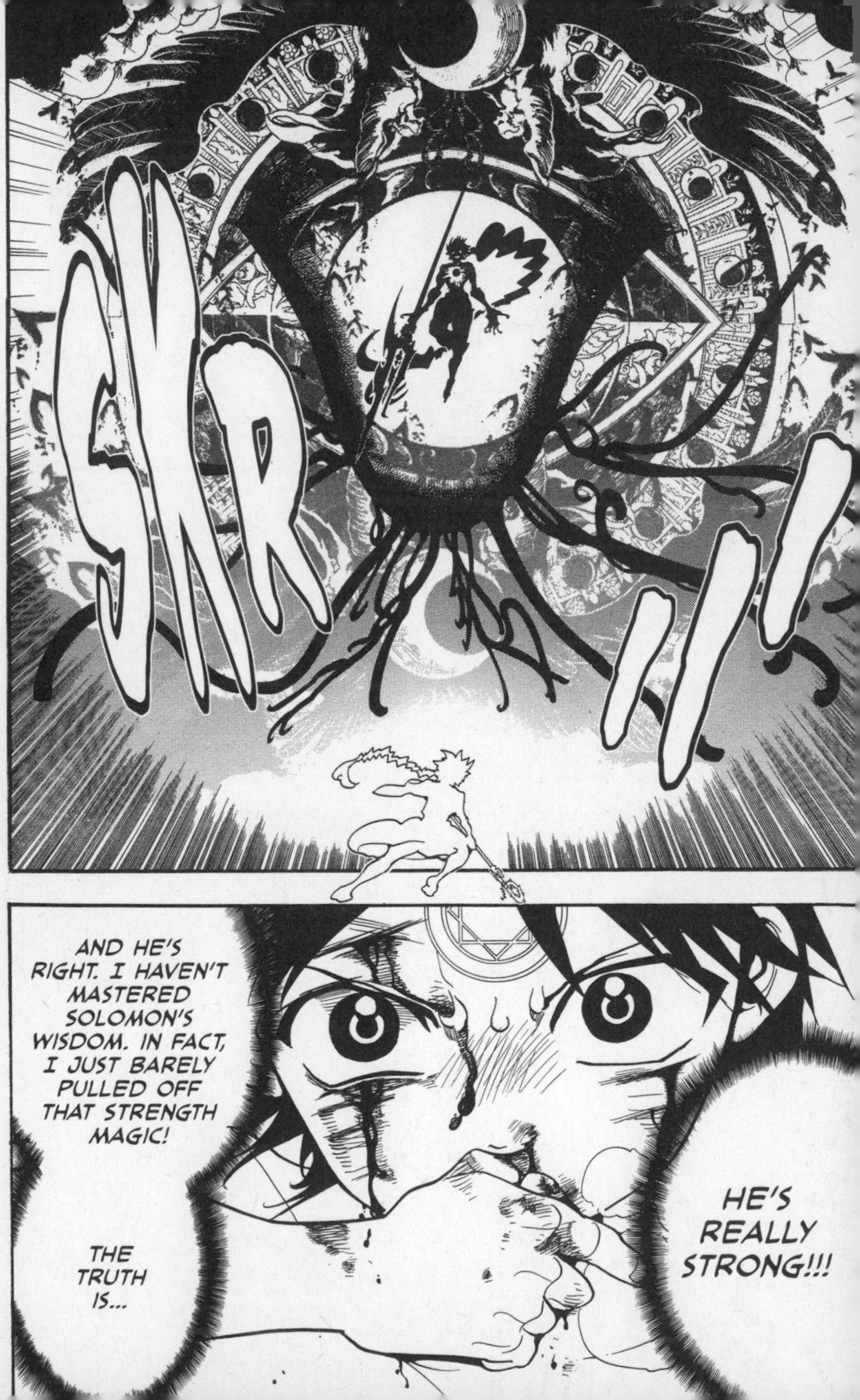

AND HE'S RIGHT. I HAVEN'T MASTERED SOLOMON'S WISDOM. IN FACT, I JUST BARELY PULLED OFF THAT STRENGTH MAGIC!
THE TRUTH IS...
HE'S REALLY STRONG!!!

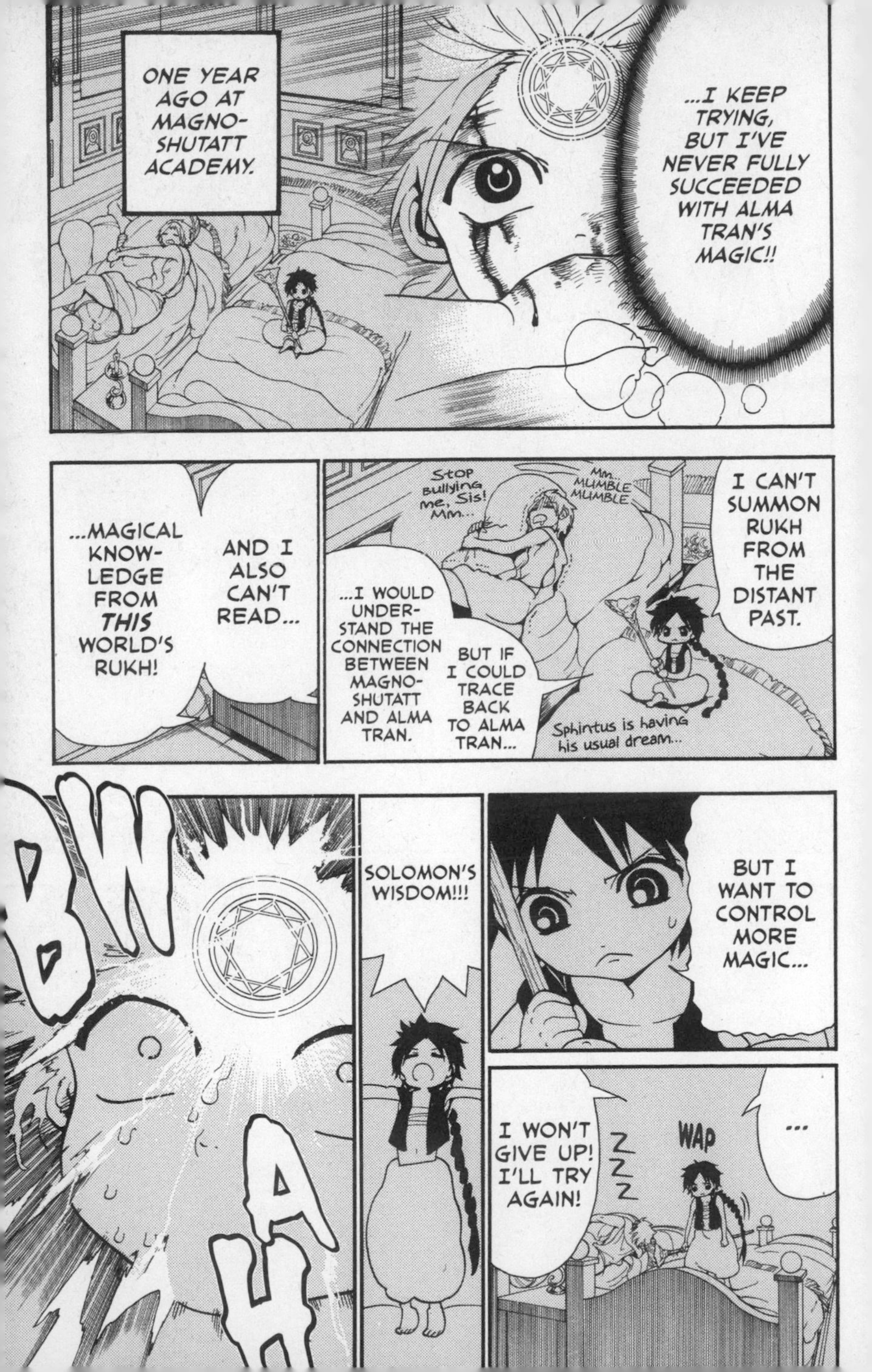
...I KEEP TRYING, BUT I'VE NEVER FULLY SUCCEEDED WITH ALMA TRAN'S MAGIC!!
ONE YEAR AGO AT MAGNO-SHUTATT ACADEMY.
I CAN'T SUMMON RUKH FROM THE DISTANT PAST.
Mm.. MUMBLE MUMBLE
Stop bullying me, Sis! Mm...
BUT IF I COULD TRACE BACK TO ALMA TRAN...
...I WOULD UNDERSTAND THE CONNECTION BETWEEN MAGNO-SHUTATT AND ALMA TRAN.
Sphintus is having his usual dream...
AND I ALSO CAN'T READ...
...MAGICAL KNOWLEDGE FROM *THIS* WORLD'S RUKH!
BUT I WANT TO CONTROL MORE MAGIC...
...
WAP
I WON'T GIVE UP! I'LL TRY AGAIN!
ZZZ
SOLOMON'S WISDOM!!!
BWAH

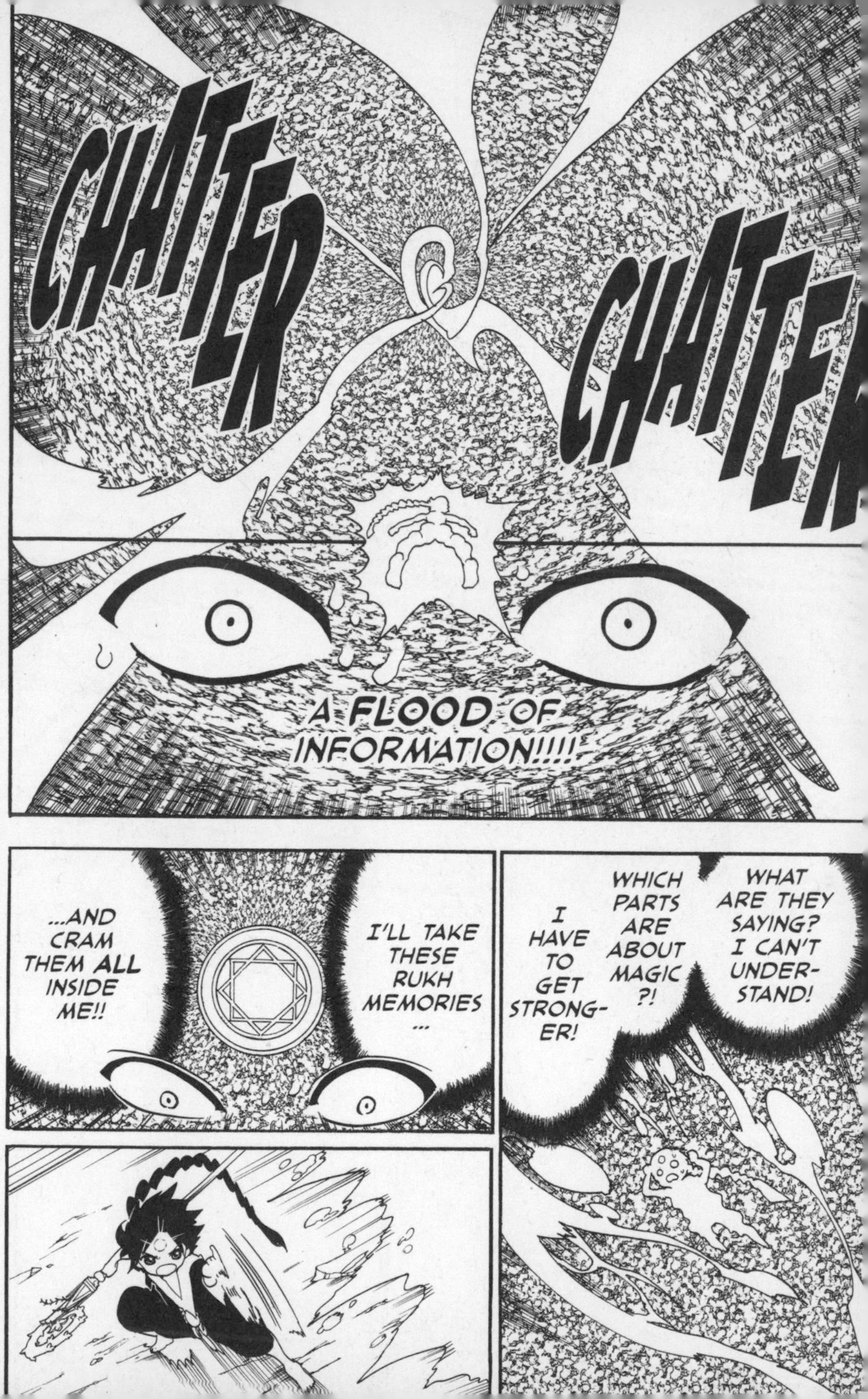
CHATTER
CHATTER
A FLOOD OF INFORMATION!!!!
WHAT ARE THEY SAYING? I CAN'T UNDERSTAND!
WHICH PARTS ARE ABOUT MAGIC?!
I HAVE TO GET STRONGER!
I'LL TAKE THESE RUKH MEMORIES...
...AND CRAM THEM ALL INSIDE ME!!

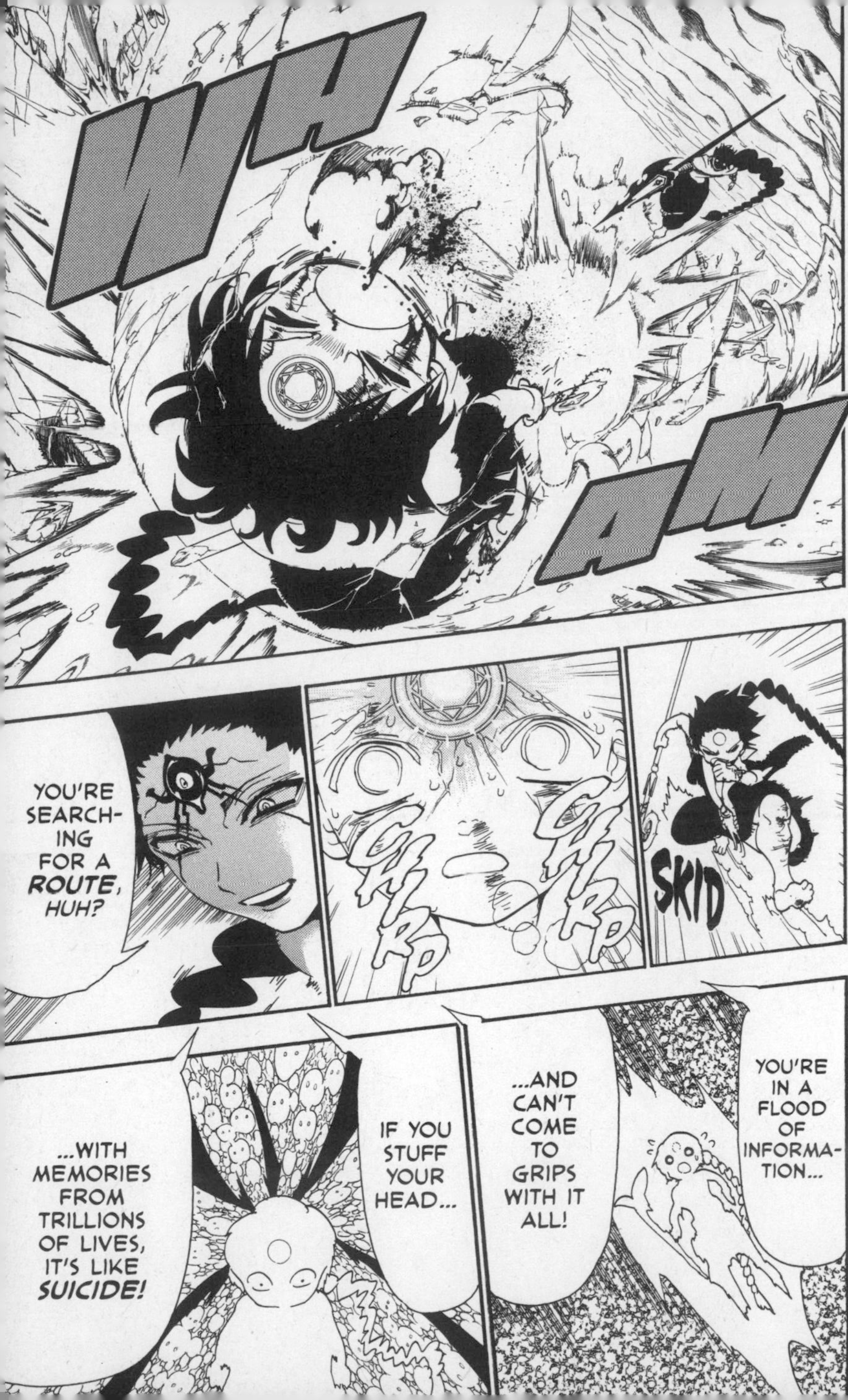
WH
A..M
SKID
CHRP
CHRP
YOU'RE SEARCHING FOR A ***ROUTE***, HUH?
YOU'RE IN A FLOOD OF INFORMATION...
...AND CAN'T COME TO GRIPS WITH IT ALL!
IF YOU STUFF YOUR HEAD...
...WITH MEMORIES FROM TRILLIONS OF LIVES, IT'S LIKE ***SUICIDE!***

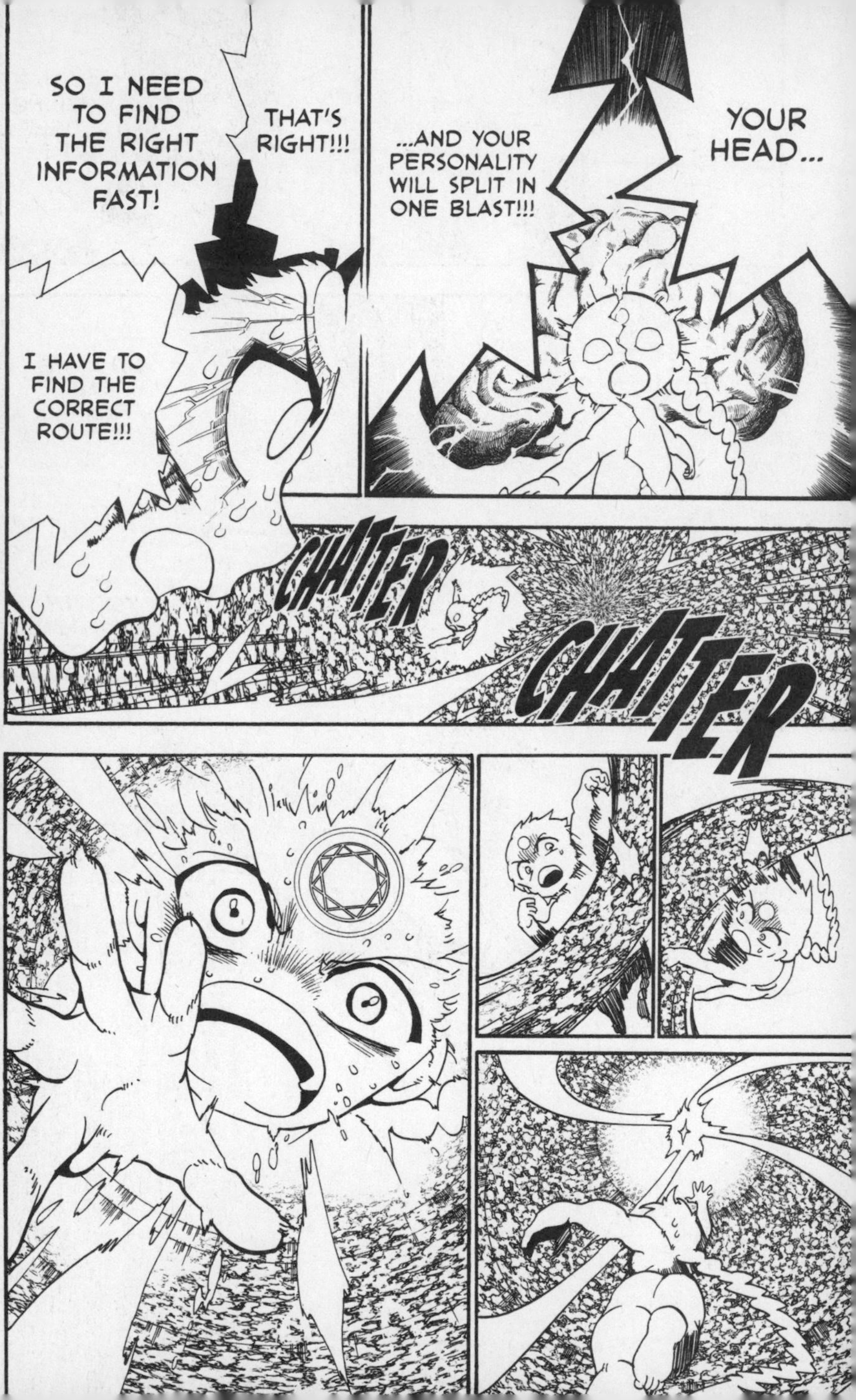
YOUR HEAD...
...AND YOUR PERSONALITY WILL SPLIT IN ONE BLAST!!!
THAT'S RIGHT!!!
SO I NEED TO FIND THE RIGHT INFORMATION FAST!
I HAVE TO FIND THE CORRECT ROUTE!!!
CHATTER
CHATTER

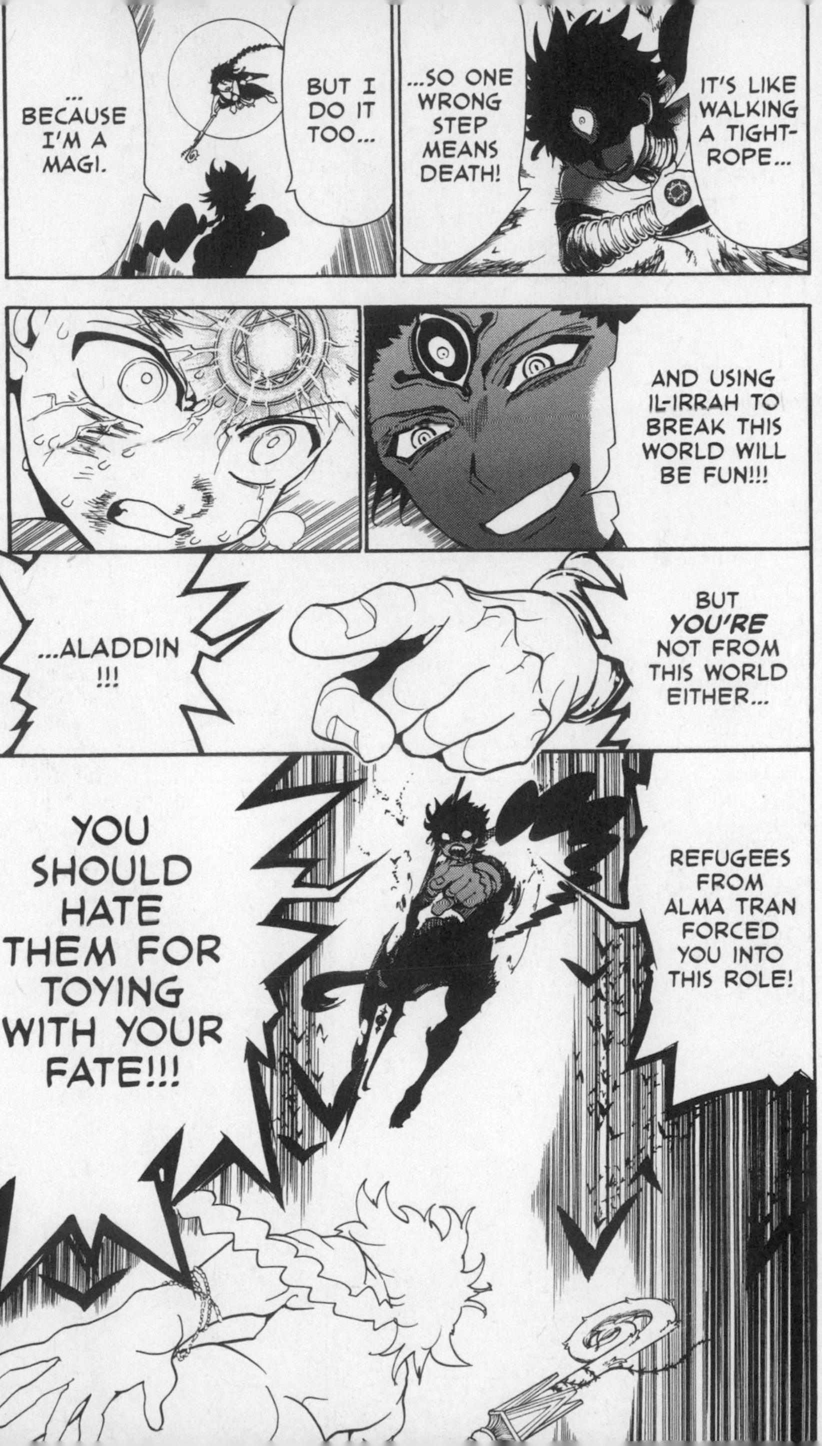
IT'S LIKE WALKING A TIGHT-ROPE...
...SO ONE WRONG STEP MEANS DEATH!
BUT I DO IT TOO...
... BECAUSE I'M A MAGI.
AND USING IL-IRRAH TO BREAK THIS WORLD WILL BE FUN!!!
BUT *YOU'RE* NOT FROM THIS WORLD EITHER...
...ALADDIN !!!
REFUGEES FROM ALMA TRAN FORCED YOU INTO THIS ROLE!
YOU SHOULD HATE THEM FOR TOYING WITH YOUR FATE!!!

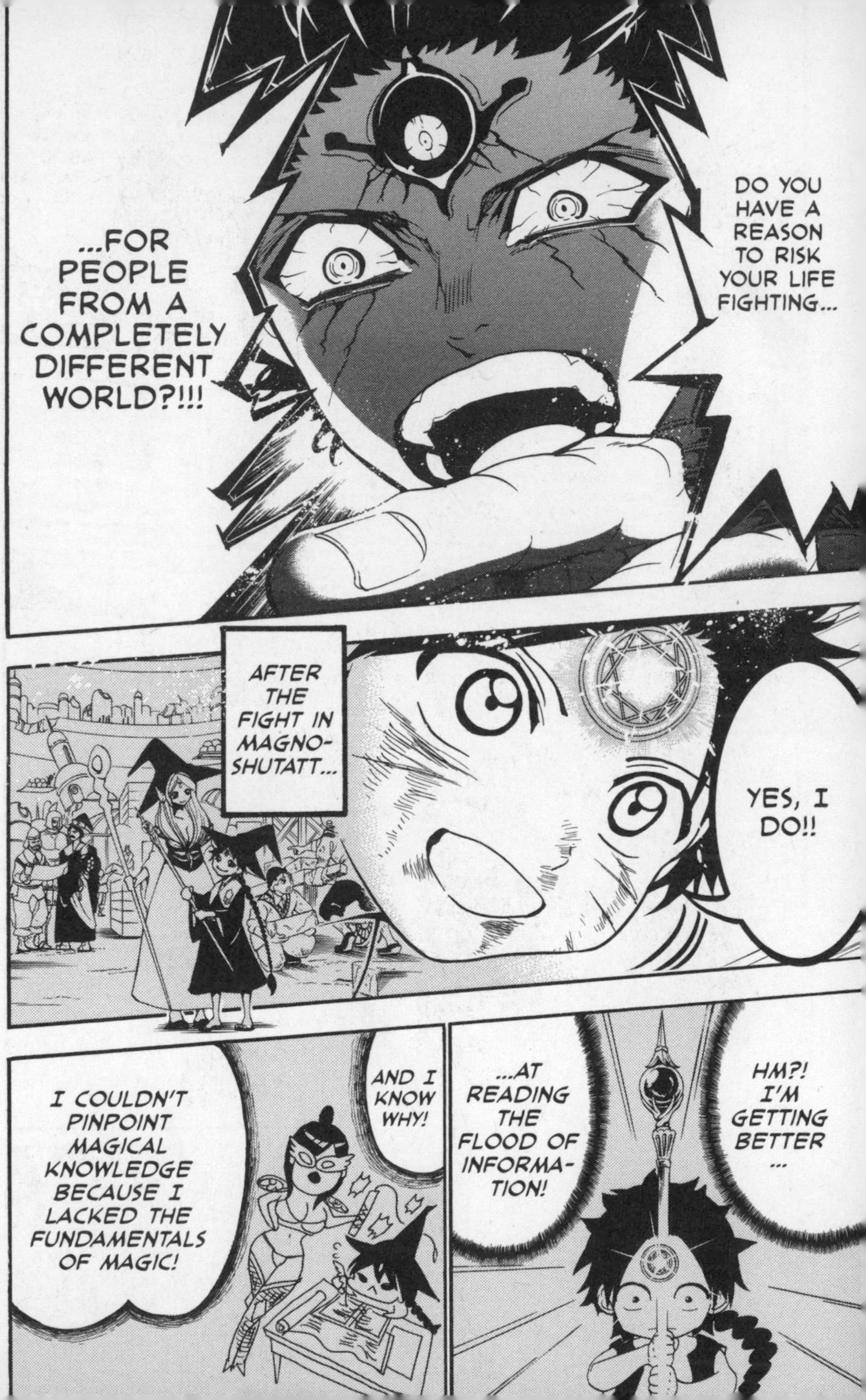
DO YOU HAVE A REASON TO RISK YOUR LIFE FIGHTING...
...FOR PEOPLE FROM A COMPLETELY DIFFERENT WORLD?!!!
YES, I DO!!
AFTER THE FIGHT IN MAGNO-SHUTATT...
HM?! I'M GETTING BETTER...
...AT READING THE FLOOD OF INFORMATION!
AND I KNOW WHY!
I COULDN'T PINPOINT MAGICAL KNOWLEDGE BECAUSE I LACKED THE FUNDAMENTALS OF MAGIC!

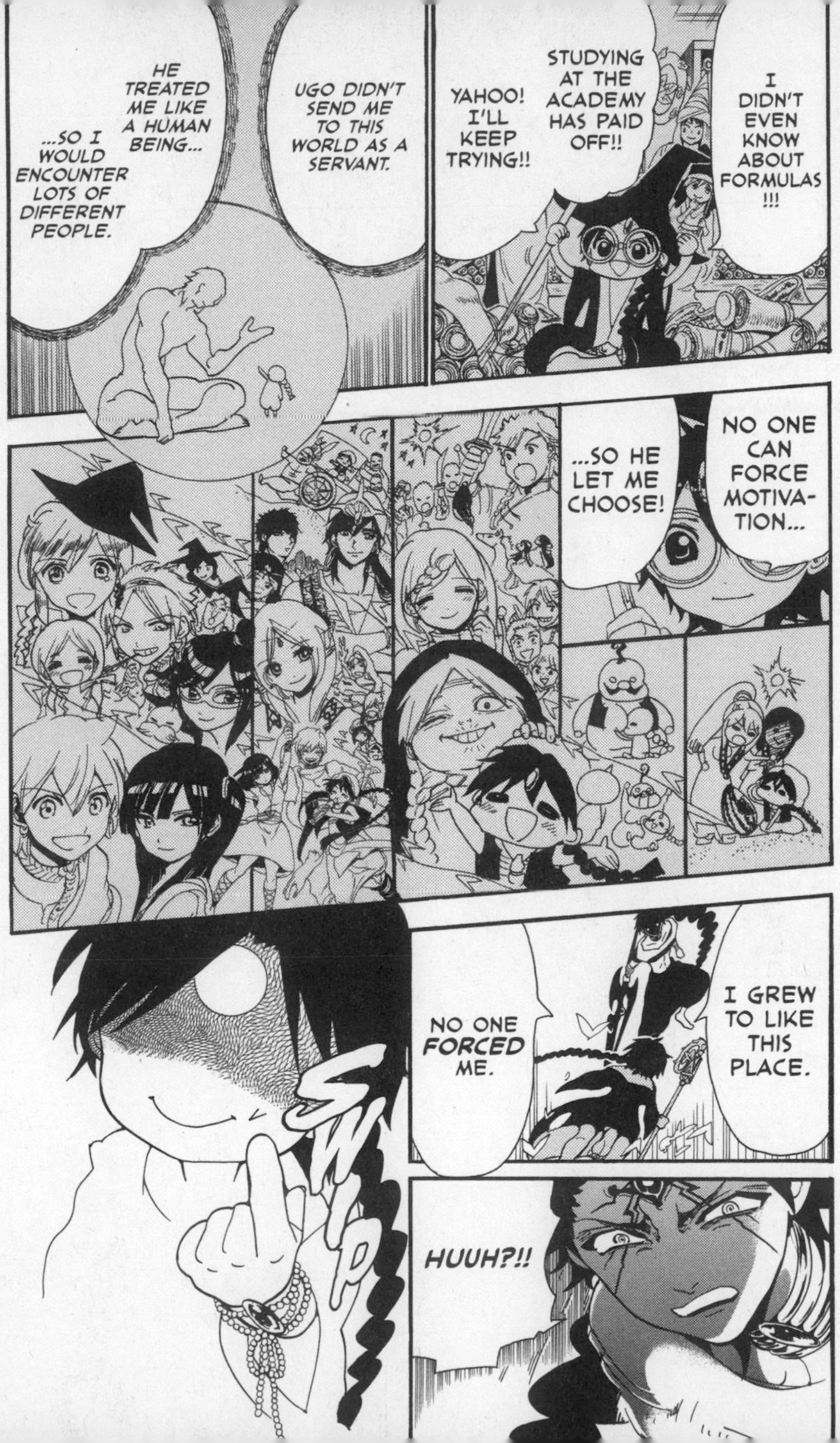
I DIDN'T EVEN KNOW ABOUT FORMULAS!!!
STUDYING AT THE ACADEMY HAS PAID OFF!!
YAHOO! I'LL KEEP TRYING!!
UGO DIDN'T SEND ME TO THIS WORLD AS A SERVANT.
HE TREATED ME LIKE A HUMAN BEING...
...SO I WOULD ENCOUNTER LOTS OF DIFFERENT PEOPLE.
NO ONE CAN FORCE MOTIVATION...
...SO HE LET ME CHOOSE!
I GREW TO LIKE THIS PLACE.
NO ONE *FORCED* ME.
HUUH?!!

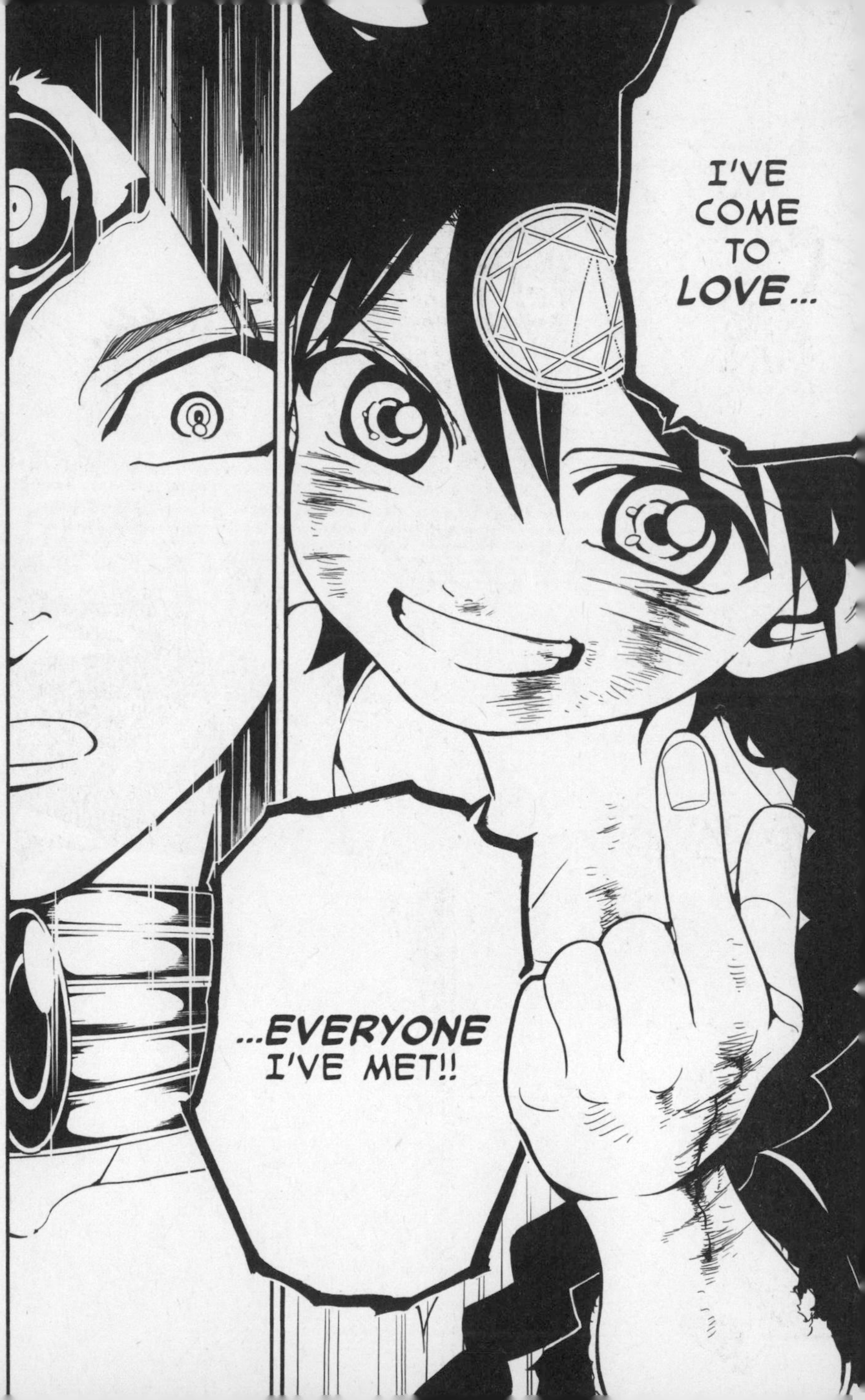
I'VE COME TO LOVE...
...EVERYONE I'VE MET!!

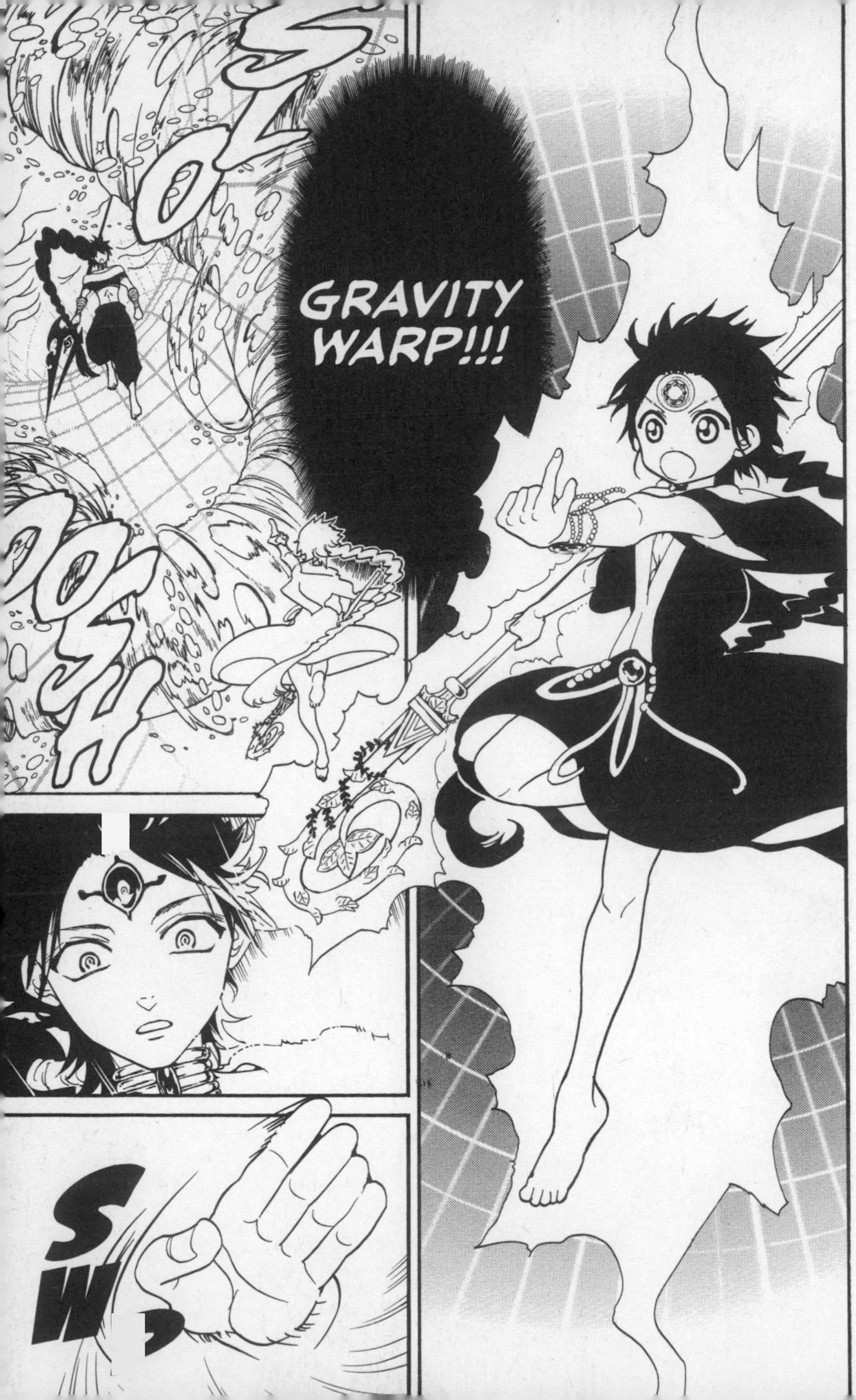
GRAVITY WARP!!!

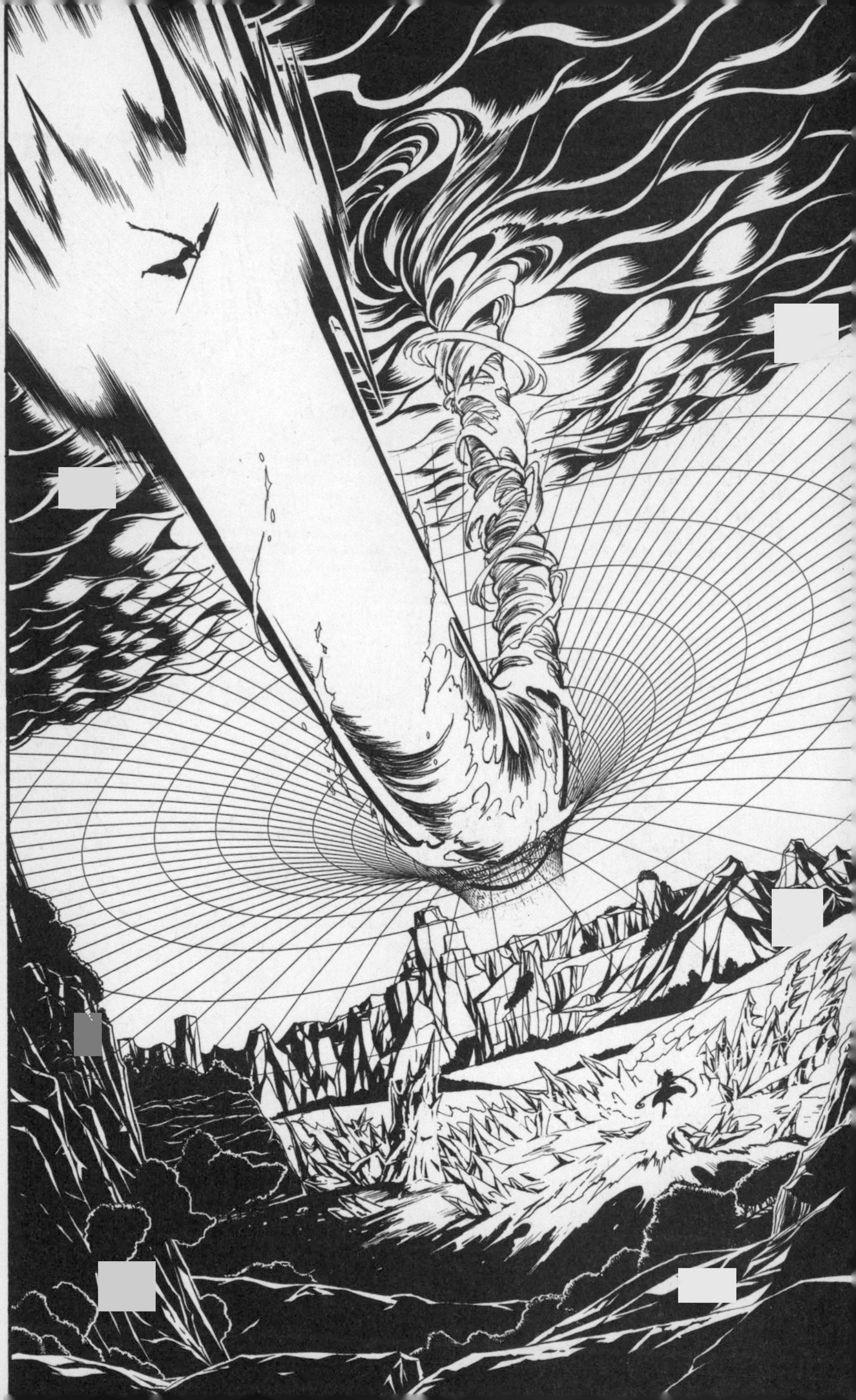

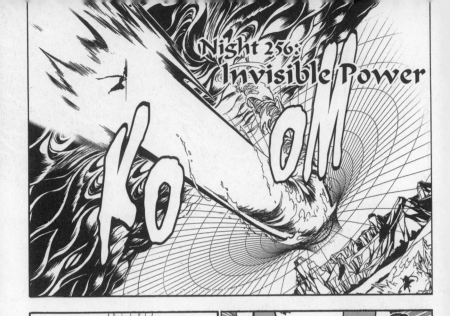

Night 256: Invisible Power

KO OM

I FINALLY SUCCEED-ED...

...IN RE-CREATING KING SOLOMON'S MAGIC!!

HUFF

HUFF

KA BOOM

...

...

I DID IT.

I...

KRUMBL KRUMBL

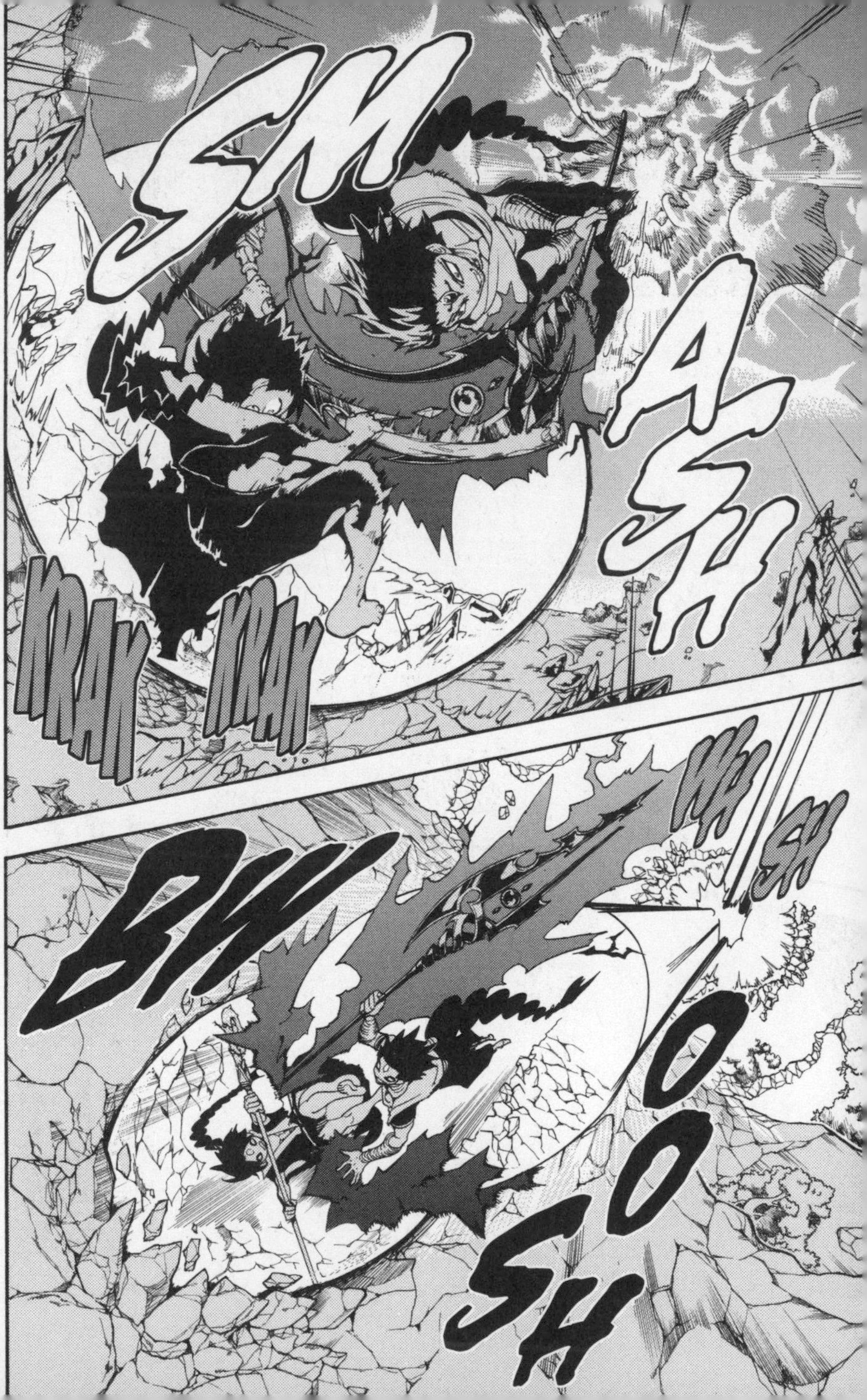
SMASH
KRAK
KRAK
WHASH
BWOOSH

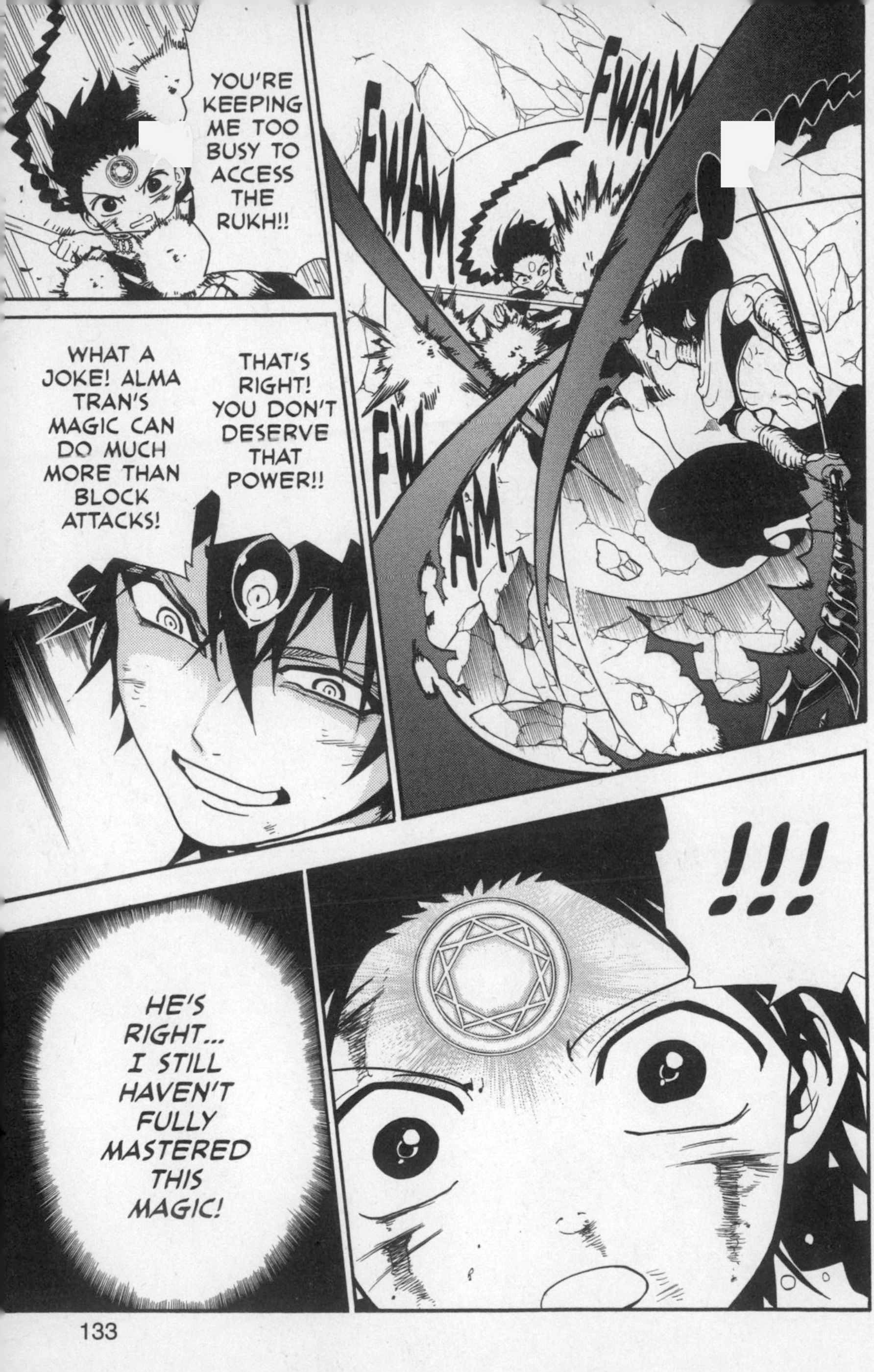
FWAM
FWAM
FW
AM
YOU'RE KEEPING ME TOO BUSY TO ACCESS THE RUKH!!
THAT'S RIGHT! YOU DON'T DESERVE THAT POWER!!
WHAT A JOKE! ALMA TRAN'S MAGIC CAN DO MUCH MORE THAN BLOCK ATTACKS!
!!!
HE'S RIGHT... I STILL HAVEN'T FULLY MASTERED THIS MAGIC!

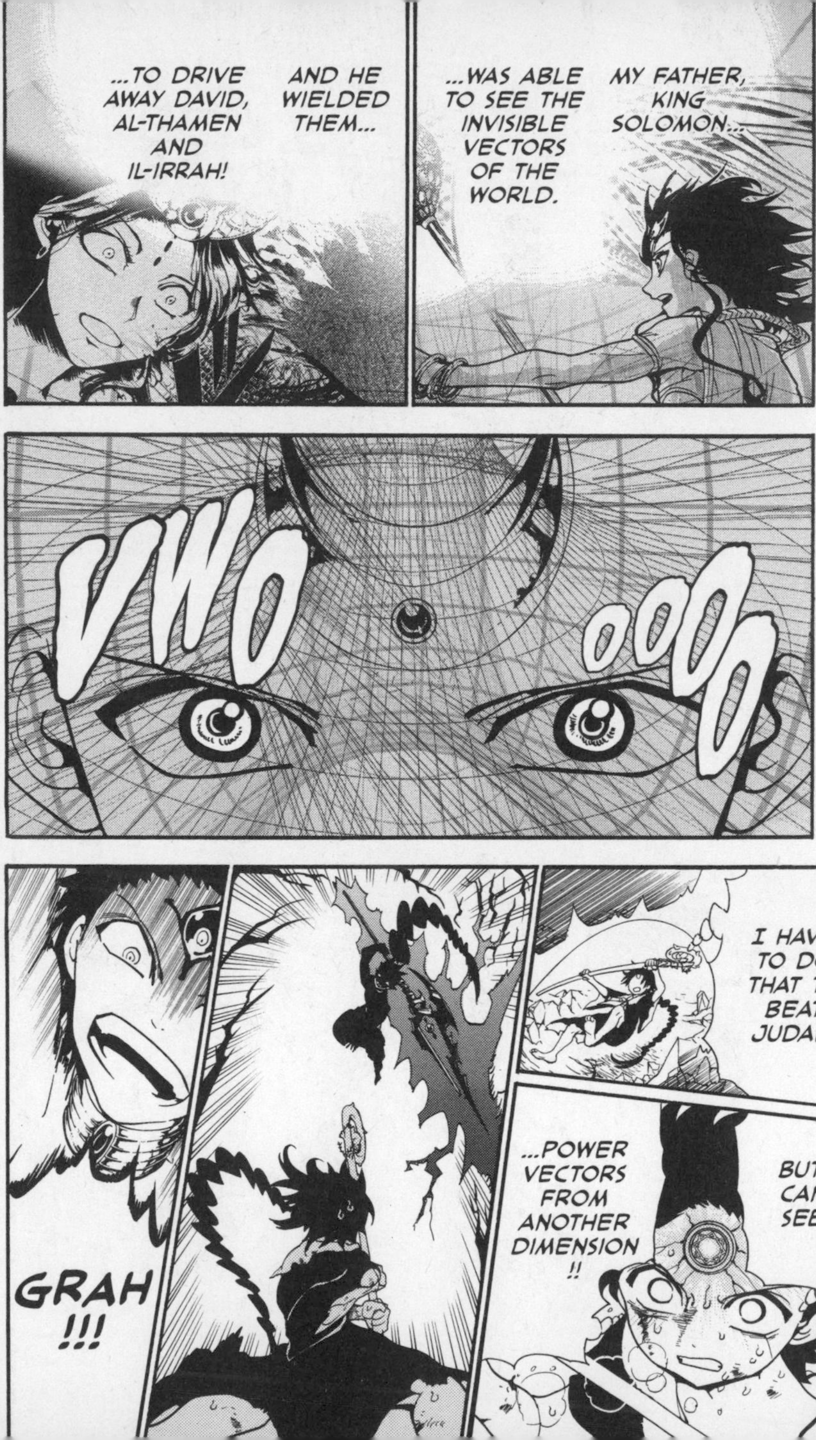

MY FATHER, KING SOLOMON...
...WAS ABLE TO SEE THE INVISIBLE VECTORS OF THE WORLD.
AND HE WIELDED THEM...
...TO DRIVE AWAY DAVID, AL-THAMEN AND IL-IRRAH!
VWO
OOOO
I HAVE TO DO THAT TO BEAT JUDAR!
BUT I CAN'T SEE...
...POWER VECTORS FROM ANOTHER DIMENSION!!
GRAH!!!

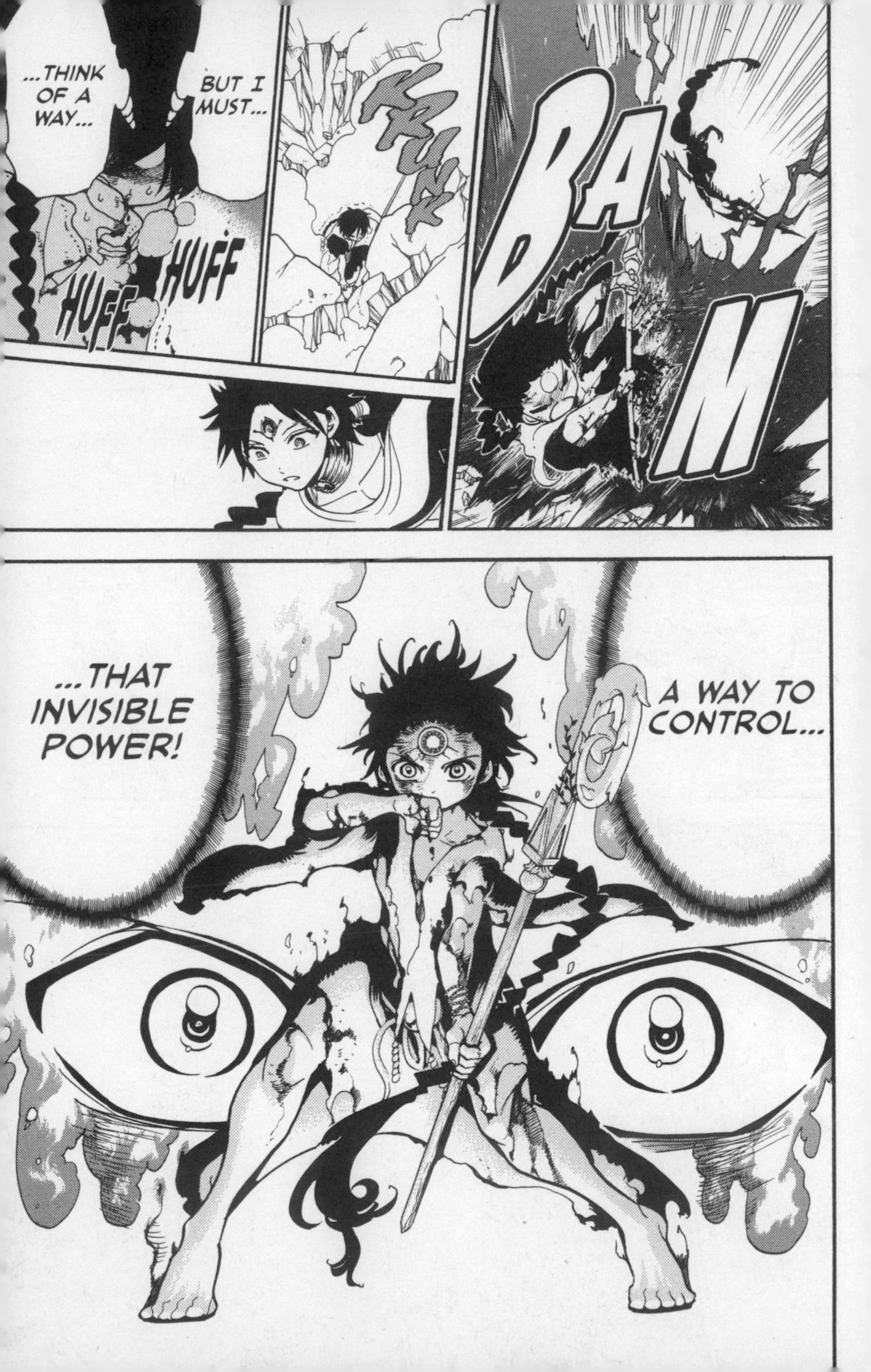
DAM
KRUNK
BUT I MUST...
...THINK OF A WAY...
HUFF HUFF
A WAY TO CONTROL...
...THAT INVISIBLE POWER!

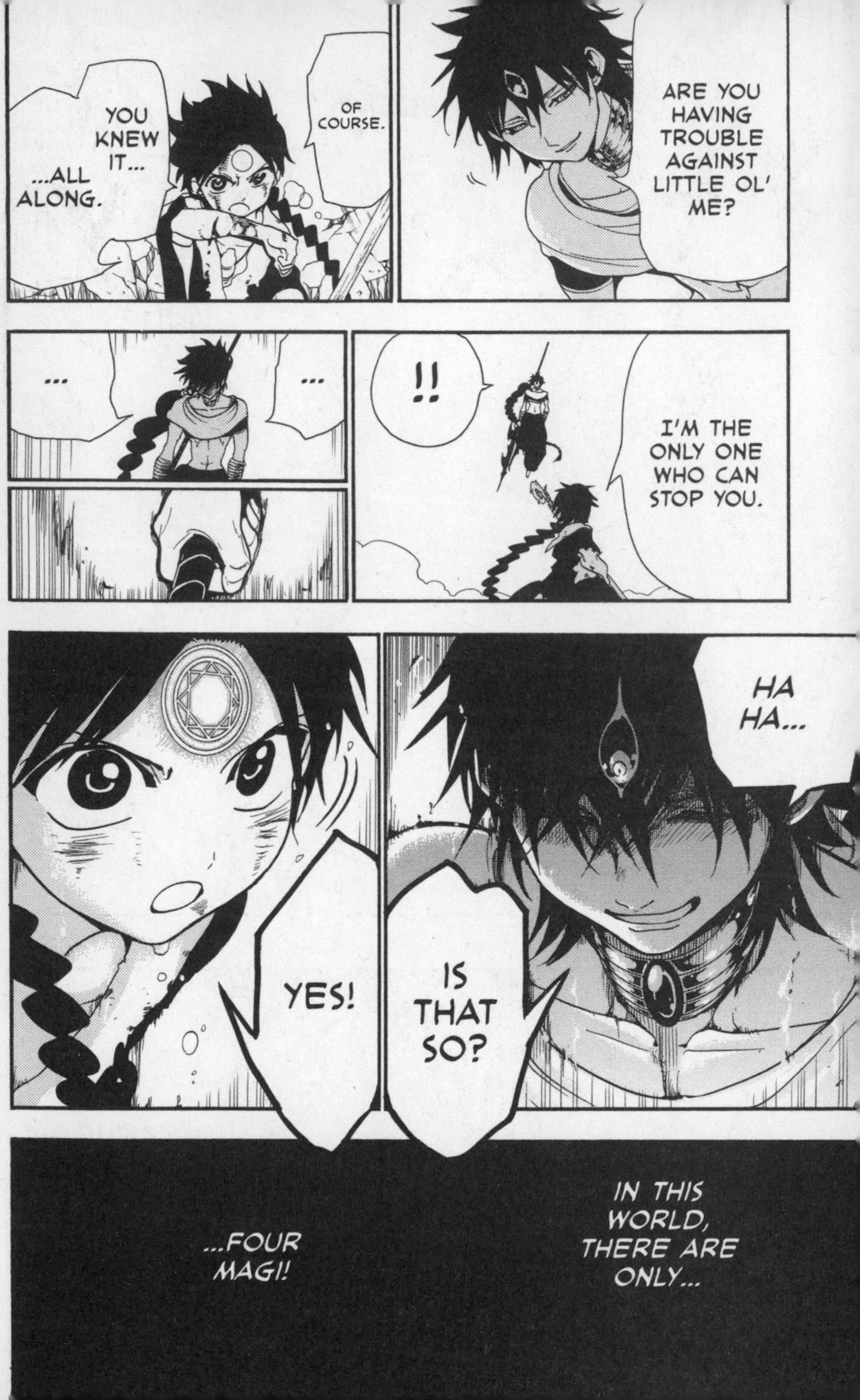
ARE YOU HAVING TROUBLE AGAINST LITTLE OL' ME?
YOU KNEW IT...
...ALL ALONG.
OF COURSE.
I'M THE ONLY ONE WHO CAN STOP YOU.
!!
...
...
HA HA...
IS THAT SO?
YES!
IN THIS WORLD, THERE ARE ONLY...
...FOUR MAGI!

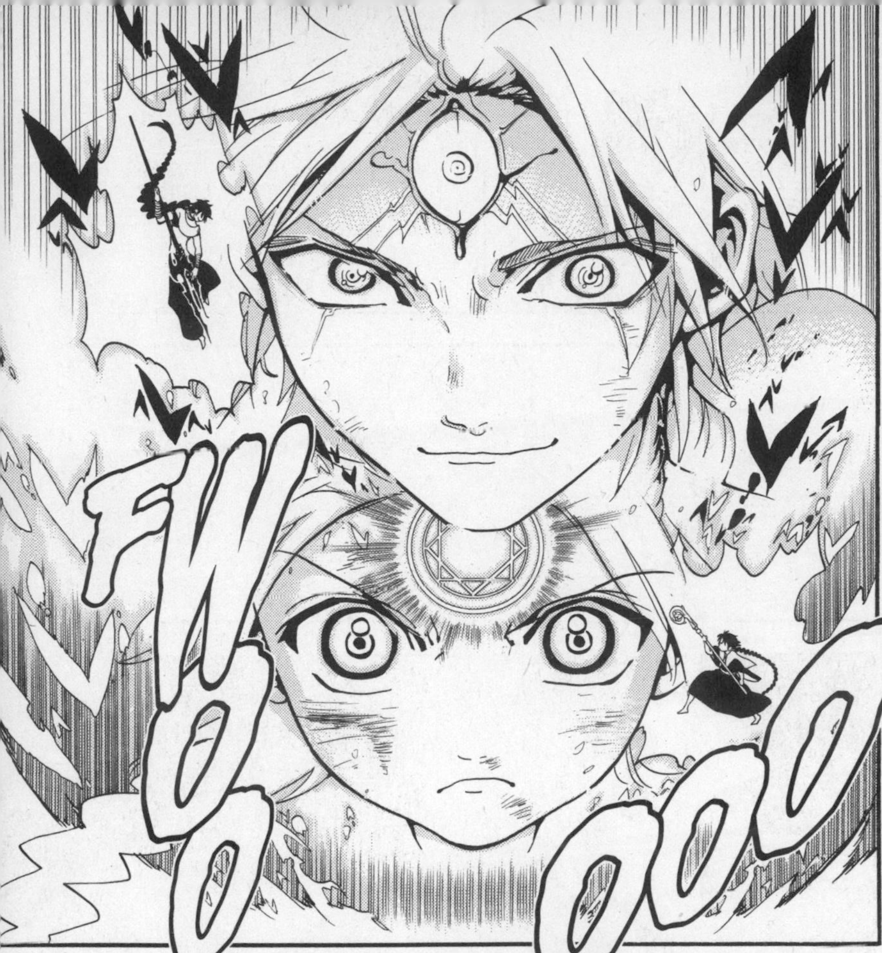
FWOOOOOO

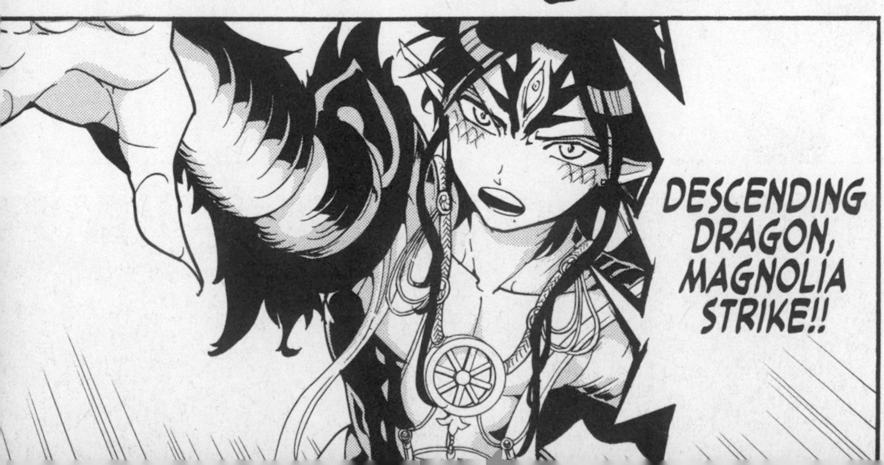
DESCENDING DRAGON, MAGNOLIA STRIKE!!

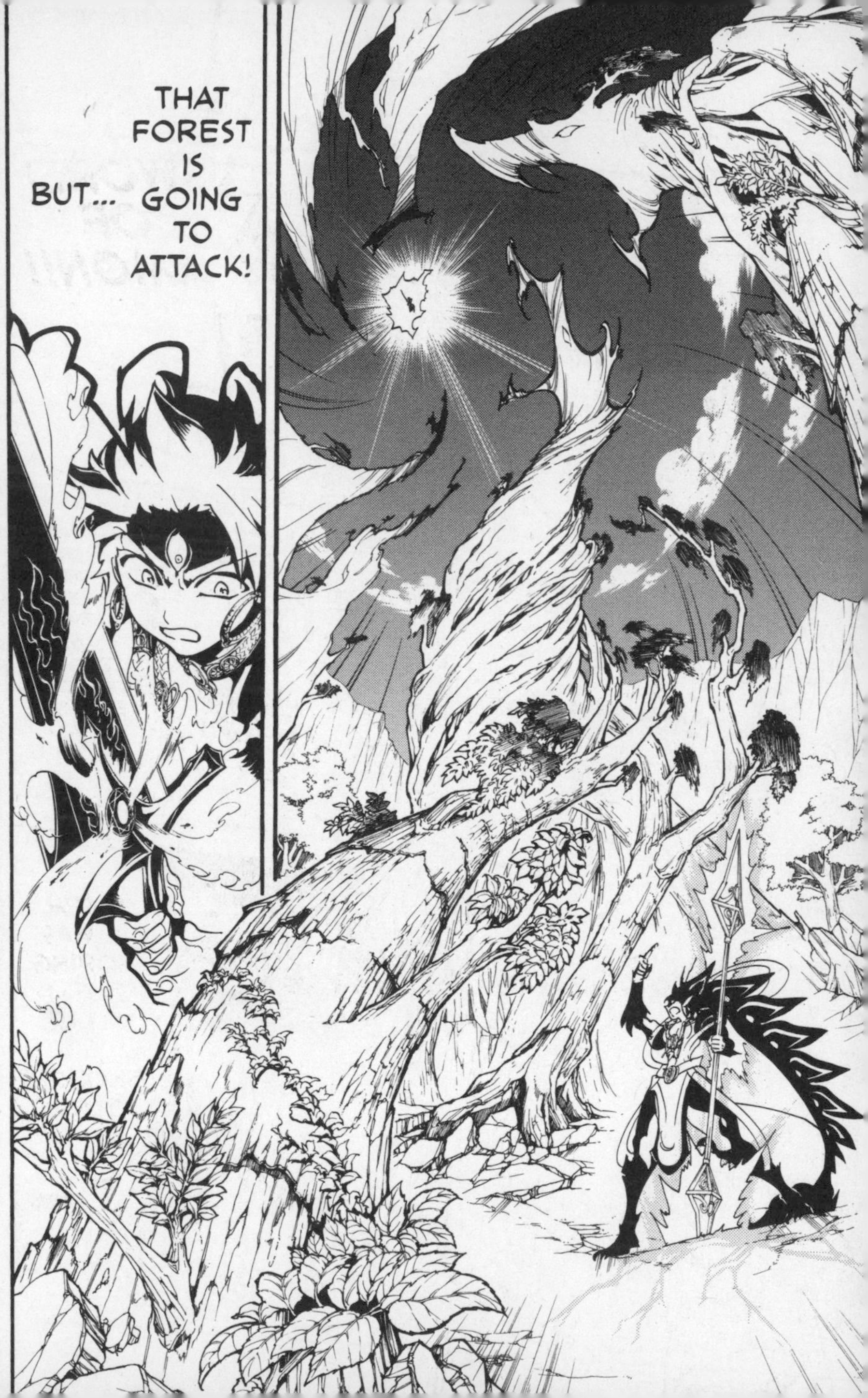
THAT FOREST IS GOING TO ATTACK!
BUT...

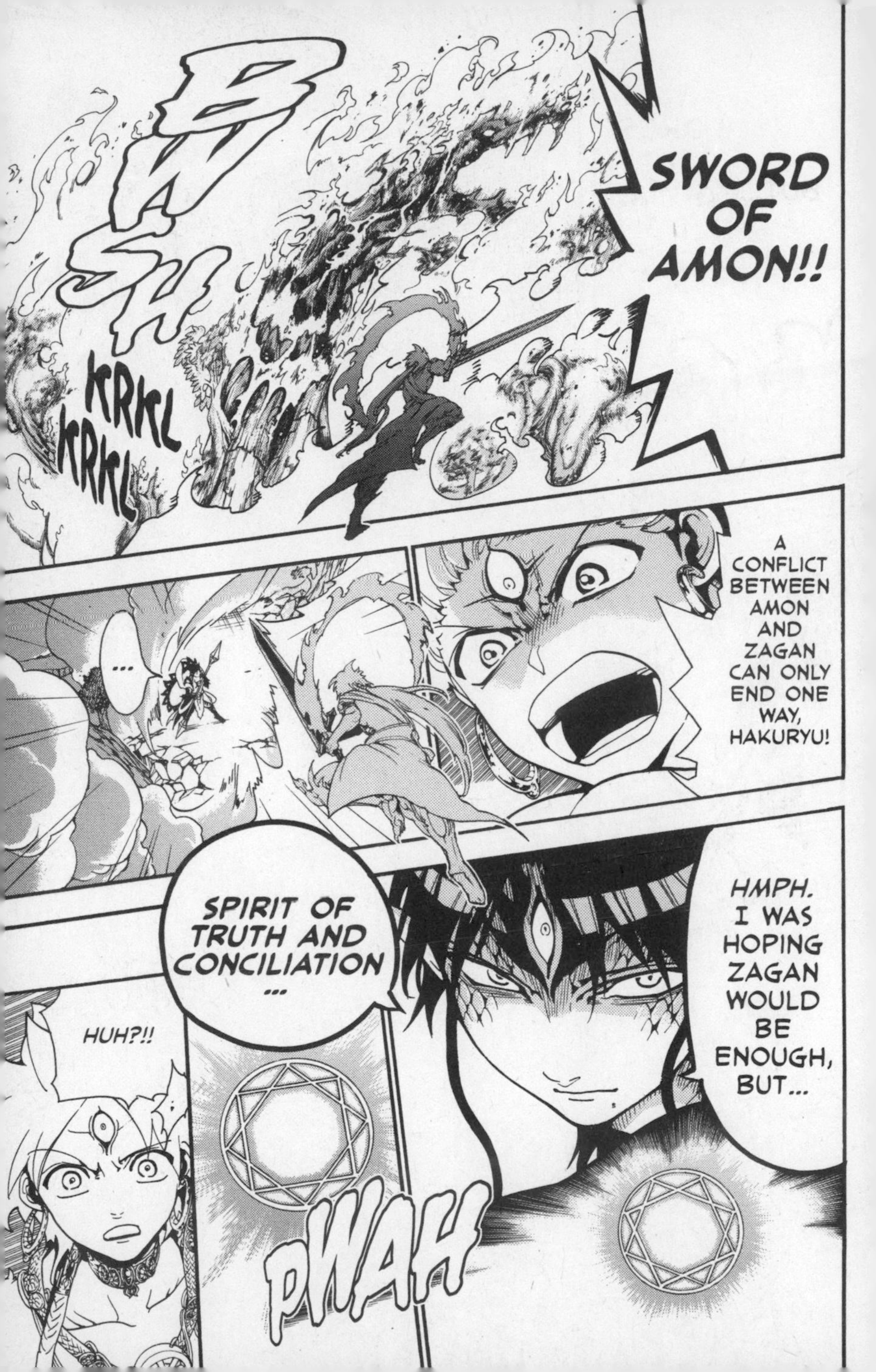
SWORD OF AMON!!
BASH
KRKL KRKL
A CONFLICT BETWEEN AMON AND ZAGAN CAN ONLY END ONE WAY, HAKURYU!
...
HMPH. I WAS HOPING ZAGAN WOULD BE ENOUGH, BUT...
SPIRIT OF TRUTH AND CONCILIATION ...
PWAH
HUH?!!

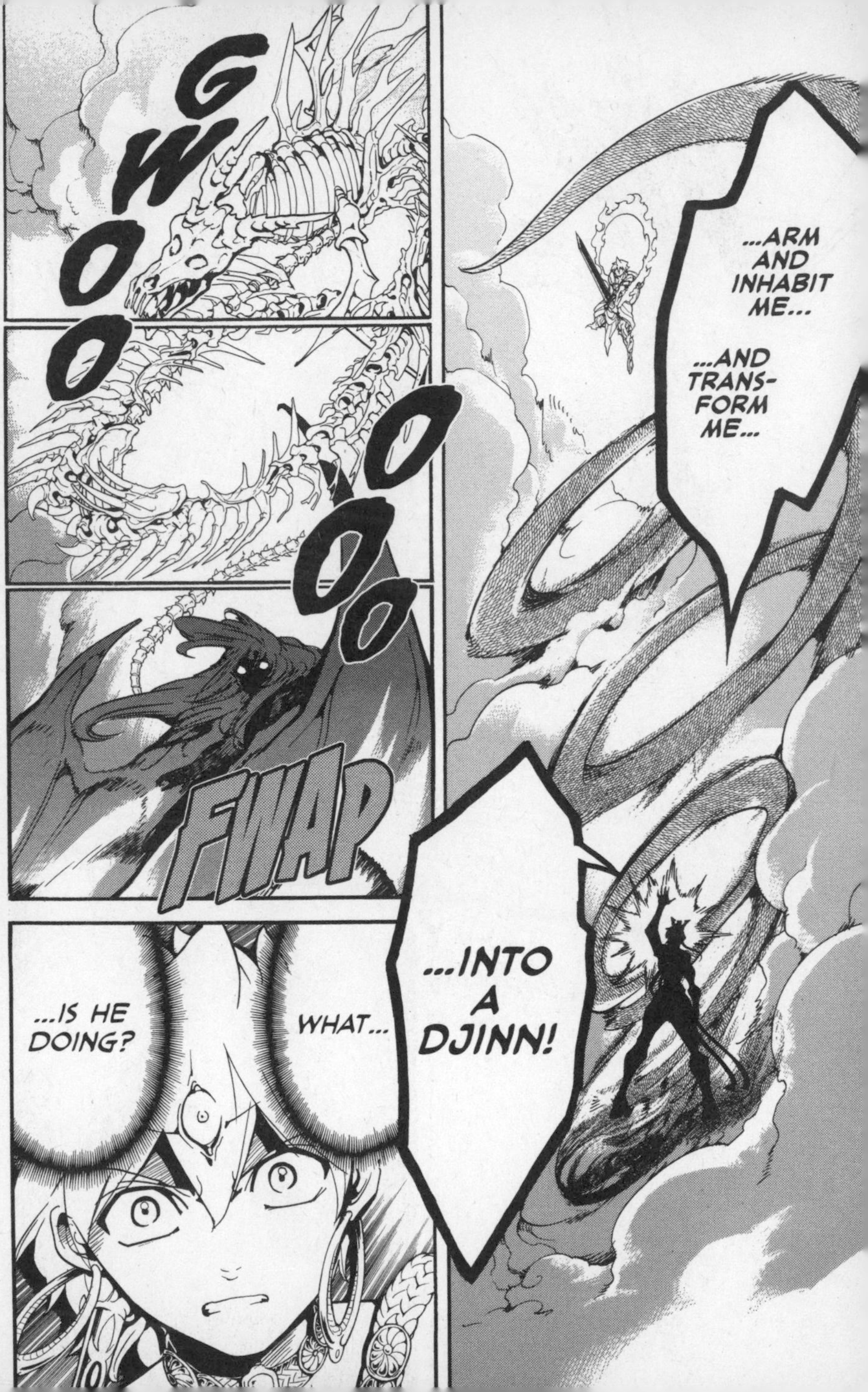
...ARM AND INHABIT ME...
...AND TRANS-FORM ME...
...INTO A DJINN!
GWOOOOO
FWAP
WHAT...
...IS HE DOING?

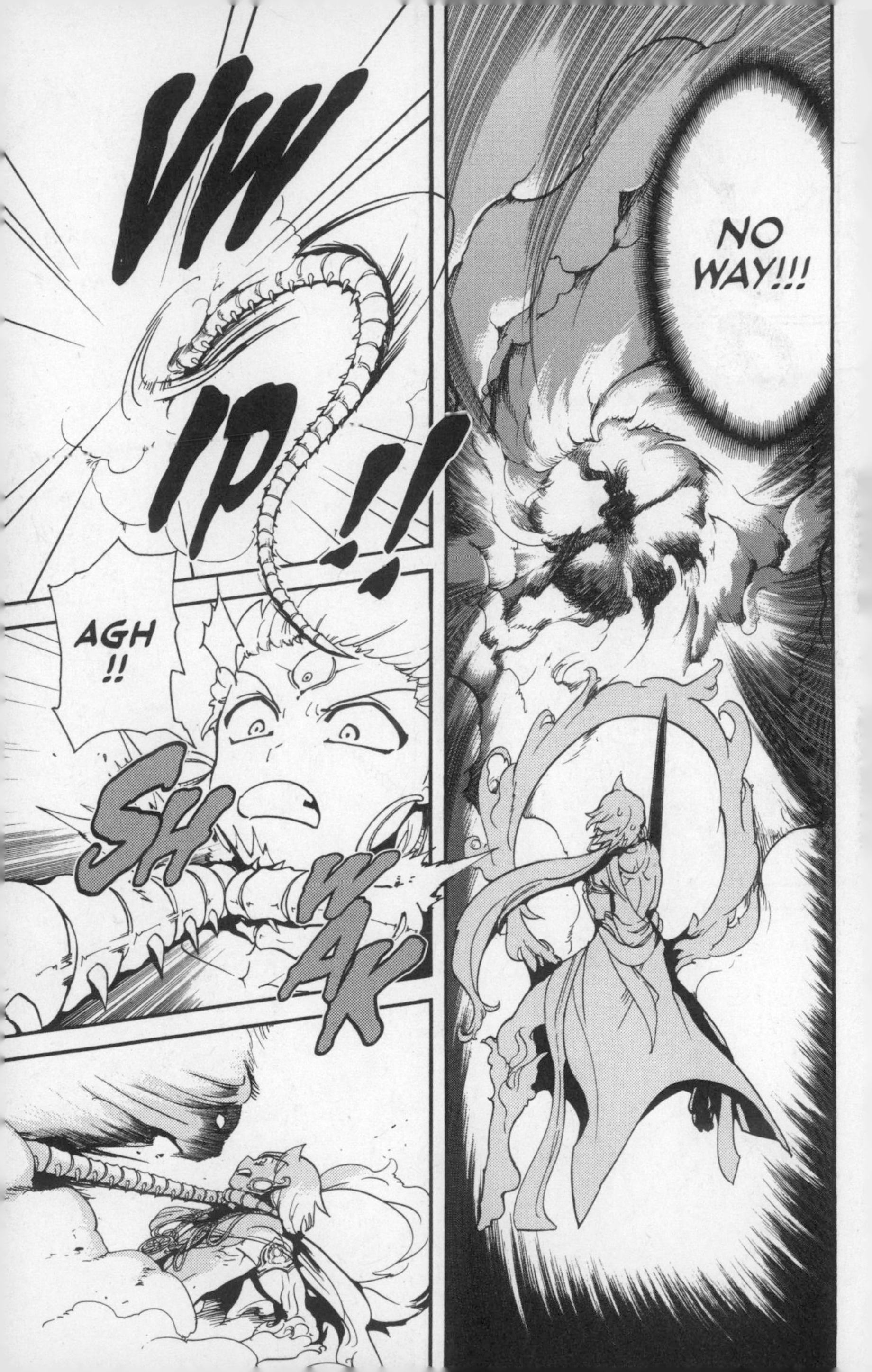
NO WAY!!!
WHIP!!
AGH!!
SHWAK

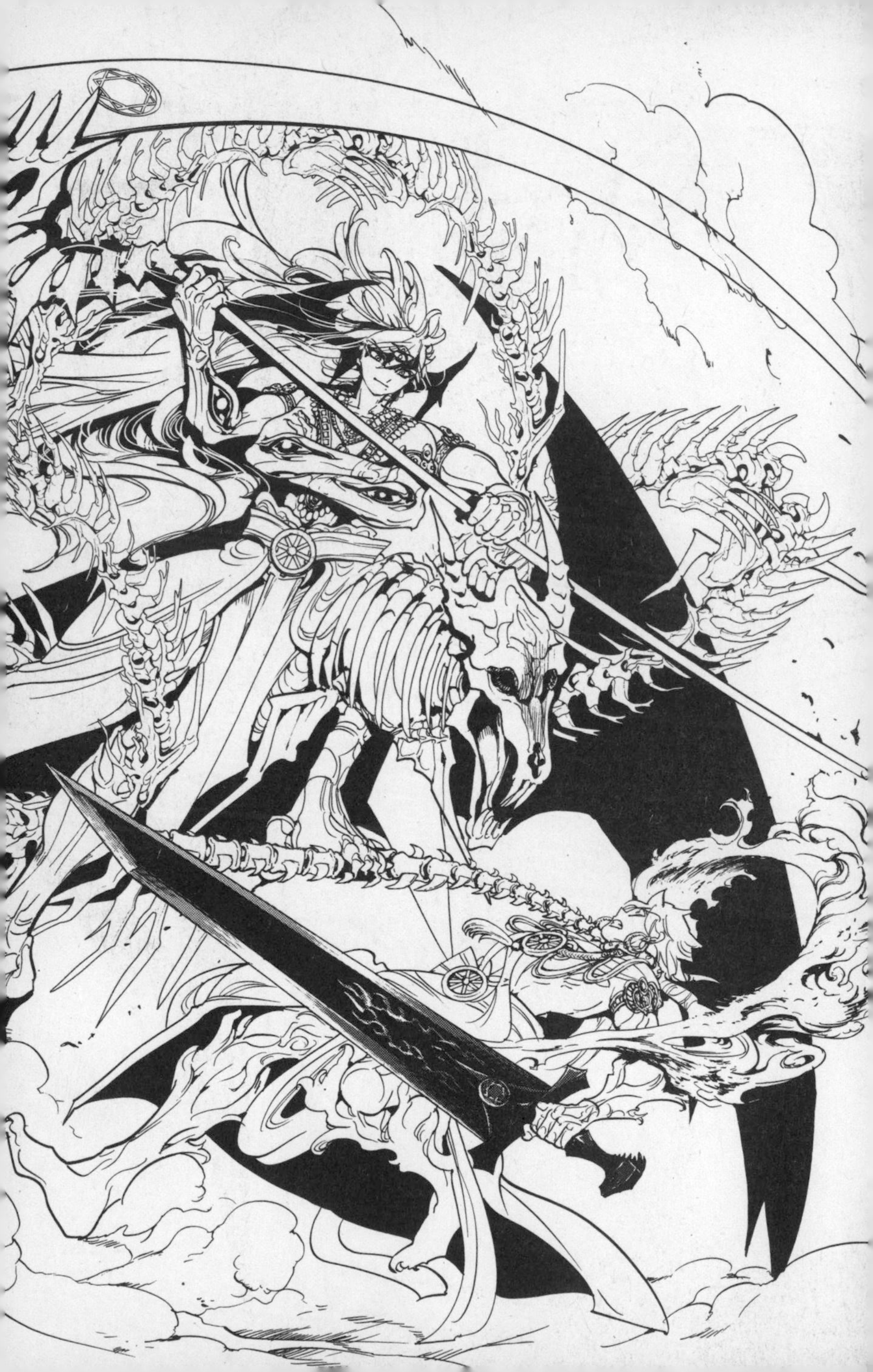

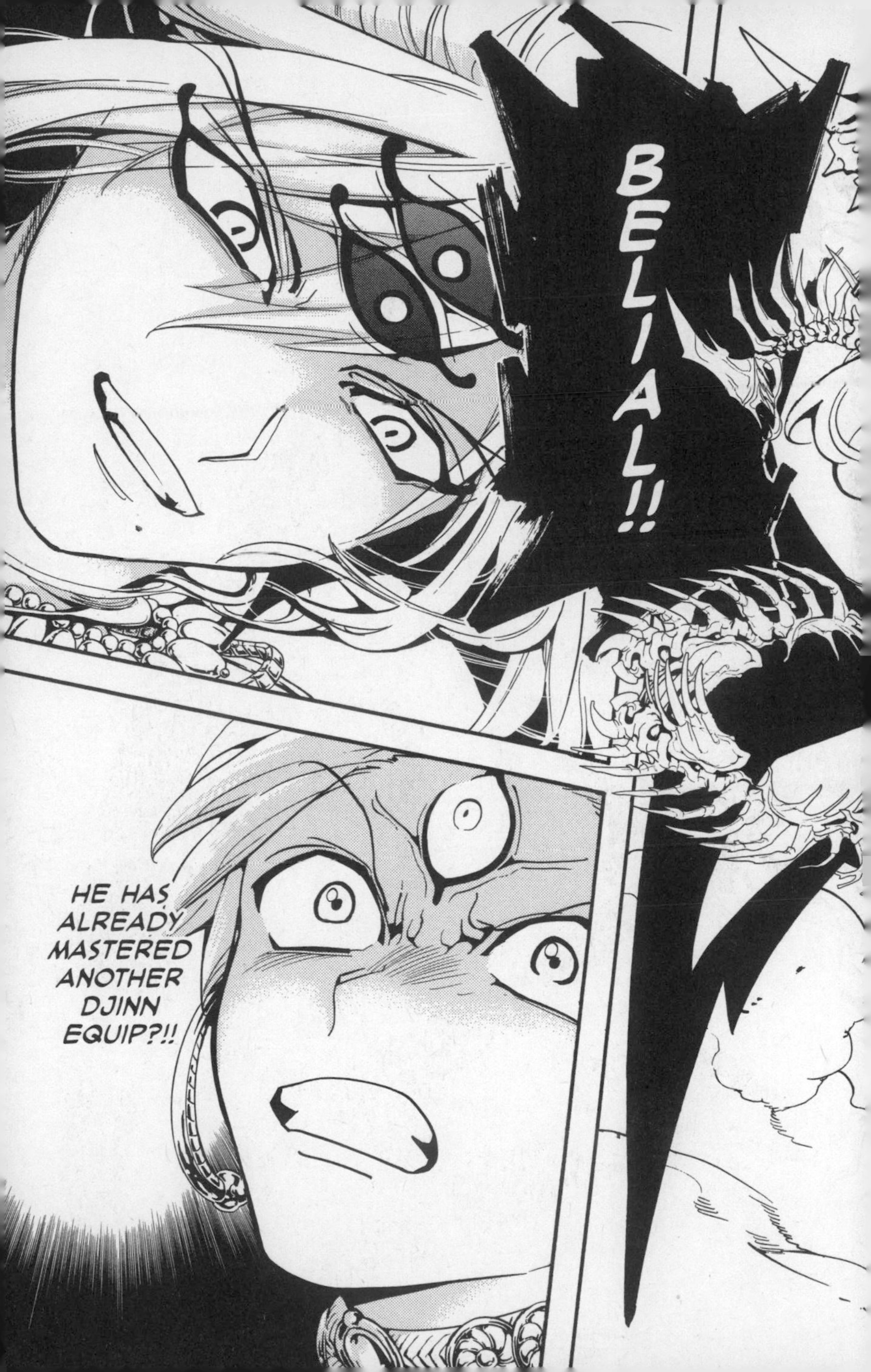
BELIAL!!
HE HAS ALREADY MASTERED ANOTHER DJINN EQUIP?!!

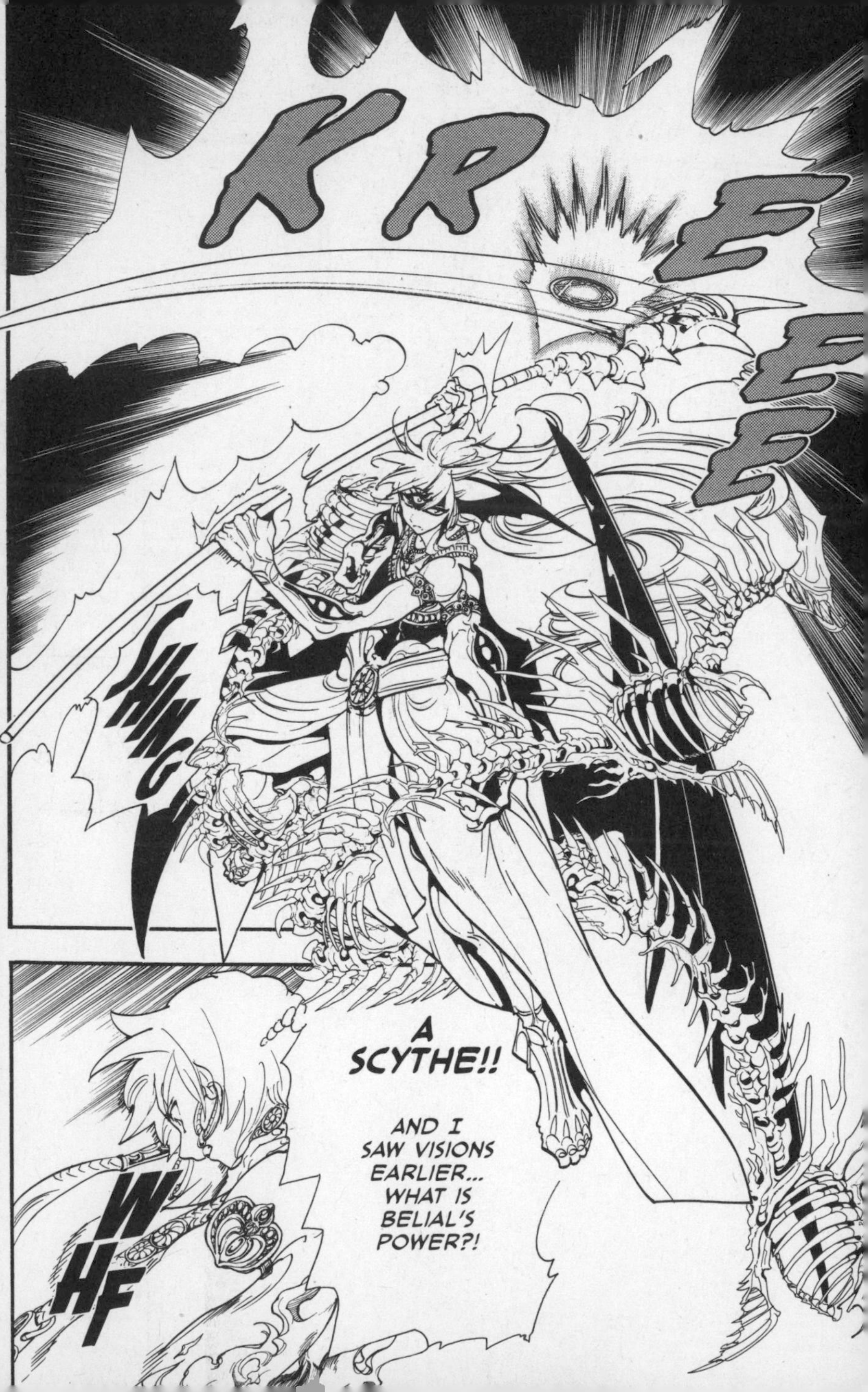
KREEE
SHING
A SCYTHE!!
AND I SAW VISIONS EARLIER... WHAT IS BELIAL'S POWER?!
WHF

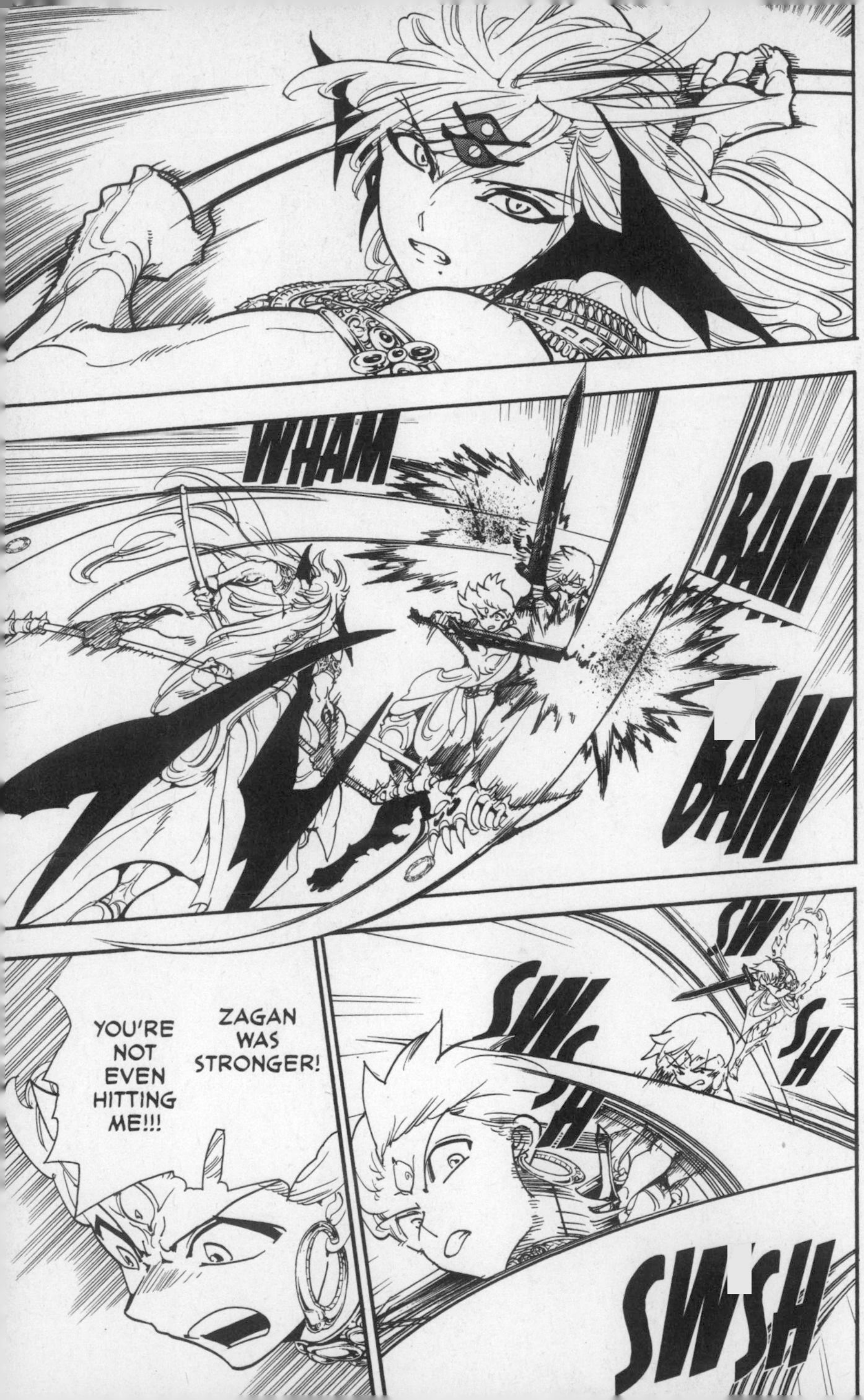
BAM
BAM
WHAM
SW
SWSH
SH
SH
SWSH
ZAGAN WAS STRONGER!
YOU'RE NOT EVEN HITTING ME!!!

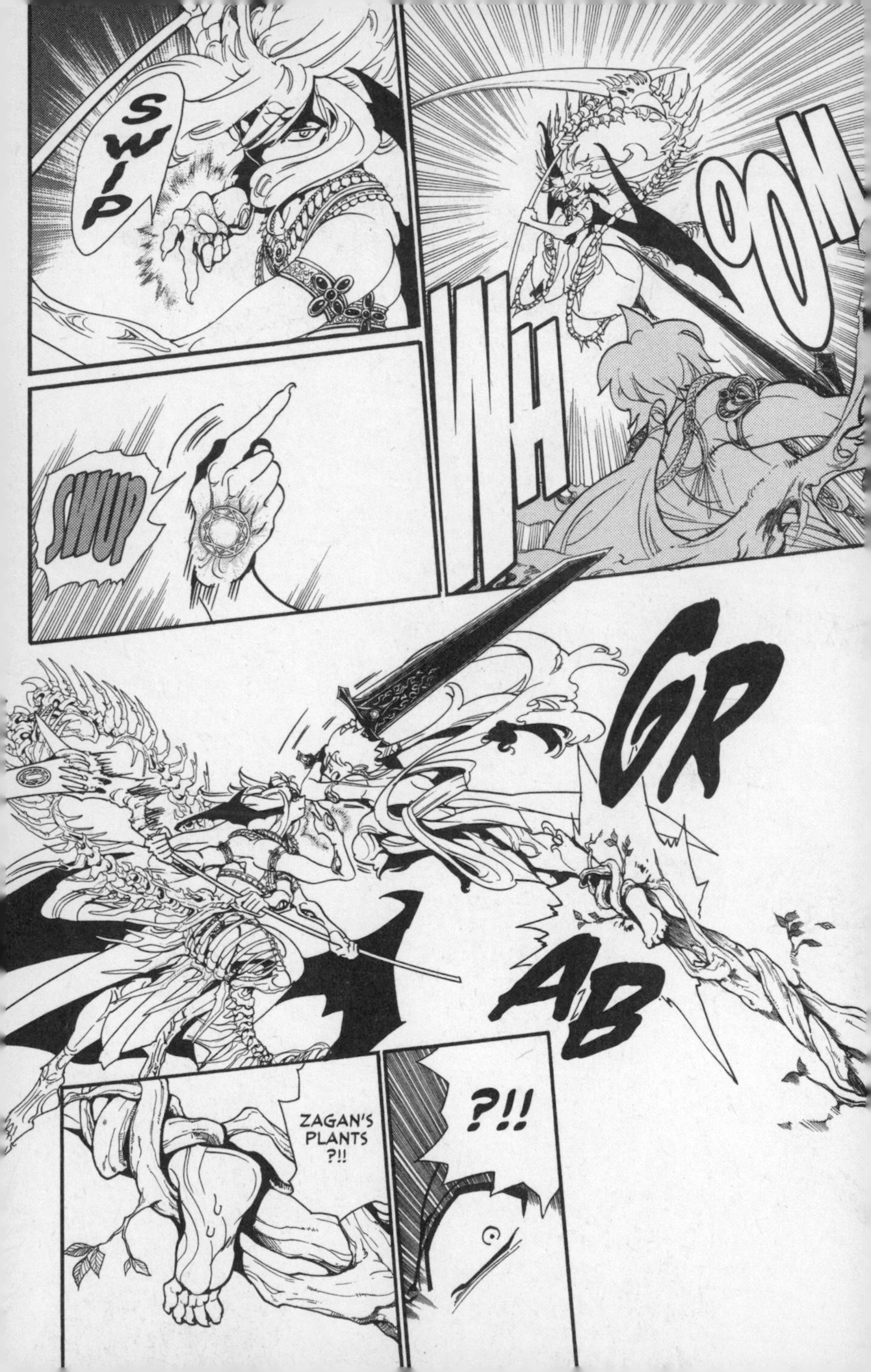
WHHOOM
SWIP
SWUP
GRAB
?!!
ZAGAN'S PLANTS ?!!

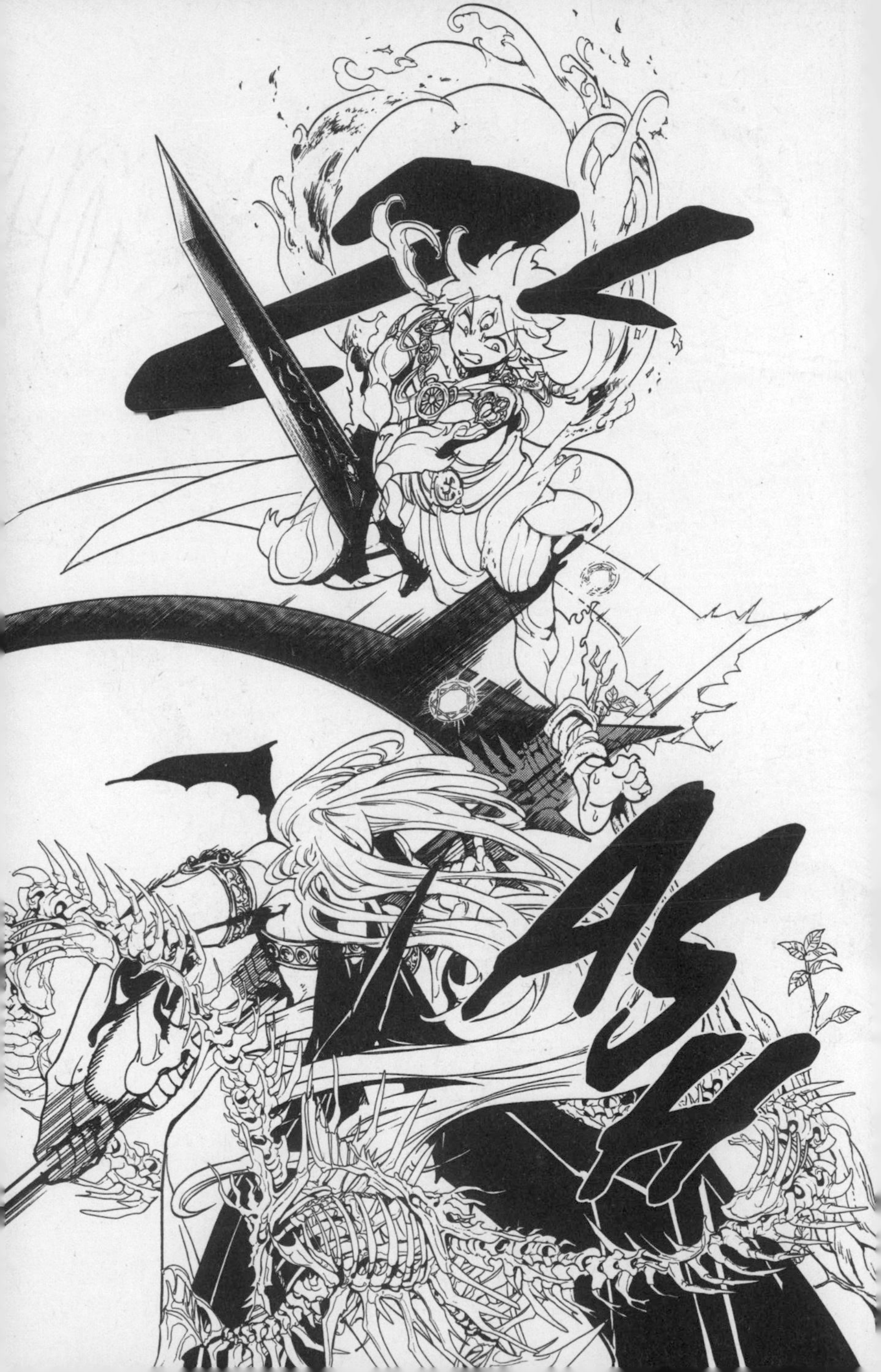

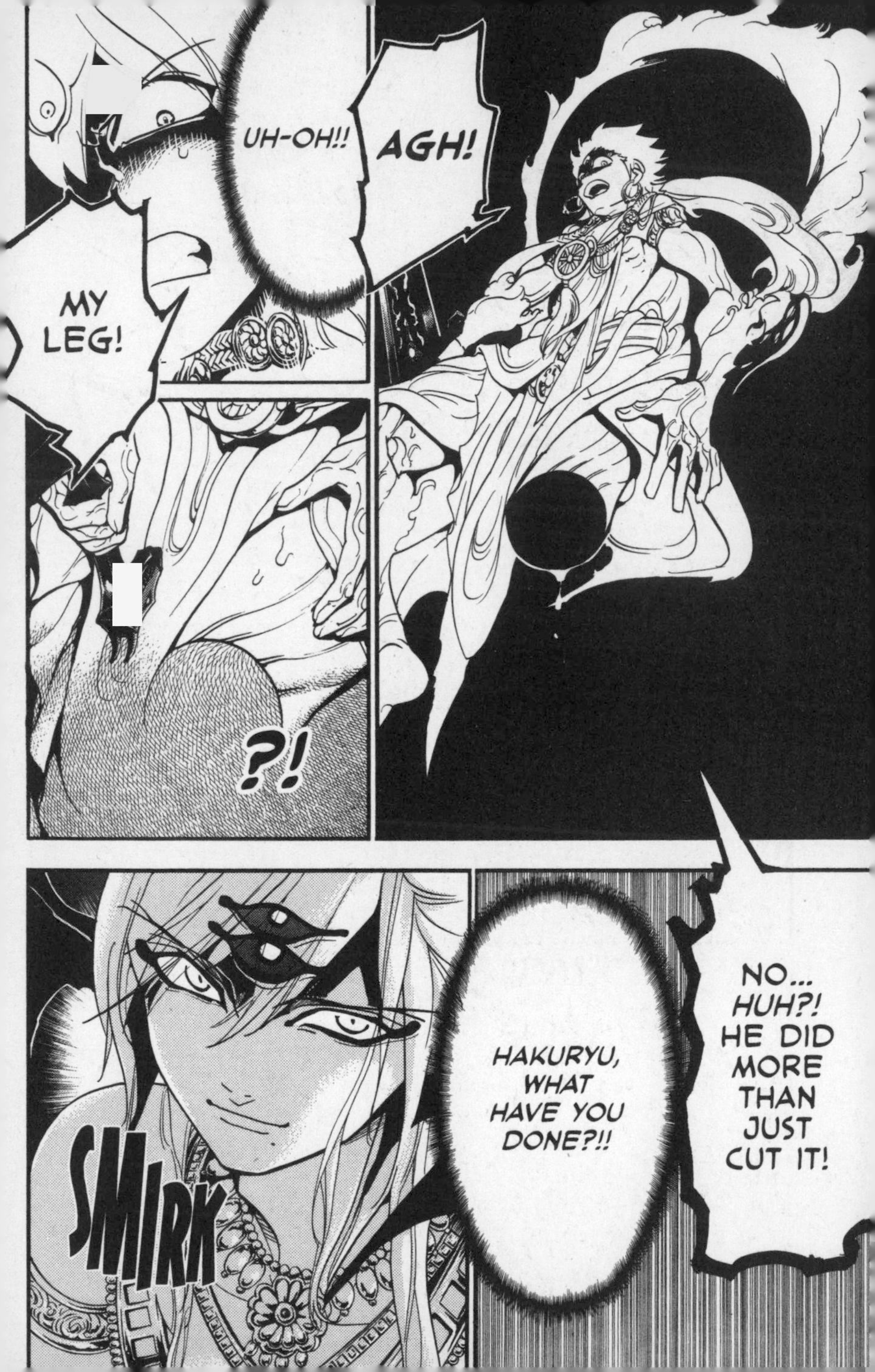
AGH!
UH-OH!!
MY LEG!
?!
NO... HUH?! HE DID MORE THAN JUST CUT IT!
HAKURYU, WHAT HAVE YOU DONE?!!
SMIRK

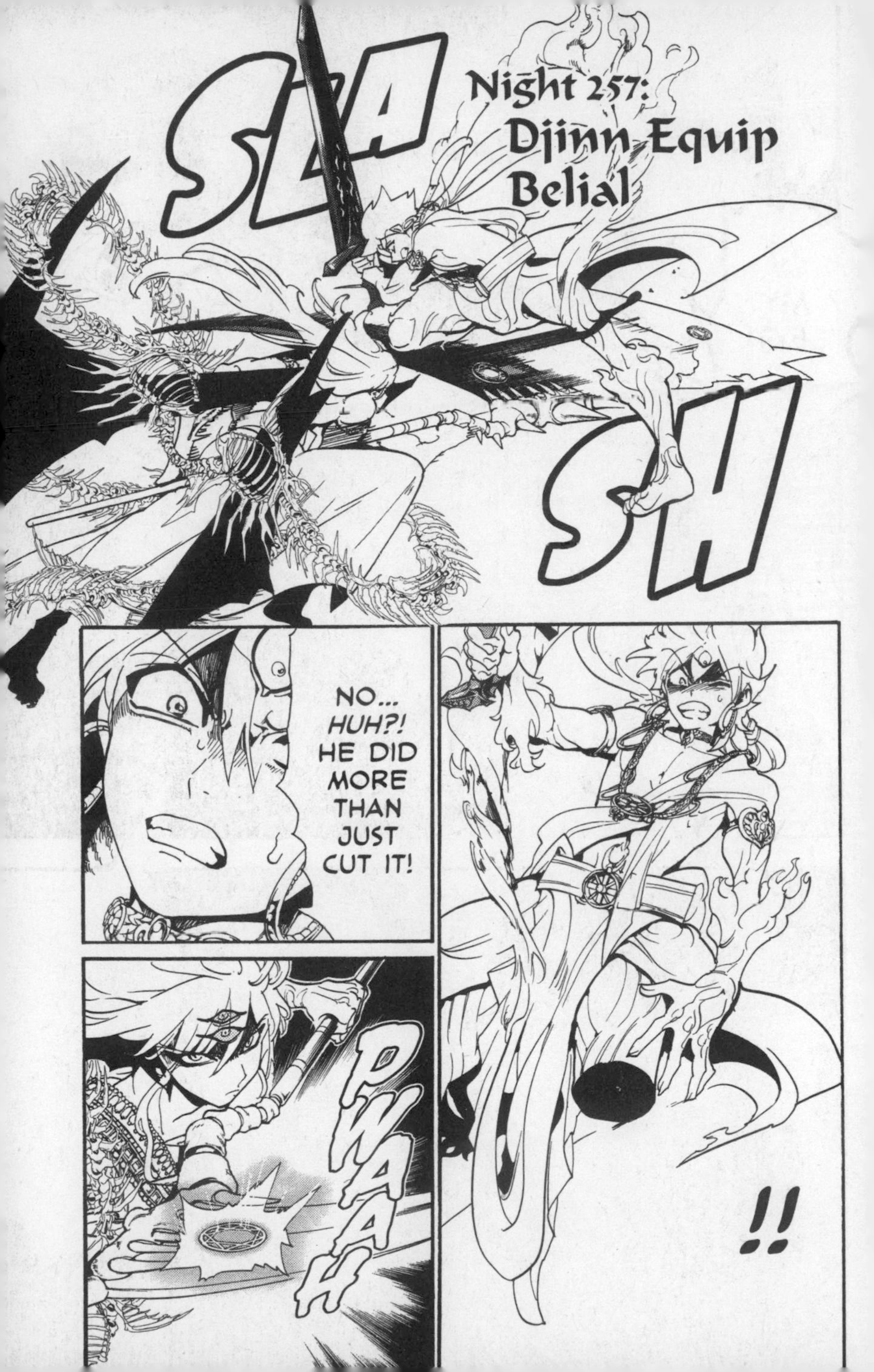
Night 257: Djinn Equip Belial
SLA
SH
!!
NO... HUH?! HE DID MORE THAN JUST CUT IT!
PWAAH

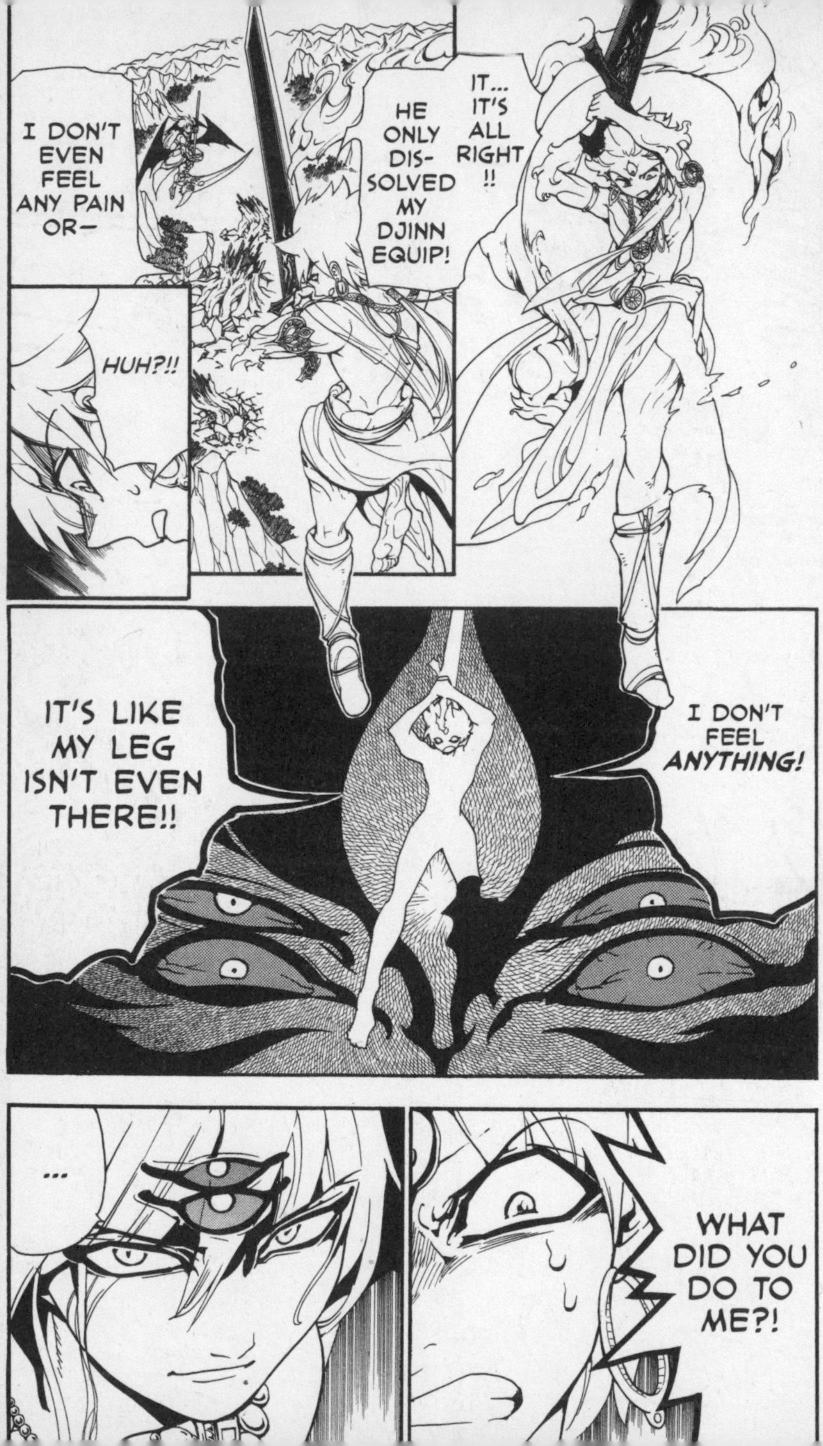
IT... IT'S ALL RIGHT!!
HE ONLY DIS-SOLVED MY DJINN EQUIP!
I DON'T EVEN FEEL ANY PAIN OR—
HUH?!!
I DON'T FEEL ANYTHING!
IT'S LIKE MY LEG ISN'T EVEN THERE!!
WHAT DID YOU DO TO ME?!
...

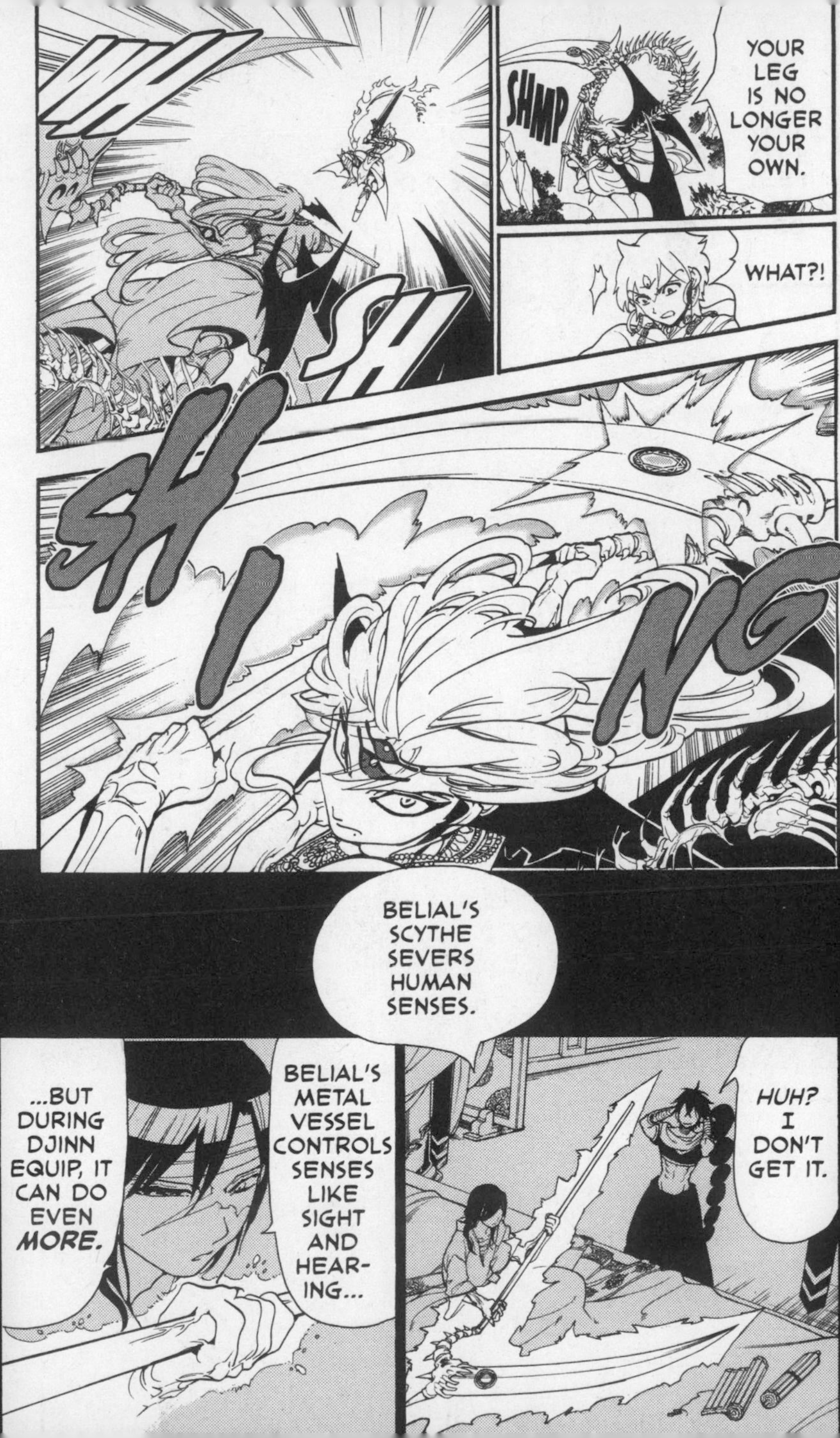
SHMP
YOUR LEG IS NO LONGER YOUR OWN.
WHAT?!
WHH
SH
SHIING
BELIAL'S SCYTHE SEVERS HUMAN SENSES.
HUH? I DON'T GET IT.
BELIAL'S METAL VESSEL CONTROLS SENSES LIKE SIGHT AND HEAR-ING...
...BUT DURING DJINN EQUIP, IT CAN DO EVEN ***MORE.***

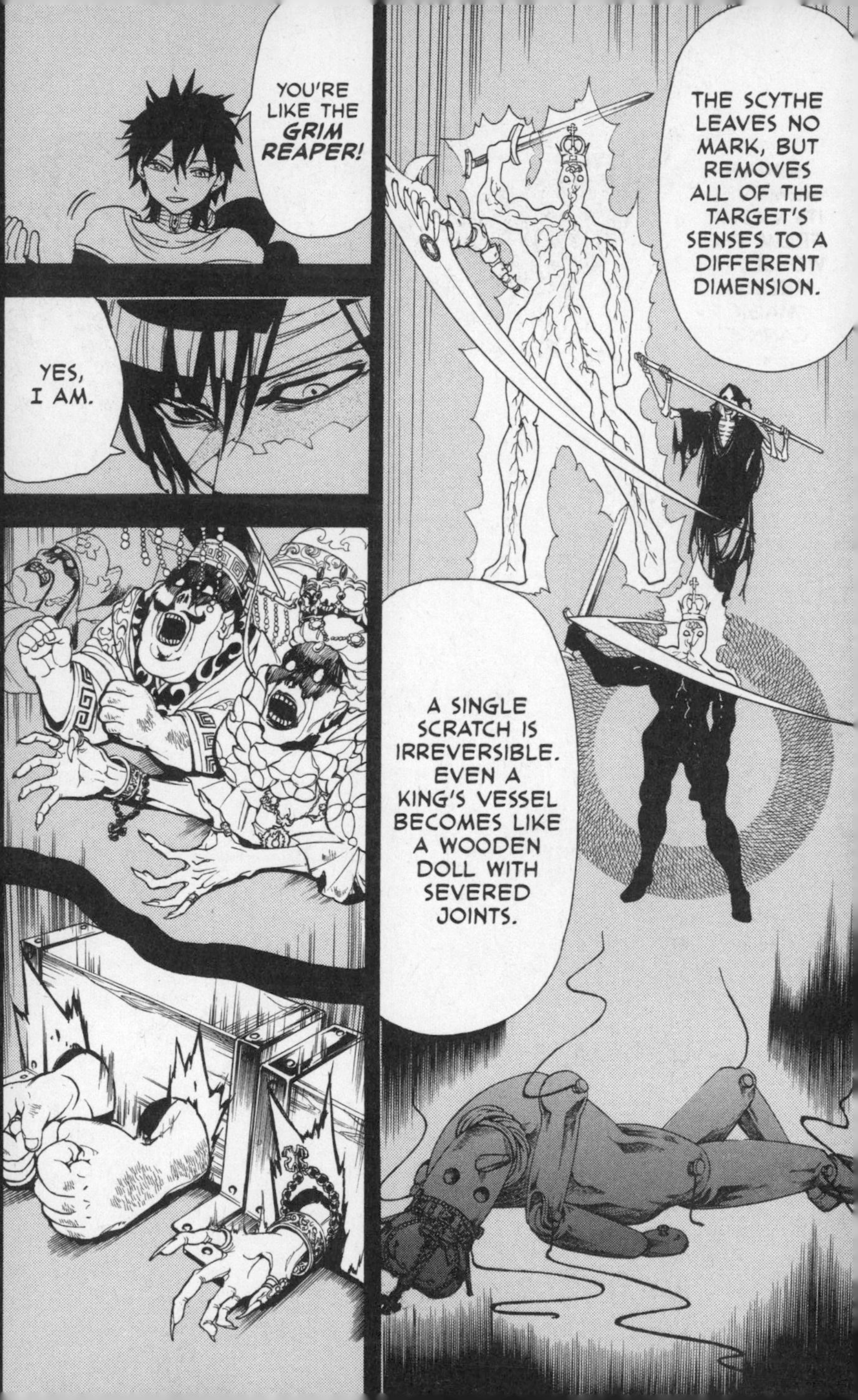
THE SCYTHE LEAVES NO MARK, BUT REMOVES ALL OF THE TARGET'S SENSES TO A DIFFERENT DIMENSION.
A SINGLE SCRATCH IS IRREVERSIBLE. EVEN A KING'S VESSEL BECOMES LIKE A WOODEN DOLL WITH SEVERED JOINTS.
YOU'RE LIKE THE *GRIM REAPER!*
YES, I AM.

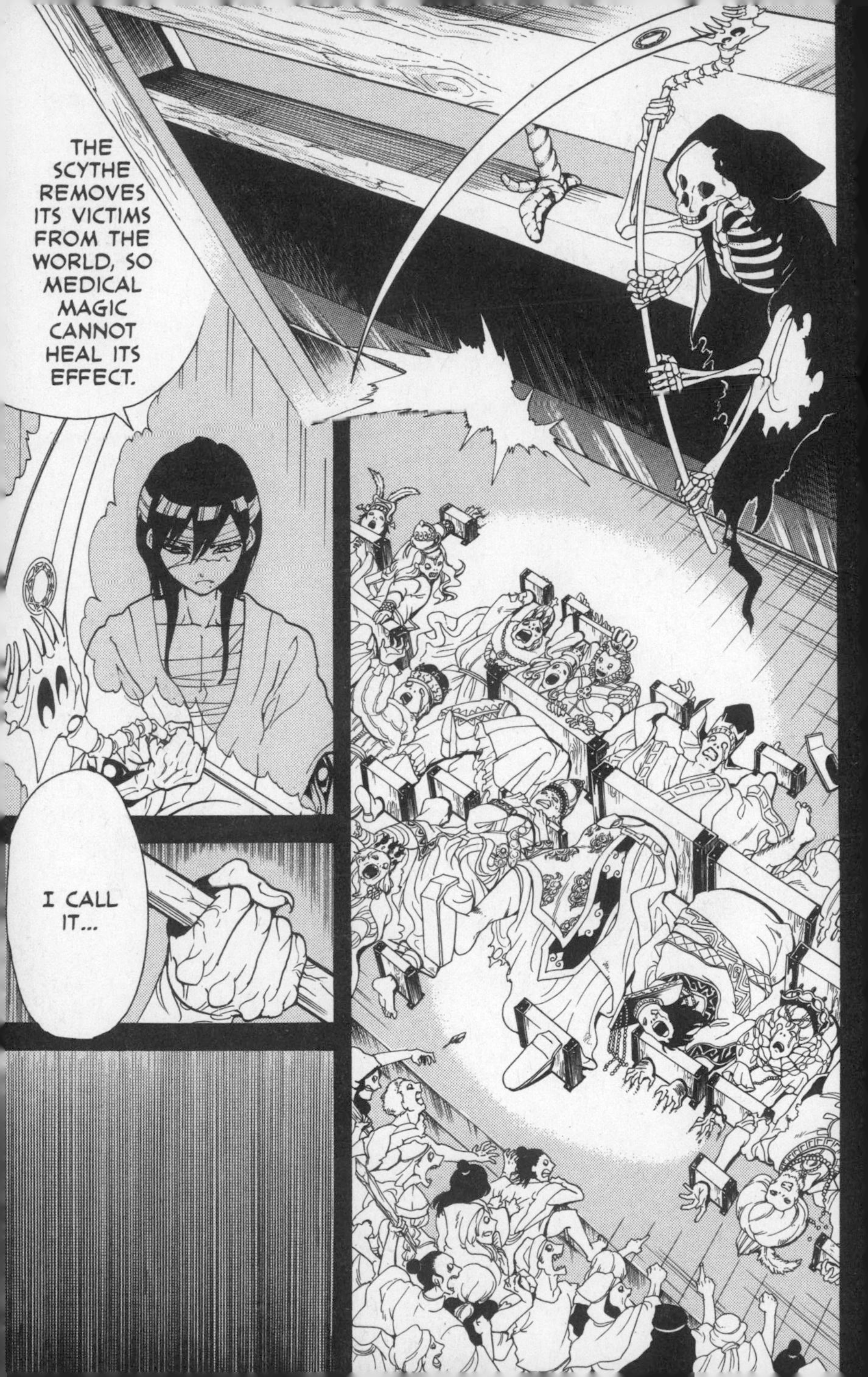
THE SCYTHE REMOVES ITS VICTIMS FROM THE WORLD, SO MEDICAL MAGIC CANNOT HEAL ITS EFFECT.
I CALL IT...

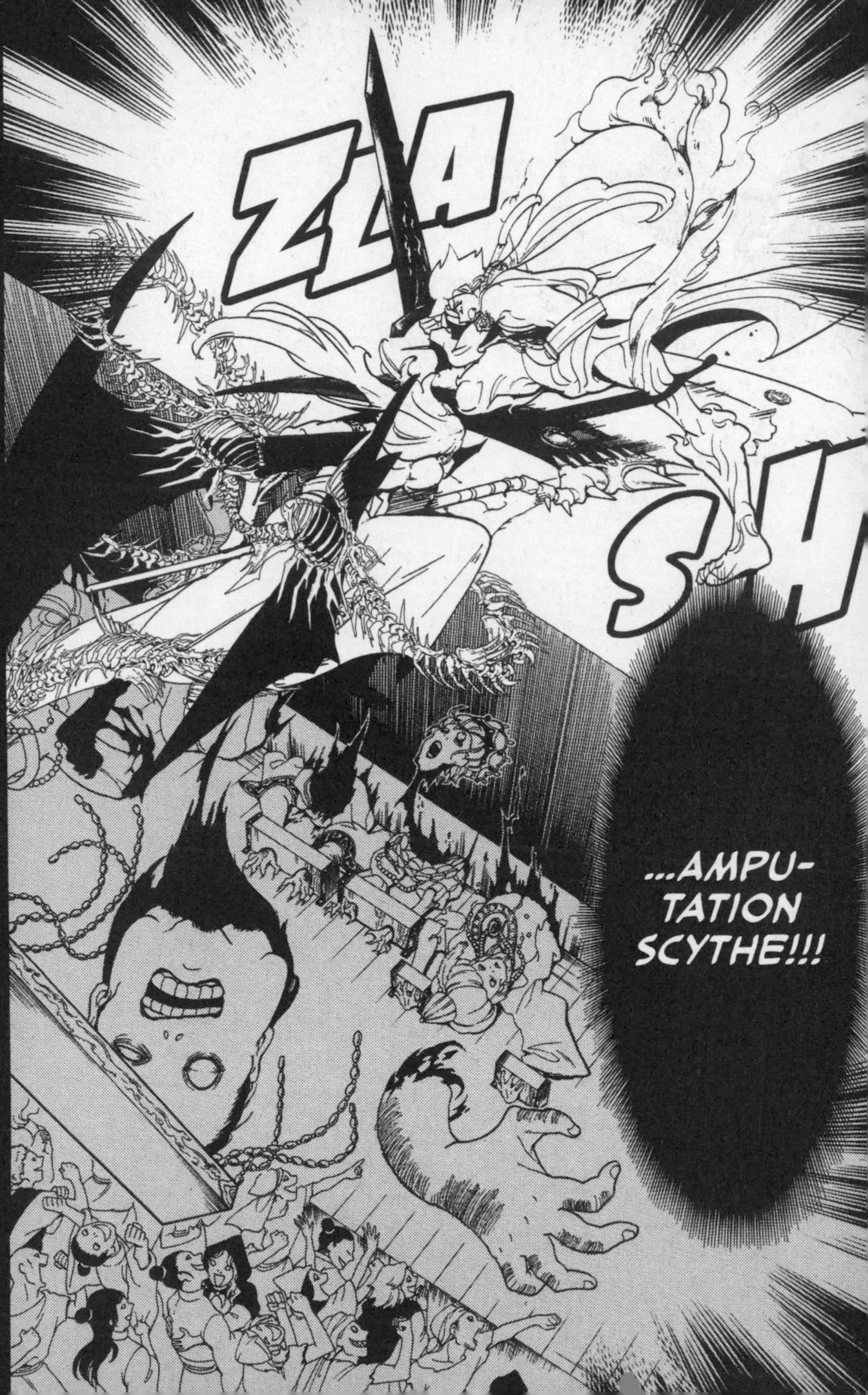
ZA
SH
...AMPU-
TATION
SCYTHE!!!

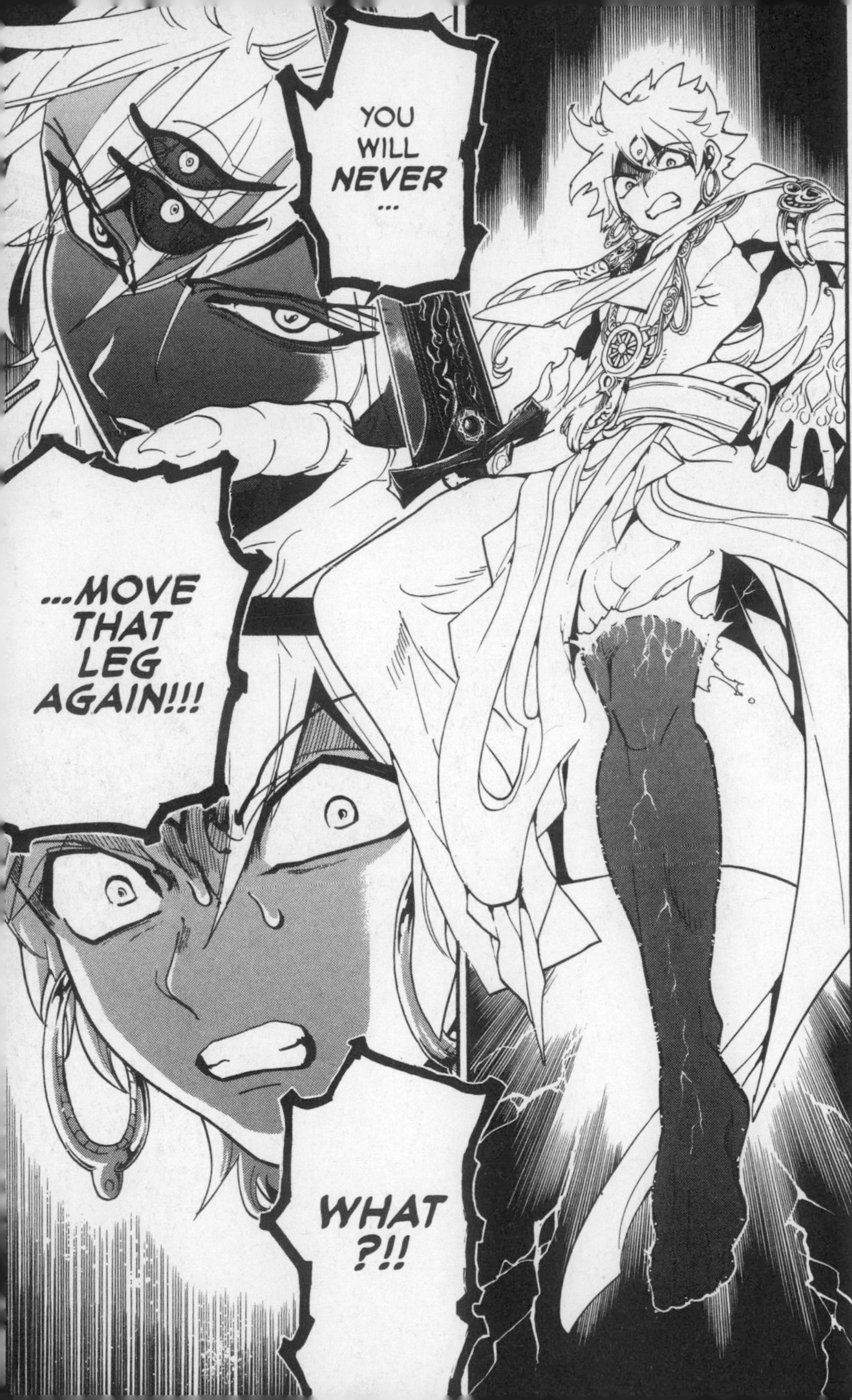
YOU WILL NEVER ...
...MOVE THAT LEG AGAIN!!!
WHAT ?!!

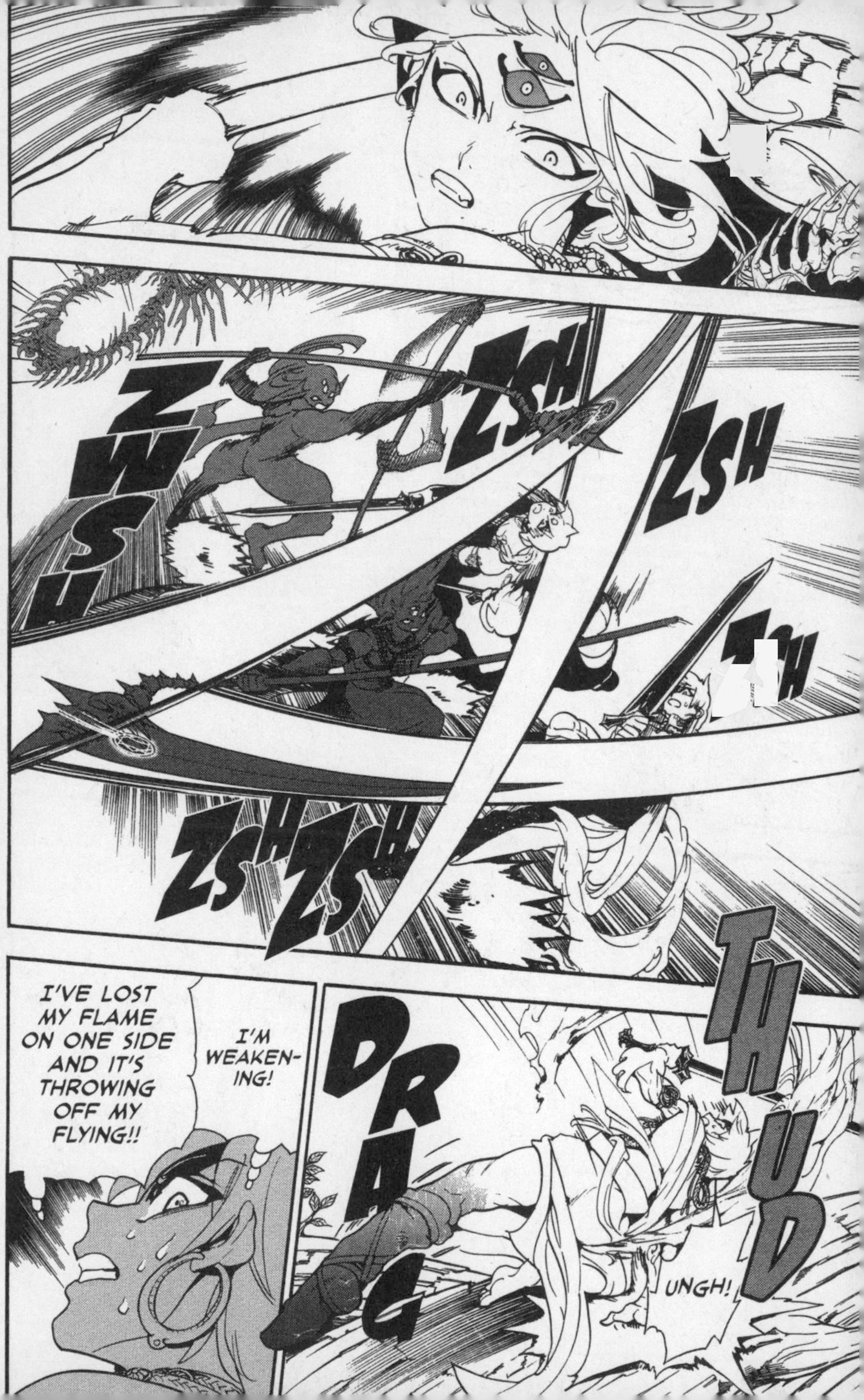
ZSH
ZSH
ZWSH
ZSH
ZSH
THUD
DRAG
UNGH!
I'M WEAKEN-ING!
I'VE LOST MY FLAME ON ONE SIDE AND IT'S THROWING OFF MY FLYING!!

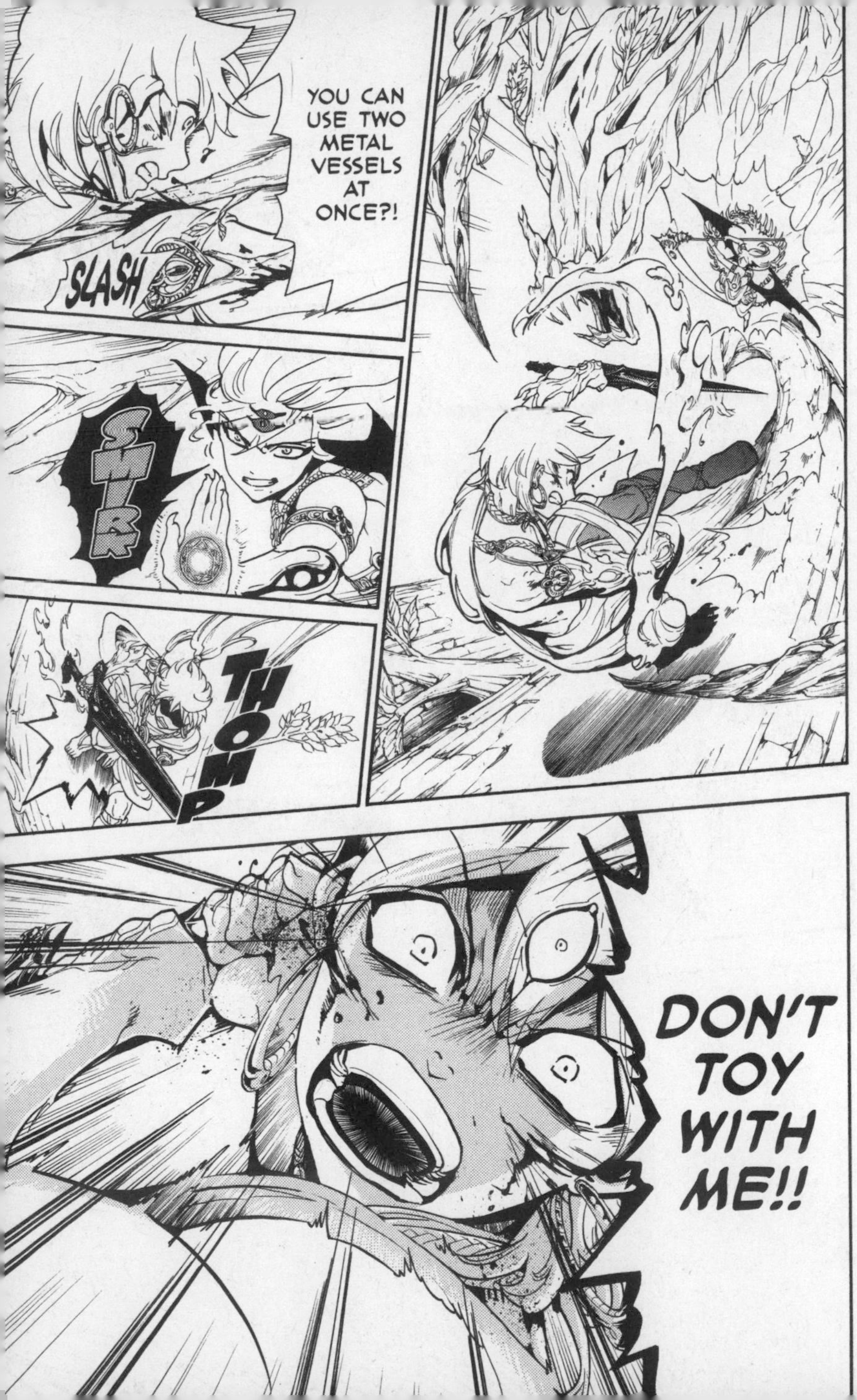
YOU CAN USE TWO METAL VESSELS AT ONCE?!
SLASH
SMIRK
THOMP
DON'T TOY WITH ME!!

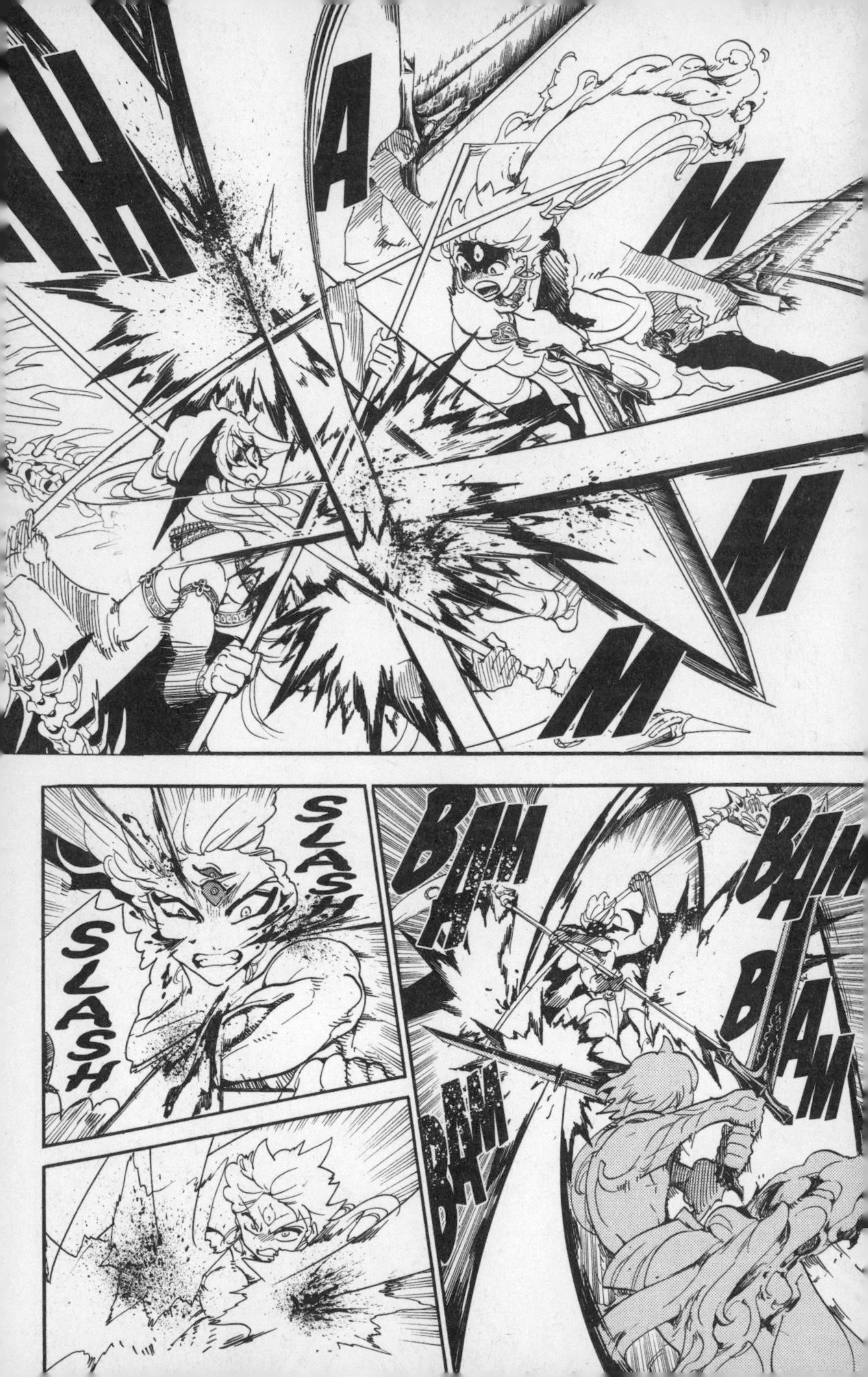
BAM
BAM
BAM
BAM
SLASH
SLASH

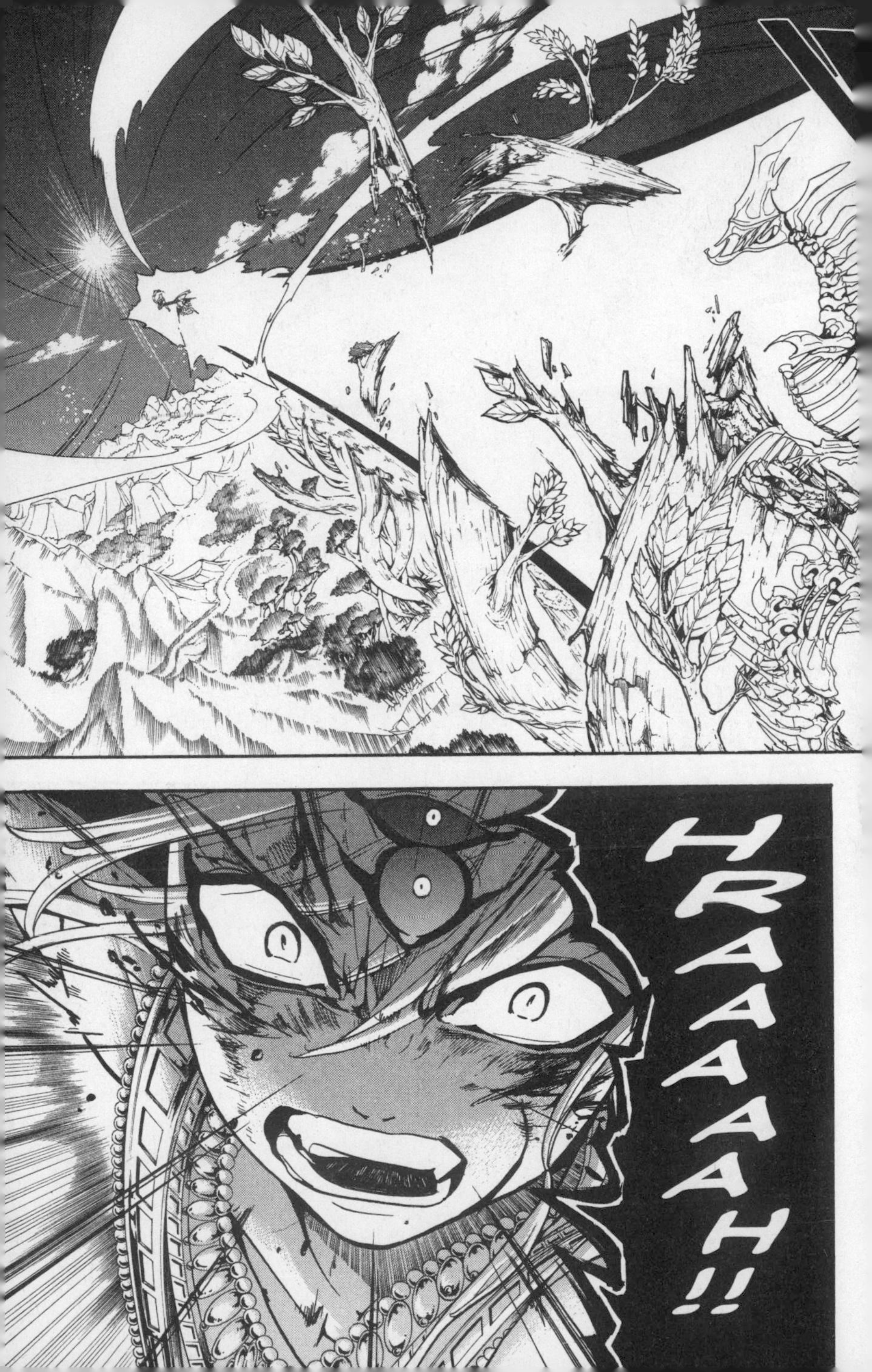
HRAAAAH!!

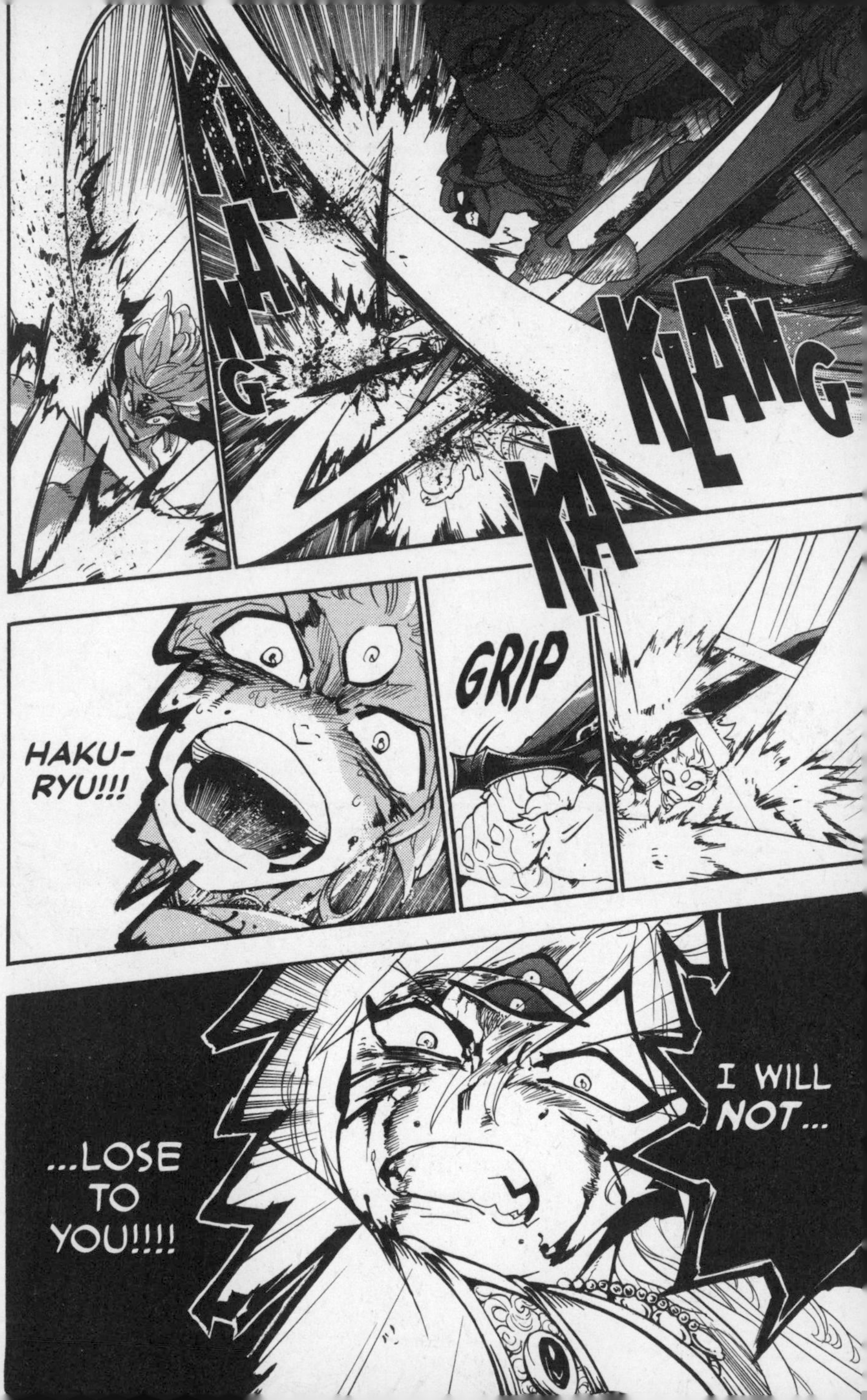
KLANG
KA
KLANG
GRIP
HAKU-RYU!!!
I WILL NOT...
...LOSE TO YOU!!!!

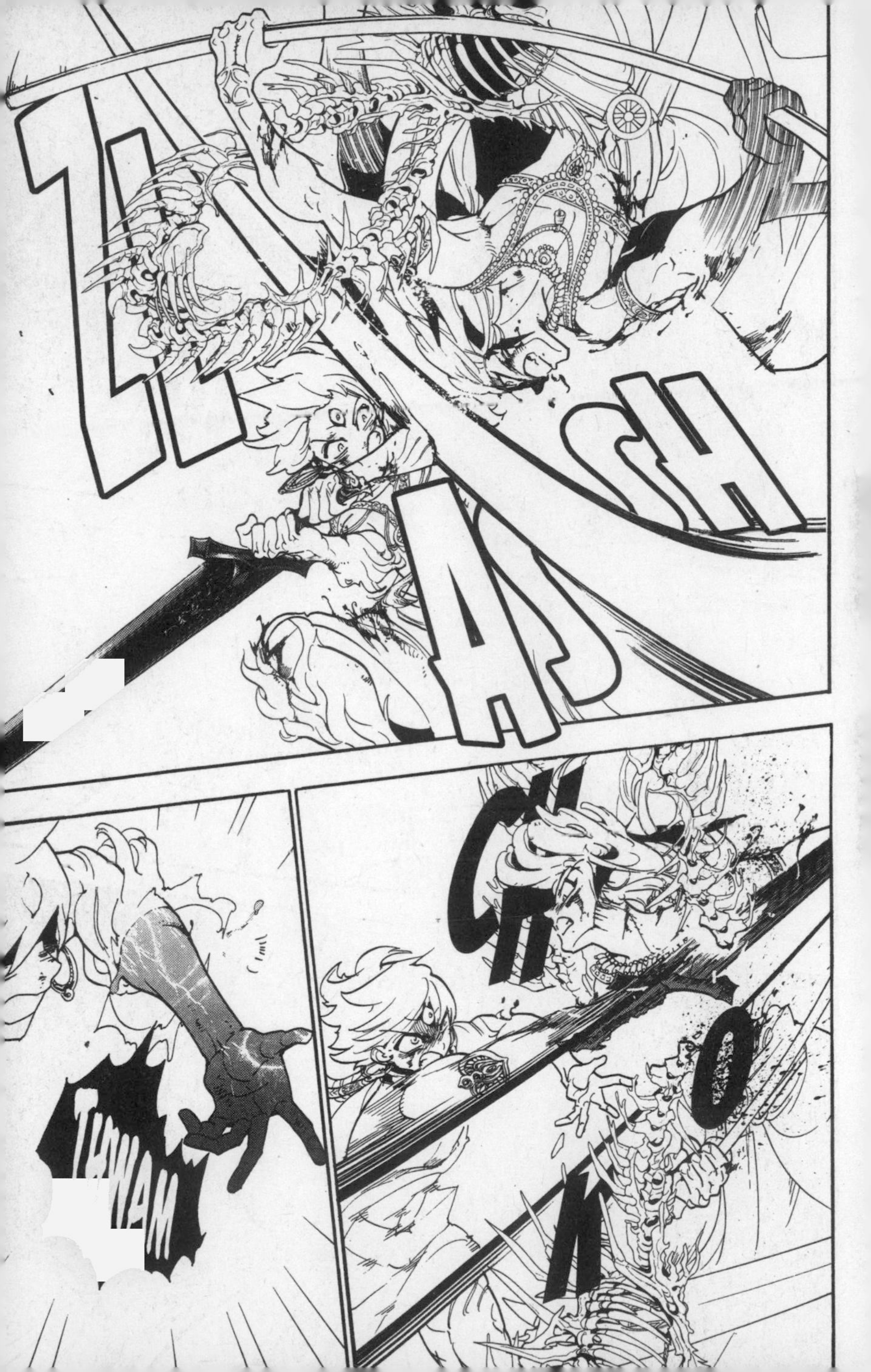
THWAM

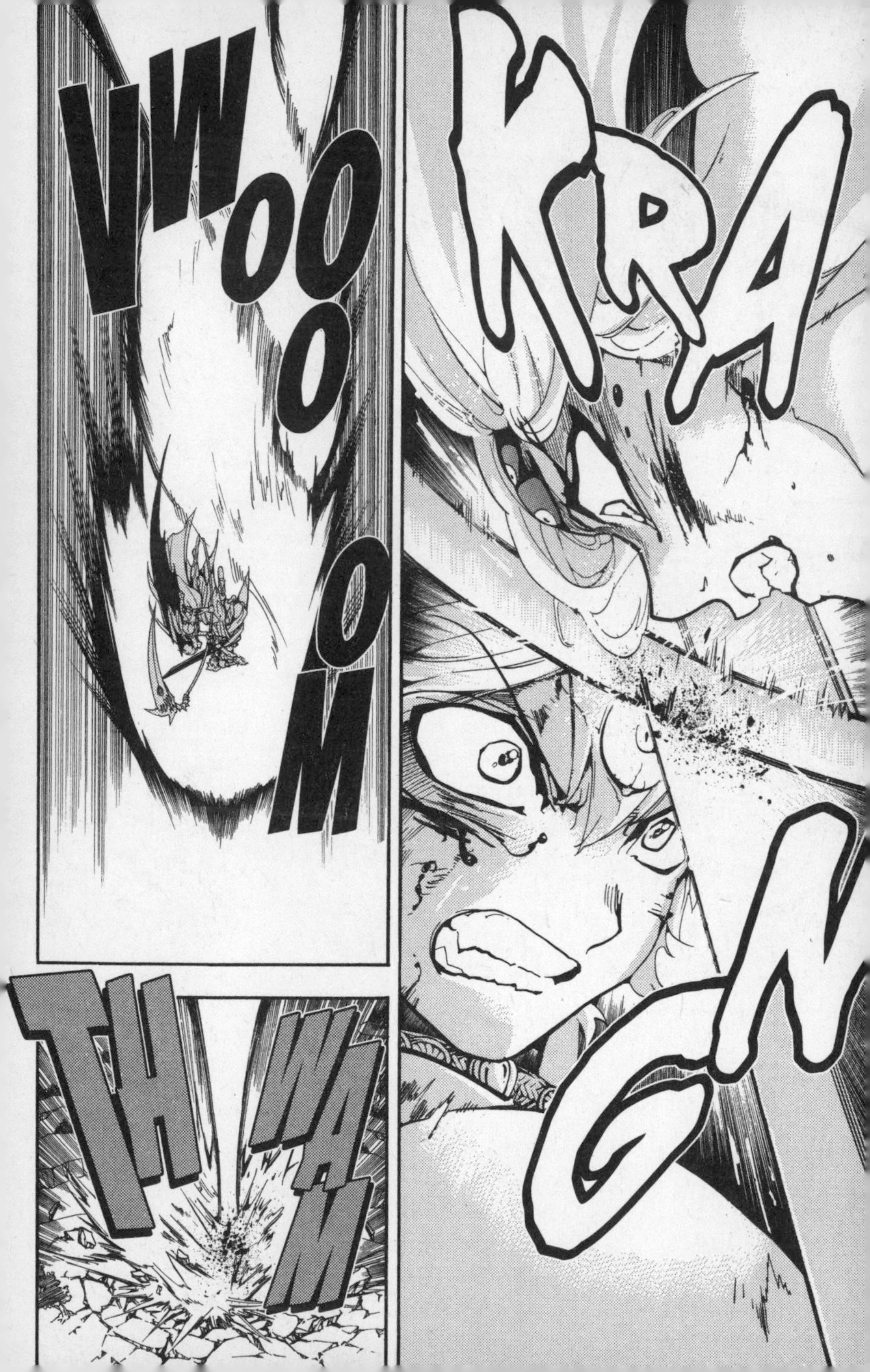
KRA
GN
VWOOOOM
THWAM

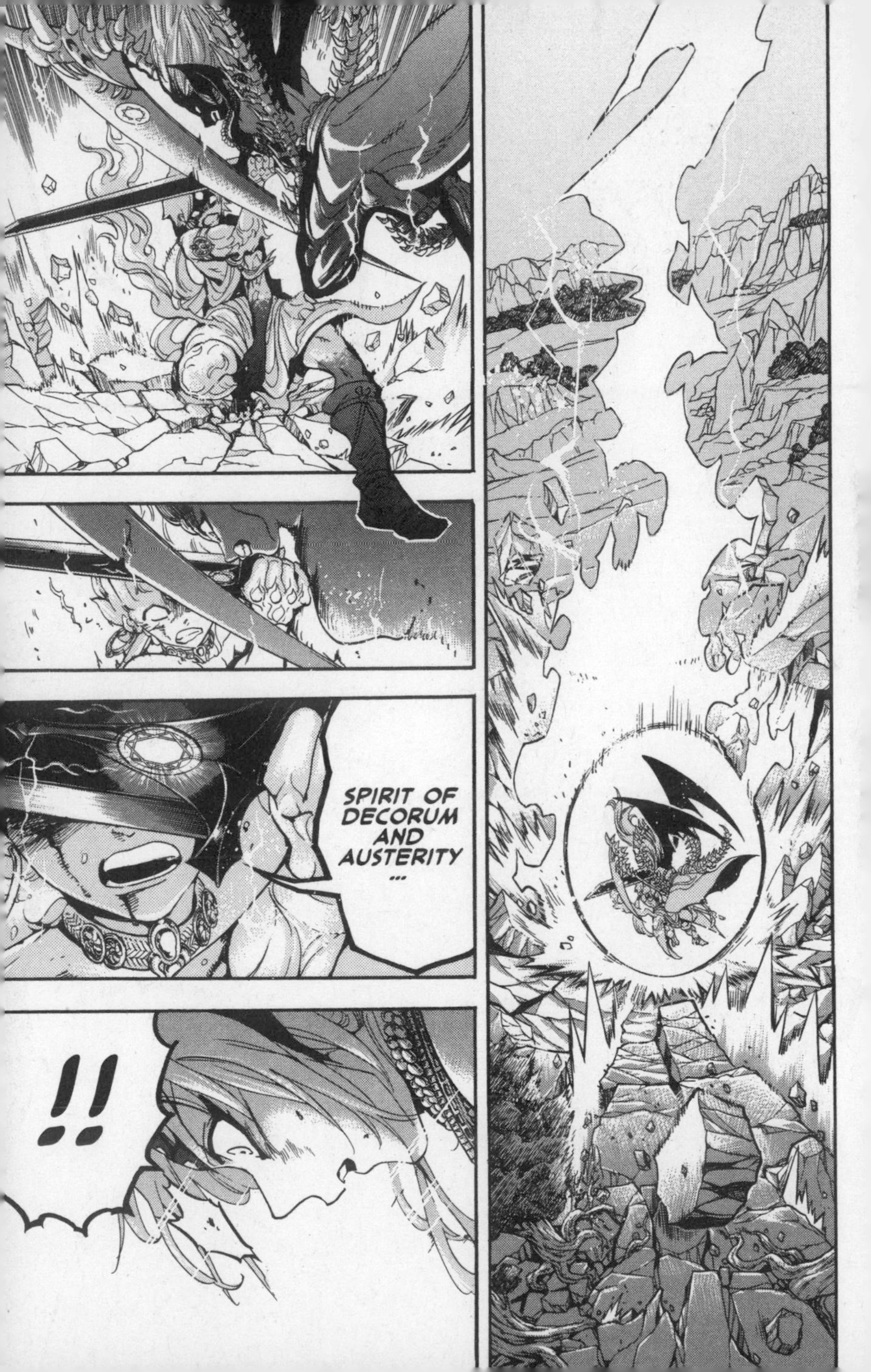
SPIRIT OF DECORUM AND AUSTERITY ...
!!

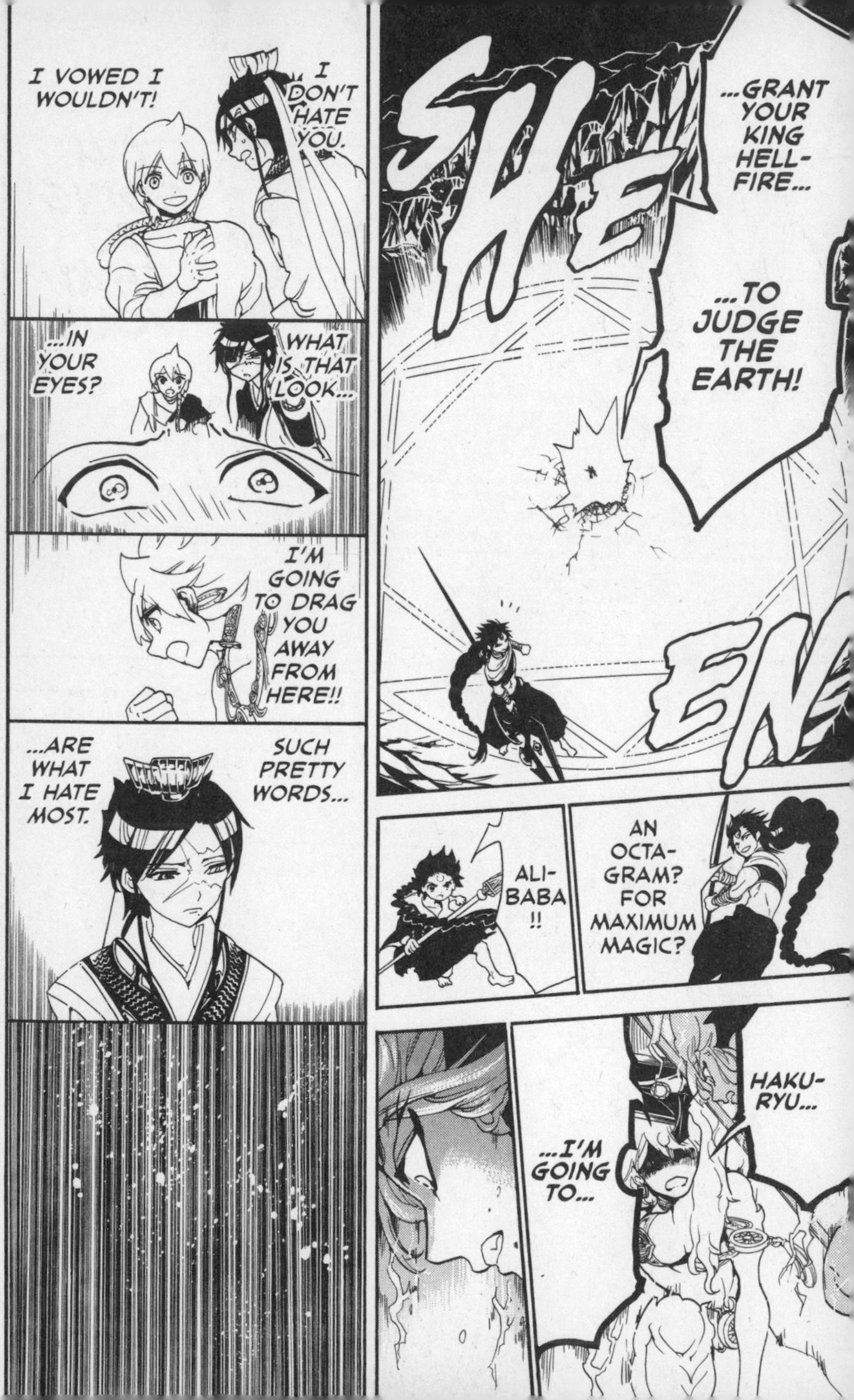
...GRANT YOUR KING HELL-FIRE...
SHE
...TO JUDGE THE EARTH!
EN
AN OCTA-GRAM? FOR MAXIMUM MAGIC?
ALI-BABA!!
HAKU-RYU...
...I'M GOING TO...
I DON'T HATE YOU.
I VOWED I WOULDN'T!
WHAT IS THAT LOOK...
...IN YOUR EYES?
I'M GOING TO DRAG YOU AWAY FROM HERE!!
SUCH PRETTY WORDS...
...ARE WHAT I HATE MOST.

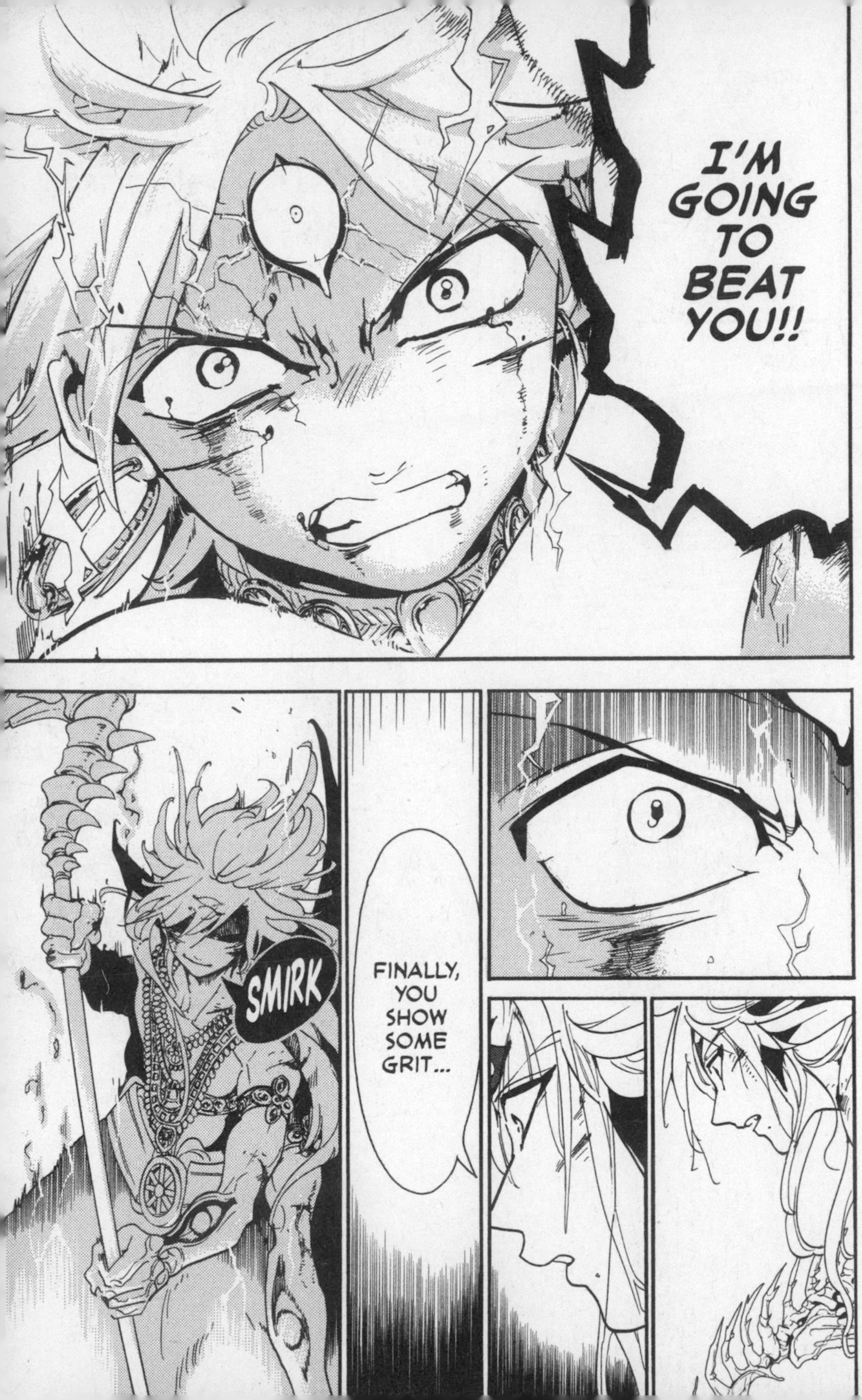
I'M GOING TO BEAT YOU!!
FINALLY, YOU SHOW SOME GRIT...
SMIRK

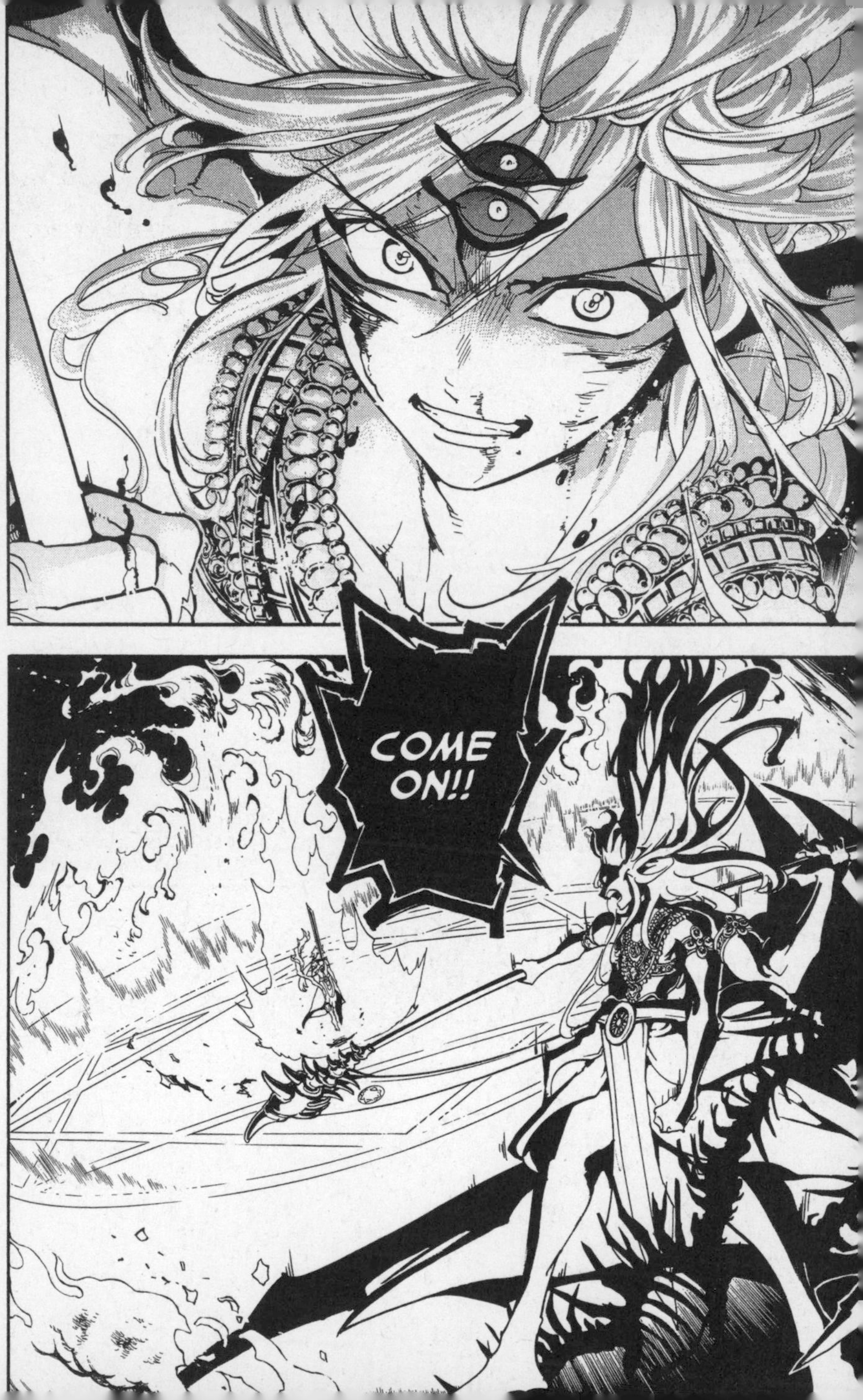
COME ON!!

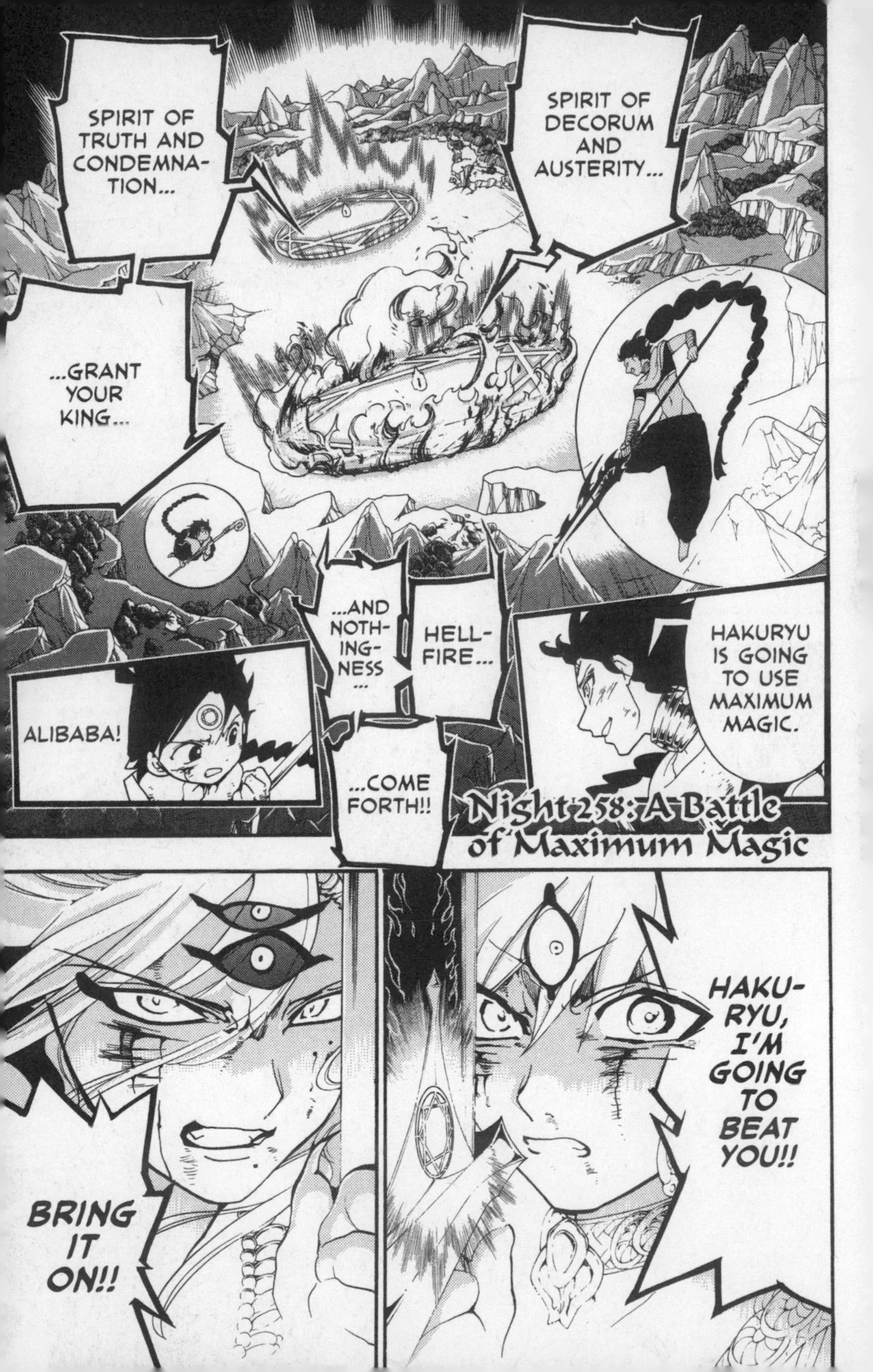
SPIRIT OF DECORUM AND AUSTERITY...
SPIRIT OF TRUTH AND CONDEMNATION...
...GRANT YOUR KING...
HAKURYU IS GOING TO USE MAXIMUM MAGIC.
HELL-FIRE...
...AND NOTHINGNESS...
...COME FORTH!!
ALIBABA!
Night 258: A Battle of Maximum Magic
HAKURYU, I'M GOING TO BEAT YOU!!
BRING IT ON!!

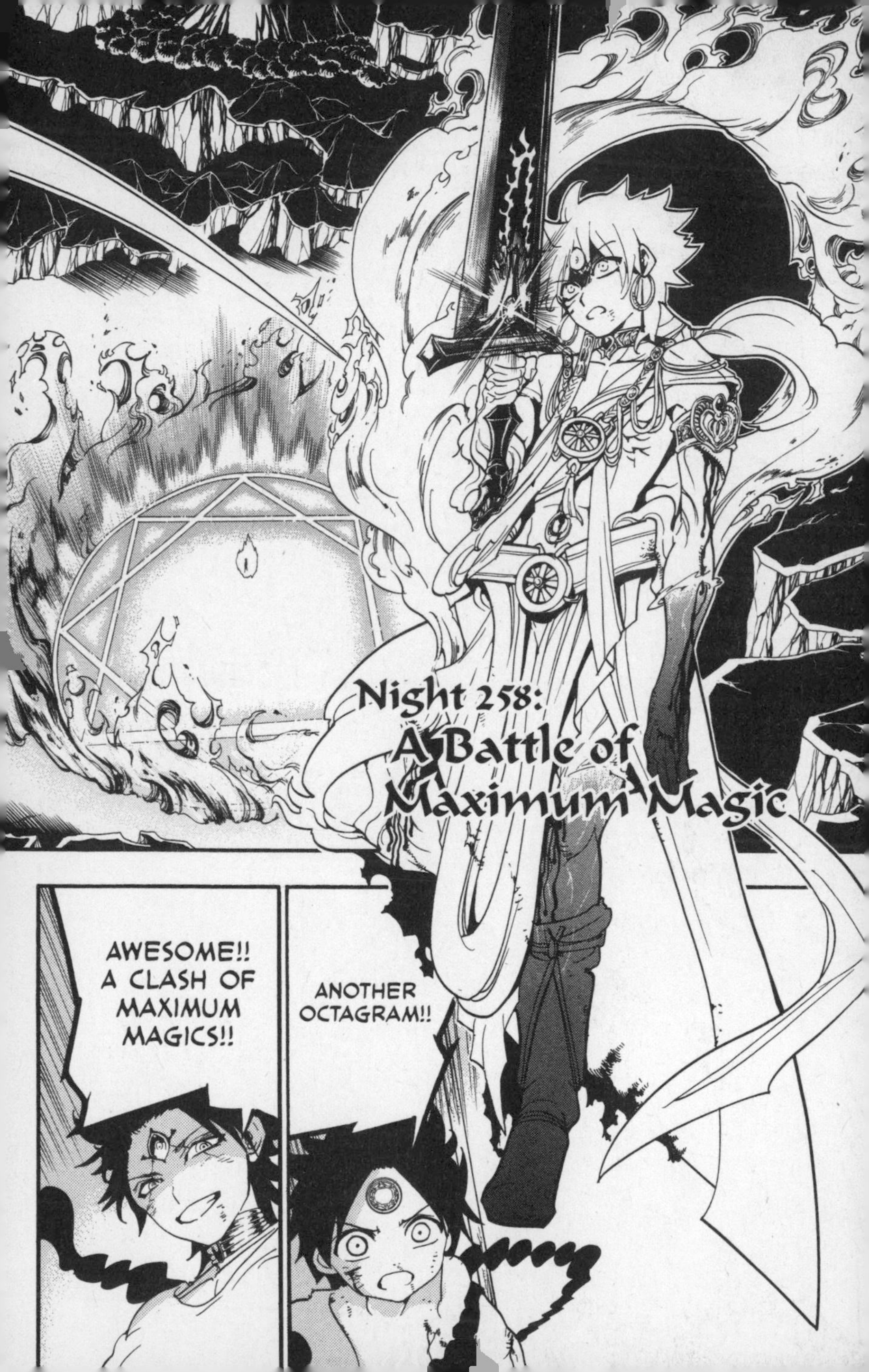
Night 258:
A Battle of Maximum Magic
ANOTHER OCTAGRAM!!
AWESOME!! A CLASH OF MAXIMUM MAGICS!!

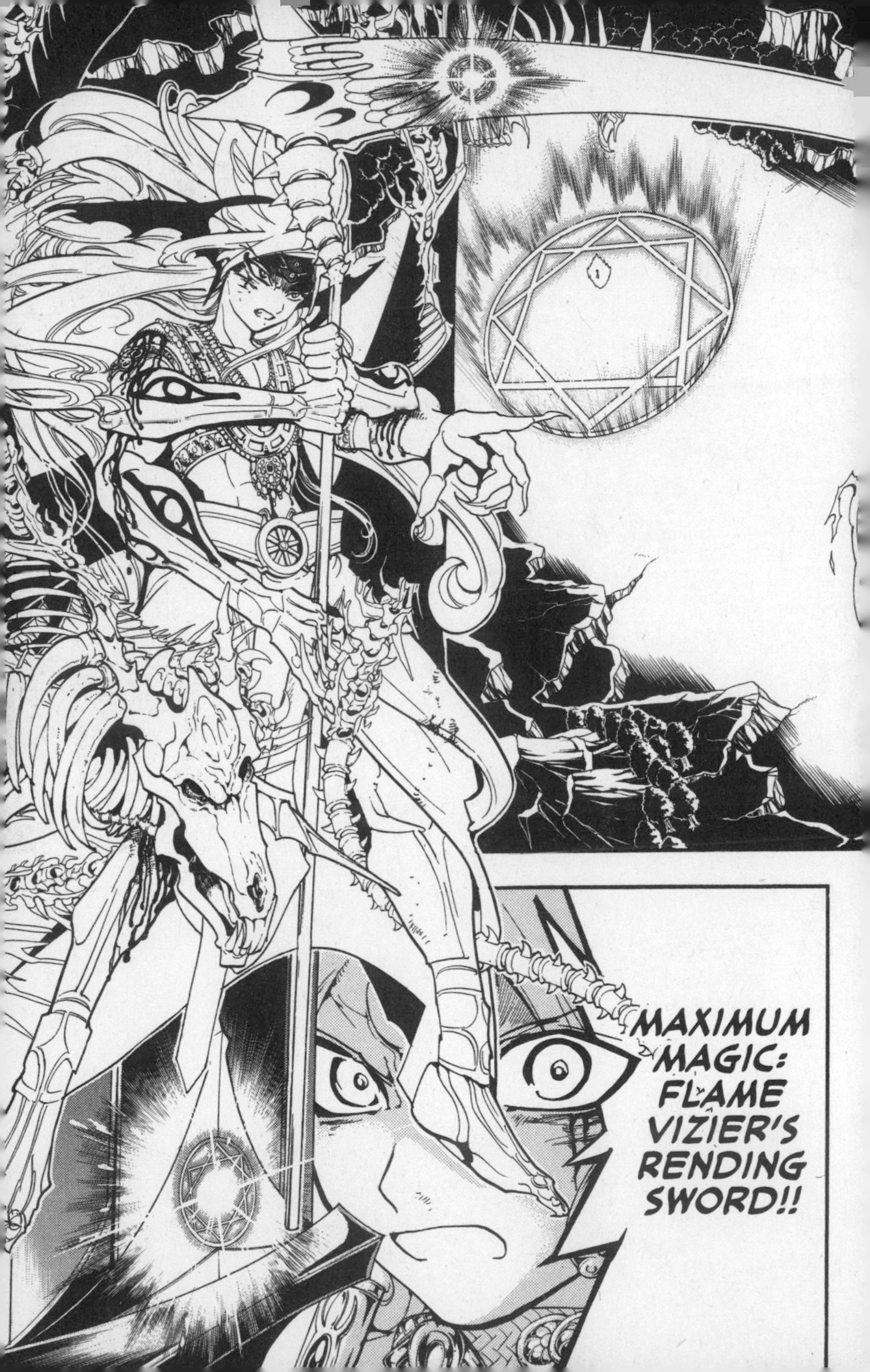
MAXIMUM MAGIC: FLAME VIZIER'S RENDING SWORD!!

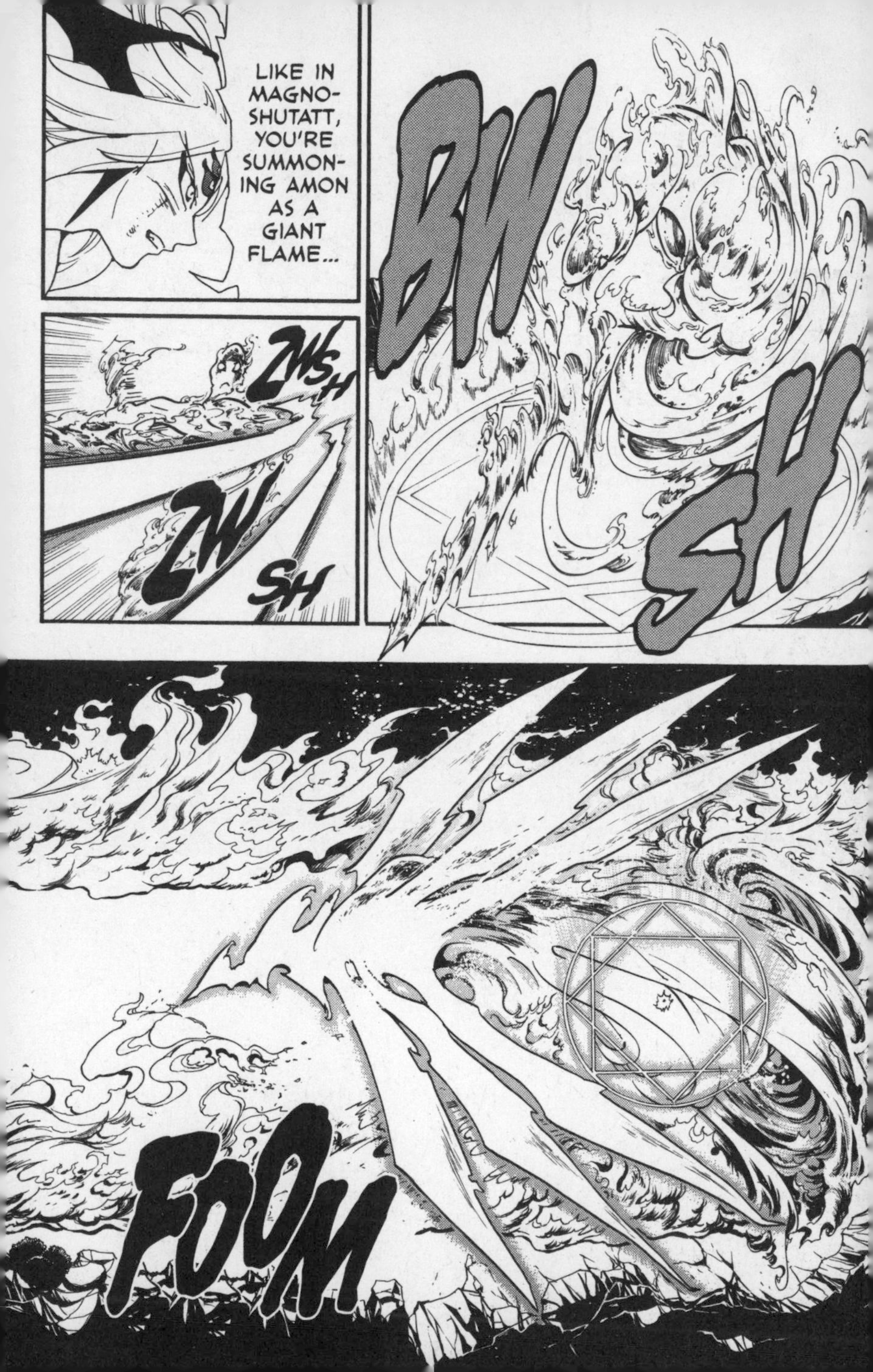
BW
SH
LIKE IN MAGNO-SHUTATT, YOU'RE SUMMONING AMON AS A GIANT FLAME...
ZWSH
ZW
SH
FOOM

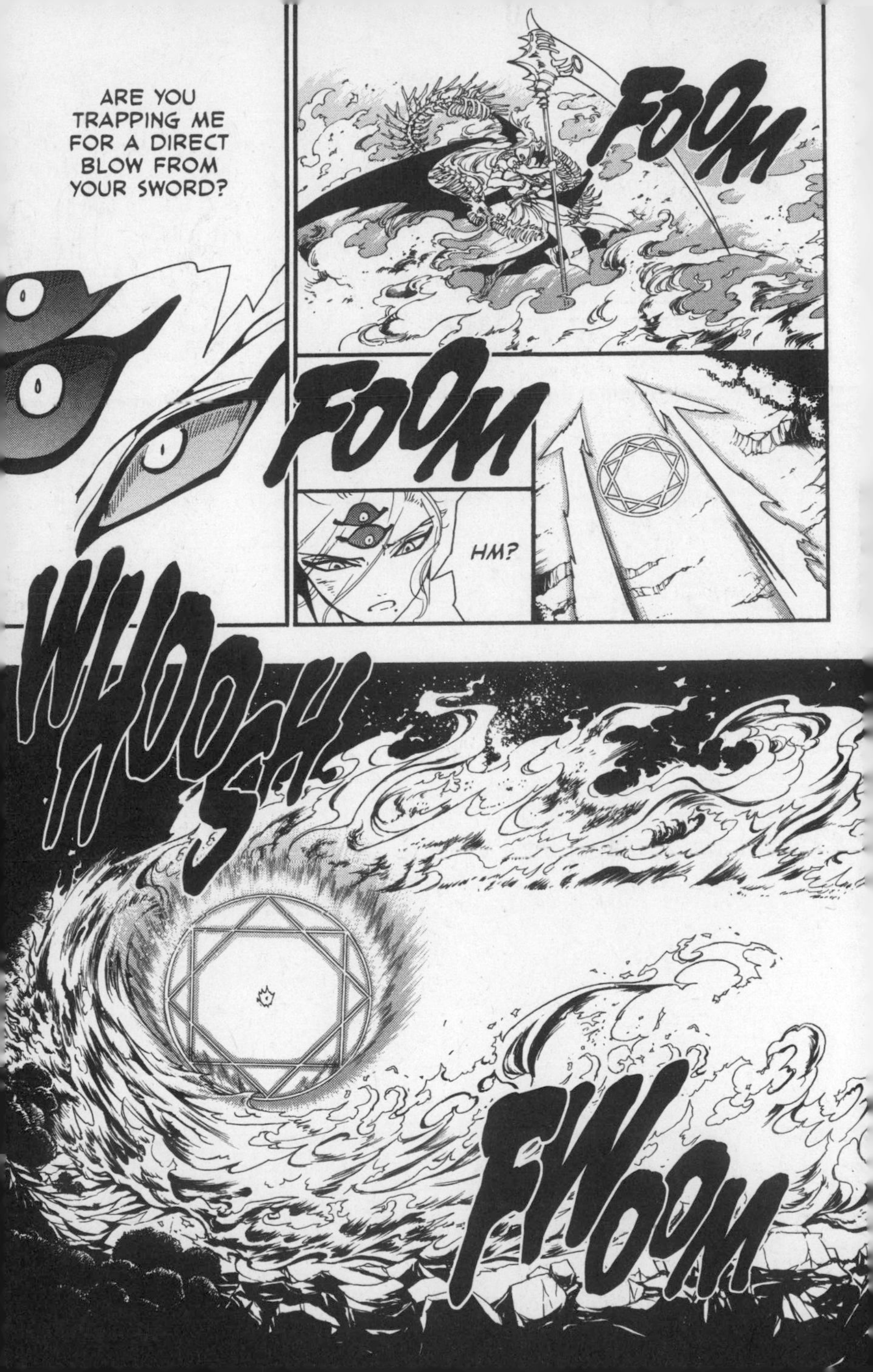
FOOM
FOOM
HM?
ARE YOU TRAPPING ME FOR A DIRECT BLOW FROM YOUR SWORD?
WHOOSH
FWOOM

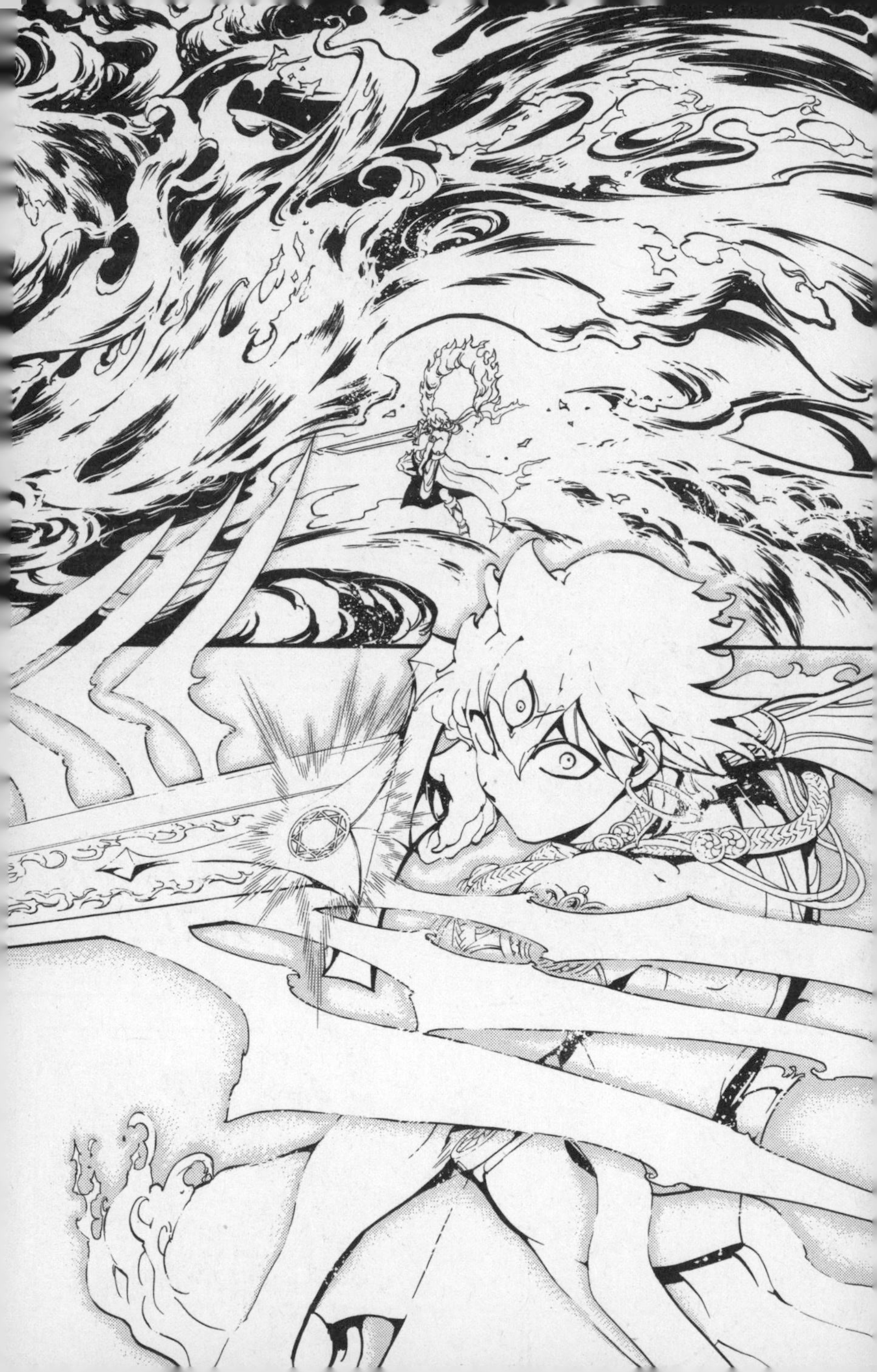

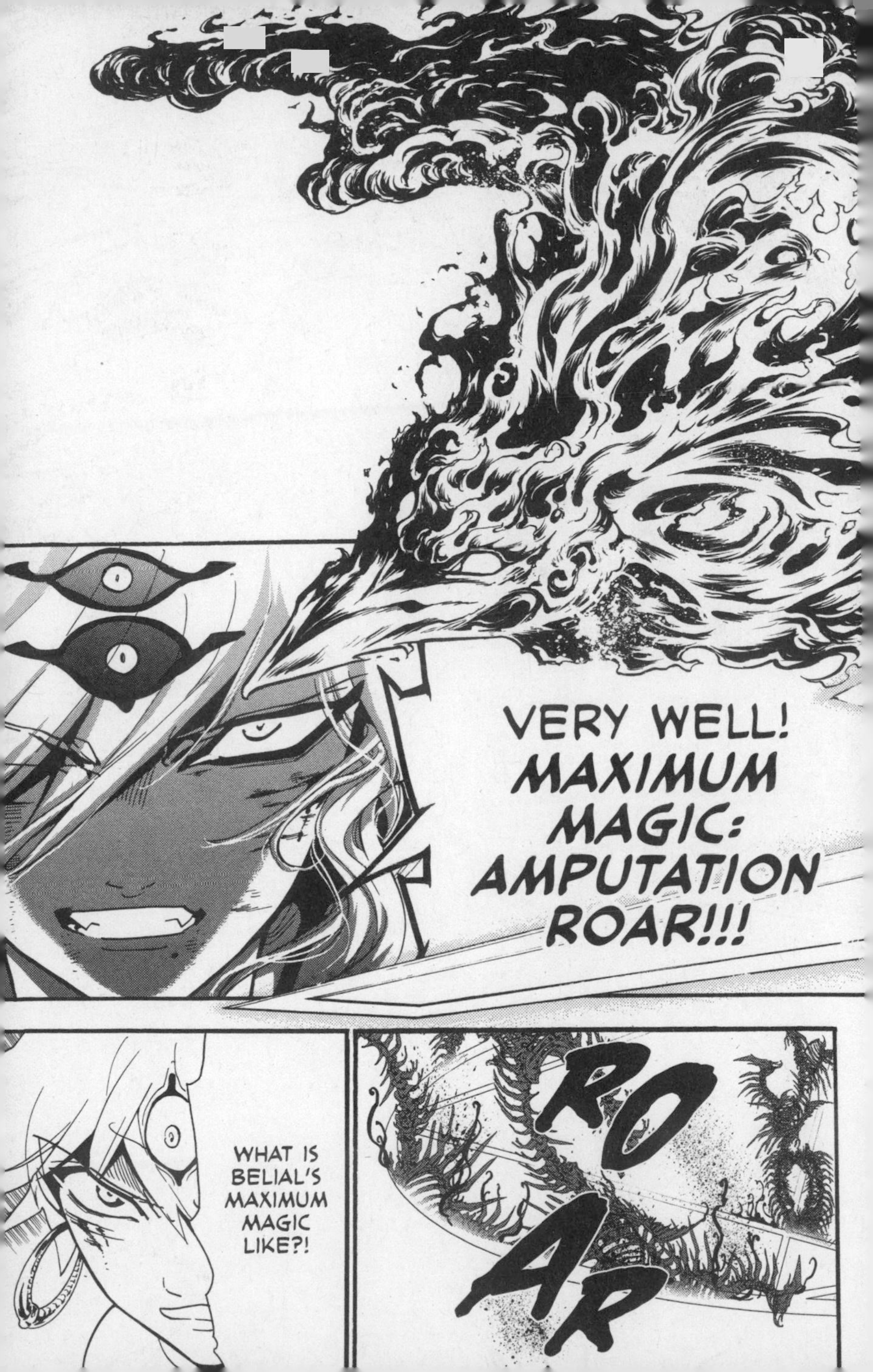
VERY WELL! MAXIMUM MAGIC: AMPUTATION ROAR!!!
ROOAR
WHAT IS BELIAL'S MAXIMUM MAGIC LIKE?!

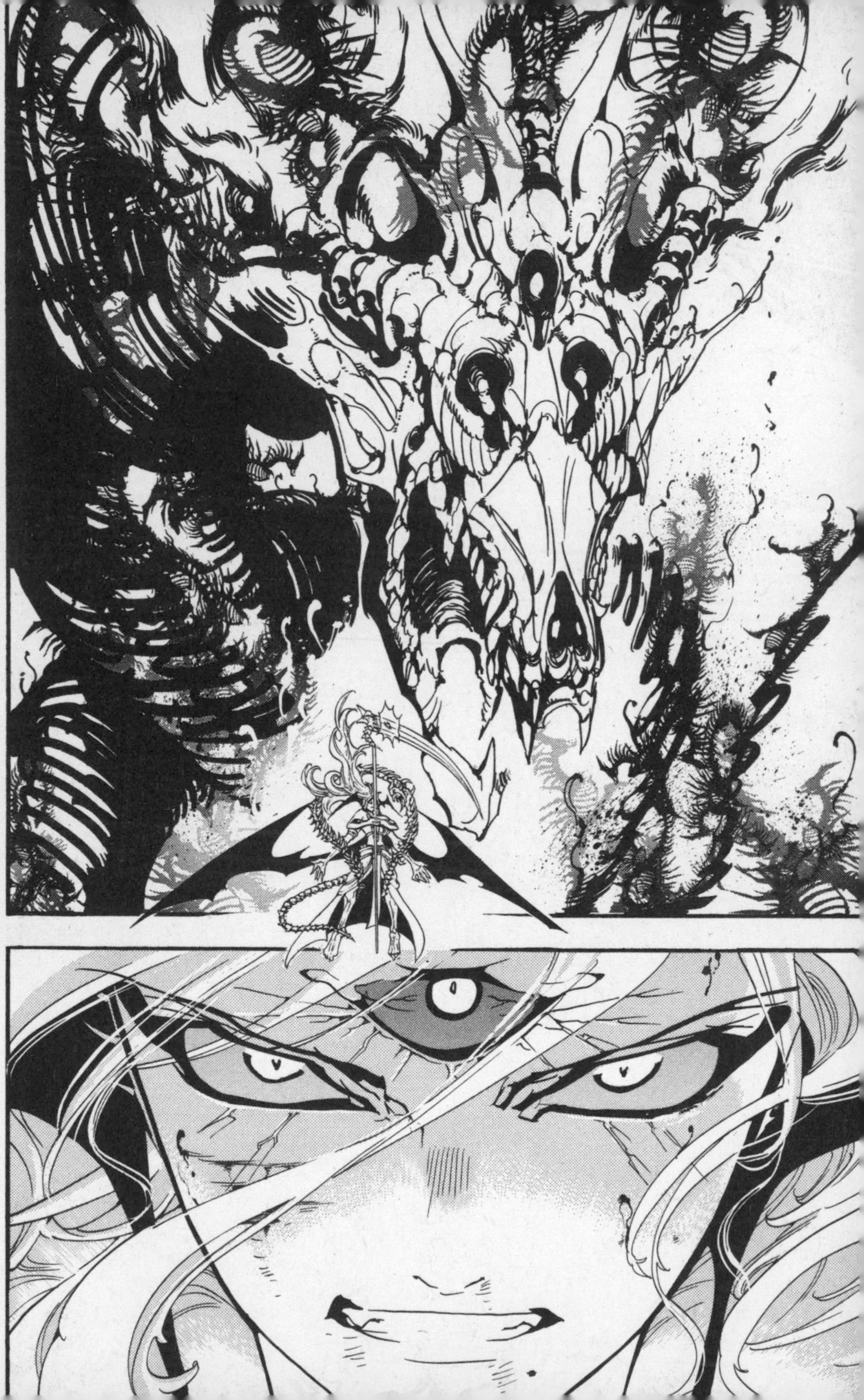

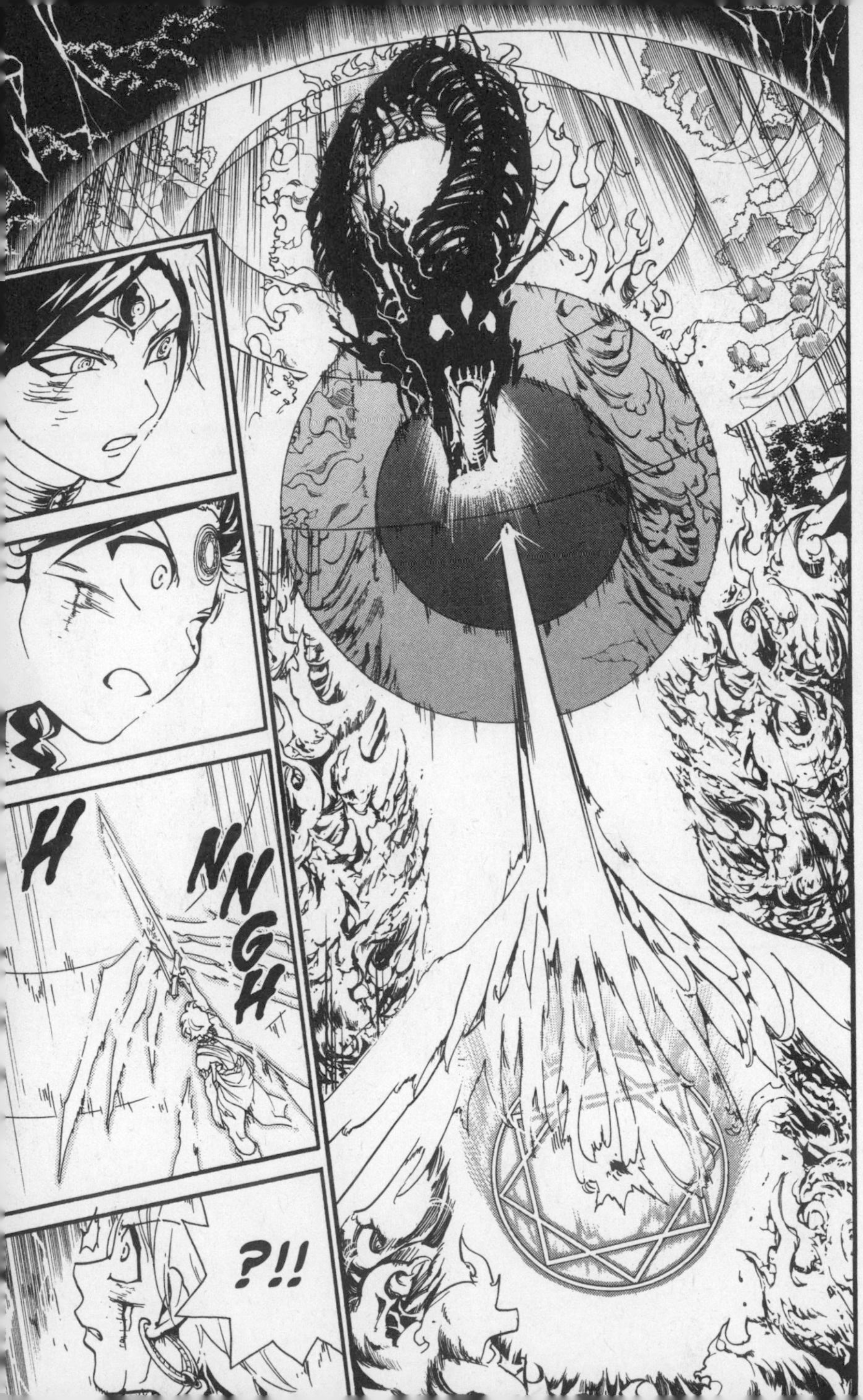
HNNGH
?!!

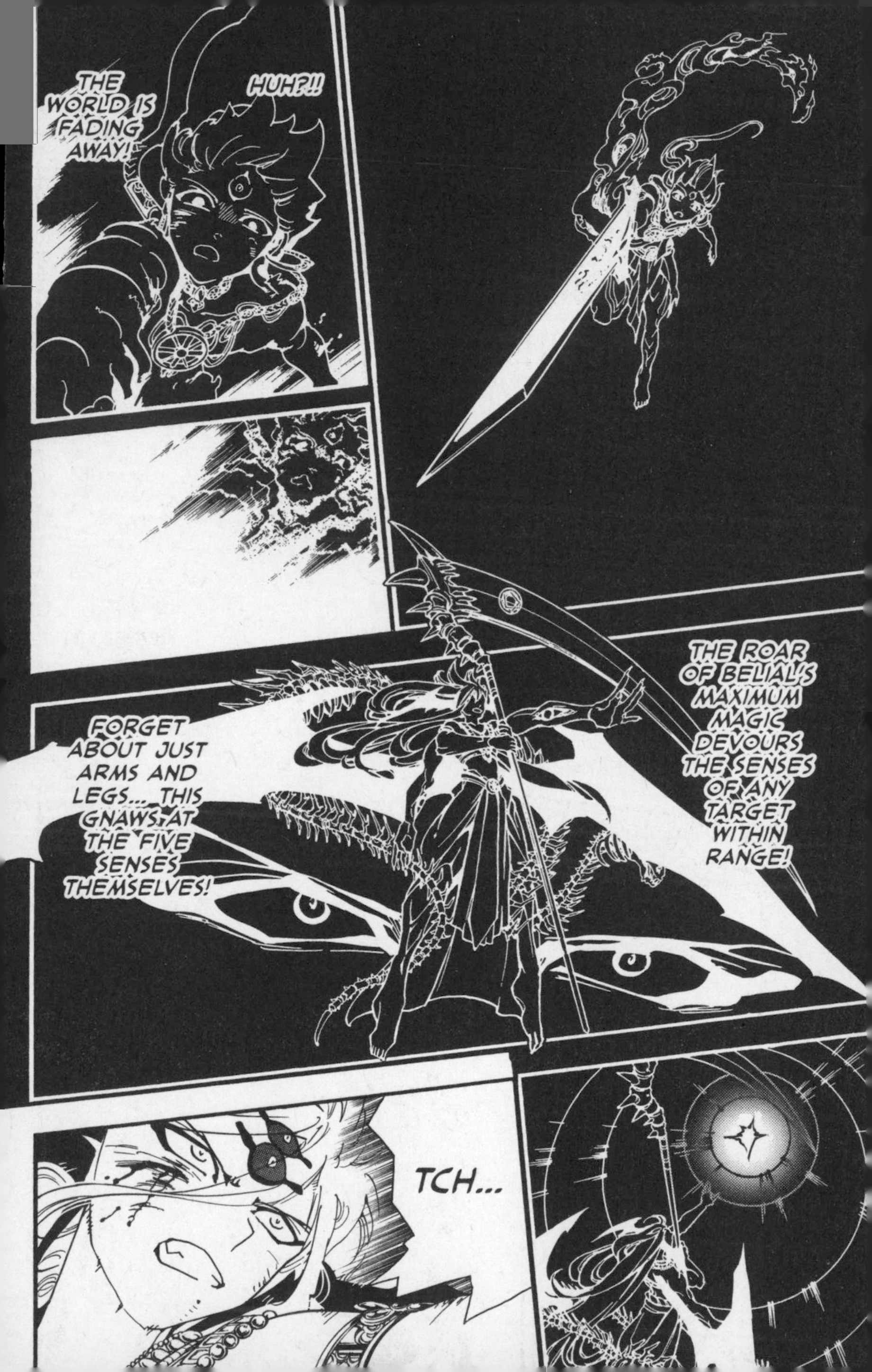
HUH?!!
THE WORLD IS FADING AWAY!
THE ROAR OF BELIAL'S MAXIMUM MAGIC DEVOURS THE SENSES OF ANY TARGET WITHIN RANGE!
FORGET ABOUT JUST ARMS AND LEGS... THIS GNAWS AT THE FIVE SENSES THEMSELVES!
TCH...

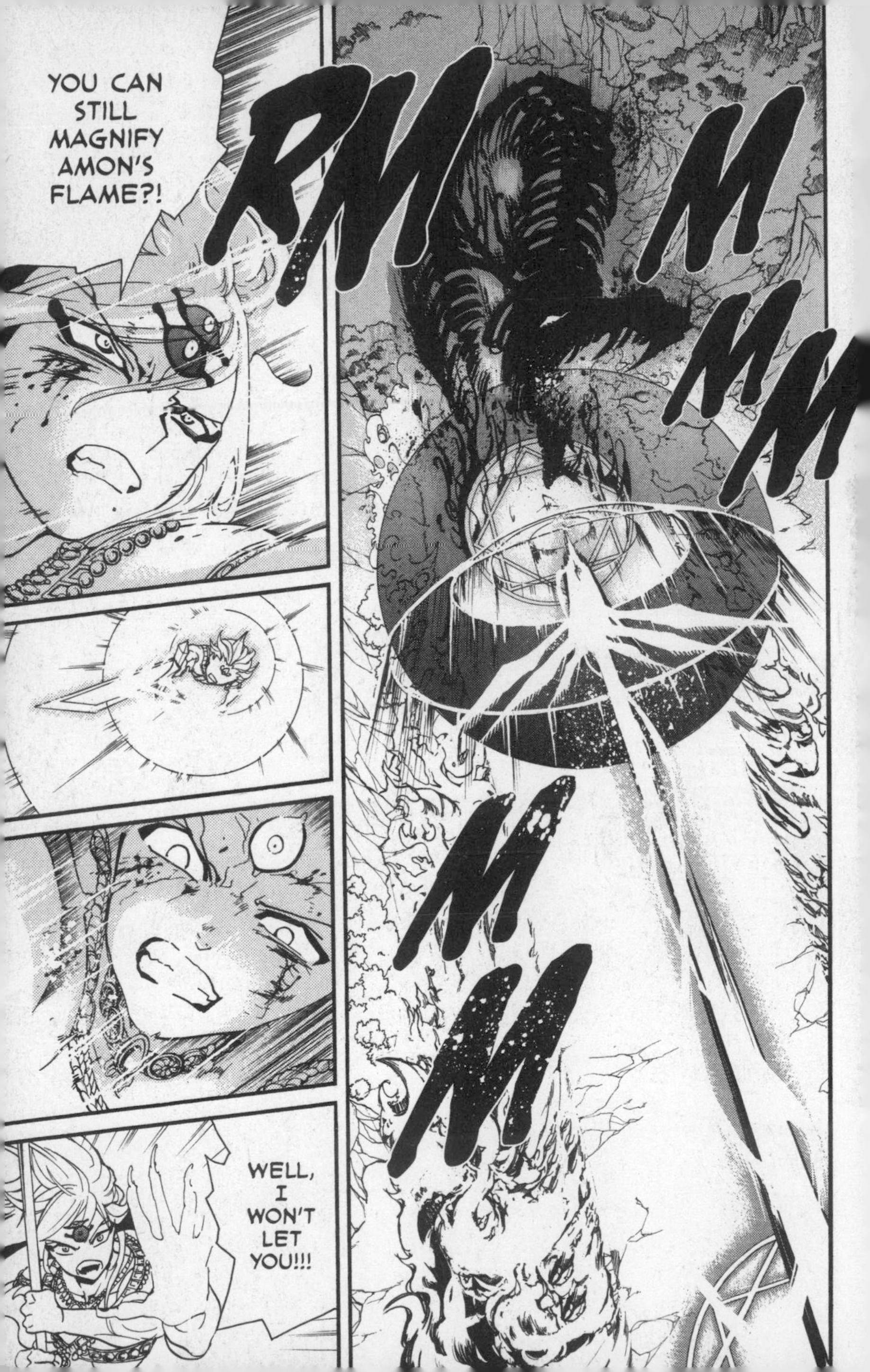
RMMMMMM
YOU CAN STILL MAGNIFY AMON'S FLAME?!
WELL, I WON'T LET YOU!!!

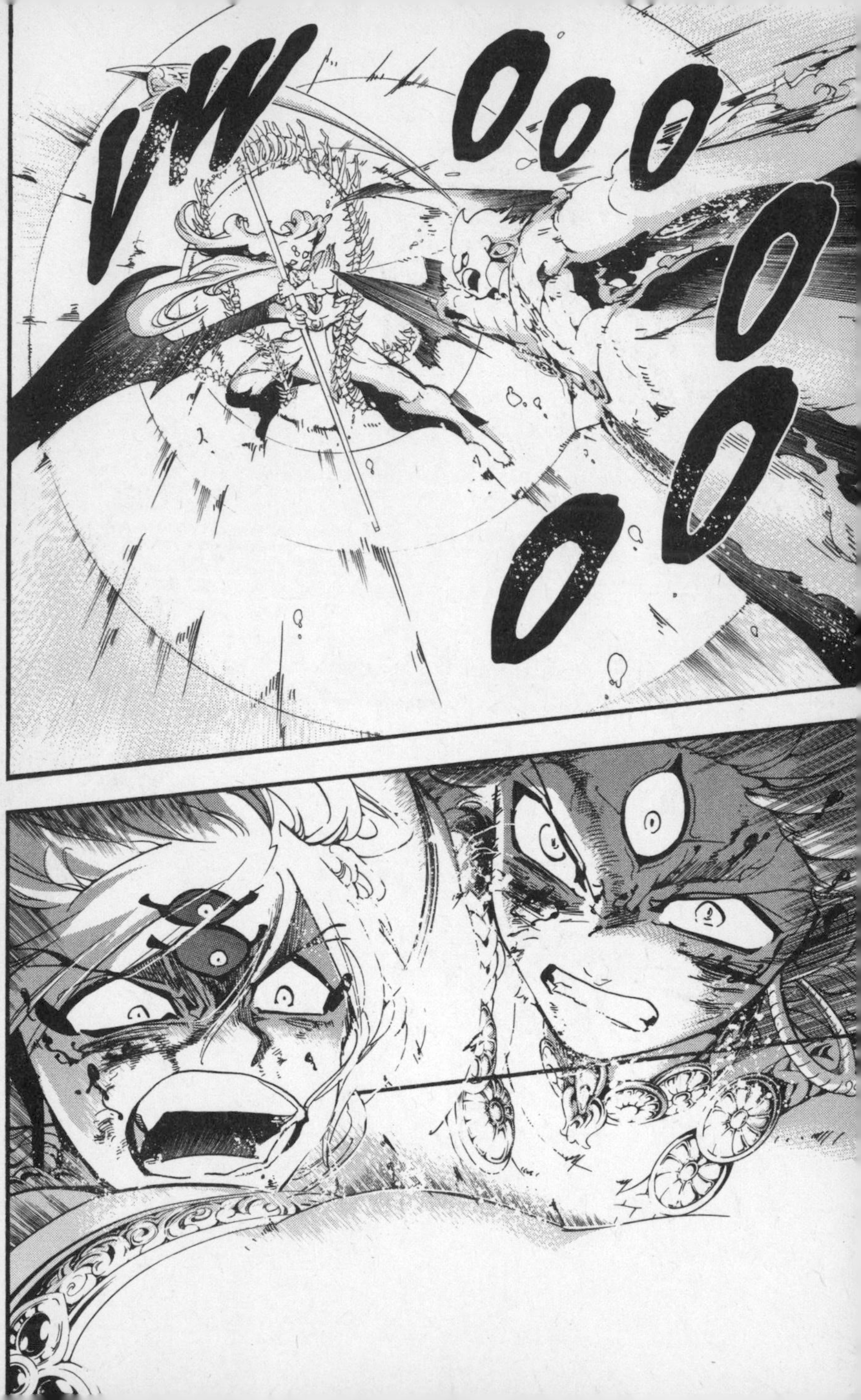

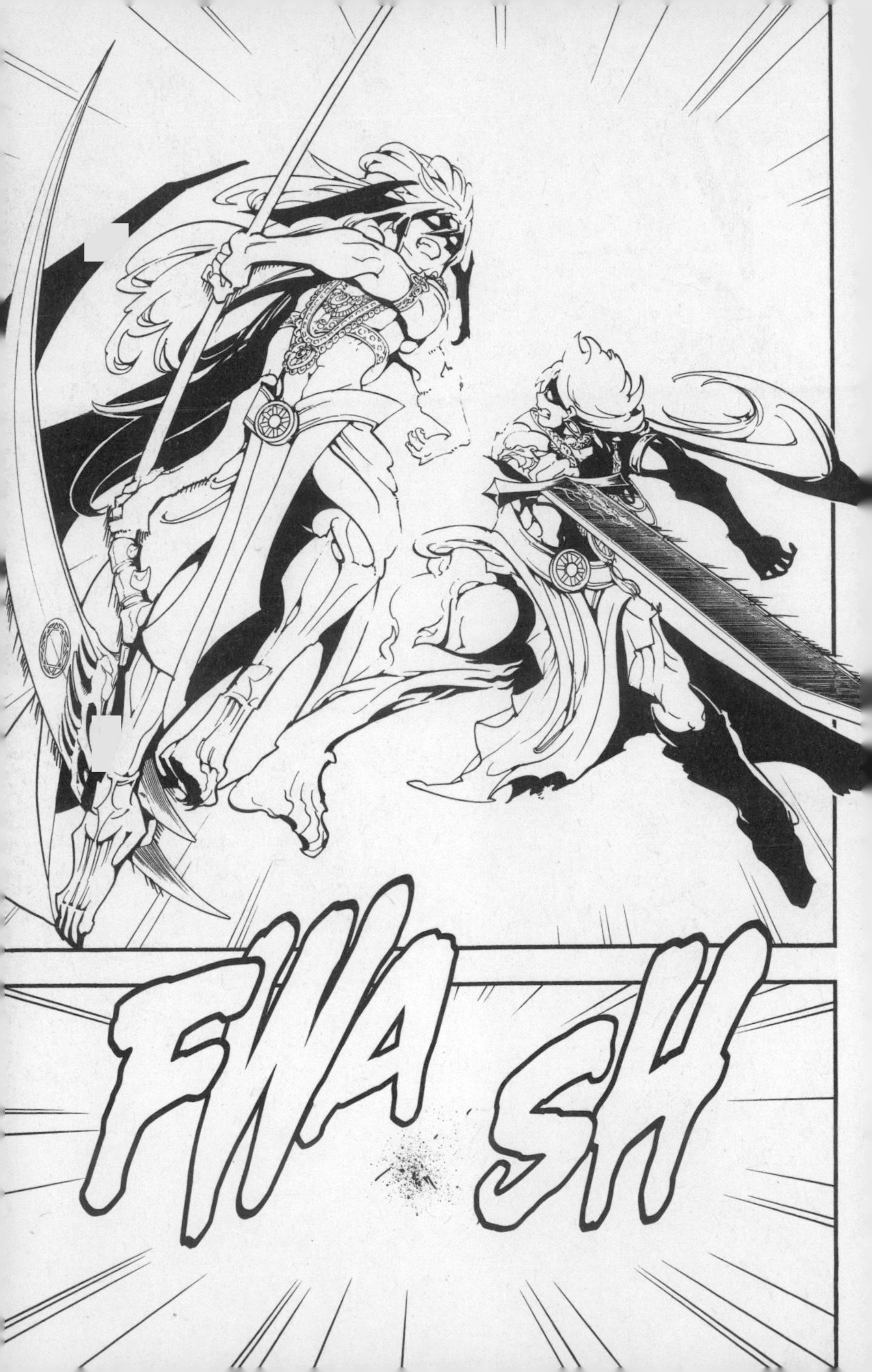
FWASH

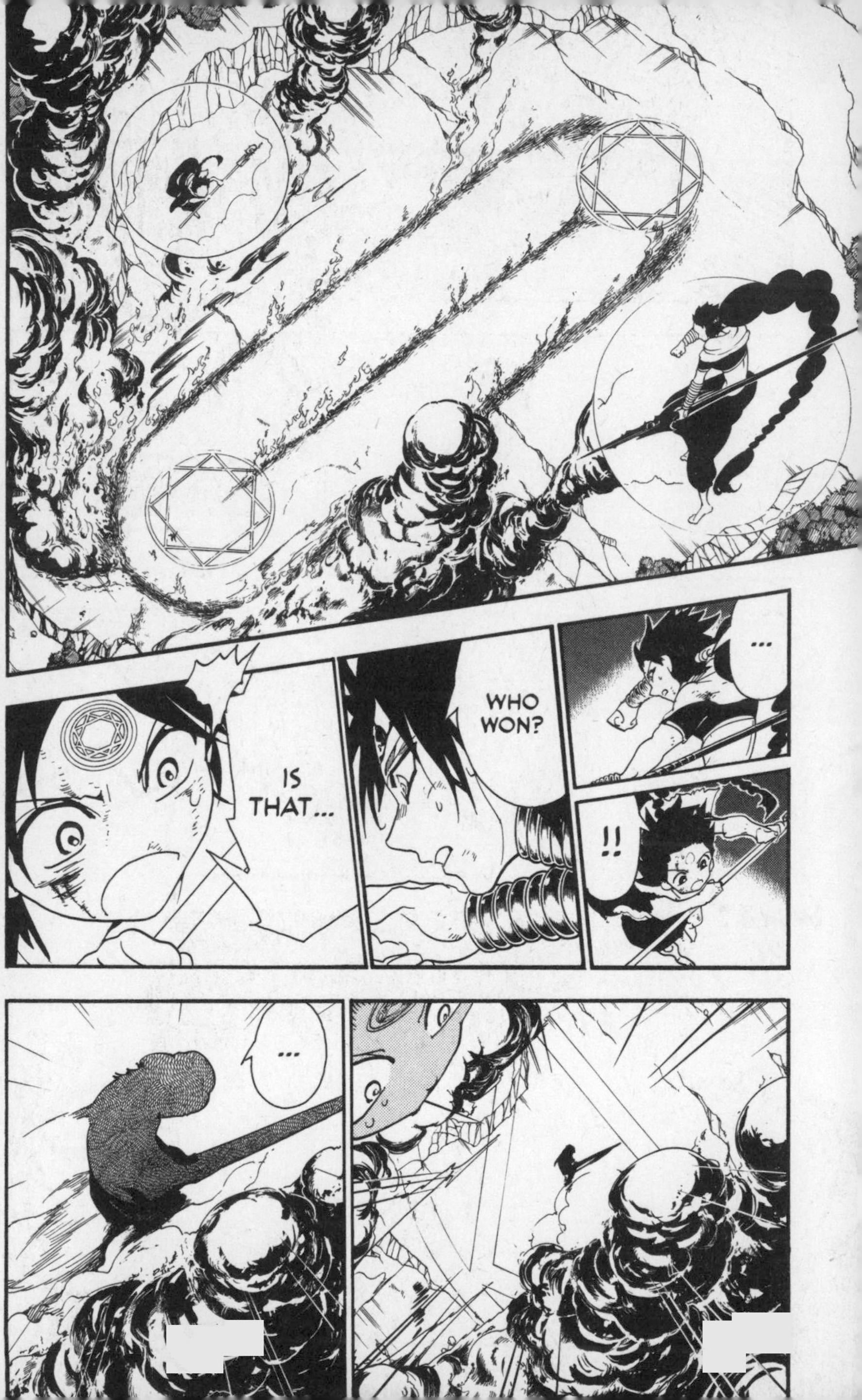
...
!!
WHO WON?
IS THAT...
...

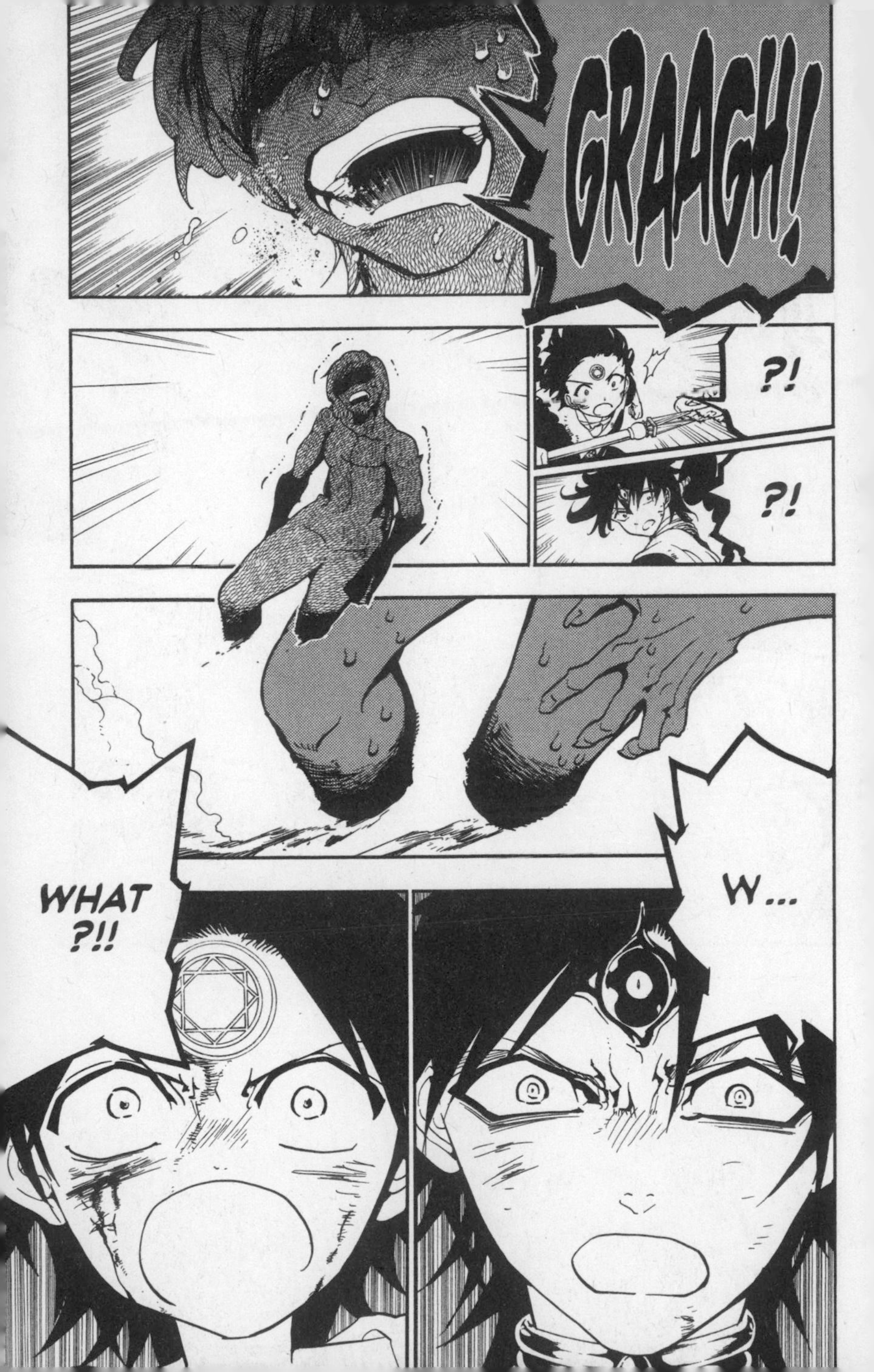
GRAAGH!
?!
?!
W...
WHAT ?!!

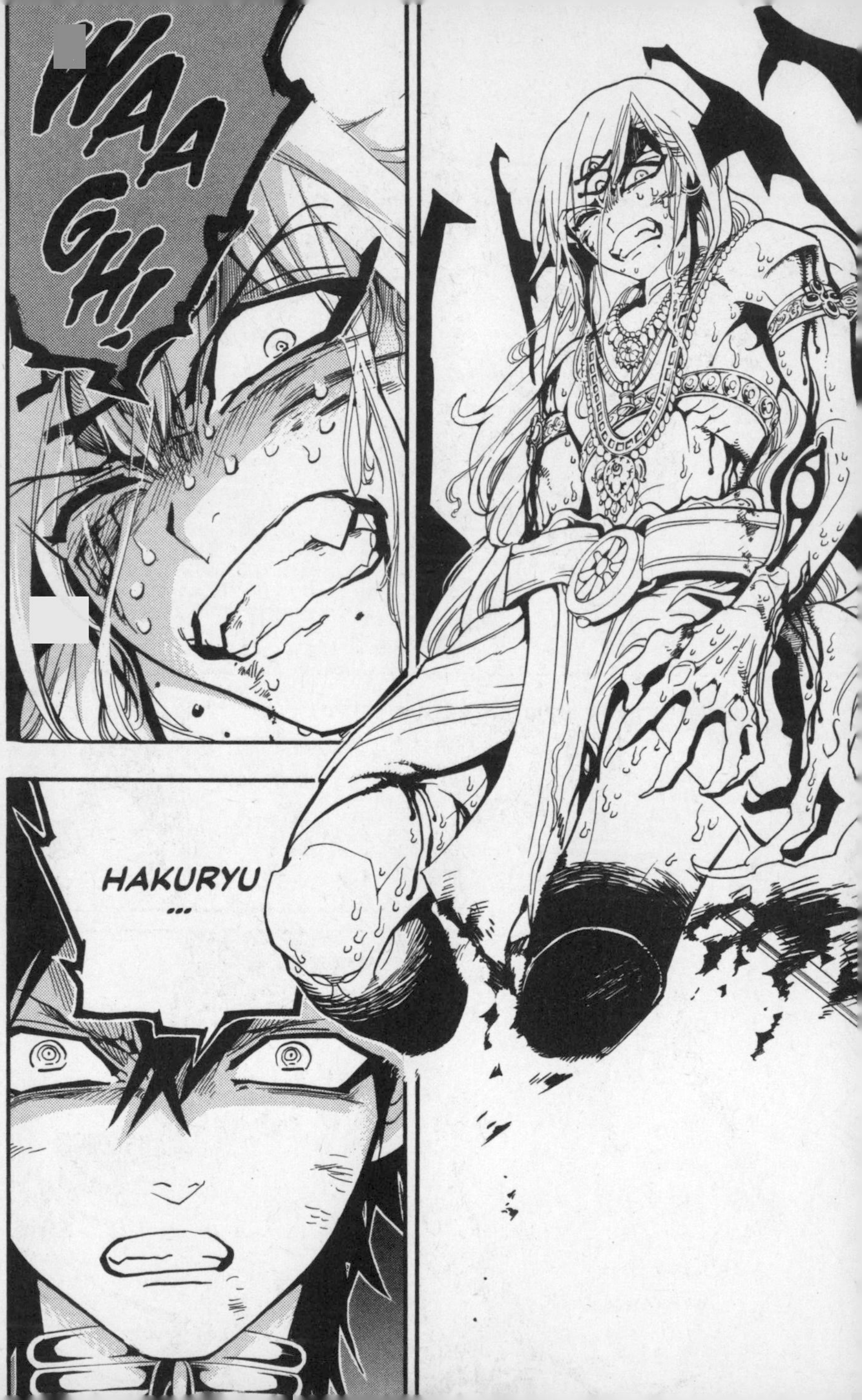
WAAGH!
HAKURYU...

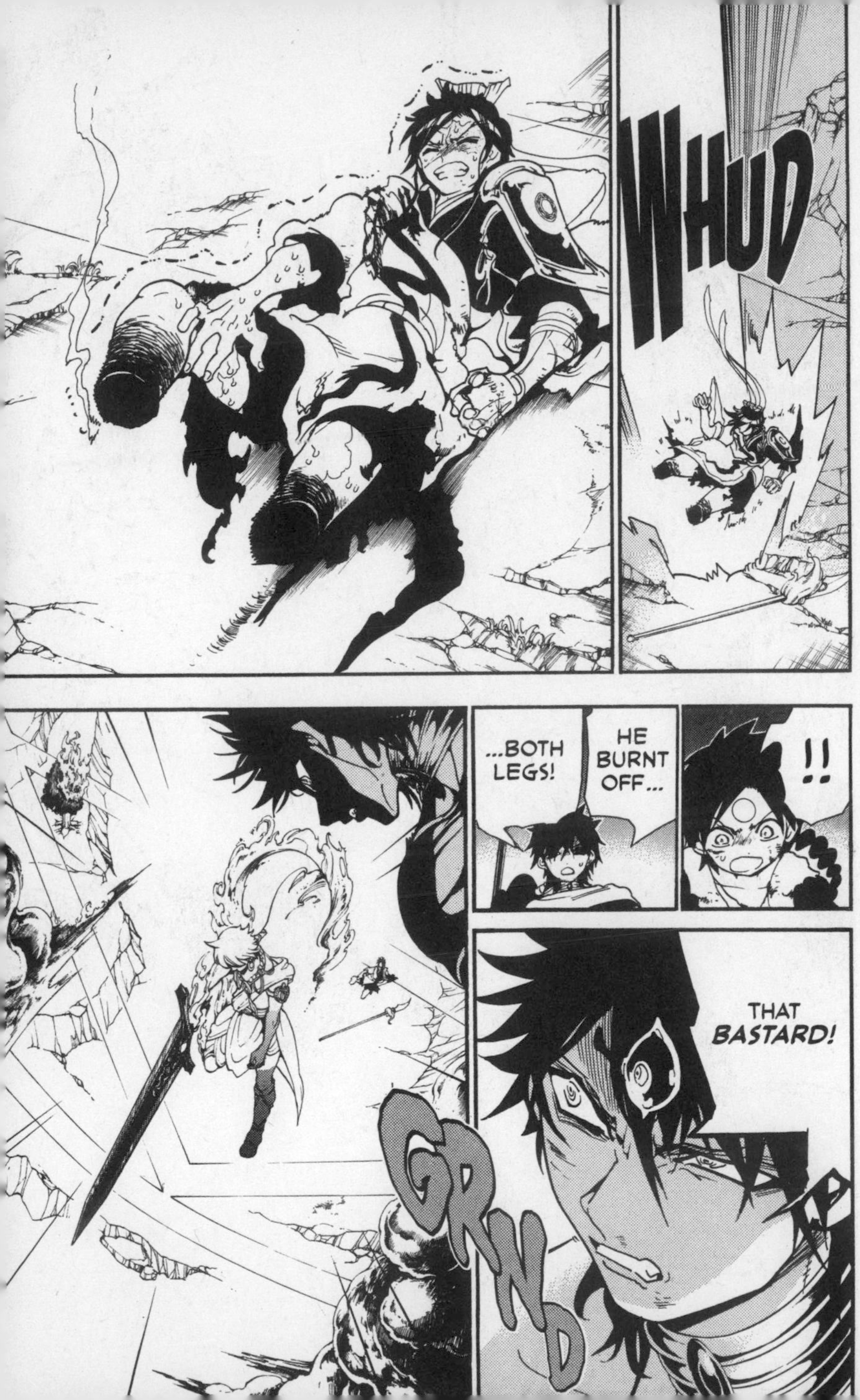
WHUD
!!
HE BURNT OFF...
...BOTH LEGS!
THAT BASTARD!
GRIND

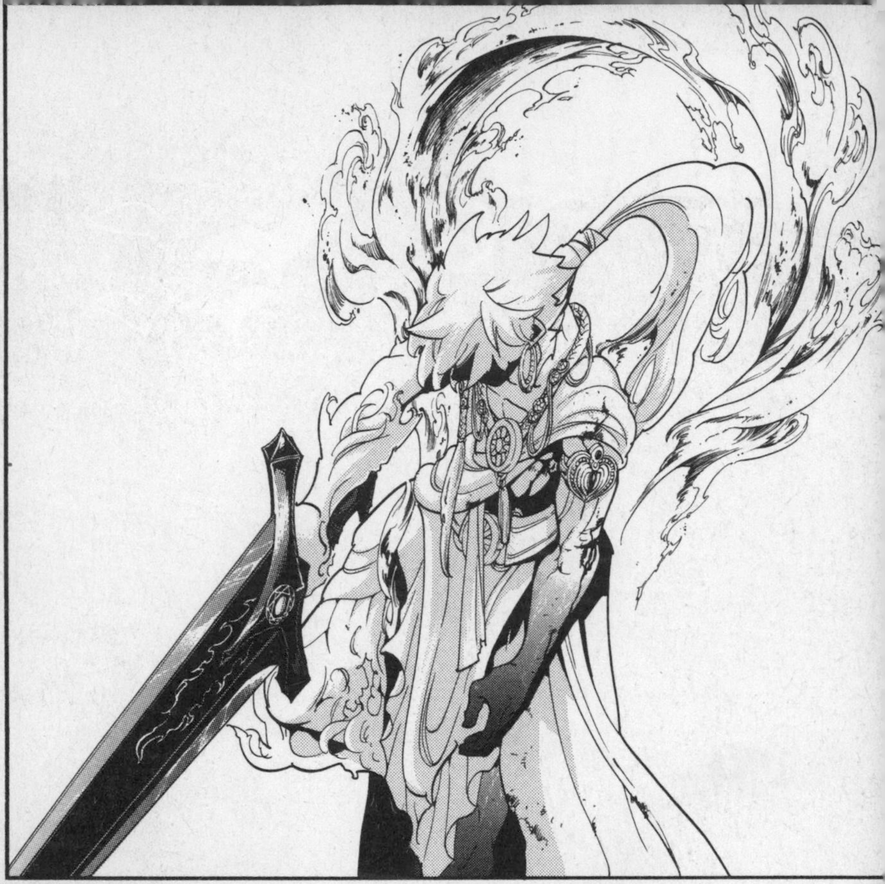

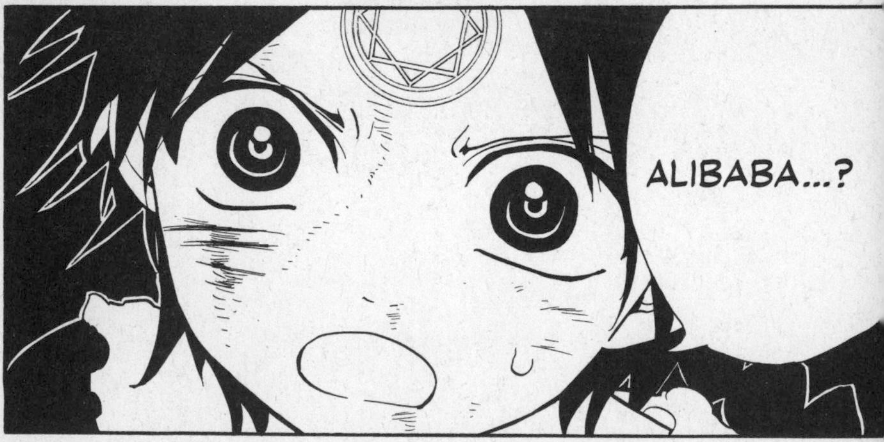
ALIBABA...?

MAGI
The labyrinth of magic
26

Staff

▧ Story & Art
Shinobu Ohtaka

▧ Regular Assistants
Hiro Maizima

Yuiko Akiyama

Megi

Aya Umoto

Mami Yoshida

Yuka Otsuji

▧ Editors
Kazuaki Ishibashi

Makoto Ishiwata

▧ Sales & Promotion
Tsunato Imamoto

Yuta Uchiyama

▧ Designer
Yasuo Shimura + Bay Bridge Studio

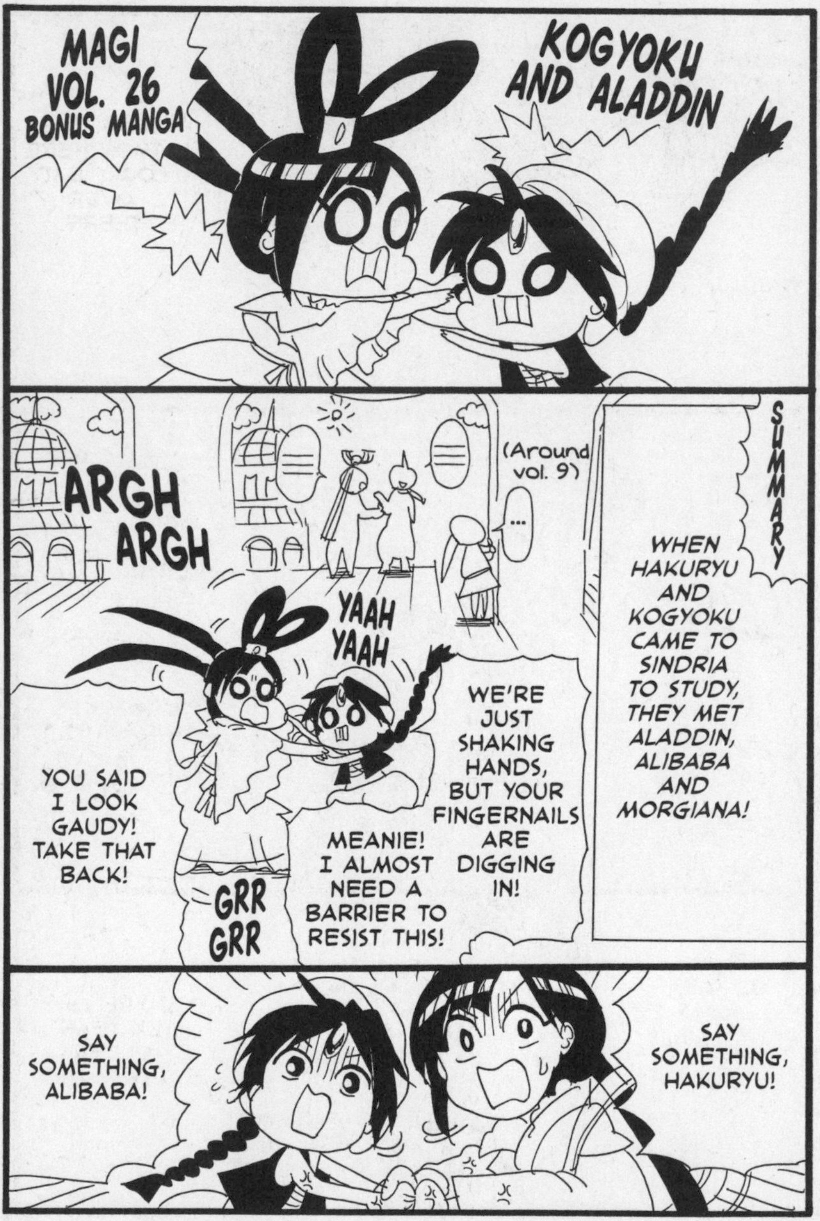
KOGYOKU AND ALADDIN
MAGI VOL. 26 BONUS MANGA
SUMMARY
WHEN HAKURYU AND KOGYOKU CAME TO SINDRIA TO STUDY, THEY MET ALADDIN, ALIBABA AND MORGIANA!
(Around vol. 9)
...
ARGH ARGH
YAAH YAAH
WE'RE JUST SHAKING HANDS, BUT YOUR FINGERNAILS ARE DIGGING IN!
MEANIE! I ALMOST NEED A BARRIER TO RESIST THIS!
YOU SAID I LOOK GAUDY! TAKE THAT BACK!
GRR GRR
SAY SOMETHING, HAKURYU!
SAY SOMETHING, ALIBABA!

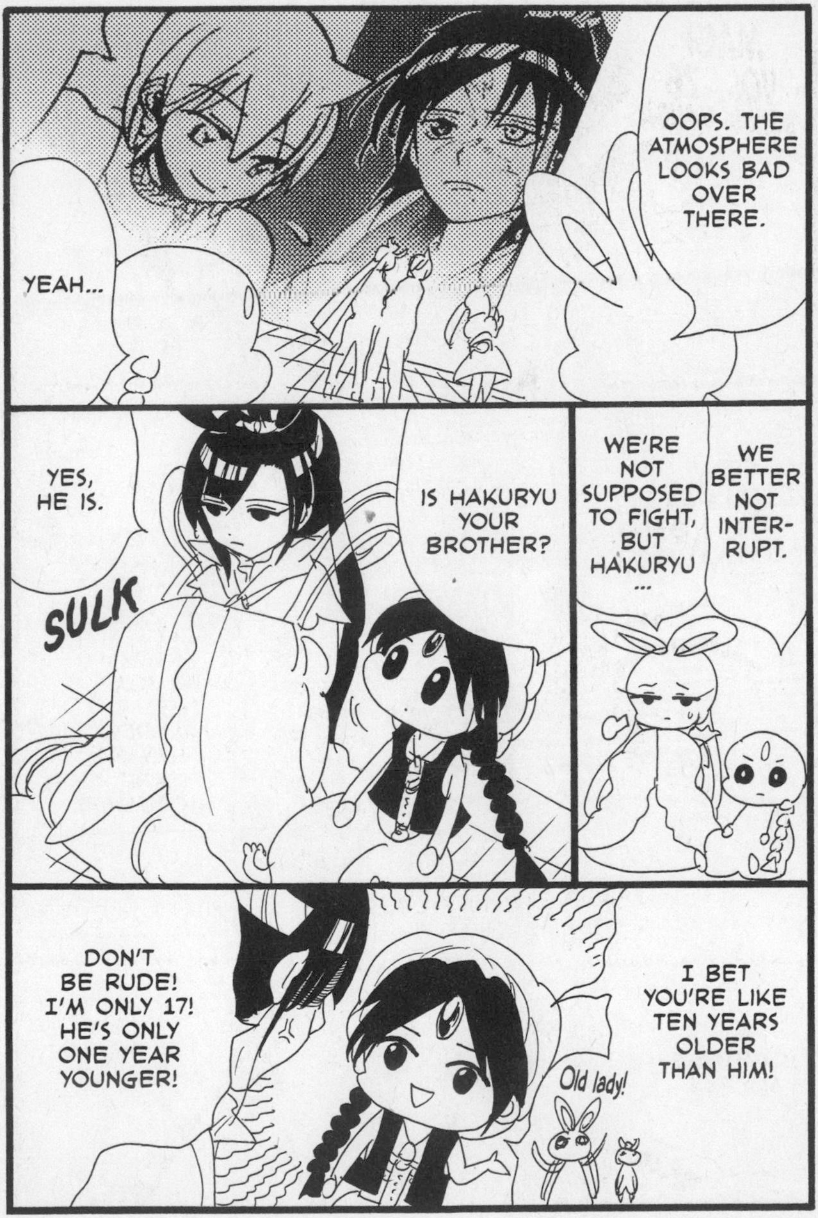
OOPS. THE ATMOSPHERE LOOKS BAD OVER THERE.
YEAH...
WE BETTER NOT INTER-RUPT.
WE'RE NOT SUPPOSED TO FIGHT, BUT HAKURYU ...
IS HAKURYU YOUR BROTHER?
YES, HE IS.
SULK
I BET YOU'RE LIKE TEN YEARS OLDER THAN HIM!
Old lady!
DON'T BE RUDE! I'M ONLY 17! HE'S ONLY ONE YEAR YOUNGER!

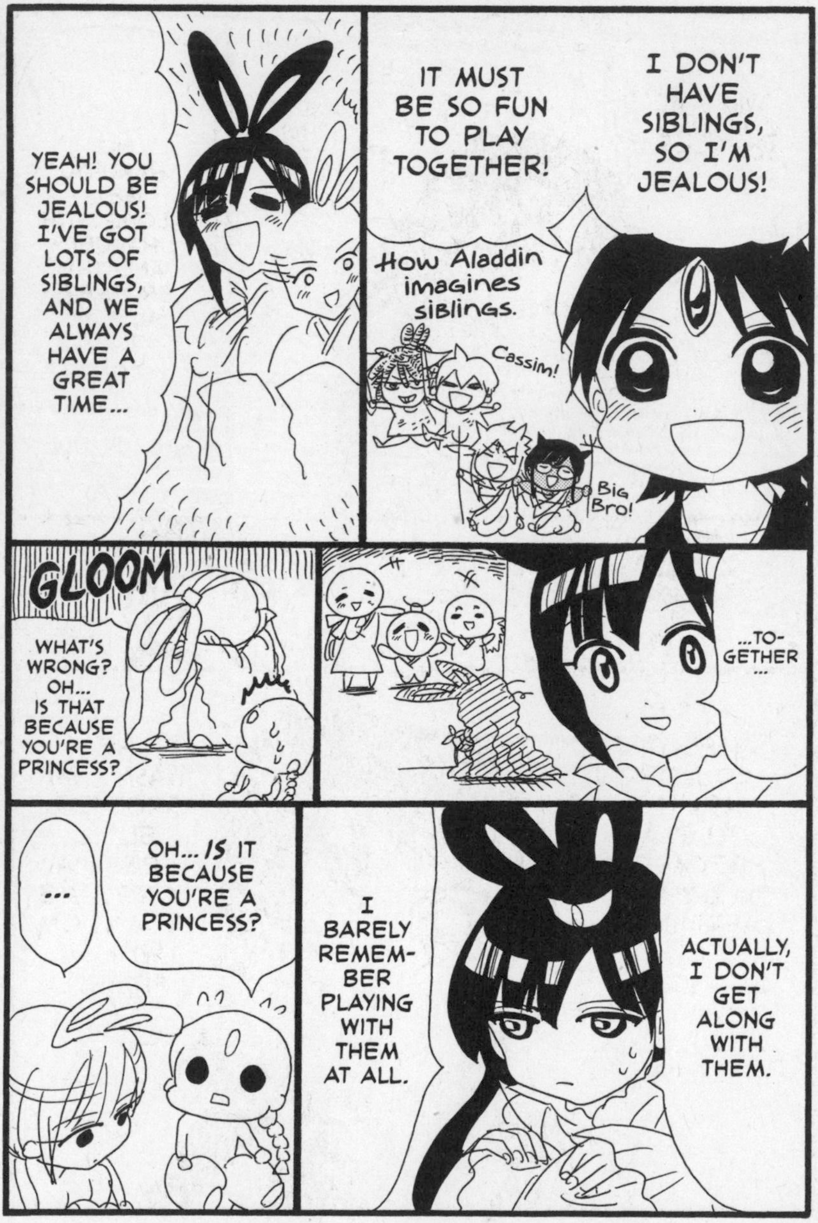
I DON'T HAVE SIBLINGS, SO I'M JEALOUS!
IT MUST BE SO FUN TO PLAY TOGETHER!
How Aladdin imagines siblings.
Cassim!
Big Bro!
YEAH! YOU SHOULD BE JEALOUS! I'VE GOT LOTS OF SIBLINGS, AND WE ALWAYS HAVE A GREAT TIME...
...TO-GETHER ...
GLOOM
WHAT'S WRONG? OH... IS THAT BECAUSE YOU'RE A PRINCESS?
ACTUALLY, I DON'T GET ALONG WITH THEM.
I BARELY REMEM-BER PLAYING WITH THEM AT ALL.
OH... IS IT BECAUSE YOU'RE A PRINCESS?
...

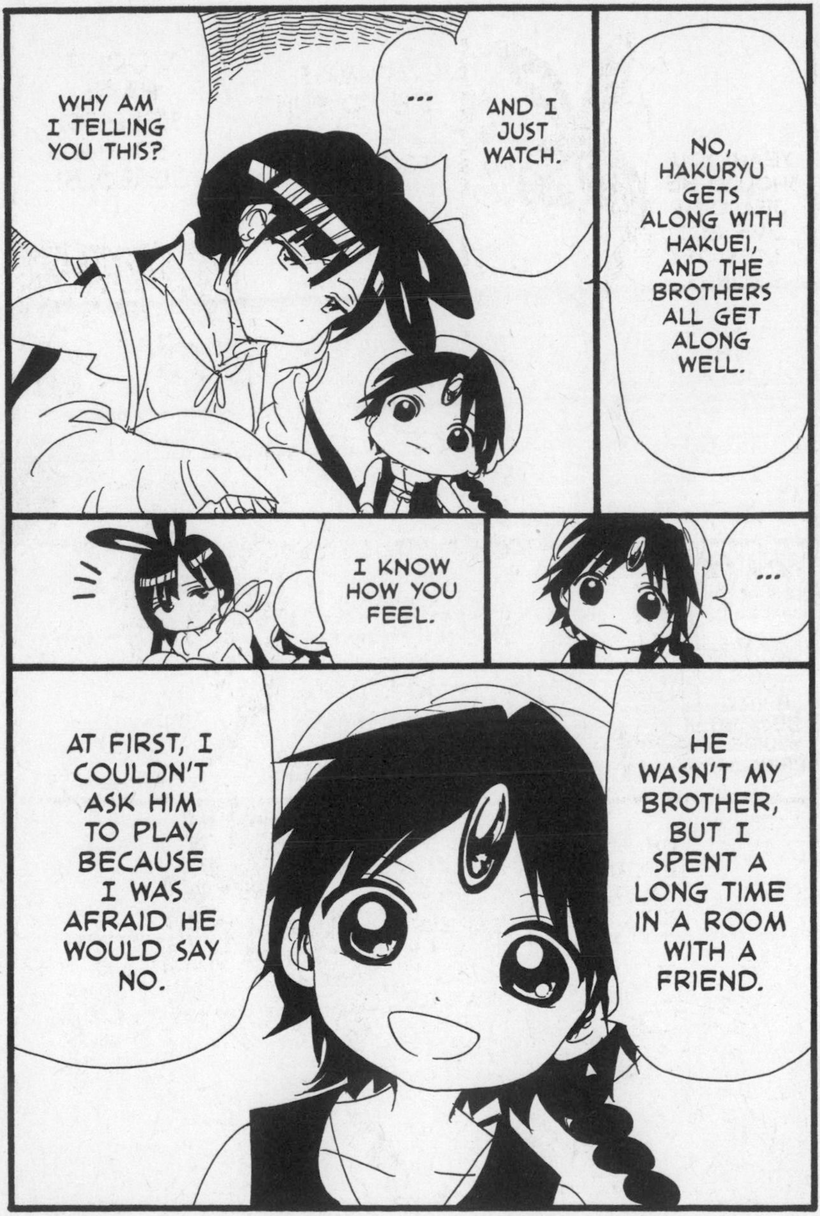
NO, HAKURYU GETS ALONG WITH HAKUEI, AND THE BROTHERS ALL GET ALONG WELL.
AND I JUST WATCH.
...
WHY AM I TELLING YOU THIS?
...
I KNOW HOW YOU FEEL.
HE WASN'T MY BROTHER, BUT I SPENT A LONG TIME IN A ROOM WITH A FRIEND.
AT FIRST, I COULDN'T ASK HIM TO PLAY BECAUSE I WAS AFRAID HE WOULD SAY NO.

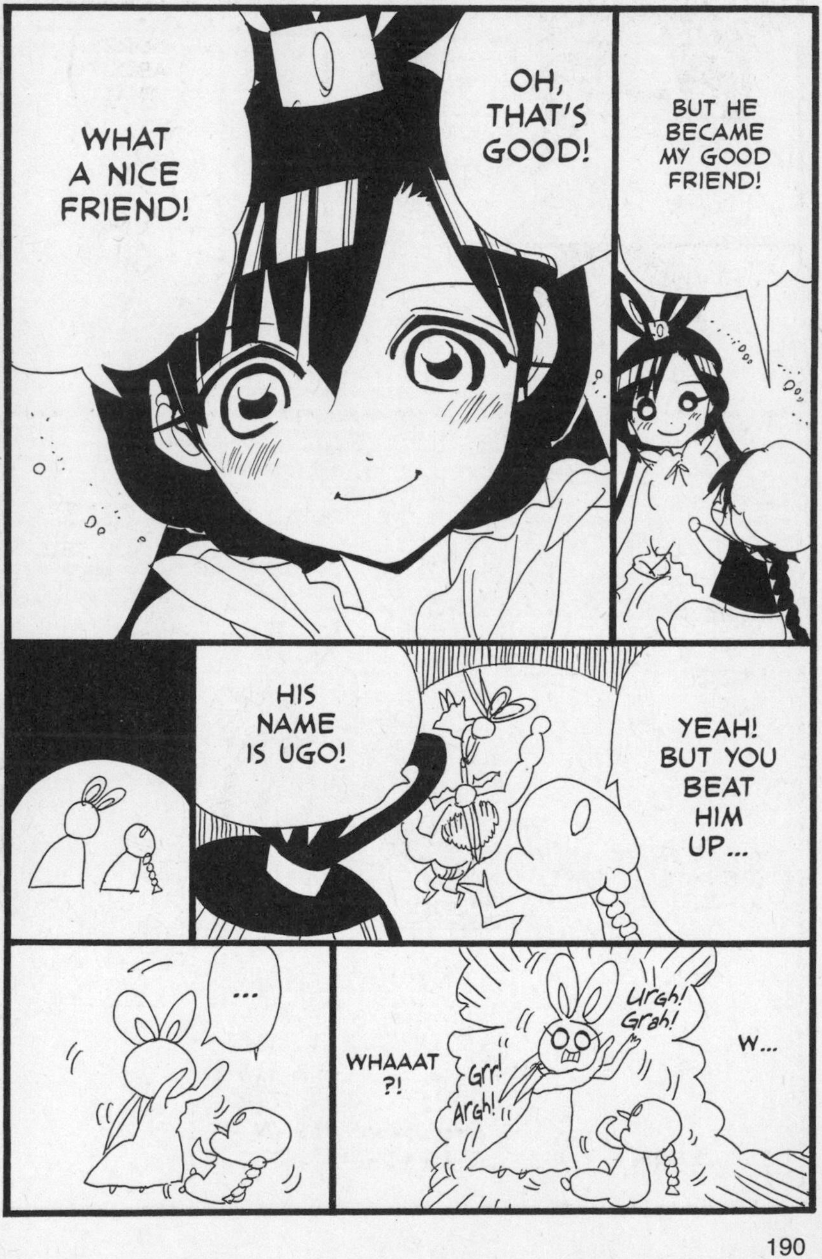
BUT HE BECAME MY GOOD FRIEND!
OH, THAT'S GOOD!
WHAT A NICE FRIEND!
HIS NAME IS UGO!
YEAH! BUT YOU BEAT HIM UP...
W...
Urgh! Grah!
Grr! Argh!
WHAAAT?!
...

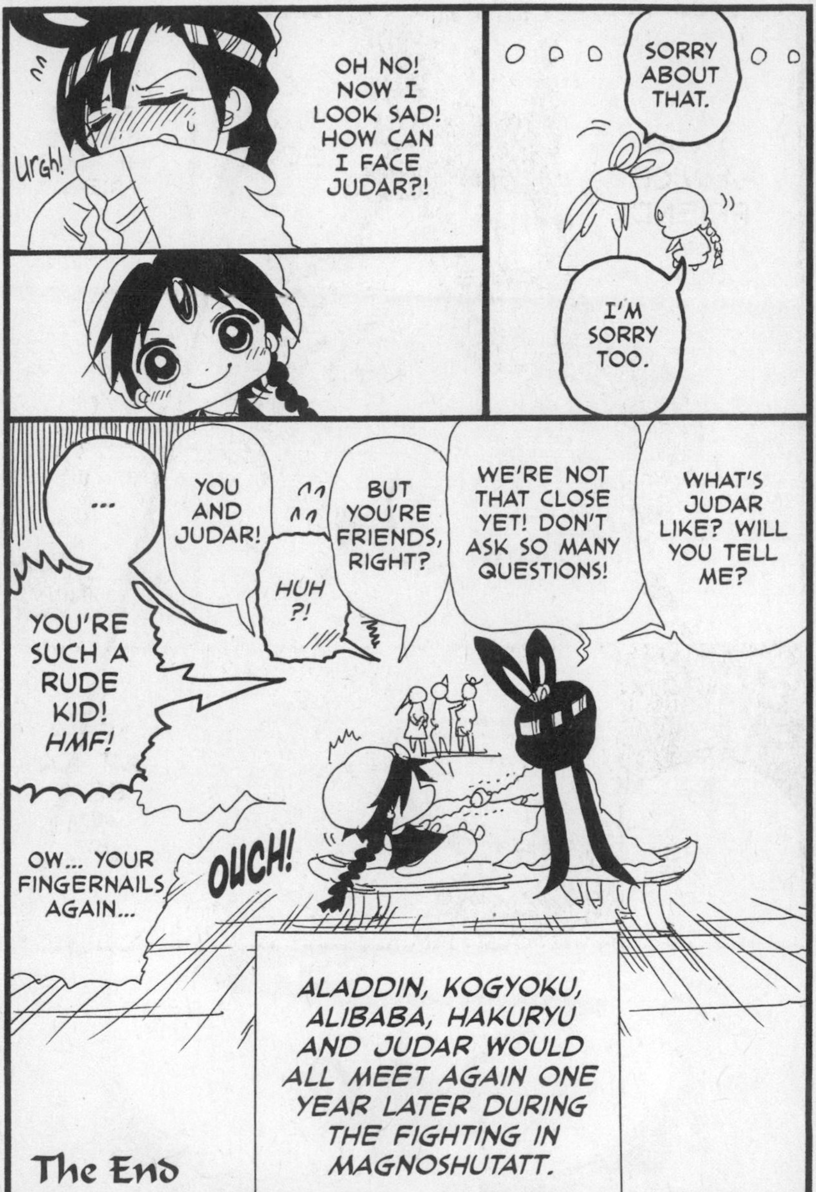
SORRY ABOUT THAT.
I'M SORRY TOO.
OH NO! NOW I LOOK SAD! HOW CAN I FACE JUDAR?!
Urgh!
WHAT'S JUDAR LIKE? WILL YOU TELL ME?
WE'RE NOT THAT CLOSE YET! DON'T ASK SO MANY QUESTIONS!
BUT YOU'RE FRIENDS, RIGHT?
HUH?!
YOU AND JUDAR!
...
YOU'RE SUCH A RUDE KID! HMF!
OUCH!
OW... YOUR FINGERNAILS AGAIN...
ALADDIN, KOGYOKU, ALIBABA, HAKURYU AND JUDAR WOULD ALL MEET AGAIN ONE YEAR LATER DURING THE FIGHTING IN MAGNOSHUTATT.
The End

You're reading the
WRONG WAY

◇◇◇◇◇◇◇◇◇◇◇◇◇◇◇◇◇◇◇◇◇◇

MAGI reads from right to left, starting in the upper-right corner. Japanese is read from **right** to **left**, meaning that action, sound effects, and word-balloon order are completely reversed from English order.

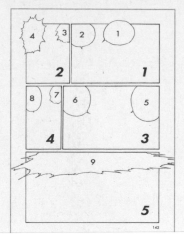